PRAISE for

The Only Del

"A marvellously re-imagined life of legendary Hall of Famer Ed Delahanty. Replete with authentic turn-of-the-19th Century vernacular, W.G. Braund's thoroughly researched historical narrative reveals "the greatest batsman in the land" as a deeply loving, tragically fated man."

Richard Orendeker, Author of *The Phillies Reader*

"A fascinating look at one of baseball's greatest hitters. Not only does this book capture the details of Ed Delahanty's amazing career, with extraordinary insights it provides a look at his tumultuous life off the field. A super read."

Rich Westcott, sports historian and author of 26 books

The 19th century's biggest star, Ed Delahanty was a five-tool player before the term existed. Will Braund wonderfully recounts Ed Delahanty's life in an engaging story.

Scott Butler, *So You Think You're a Philadelphia Phillies Fan* author, *The Phillies Baseball Blog* founder

To my amazing bride for condoning my passion for baseball and for everything she does.

The Only Del

© 2017, W. G. Braund / Out Of The Park Worldwide.
All rights reserved.

No part of this book may be used or reproduced by any means, graphic, electronic, or mechanical, including photocopying, recordiing, taping or by any information storage retrieval system without the written permission of the author/publisher except in the case of brief quotations embodied in critical articles and reviews.

Contact info
Out of the Park Worldwide
22 Waterhouse Crescent • Bancroft, ON K0L 1C0 • Canada

ISBN: 978-0-0977758-7-7 - *Hardcover*
ISBN: 978-0-0977758-8-4 - *Softcover*
ISBN: 978-0-0977758-9-1 - *e-book*

Niagara Falls Illustration
Frederic Edwin Church

Book Design
timmyroland.com

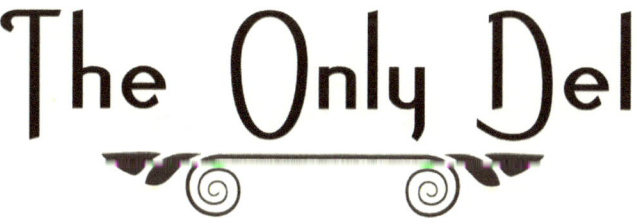

The Only Del

the greatest batsman in the land

The Only Del

Chapter One

Born with a Bat for a Rattle

"When in the name uv the sweet baby Jaysus in velvet pants are we're gointa have all these bluddy rocks out uv here?" freckle-faced Fergus Maloney called out to his friends from Central High School as they struggled to lay out a baseball diamond on the vacant lot beside Fire Engine House Number Five.

"Lord thunderin', we've bin at this fer nigh onta six hours now, lads," groaned slope-shouldered and generally high-spirited Shaymus Finnegan, whose cheekbones seemed ready to burst through his sallow skin. He stopped picking up stones long enough to draw a ladle full of cold water from a fire bucket, pour half its contents onto his shock of curly red hair, and take a big swallow.

"Keep at it, shirkers, else it's not gointa be ready for tomorrow," fifteen-year-old Ed Delahanty told his friends as he picked up a boulder and effortlessly flung it into a wheelbarrow, rattling and nearly knocking the rusty old thing over.

Ed was tall and square-shouldered, with clear ocean green eyes, a dimple in the center of his square chin, and wavy light brown hair under his sweaty flat cap. His attitude and carriage were self-assured, laid-back but at the same time ready-for-anything. His rugged good looks made him popular with the high school girls, who did their best not to be caught staring when he passed them in the halls.

"The teamsters' field's a helluva lot rockier than this," muttered straw-haired, soft-spoken Logan O'Shea, who was exhausted and just wanted to go home and rest up for tomorrow's big game. He'd be doing the twirling for the Fire Engine House Number Five team.

The Only Del

The firemen were letting the boys do most of the work, though they'd begun the job by smoothing the uneven lot with an old plowing blade dragged by two of the horses from the team that pulled their engine wagon. Most of the fire fighters were busy washing the hook-and-ladder. Two tossed hay up into the loft. Four others were trying to harmonize well enough to get up a barbershop quartet, but the baritone was drowning the others out.

In a far corner of the sleeping quarters a frail old fireman sat on his bed peering at a stereopticon into which he'd loaded pictures of scantily-clad French dancers. "My, but women are beautiful things," he murmured to himself.

Salt-and-pepper haired Mike Whalen, a veteran of the Cleveland force from the days when it was still made up of volunteers, watched the boys work. He thought back to a game in the Firemen's League between the Screw Guzzles and the Red Hots that had sent three men to the hospital and sipped from a bottle of Doyle's Hop Bitters he kept in his back pocket. The tonic was a blend of hops, dandelion, mandrake roots, and grain alcohol. He restored the bottle to his pocket and picked up a lantern to polish.

"That Delahanty kid's a real fire plug," he said to no one in particular.

"Where's that come from anyway?" asked twenty-year old Sean Murphy, who'd been hired to complement the station's crew after Davey Callaghan had been badly burned in the tannery blaze. Murphy was patting the head of the scrawny Dalmatian that herded the horses to safety after the crew reached the scene of a fire. "I know it's what you call a stocky fella, but what *is* a fire plug?"

"The water mains were made from hollowed-out logs back in the day," Whalen explained, setting down the lantern and pulling a pipe from his pocket. "When we got to a fire we'd dig up the cobble stones down to the main and bore a hole into it so the hole'd fill up with water. Then we'd draft it with the steam pumper. When we finished fightin' the fire, we'd seal the main with a plug. The next time there was a fire in the neighborhood, we'd dig up the plug and not have to cut into the main again."

Back on the lot, Shaymus Finnegan stuck his newsie cap onto his sopping

the greatest batsman in the land

head and went back to working and talking. "I know it sounds crazy, but I heard tell the Teamsters' first baseman is usin' a *glove,* an old brakeman's glove he found at the railyard."

"Me father says sum fella that plays fer Saint Louis is wearin' one," said Fergus Maloney. "Uv course all the other players laugh at him."

"Can ya blame 'em?" asked Shaymus. "*Cricket* players don't use gloves, ball players ought not to either. The measure uv a player's the number uv calluses on his hands and how many fingers he's had broken. Wearin' a glove just ain't manly."

"Well Albert Spalding, the twirler that won fifty games a couple uv times for Boston, started wearing one when he went to Chicago and switched over to first base," said Logan O'Shea. "Now that he's retired he's started up a sports equipment company that makes baseballs and fingerless gloves with padded palms."

"Can yas picture Jimmy McCormick goin' out ta the pitcher's box wearin' a glove?" Fergus asked the others.

"Or Sure Shot Dunlap goin' out ta second base wearin' one?" asked Ed Delahanty.

"Didn't George Wright make a wad of money selling mouthpieces for catchers?" asked Logan.

"He did so," said Fergus, "calls um rubbers. And apparently Deacon Jones has talked Spalding into makin' *masks* fer catchers."

"Masks? Muther Mary uv God!" exclaimed Shaymus Finnegan. "You must be daft."

"Have ya taken leave uv your senses?" asked Ed.

"Oim serious," insisted Fergus. "Some Ivy League catcher got his face beaten up cuz his twirler was throwin' curve pitches. So his manager took a fencin' mask and put padding in the chin and the forehead and Spalding's sellin' the things out uv his catalogue. Claims the padding's made from imported dog skin."

"The catchers'll look like they've got a bird cage on their face if they wear those get-ups," chuckled Ed.

The Only Del

"Well the catchers might just wear them, what with the new rule and all," said Shaymus.

"He's right," said Fergus. "They can't let a two-strike foul tip bounce before they catch it for an out anymore. They're gointa have to move up a lot closer ta the plate."

"I suppose we should start using the new rules when we play," mused Logan. "The National League's put one in that every pitched ball is gointa be called a ball or a strike. Nine balls and the batter gets a walk."

"The League's abolishing all bound outs, not just the foul balls on third strikes. And they're lettin' the twirlers throw overhand," added Shaymus.

"Saints preserve us, what'll be next?" asked Ed. "Are they gointa say the twirler doesn't have to pitch the ball where the batter wants it?"

"If I had me druthers I'd stay and chew the rag 'til the cows come home, but oive got to head home or I'm sure ta be in the soup," said Fergus. "Me dear muther's all in a lather about the president bein' shot. She thought Garfield was gointa be our best one ever - 'cept fer Lincoln maybe. And now the poor man's fightin' fer his life."

"Is he gointa make it?" asked Logan.

"Twelve doctors on the platform of the train station rooted around inside him with their fingers for the bullets," said Fergus. "They got the one in his arm easy enough, but they had a helluva time diggin' out the one in his back. They say it wasn't fatal, the thing didn't hit any vital organs. They expect the president to live."

"A terrible thing it was," sighed Ed. "Garfield's two boys were with him. They were on their way to see their muther."

"Well mine is sure ta skin me alive if oim not home in time fer dinner," said Shaymus.

Ed looked around the cleared lot. "I guess this'll have to do then," he told the others as he grabbed the handles of the wheelbarrow to take it back to the fire hall. "We're down ta pebbles at least. It's not like infielders aren't used to *those*."

the greatest batsman in the land

The fire hall team played the teamsters' sons the next day at noon. Some of the players had shown up at eleven. It was taking people a while to get used to the new Standard Time the railways had shoved down the nation's throat. Webb C. Ball's jewelry store had a huge chronometer in its window and a lot of people went to admire it and to find out what the damn time was. Others set their clocks and watches by factory whistles.

Ed started the game behind the plate. If the hitter asked the twirler to give him low pitches he caught the ones the batter missed on one bounce. If he asked for high pitches Ed caught them on the fly. He got one foul tip in the ear and two in his right thigh. They stung a little but they were nothing Ed couldn't handle and it wasn't as if he wanted to - or could - leave the game, substitutions weren't allowed

"It's lucky for me you don't throw very hard," he teased Logan.

Ed nailed three runners trying to steal and pegged out another who'd taken too big a lead off third. Later he played first base, adroitly scooping low throws from the other infielders out of the gravel and using his height to reach for high throws. Sometimes he caught with both hands, sometimes with just his left. His palms were hard and callused from all the baseball he played and even the hardest throws didn't bother him. He played second base for the final three innings, ranging far to his left and right to keep the teamsters' sons' grounders from reaching the outfield and snagging several line drives as well. Wherever he was stationed, Ed made plays his teammates wouldn't even have attempted.

At the round marble plate, Ed called for nothing but high ones from the other team's portly left-handed twirler and drove in eight of his team's twelve runs with two doubles, a triple, and a home run that bounded all the way to the fire hall stables. Sixteen-year-old Colleen Dougherty was at the game. She sat with three other girls who were attractive, but paled in comparison. Colleen wore a soft curve bustle dress with an elongated tight bodice and a square neckline. She had dancing green eyes and a peaches and cream complexion. Her glossy hair was pulled back at the sides into clusters of ringlets.

Shaymus poked Fergus when he spotted Colleen standing up and looking for Ed. "She a fizzin' beauty, that one."

The Only Del

"A comely bird she is ta be sure," agreed Fergus.

"She's got the eyes fer Mush," said Shaymus.

"That she does. They're liable ta pop right out uv that pretty head uv hers."

Colleen cheered Ed's every move but almost swooned when he ran full tilt into Fergus Maloney when the two charged after the same foul pop fly. She stood up and yelled, "Edward? Are you hurt?"

Her friends giggled. Colleen gave them a withering look, smoothed her dress, and sat back down. She embarrassed Ed after the game ended, coming up to him while he and his mates were celebrating their win. "Me muther says that if you were to leave a calling card at our door some time tomorrow morning we'd be delighted to receive you for tea in the afternoon," Colleen told Ed, who blushed as his friends grinned and elbowed one another.

"Oi . . . Oi . . . Oim glad to hear it and oid be happy to leave a card at yer house in the mornin'," Ed managed to get out. Colleen smiled and went to join her friends.

"A right bold one, she is," chuckled Fergus.

"So, you'll be startin' with tea and scones will ya, Edward Delahanty?" teased Shaymus. "And what'll ya be nibblin' on after that?"

"I'm thinking he'll be nibbling the girl's ears soon enough," said Logan, who hadn't the slightest experience with girls and could only imagine.

"And if he gets jammy," said Fergus, "it's on ta fondle her diddies, off with her drawers, and off to the races."

"She's a game bird she is, they'll be snogging before the night's done," chortled Shaymus.

"Lay off, you wankers! That's beyond the pale," Ed silenced them, menacingly waving his bat in their direction. "There'll be no such shenanagans with Colleen, she's no scrubber. Oill be thankin' yas all ta keep a civil tongue when yas speak uv her."

the greatest batsman in the land

The boys headed into the fire hall, where they threw buckets of water on one another to wash off the dirt and sweat. Then they soaked down the horses and joined the firemen, who were sitting out front of the hall. Several had watched the game.

"'Twas a grand performance you gave today, young Delahanty," said Patrick Leahy, the lanky fellow in charge of the hall's inventory of ladders, buckets, hoses, nozzles, respirators, and the stout tan cowhide helmets that led some people to call fire fighters leatherheads.

Fred Farrand, the fire hall captain, had watched some of the game. He tugged on his suspenders and told Ed, "I swear you can hit a ball farther than any boy in Cleveland. You must have been born with a baseball bat for a rattle."

Embarrassed at being singled out for praise, Ed changed the subject. "Do yas figure Pud Galvin'll pitch all three games when Buffalo comes in next week?" he asked no one in particular. "He says that monkey testosterone he takes works such wonders he could pitch fifteen innings five days in a row."

"I expect Jimmy O'Rourke'll use Jack Lynch for one uv them," said Leahy. "Even the little steam engine can't pitch *every* day."

"A tricky one, he is," said Mike Whalen. "Picked three uv the Blues off first the last time he was here."

"Galvin's full uv the jiggery-pokery," chuckled Leahy.

"He's a four-flusher," said Shaymus.

"Do yas think Big Dan Brouthers'll sock another ball over the fence?" asked Ed. "He's done it five times this year."

Sean Murphy joined them. He was waving a copy of the *Cleveland Leader* he'd been reading in the outdoor privy. "Did you fellas hear what happened?" he asked excitedly.

"Did the president die?" asked Fergus.

"No. But William Bonny surely did. Some sheriff name uv Pat Garrett shot and killed him in New Mexico."

The Only Del

"They got *Billy the Kid?*" blurted Ed. "What happened?"

"Apparently he spent the last four years in Lincoln County, New Mexico," said Murphy. "Got mixed up in a war between cattlemen and picked the wrong side. He shot the sheriff and his deputy and then went into hiding for two years. The new sheriff, this Pat Garrett, finally caught him and threw him in the Lincoln jail. A few weeks ago while Garrett was out uv town on business the Kid grabbed a guard's six-shooter and shot him. Another guard ran after Billy and the Kid shot him too before stealing a horse and riding off."

"I remember reading about that," said Leahy.

Enjoying that the group was hanging on his every word, Murphy continued his account. "Garrett heard tell the Kid was holed up in Fort Sumner and he and two deputies lit off after him. Here, I'll read you what Garrett told the reporters."

He unfolded his newspaper, found the article, and started reading to the others. "My deputies and I spotted him outside of a Mexican's house. We went in but couldn't see anybody. Then the Kid burst through the door in his stocking-feet, carrying a revolver in his right hand and a butcher knife in the other. He backed away from us, raised his pistol, and pointed it at my chest. I threw my body to the side, drew my revolver, and shot twice. I hadn't needed to fire the second shot. The first one killed him."

"That's quite the story," said Mike Whalen.

"And a *story* it might just be," said Murphy. "Apparently one of Garrett's deputies said the Kid wasn't carrying a pistol when he went into the house, just a knife."

"How long has it been since Wild Bill Hickok was shot?" asked Fergus Maloney.

"I was ten when it happened, so it must uv been five years ago," said Logan.

"What's that on the wall?" Ed asked Patrick Leahy.

"I looks like one uv the things you talk into and somebody all the way across town can hear you," said Fergus.

the greatest batsman in the land

"That's exactly what it is," said Leahy. "Department's putting one in every station. It's a telephone. We're still gointa have the alarm bells ring here in the station when there's a fire, but we can use that to call headquarters to find out how big the fire is and decide how many hook-and-ladders we need."

"How does it work?" asked Ed.

"I'll show you," offered Leahy. "The fella that's putting them in taught me." He went over and took the cone-shaped device that was attached to the hanger. He put it to his ear, cranked a lever on the side of the box, and then pretended to speak into the telephone. "Hello. Hello. Operator? This is Patrick Leahy down at Fire Engine House Number Five. Can ya put me through to City Hall? Oid like to tell yer man the mayor what a rotten job he's doin' uv running this burg."

Everyone laughed.

"Apparently your voice goes through the wires they're stringing from the ugly new poles along the streets," explained Leahy. "The installer fella said pretty soon *everybody*'ll have one uv these contraptions."

"Does that mean the missus'll be able to call me at the pool hall and tell me ta get me lazy arse home?" asked Mike Whalen.

Everyone laughed again. Fergus went over and pretended to make a call. "Operator? Connect me with Colleen Dougherty's house. Hello? This is Fred Farrand down at the fire house. We just got word there's some young hooligan name uv Ed Delahanty startin' fires in your neighborhood and terrorizin' young girls like your daughter. You'd best keep her under lock and key and make sure she doesn't go near this Delahanty character. He's nuthin' but trouble."

Ed grabbed Fergus, easily wrestled him to the ground, and then sat on him.

"Uncle! Uncle!" protested Fergus. "Get off, ya big lug! Yer smotherin' the life out uv me. There'll be a coroner's inquest inta how some hot shot baseball player squeezed the life out uv a teammate cuz they smashed into each other on the ball field and the hooligan's girl nearly up and feinted."

The Only Del

Chapter Two

No Dogs or Irish Allowed

Ed got to his small, red brick house on Phelps Street between St. Clair and Superior at 5:30. He was often late for supper because he'd been playing ball. His father arrived home just after Ed, having stopped on his way to play handball. He wore a brown sack suit with narrow lapels, a wingtip collar, and a slightly dented derby. His small bow tie with short, pointed ends would have been the height of fashion in the '70's but it wasn't now. Ed noticed that DELAHANTY was printed on his brief case and remembered how when he was eight years old his father had explained to him that, even though they came from Ireland, the family name was originally French and that de la hanté meant "of the haunted". Ed thought that was a little spooky, but he'd enjoyed telling the other kids in his third grade class.

"So yer *haunted* then are yas?" Fergus Maloney had asked Ed.

"I suppose so."

"Well then, when we have the school costume party and other kids are dressed up as ghosts you can just come as yerself."

"When are you ever gointa start thinking about finding a job?" his father asked him after he'd finished his dinner and pushed his plate aside. The meal had been brown bread fried in bacon fat and coddle - layers of thinly-sliced and battered pork sausages, with mashed potatoes and onions. Most of the men Ed knew apart from the fire fighters worked at the Cleveland Worsted Wool mill, the California Powder Company where they made dynamite, the Cleveland Lorain & Wheeling Railroad yards, the Standard Oil Company refinery, or the shipyards. Ed knew he didn't want to work at some five cents an hour pick-and-shovel job.

The Only Del

A lot of young Irishmen had left home to lay railway tracks or work in Pennsylvania coal mines. Ed's grandfather, who'd married Mary Phelan of Knockbodaly, had worked on the Barrow River Canals in County Kilkenny in the 1850's. Ed's father James had been a day laborer when he came to America. He got a job as a stoker at the Cleveland Gas Works and then worked as a teamster. Ed's mother Bridget, who married James when she was seventeen, lost her first child - a girl - to scarlet fever before giving birth to Ed. Another girl had died before her third birthday. Bridget's prayers were answered though and she had four more boys and two girls after Ed, who would always be the apple of her eye and get the lion's share of her affection. She took in boarders to help support her growing family and ran the household without ever bothering to ask for her husband's opinion.

At Cleveland High School, Ed studied geometry, natural science, book-keeping, rhetoric, and mechanics. He was a good student, but there was no subject that interested him much. He just wanted to play baseball. Ed knew that close to half of the players in the major leagues were of Irish descent. Back home their grandfathers had played the ancient Irish stick and ball game of hurling - Ed's grandfather had been the best hurley player in all of Kilkenny - and the sons and grandsons had inherited hand-eye coordination and a knack for smacking a ball a long way.

All of Ed's heroes were Irish - Pud Galvin, Jim O'Rourke, Smiling Mickey Welch, Tony Mullane, and Roger Connors. His biggest hero though was Mike "King" Kelly of the Chicago White Stockings. He was the first man to play off the bag at first and to purposely foul off pitches until he got one to his liking. Ed knew that Kelly resided in the Palmer House, one of Chicago's finest hotels. That'd be the life for Ed Delahanty.

The Blues were at home, so early Saturday morning the boys crossed St. Clair on their way to catch an omnibus to Kennard Street. They were careful as always to keep an eye out for the droppings of the horses that pulled the ice, milk, and bread wagons. The Cleveland City Council was considering the purchase of some of the new street-cleaning machines to solve the problem. The boys heard the clopping of hooves and stepped out of the path of a bakery wagon. Some folks had started getting their bread at the new A&P store, but most people in the neighborhood were

the greatest batsman in the land

still attached to McFingle's Bread & Pastries and to Davey, their voluble young driver.

"Fresh out uv me muther's oven at five this mornin'," he'd always tell his customers. Ed liked to pat Davey's horse, an old piebald mare named Daisy. She was almost blind, but she knew the route so well she could have navigated it in her sleep.

Three foppishly dressed boys were smoking in front of Chalmers Fine Tobaccos. Ed and his friends recognized them. They were the best-dressed seniors at Central High School.

"Well, if it isn't Ed Delahanty and his paddy posse," sneered weasel-faced Jeffrey Forrester. He was the most arrogant of the bunch, which was really saying something. His father, the president of the City Bank, was undoubtedly holding court at the Cleveland Yachting Club this morning in preparation for the annual regatta at Put-in-Bay. Forrester's mother was never seen anywhere without her emerald necklace and fur wraps.

"Off to find some four-leaf clovers are you, lads?" taunted Forrester.

"Oh, I'm certain the Cat-licks have more important work than that this fine day," said Thomas Spencer, whose father was a foreman at the Cleveland Rolling Mill Company. Ed knew that a lot of Irish laborers were working on the erection of a huge furnace near the Cuyahoga River for Spencer's father. "The bog trotters are likely off to search for a leprechaun and a pot of gold."

"Or a pot to piss in," chortled pimply Charles Bolton, an obnoxious snob who called Irish people green niggers. "Do you gents know why Jesus wasn't born in Ireland?" he asked the others. "God couldn't find three wise men or a virgin."

"Did you gents hear the one about the Irish road crew?" Forrester asked his smarmy friends.

"I don't believe I have," answered Spencer.

"No? Well it seems two paddies were working for the public works department. One would dig a hole and the other would follow behind and fill it in. They worked up one side of the street and back down the other side, and then moved onto the next street. They were working feverishly

The Only Del

when a man who'd been watching came up and told them he couldn't understand what they were doing. So the one paddy explained that there were normally three of them, but today the fellow that planted the trees had called in sick."

As Spencer and Bolton laughed, Ed and his friends did their best to ignore them; they'd been subjected to such indignities their whole lives. Ed still seethed whenever he passed a hotel with a sign that read "No dogs or Irish allowed." He just wanted to get to the ballpark but the dandies weren't finished.

"What is it they call a shovel down at your father's mill?" Forrester asked Spencer.

"Why, that would be an Irish spoon, Master Forrester," Spencer told him.

"And what is it that they call a wheelbarrow?"

"A wheelbarrow? That's an Irish buggy."

"And pray tell me, my good man, what do they call bricks?"

"Everyone knows that bricks are referred to as Irish confetti."

Ed stopped and glared at Spencer.

"Hey, Maloney," Spencer said to Fergus. "Is your dear mother still doing laundry, I have some underwear that needs cleaning."

"Did you shit yer knickers again?" asked Ed.

Spencer stepped up to face Ed eye-to-eye. "You shillelagh-swinging pot licker," he snarled. "It's high time someone taught you spud suckers your place."

"What's the matter, Spencer?" Ed asked. "Did somebody steal your lunch money again?"

Spencer clenched a fist and swung as hard as he could. Everyone inhaled as the blow landed squarely on Ed's jaw.

"Ouhh!" screeched Spencer.

Scarcely affected by the feeble punch, Ed stood smiling and chuckling at Spencer, who had almost certainly broken his hand.

"I guess you're only used to hittin' servant girls with those dainty hands

the greatest batsman in the land

uv yours," Ed mocked Spencer.

Bolton and Forrester stepped up to avenge their friend's humiliation. Ed turned to face them and they quickly backed away. Spencer's boater had fallen off his head. Ed picked it up and straightened its ribbon. "You'll not be needin' this, what with winter on the way and all," he told Spencer before putting his fist through it and shoving it down over Spencer's head all the way to his neck. He looked ridiculous. He and the other dandies glared at Ed and left.

"Why didn't you hit him back?" Fergus asked Ed as Bolton and Forrester hustled Spencer away.

"The *firemen* may be mostly Irish, but most of the police are limeys. Whose side d'ya think they're gointa take if they get called to a street fight? The way I left things, those three'll be too ashamed to tell anybody what happened and there'll be no more to it."

"But we *should* ask Spencer in front of all his friends at school how he broke his hand," chuckled Logan.

The boys reached the Kennard Street Ballpark just in time for the Blues' morning practice. The players liked the teenagers and let them shag flies and even take a few swings during batting practice the odd time. They thought they were pretty good for their age - especially the Delahanty kid. When he got a chance to bat after all of the Blues had their turns, Ed strode to the plate with the nonchalance of a veteran. He drew a line in the dirt and raised the barrel of his big bat behind his head. When the pitches came in he waited until the last instant and then lashed at them seemingly without effort, smashing line drives intended to do harm to anyone who got in their way.

"Oive got a feelin' dat big lad's gointa do Irish folks proud afore long," Mike Moynahan told the other Blues from the Emerald Isle after Ed had drilled three balls in a row to the deepest regions of the field. "He's got major leaguer written all over those muscles uv his."

"He sure puts a wallop into the ball," agreed Mike McGeary, who'd played for the Philadelphia White Stockings in the short-lived National

The Only Del

Association. He didn't hit the ball anything like Ed did. McGeary hadn't homered once in his twelve years of professional baseball.

"He runs like a colt too he does," said outfielder Mike Muldoon from Westneath County, twisting the end of his mustache as he was wont to do.

"And did you see him the play the infield?" asked Moynahan. Cleveland's diamond was one of the few dirt or "skinned" ones still in use. "He gets to grounders like greased lightnin'. He watches the ball into his hands and scoops it out uv the dirt like a sweet sixteen acceptin' a box uv bonbons."

As Ed and Logan headed to the firehall after watching the Blues coast to a 9-0 win over the Detroit Wolverines they talked about which feud was worse, the Earps and the Clantons or the Hatfields and the McCoys. The *Cleveland Plain Dealer* had just reported receiving a message from the *Associated Press* that Kentucky storekeeper Ellison Hatfield, the brother of William "Devil Anse" Hatfield, had been shot. The *Dealer* reminded its readers that Devil Anse had mortally wounded Harmon McCoy during the War and Hatfield's son Johnse had precipitated the bitter quarrel by eloping with Randall McCoy's daughter Rosanna. Ellison had died from his wounds and three of McCoy's sons had now been murdered in retaliation. The *Tombstone Daily Epitaph* had recently related the details of the Gunfight at the O.K. Corral. It was all the talk among the boys at Cleveland High School these days.

"The Blues let you lads practice with them again this morning?" Mike Whalen asked when the boys arrived at the fire hall.

"That they did," answered Shaymus Finnegan. "Then they laid a beatin' on the Wolverines."

"Seems you lot are at the ballpark every chance you get," said Whalen. "Yas spend near as much time there as ya do *here*."

"Sure then, you must be a tad thirsty," said Sean Murphy. "By any chance would yas be wantin' ta share a pail uv cold beer?"

"Does a duck's dong drag in the weeds?" Whalen asked the other firemen. "A course the lads'd like some beer."

the greatest batsman in the land

"It'd be just what the doctor ordered," said Ed, licking his lips as Murphy handed the boys a bucket with foamy suds spilling out the top.

"Mush was in a street brawl on the way to the park this morning," Shaymus told the firemen who were no longer on call but were playing cards and drinking instead of heading home to their wives.

Ed was no stranger to drink. A short walk from his house there was a saloon in which you could buy two jugs of beer for a nickel or a shot of whiskey for the same and a billiard parlor that served whiskey as well.

Mike Whelan took a close look at Ed's face. "I don't see a mark on him," he told Shaymus. "What kinduva brawl was it?"

Shaymus laughed. "One of the swells from the high school that thinks their shite don't stink insulted us and then punched Ed right in the jaw. Mush just stood there like he'd been brushed with a feather. The little prick broke his hand and the three of them tucked their rich tails between their legs and tore off like a herd uv frightened toads."

The fire hall erupted in laughter. Ed smiled and took a generous swallow of beer.

"Why is it you lads call Ed Mush?" Sean asked the boys.

"Have ya never taken a look at a baseball after Ed's had a few licks at the thing?" Logan asked Murphy.

"It looks like it's bin run over by a ruddy freight train," said Shaymus.

Strapping six-footer Darcy Flanaghan and Brian Kincaid, the firehall's willowy engine driver, had been arm wrestling but they'd taken a break to listen to Shaymus tell the story. Kincaid was glad of the reprieve, he was losing badly.

"Hear then, why don't we have young Edward arm-wrestle Flanaghan?" he suggested.

"Dat's hardly fair," protested Flanaghan. "Oive got ten years and twenty pounds on the lad."

"Afeared the boy might just beat ya, Darcy?" asked Mike Whalen.

"No, but ..."

"No but's about it, then. Let's have it," said Whalen.

 The Only Del

The firemen started getting out their money and laying bets on the outcome. The ones who bet on Ed got 5-1 odds. As usual it would be best two-out-of-three. Flanaghan won the first match in a couple of minutes, but not as decisively as his fellow smoke eaters would have expected. Anxious looks were exchanged. Ed took another slug of beer, wiped his mouth on his sleeve, and belched like a stevedore. When he grinned at his friends the men who'd bet on Flanaghan looked even more worried.

"If I drop ten dollars on Flanaghan the wife's gointa wonder why I can't give her grocery money this week," whispered Kincaid.

"Who did Whalen bet on?" asked Murphy.

"The kid," Kincaid whispered back before spitting a stream of tobacco juice into a brass cuspidor. Murphy gulped.

Ed won the next match in just under three minutes. Flanaghan was getting tired. He'd expected to win two in a row with relative ease. "Me hand's all sweaty," he told the men who'd crowded around to watch. They smiled and nodded their heads.

Ed won the third match in less than a minute, slamming Flanaghan's arm down on the table in triumph. Flanaghan groaned and looked apologetically at the friends who'd just lost a bundle. Mike Whalen grinned as he moved among the crowd collecting his winnings.

"Sunnuvabitch, that kid's strong," said Brian Kincaid. "No wonder he can hit a baseball as hard as he does."

Ed was in good spirits, but he wished he'd bet on himself. "Gotta go, gents," he told the firemen. "Me mum'll be on the warpath if oim late again tonight."

His mother *was* up in arms. Each of Ed's younger brothers had taken a liking to baseball thanks to their big brother's heroics on the diamond. She feared none of them would ever get serious and earn a decent living.

Chapter Three

Comin' Home with Rocks in Me Pocket

Engine House Number Five sponsored several tournaments on their new baseball field. Invariably the boys who spent so much of their time at the station house came out on top and it was usually due to the hard-hitting and skillful fielding of Ed Delahanty. The firemen won a small fortune betting on the Irish lads when they played against sides with bigger and more experienced nines.

"Where is it you'll be goin' now, Mush?" Sean Murphy asked Ed after he'd hit three triples and scored five runs in another Engine House Number Five victory.

"Saint Joseph's College. It's on Woodland, not far from the high school," answered Ed, who was now six-foot one and 175 pounds. "Me muther has high hopes uv me endin' up in some fancy job and dressin' like a dandy. She signed me up for *bookkeeping* uv all things. I'd rather shovel shite than be a damn *book*keeper!"

"No, I mean where are you goin' ta be playin' ball. You're gettin' far too good fer these penny-ante tournaments *we* put on."

"I've been asked to play on the other side uv the river," Ed told Murphy. "It's semi-pro. I'll get four dollars a game."

Sean whistled. "They play a high level uv ball across the river from what I hear. But it's a pretty rough crowd. Keep yer head up over there, else some ruffian'll knock it clear off."

The Only Del

The games on the west side of the Cuyahoga were played at a park not far from the shoreline. The infield was smooth, the play was hard. A lot of the dirty-faced older boys were toughs raised in the squalor of the Bend - or worse the shacks of Whiskey Island. The twirlers 'accidentally' sent pitches not where Ed requested them, but towards his head.

Now the throws were harder and they did hurt Ed's hands, but just a little. It was not as easy to steal bases on the catchers in this league. And when you did you could count on the ball being slapped hard into your back - or your face - even if you were safe by a mile. Ed excelled in spite of the rough treatment, he could take it. He got into a few shoving matches, but when a particularly nasty third baseman tried to punch him Ed grabbed his arm and nearly broke it. Word got around about how strong Delahanty was and that the big kid was not to be trifled with. Even the meanest louts gave him a wide berth.

Ed did so well he was invited to play for the Cleveland Shamrocks, who played against the best semi-pro teams in northern Ohio and even took on American Association clubs. Before long, Ed was the Shamrocks' best hitter. Their manager claimed that even though he was paying him only four dollars a game, Ed was his most expensive player since he hit two, three, or sometimes four baseballs over the fence into the Cuyahoga River or the nearby shipyards almost every time he played.

Ed liked having some money in his pocket. He bought beer for his buddies and sarsaparillas for Colleen. He saw other girls from time to time, but none of them were as pretty and smart as Colleen. He often took her to Clifton Park, which was located along the bluffs of Lake Erie in the northwestern corner of Lakewood, a short ride from Cleveland on the Rocky River Railroad. The park had beaches and boating, picnic groves, a dancehall, and beer garden. Colleen attracted plenty of admiring glances. The bustle had made a dramatic comeback in women's fashion. Now it was worn lower and it made sitting a challenge, especially in a small boat. In parlor rooms chairs were giving way to love seats. Regular-sized chairs couldn't accommodate the voluminous new bustles and it would hardly be proper for a lady to stand in the presence of men.

the greatest batsman in the land

Colleen, who was wearing her hair up now, wore navy blue, bottle green, or deep wine dresses in the fall and winter and cotton ones in the spring and summer. The layered, pleated, draped and severely-tailored dresses a stylish woman now wore were high-necked and modest, but the bodice and wired Kabocorset underneath produced a wasp-waisted hour-glass figure that in Colleen's case could hardly go unnoticed. When Ed took her punting she would twirl her parasol contentedly as he propelled the skiff along the lakeshore with his powerful arms. Sometimes another swain would try to outrace Ed and be humiliated in front of his girl when Ed effortlessly left the other boat in his wake.

Colleen loved to kiss and hold hands when they went for walks, but that was all. Too many of her friends had been sent away to have their babies in secret, or for something even worse. No matter what exciting new sensations she felt when Ed touched her, she was determined not to end up 'in the family way'.

Ed hated the classes at St. Joseph's College and he didn't like the fact that there were no girls there. But they did have a baseball team.

"A holy terror, he is," Father Jonas told the stranger sitting next to him in the stands one afternoon after classes had finished for the day. He wore a cheap suit that showed the effects of too many train and coach rides. Ed had just pulled up at third base after yet another extra-base hit. "And strong! I've never seen such a powerful boy ... well, young man, as Edward Delahanty. He's not exactly a model student though," he chuckled. The stranger looked puzzled. "Let's just say if I had a business, I wouldn't want him keeping *my* books."

Ed was on his way out of the ballpark one afternoon when he noticed that the stands weren't completely empty, even though the game had ended almost half an hour before. There was a raven-haired girl with emerald green eyes and pouty lips sitting by herself. She was wearing a Catholic girls' school uniform. Ed had noticed her in the stands a couple of times before but then she'd been with other girls. She got up and came over.

The Only Del

"Was that a major league scout come to see you play, Ed Delahanty?" she asked in a lilting voice.

"'Twas," answered Ed. "And it seems you know *my* name but I've not had the pleasure uv yours."

"It's Katie. Katie McKonechy. Oim a senior at Saint Malachi's School for Girls."

Ed looked puzzled.

"The new one they've just built on the heights. At Pearl and Washington."

"The one you can see from the river?"

"The very one. What's it like at *this* school then? Must be fun havin' nuthin but other boys to stare at."

"I manage to stay awake most days."

Katie chuckled. "Do ya get *thirsty* playin' hard like ya do, Ed Delahanty?"

"As a matter uv fact I do. Would ya care ta go somewhere for a sarsaparilla?"

"That ud be nice. Something a wee bit stronger'd be even nicer."

Ed smiled. "There's a billiard parlor not far from here that serves up a fine pitcher uv beer. Have you ever played?"

"Once or twice."

Katie turned some heads when they went into the place, but she played a mean game of pool. Ed had a hard time beating her. She matched him beer for beer as well.

"Can I see ya home then, Katie McKonechy?" asked Ed when he noticed it was getting dark outside.

"Oill be fine. Oive just to jump on a trolley and oill be home in two shakes uv a lamb's tail. Thanks for the fun and games … and the beer."

"Will ya be cumin' to another game anytime soon?"

"I might," said Katie over her shoulder.

the greatest batsman in the land

Completely bored with his bookkeeping lectures, Ed often read the newspaper in class. One day, among advertisements placed by Hiram Bushnell, a stationer and printer, the Fairmount Steamboat Company, and Mrs. May, who purported to be a psychic medium, a notice caught his eye.

It read . . .

> *"Players sought for a new league. Quality men of 18 to 21 years of age are invited to submit applications by post for a place on one of the eight Ohio State teams stating their height, weight, positions they have played and any batting or fielding records they may have."*

Mansfield had been fielding top-notch nines for two decades, just not professional ones. Now, in 1887, they'd hooked up with seven other cities to form the Ohio State League. It was financed well enough to not only pay the players' room and board, but to send them around in high class train accommodations as well.

Ed wasted no time sending in his application. A reply came back two weeks later from Sandy McDermott, the manager of the Mansfield ball club, offering him a spot. McDermott had heard that young Delahanty was literally knocking the ball out of the park. Ed didn't get McDermott's letter. His mother had opened and read it. "I'll be damned if I'm gointa let me dear boy run off to play a game instead of stayin' home and makin' somethin' uv himself," she said to herself. She burned the letter in the kitchen stove.

Ed was glad when he saw Katie McKonechy at his next game. She was alone again, fanning herself with her parasol. The temperature was in the nineties. She waited for him after the game.

"Look at you, Ed Delahanty," she said when she saw how soaked his uniform was.

"I sweated three buckets out there this afternoon."

"It's good you ended it with that home run or we might have all perished. What's say we go and cool off somewhere?"

Ed looked at her. "I can't think of . . ."

The Only Del

"I know a place that's closer than the pool hall."

The place turned out to be a secluded cove along the river surrounded by elm and maple trees. There wasn't a sole in sight.

"Let's get you out uv that sweaty uniform," said Katie after she set down her parasol. She unbuttoned his shirt and looked admiringly at his powerful chest. "You can take care uv the rest."

With that *she* began to undress. In a moment she was completely naked. Ed stood stock still staring at her lovely white body. Then she dove into the water. When she surfaced she pulled the hair back from her eyes and said, "Yer not gettin' any cooler standing there like that, Edward Delahanty."

He tore off the rest of his uniform and dove in after her. Katie giggled and swam away from him. Then she stopped. Ed rammed right into her, his groin up against her rear end.

"That's quite the rudder you've got there, Mister Delahanty."

Ed blushed. "Oh. I'm sorry, I ..."

"There's no need to be sorry for *that*. A girl'd take it as a real insult if she stripped down to her birthday suit and a fella didn't get excited."

When she rubbed her bottom up and down against his swollen member Ed gulped.

"Go ahead and put it in," said Katie.

"But what about ..."

"It's not the time uv the month for me ta have a baby. But just in case, before your rudder bursts pull it out and let him go on me backside."

Ed did exactly as he was told. It didn't take long.

"You *were* excited out there," Katie told Ed as they lay on the grass a few minutes later.

"Do you think I could put him back inside again?" asked Ed. "It might last a bit longer."

It did. It lasted even *longer* the third time.

the greatest batsman in the land

Phil Osborne, one of the Shamrocks' twirlers, stopped at a tobacco shop one morning to get a pack of cross-cut cigarettes. Sandy McDermott was there buying cigars.

"Sandy, you old dog. How's the missus?" asked Osborne.

"Oive just come from the chemist's," said McDermott. "Pearl needed more laudanum for her cough. The doctor won't say so, but I hear tell the stuff's really just opium. The dear sole's gointa be speakin' Chinese before long."

Osborne chuckled. "Is it true yer managin' the Mansfield nine in the new Ohio state league, Sandy?" asked Osborne.

"That I am, Phil."

"Have you got all the players you need?"

"I'd like to get *you*, Phil, but you're happy with the Shamrocks, are ya not?"

"It's more than happy I am with the Shamrocks. But I was playin' pool with Ed Delahanty the uther night and he said he'd put in an application ta play fer Mansfield. Why in the name uv Pete did ya not take him? The fella's the best young player in Ohio."

"Of course I'd want Delahanty, ya darn fool. I sent him a letter sayin' I'd be happy ta have him on me club and he never wrote me back."

"Ya don't say."

"I tried to telephone him, but the operator said they must not have one."

"Someone told me when Delahanty's not playin' pool or baseball he spends a lot uv time at the fire engine house at the north end of Phelps Street," said Osborne.

"I'm gointa ta head there right now. The wife'll just have to carry on coughing for a spell." He grabbed his cigars, left a nickel, and hurried out.

McDermott found Ed, as expected, at the fire house. He was drinking beer and swapping jokes with Shaymus and Sean Murphy. Murphy said, "Missus Feeney shouted from the kitchen, 'Is that you I hear spittin' in the vase on the mantle piece, Paddy?' 'No,' says himself, but oim gettin' closer every try.'"

The Only Del

"Delahanty, is that you?" asked McDermott after looking around and picking out the largest of the boys in the group.

"I'm Delahanty," Ed replied, setting down his mug and sitting up straight.

"Why did you not answer me letter?"

"Who are you?"

"Sandy McDermott. I run the new Mansfield ball club. I wrote you saying I'd like ya ta play for us. I never heard back."

"Well I never got the letter."

"Never mind. It's no matter now I've found you. Hop on the Lorain and West Virginia Line next week and come see me as soon as you get to Mansfield. I'll have a contract waitin' for ya for fifty dollars a month."

Ed's face lit up at the prospect of making that kind of money. It was more than his hard-working father earned. Shaymus patted him on the back of his big shoulders.

McDermott pulled his billfold out of his pocket and handed Ed a twenty dollar note. "Here's a small advance and enough for your ticket. We'll see if we've got a uniform big enough to fit you. Your letter said you can play pretty near any position we got."

"That's right," said Ed. "Oive played um all, 'cept twirler."

"Well, I'll put ya to the test and see how you make out," said McDermott.

Ed hurried home. His mother was making brown bread and beef stew when he burst through the door.

"What have you done, muther?" Ed demanded.

"What is it you're talkin' about?" she asked innocently.

"You know exactly what oim talkin' about. Where is the letter from the Mansfield club?"

"I . . . I . . . threw it into the woodstove."

"You what!"

"Drat you and your darned baseball. It's ruinin' our family. All your little

the greatest batsman in the land

bruthers can talk about is how they want to grow up and play baseball just like their big bruther the hero. I give the lads chores to do and the next thing I turn around and they've run off to play ball. It's a fine example you've set for them."

"Listen, muther. I love you very much, but I am gointa quit you and play ball and that's all there is to it."

"Well it's a damn fool-hearted thing yer doin', it's sure ta be the ruin uv ya."

"Just wait and see, muther. Before long I'll be comin' home with rocks in me pocket."

Ed celebrated his nineteenth birthday with his friends at the fire hall. Then he took Katie McKonechy to see a show and after it they wrestled in the back of a buggy he'd rented. He told her he wouldn't be seeing her for a while, that he was going away to play baseball for money. Katie told Ed that she was leaving town as well. Her mother had met a man who was taking them to live on his ranch in Colorado.

Ed couldn't afford a train ticket to Mansfield. He'd already spent his advance and his bonus showing off for the neighborhood and buying a five-dollar tweed suit and a fifty-cent collar. So, when it was time to go, he hopped a freight car on the CCC Railroad south and jumped off at Crestline. He would have walked all the way from there into Mansfield but a buckboard pulled by a brace of gray geldings drew up alongside him just as he was stealing an apple from a tree along the side of the road.

"You the fellow that's coming to play for the Pioneers?" asked the driver as he pulled on the reins to stop. He was a big man with deep-set eyes, a huge red mustache, and thick eyebrows. He was wearing dungarees and suspenders.

"I am," said Ed, shoving the apple into his pocket for later.

"You've got soot all over you. Were you on that freight train that came through a while back?"

"I was."

"Well, climb in and I'll take you to the Saint James Hotel. I suppose you'll be moving to Jenkinsons' boarding house as soon as a room opens up."

The Only Del

"Much obliged," said Ed, jumping into the rig and setting his new grip on the bench beside him.

"You'll like it there. Missus Jenkinson puts out a good spread every night and her pies are delicious. You'll be filling out that thin frame of yours in no time flat. Name's Wirtz, Henry Wirtz."

"Are there a lot of German folks in Mansfield?" asked Ed.

"Quite a few," said Wirtz, urging his buggy forward with a click of his tongue and a sharp crack of his horsewhip. "Most of us have been here long enough to have lost our accents."

"I'm Ed . . . Ed . . ."

"Delahanty," Wirtz finished for him.

Ed looked stunned. "How did ya know?"

"You're the talk of the town, son. The people here are all mad for baseball. The new team's all folks want to talk about. Everybody's hoping you're as good as they say you are."

Ed looked around. It was a hilly area with fertile land dotted with apple orchards and what looked to be prosperous farms on either side of the Mohican River. Ed wondered which one belonged to Wirtz. "There sure are a lot uv apple trees around here."

"We can thank John Chapman for those."

"John Chapman? Who was he?"

"He was born in New England and he imbibed a remarkable passion for the rearing of apple trees from seed as a boy. He first made his appearance in western Pennsylvania and then made his way into Ohio, keeping on the outskirts of settlements like Mansfield, which was just a one-horse town back then. Chapman would clear spots on the banks of streams, plant his seeds, enclose the ground, and then leave. When settlers like my father began to flock in and open their clearings, Johnny was ready for them with his young trees. We've got had a small monument to him in the town square."

"To John Chapman?" Ed asked.

"To Johnny Appleseed," said Wirtz.

the greatest batsman in the land

"I thought people'd just made that story up," said Ed. He saw a huge assembly of buildings ahead.

"We're not a one-horse town anymore. Mansfield is getting to be quite a manufacturing hub thanks to the four railroad lines that run through."

They passed the South Bend Iron Works, Ellsworth & Co. Bending Works, the Mansfield Paper Box Company, the Buckeye Suspenders Company, the Mansfield Buggy Company where Wirtz's buckboard had been assembled, and Kraus and Company.

"Kraus is a relative of mine," said Wirtz. "He makes self-recommending churns. I'll have to ask him some day exactly how a churn can recommend itself."

Then they passed Hautzenroeder & Company. "When you get to the ball park, you'll see a big sign on the outfield fence advertising Hautzenroeder's cigars," Wirtz told Ed. "He's my cousin. They're pretty smooth if I do say so myself. Any player that hits the ball over the fence gets a box of them. Nobody has yet. Do you like cigars, Edward? From what I hear you might just win a few boxes."

Once they reached downtown they passed W.J. Jackson & Co., Jobbers of Fruit and Produce, which was appropriately located on Mulberry Street, H.L. Reed's Department Store, a park with a fountain and a canon that had probably seen service during the war, the Faust & Wappner Fine Furniture store, Crawford & Taylor Crackers, and the telegraph office. Wirtz pulled the rig up in front of the St. James. A policeman was leaning against a post out front. It was a quiet town. It looked as though he was about to fall asleep.

"John, I mean Officer Englehart ... I've brought the young fellow everybody's been talking about," Wirtz called out to Englehart.

"The Irish fella? The baseballist?" asked Englehart.

"You're no Sherlock Holmes, John," chuckled Wirtz. "Delahanty's his name. You must be the only person in town who doesn't know that. He's going to stay here until there's a room for him at Jenkinson's."

"You have to try her apple pie," said Englehart.

"Oive heard," replied Ed.

The Only Del

As he climbed out of Wirtz's rig a small, dark-haired man came out of the St. James. Ed noticed that the left sleeve of his suit was empty. A man with a flowing mustache followed him.

"Is that you, Delahanty?" asked the man in the lead.

"I'm Delahanty," answered Ed.

The man stepped down off the boardwalk and shook Ed's hand with the only one he had. The other man shook Ed's hand vigorously and then spat a stream of tobacco juice onto the street, just missing a large, steaming pile that one of Wirtz's geldings had just deposited. "Bob Allen, shortstop and outfield," he told Ed.

Allen was the same age as Ed but a little shorter. He was from Marion, an hour's train ride away.

"The other players will be glad to hear you made it. We could sure use a strong batsman," said the one-armed man. "Young Bob here's really the only man we've got that you could call a hitter. George England's the name. I pitch for the Pioneers every third game or so. Sandy McDermott sent me down to wait for you. We thought you'd be on the nine o'clock train. He said he gave you money for a ticket."

"Pleased ta make yer acquaintance, George. I … I … missed the train. Had to jump on a freight. This man was good enough to give me a ride into town," said Ed, indicating Wirtz.

"Good luck, Delahanty," said Wirtz as he flipped the reins up and down and his buckboard jerked away down the street.

Sandy McDermott had Ed catch and lead off in the Pioneers' first game against the Akron Acorns and he made a great first impression with three hits in five at bats. He started the second game behind the plate as well but a foul tip put him on the bench for a few days. Most of the time Ed played second base, but he played first, third, shortstop, left field, and right field too. He led the Pioneers in hits, runs, doubles, triples, and home runs even though he was the youngest player on the team. He was happy when Wirtz's prediction came true and he won two boxes of Hautzenroeder cigars for hitting balls out of the park.

the greatest batsman in the land

Ed enjoyed playing with the Pioneers' Irishmen: Jim Green, who was the oldest player on the team at 33, George "Legs" Mallory, who pitched - usually with less than impressive results, quick-witted Frank O'Brien, who generally rode the pines but played right field the odd time, and Mickey Kelly, who usually played centerfield but took a few turns in the pitching box and lost every time he did. They drank whiskey at the St. James after the games. Bob Allen, George England, and most of the other players drank the inexpensive beer Mansfield's German population brewed.

After a game in which Ed and Bob had each smacked three extra-base hits Allen introduced him to a friend who had come to see him play. He was a tall, clean-shaven, serious looking young man, with wavy brown hair parted on one side.

"This is my good friend Warren Harding," Bob told Ed. "Warren's tried teaching, selling insurance, and the law. He's a journalist now. He's bought into his father's newspaper, the Marion Star. Warren comes to our games, but he doesn't write about us."

"I leave that to others who know what they are talking about," said Harding.

"Warren wouldn't know a twirler from a teamster," chuckled Bob.

"I generally write about politics since the Republicans won the election in Eighty-Four," said Harding.

"Warren and I fish in Whetstone Creek whenever we get a chance," said Bob, who clearly had no interest in talking politics like Harding always wanted to.

Ed thought Warren might just go a long way. For a minute he wondered if he had made the right decision to abandon an education and take his chances in baseball. It burned that his mother was so disappointed in him. When he tried to get to sleep at the St. James in spite of the noise from the saloon he often thought about her harsh words and look of utter disapproval when he'd left home.

"Yer lookin' pretty glum for a fella that just got four hits and won himself

The Only Del

a box uv Hautzenroeders," Jim Green told Ed, who was offering his cigars to the others but wore a frown. "Still feelin' bad about their third baseman, are ya then?"

The Irish contingent sat around a table in the St. James' "Men Only" saloon celebrating a rare win. The Pioneers had just beaten the Kalamazoo Kazoos thanks to heavy hitting by their young star from Cleveland.

"A little," shrugged Ed.

"Well it's only natural the man'd stick his hand up when ya hit the ball right at him. Problem was the thing was flyin' like a bluddy bullet."

"He'll have ta throw and catch with his uther hand fer a while," said Mickey Kelly, rolling a cigar with a cinnamon tip around in his fingers and smelling it.

"What's dat paper yuve got dere?" Legs Mallory asked Frank O'Brien.

"It's called the Sportin' News," said O'Brien. "They've got um down at the tobacco shop. Some fella named Alfred H Spink in Saint Louis is puttin' it out. It's full uv baseball news and ... what is it they call a player's numbers? I can never think of it."

"Statistics," Kelly told him.

"That's it. Statistics. And they've got a piece here on all the new rules. The National League's made the stolen base an official ..."

"Statistic," Mickey reminded him.

"Right. They're gointa have five balls for a walk and four strikes for an out now. They're doin' away with the batter calling for a certain kind uv pitch and the strike zone is gointa be between the batter's knees and his shoulders."

"No more callin' fer pitches where ya want 'em," mused Frank O'Brien. "That'll change things up a might."

Being the best player on the team didn't mean that Ed had special status in after game celebrations. He went to the bar and fetched a bottle of whiskey and a bowl of peanuts. Mallory continued reading about the new rules to the others. "Now the twirler can only take one forward step in his pitching delivery and the box is bein' reduced to four feet by five and a half

the greatest batsman in the land

feet so the pitching distance is gointa be fifty-five and a half feet. Home plate has to be made of rubber, not marble from now on and it's ta be a twelve-inch square."

"I suppose our league'll use most uv those new rules next year," said O'Brien.

"If it's still around," said Mallory as he downed a shot of whiskey.

Mansfield really was a baseball town and the people knew a terrific player when they saw one. They thought the young Irishman had buckets of talent and a great deal of naïve charm and charisma as well. The mayor, R.B. McCrory, was from an Irish family. The Irish had followed the Germans into the territory. McCrory was one of several baseball enthusiasts who invited Ed to his home for dinner. In his case it had a lot to do with the fact that his twelve-year-old daughter Mildred had an enormous crush on the muscular nineteen-year old and her little brother idolized Ed. The mayor showed Ed the coffee mugs he'd convinced the town council to have made with the words Mansfield Baseball and a drawing of a player who looked a lot like Ed between the numbers 18 and 87.

Ed finished the season with a .355 batting average and showed speed on the basepaths scoring ninety runs. By then the whole city had taken him to its heart. At the start of the first game of the Pioneers' last home stand he was presented with a silver-mounted rosewood bat. At the end of summer they knew that a talented player like him wasn't likely to stay in a small town like Mansfield for long and that once he was headed off to greener pastures they'd probably never see him again. The townsfolk held a special meeting and they all chipped in and bought the young hero a gold watch that he would keep until the tragic end of his life. It was inscribed "Presented to Edward J. Delahanty by the Mansfield Rooters 1887." No one could have known that one day there would be a Baseball Hall of Fame and that the watch would be put on display there.

Sadly, in spite of Ed's terrific play, the Mansfield team lost more games than they won. Frank O'Brien took over as the manager when McDermott finally tired of sitting in sixth place. O'Brien didn't fare any better than McDermott had. The new league did even worse. It sputtered to stay afloat and then sank at the end of the summer. Luckily, Ed "of the haunted" Delahanty would have a place to go.

The Only Del

Chapter Four

A Big Wheel in Wheeling

Ed went home to Cleveland in October. Though his mother was glad, now she was even more upset with him. His little brothers had heard how well he'd done in Mansfield and how much he'd been admired. His fifteen-year old brother Tom had quit attending Immaculate Conception and gone to work on the docks. He spent his free time on the sandlots hoping to be picked up by a semi-pro team. He dreamt of being as good a ballplayer as his big brother, but he was a lot smaller and couldn't hit a ball like Ed.

Joe, who was eight years younger than Ed, wasn't much bigger than Tom. He was a good student and his mother hoped he would find a respectable profession but he spent a lot of time on the sandlots too. Five-year old Frank, who was the spit and image of Ed at the same age, had one of his big brother's old bats in his hands anytime he wasn't in kindergarten even though he could barely lift them. Ed's mother prayed that two-year-old Willie would never catch the damn baseball bug.

In November Ed received a telegram from Al Buckenberger, the new manager of the Wheeling Nailers. Buckenberger had managed the Kalamazoo Kazoos to the pennant in '86. Ed couldn't remember ever talking to him, though he recalled that the other Kazoos called him Buck. George England was going to Wheeling too. But the best news of all was that Buckenberger had gone against the Ohio League directors who were trying to keep salary costs down and was going to double Ed's pay to $100 a month. At the end of the season he *would* be going home with rocks in his pockets.

At the end of March Ed hopped aboard a Baltimore & Ohio train and headed to Wheeling. This time no one stopped to give him a ride so he

The Only Del

walked the short distance to town. Several of the barns he passed had huge ads painted on one side for the Bloch Brothers Tobacco Company that read "Mail Pouch Chewing Tobacco: "Treat yourself to the best." Wheeling had become the center of West Virginia iron production, making so many nails - 50,000 barrels a year - that it had become known as the Nail City.

Ed passed the the Schmulach Brewery, the Benwood Nail Works, the Standard Match Company, and the Nail City Stogie Company and then walked across the enormous suspension bridge that led to downtown Wheeling. He stopped in the middle to look down into the river and then stepped back suddenly from the rail. He realized for the first time that he'd been having nightmares about falling. He wasn't sure whether he was falling into water in the dreams, but he got off the bridge as fast as his legs would carry him.

When he reached the city center he found the McLure Hotel on 12th Street between the Wheeling Register office and the Capitol Music Hall. Ed would like to have stayed there but it was too expensive - a $1.25 a night. He settled for the Mt. Belleview at the corner of 14th and Chapline. Some of the other Nailers were staying there, most of them on the same floor. Hotel owners tried their best to keep ball players away from their more sophisticated guests.

The Nailers loved to play practical jokes on one another. Someone got a key to the room Dewey McDougal and Jake Stenzel shared, set a tub of cold water under their bed, and then removed the slats. From their room across the hall Ed and his roommate George England heard a loud thump and a splash when the two got into bed and fell to the floor. Ed and George found a wriggling garter snake in their bed the next morning. When they got their breakfast someone had spread something on their toast and it wasn't jam or butter.

"What the devil is this?" asked George.

"Someone is gointa pay for smearin' shite on me toast. And *dearly*, uv that you can be sure," Ed announced loud enough for all the other players and a number of startled guests to hear. He held up his plate for all to see. "Which one of you blackguards snuck inta the kitchen and did this?"

the greatest batsman in the land

Everyone looked at each other. The owner rushed in to the dining room followed closely by the cook.

"What seems to be the matter, Mister Delahanty?" he asked.

"What seems ta be the matter? Look at me butter. It's brown!"

"It's supposed to be," said the cook. "It's the latest thing."

"It's called peanut paste," explained the owner. "A doctor invented it for his patients whose teeth are so bad they can't chew."

Ed regarded the toast suspiciously.

"I can assure you there is nothing wrong with it," said the owner. "Many of our guests ask for it whenever they stay here."

"Smell it," suggested the cook.

Ed picked up his plate and gingerly held the toast up to his nose. "Well, oill be a monkey's uncle," he declared. "It *does* smell like peanuts."

Everyone breathed a sigh of relief and returned to their breakfast.

An attractive, well-dressed couple passed Ed on the sidewalk on his way to the ballpark one day. The woman was so pretty Ed couldn't help but give her an admiring look. She twirled her parasol and smiled at him.

That night the woman's husband charged into Ed and George's room. George stared in horror as the man drew a revolver from his pocket.

With fire in his eyes, the man yelled at Ed. "You, sir, are a cad. I saw you making eyes at my wife today."

"D . . . D . . . Delahanty is a gentleman," George told the madman. "He would never . . ."

The man was in no mood for excuses. He aimed his gun at Ed's chest and fired three shots. Aghast, Ed stumbled back and felt about his nightshirt for blood. There wasn't any.

The irate husband stood where he was. So did George. They looked at one another and then doubled over in laughter.

Five other Nailers burst in to the room laughing their heads off. Dewey

The Only Del

McDougal and Jake Stenzel came out from behind the curtain, tears of laughter streaming down their cheeks.

"'Twas *blanks* in the gun, Ed," McDougal explained.

"You should have seen the look on your face," said Stenzel.

Al Buckenberger eventually heard about the pranks that were keeping his players up nights. At a team meeting he ordered an end to the tomfoolery. He also decreed that the players report to the ballpark every morning at ten o'clock. They were to be in bed no later than 11:30 and the players who were not among the starting nine were instructed not to leave their posts when they were taking tickets.

Ed, who stood out among his new teammates because was still clean-shaven, led off and played second base in an exhibition game against the National League's Pittsburghh Alleghenys. A huge crowd had taken the ferry to Wheeling Island where the team's directors had rented a patch of land on Fink Street near the horse car lines and erected a wooden grandstand. Ed had taken to wearing a glove and he still found it awkward. There was hardly any padding, it was just an assemblage of buckskin, sponge, string, and cloth, and it was only slightly larger than his hand, so Ed hardly saw the point. He'd considered wearing two gloves like a lot of infielders did. If you cut out the fingers you had a good enough grip to be able to throw the ball. At home in the off season he'd practiced with his mother's gardening gloves.

Pitching for the Alleghenys was short, stocky Pud Galvin. His head seemed small in relation to his massive shoulders. Ed thought it looked like a turtle peeking out of its shell. Galvin's tiny hands were too small to allow him to throw a curveball. He relied on the speed and accuracy of his shoots but they weren't as fast as they had been in his glory days with Buffalo. He was closing in on three hundred victories, but he wasn't winning forty-five a year anymore. He was struggling to win twenty-five now.

"I hear you hit like a house on fire in Mansfield last year," the Pittsburghh catcher Doggie Miller told Ed. Miller put his mask on awkwardly. He still wasn't used to wearing one. "We'll see how you do against a *major league twirler*."

the greatest batsman in the land

Ed lined Galvin's first shoot right at the Alleghenys' new second baseman, Sure Shot Fred Dunlap, who sported an enormous, drooping mustache. Fred was illiterate. Both of his parents had died when he was nine and the German couple who adopted him required him only to fetch them a bucket of beer in the morning and then he could do as he liked the rest of the day. That usually meant playing baseball, not attending school.

Sure Shot tried to get his hands on the ball but it was hit much too hard. He swore as it ricocheted off him. Ed's next time up he smashed a ball into the gap between Abner Dalrymple and Billy Sunday. After looking at ball five for a walk in his third at bat and grounding out to Sure Shot in his fourth, Ed hit a ball over the centerfield fence his last time up.

That night on their hotel veranda the Wheeling players read what the newspapers had to say about the Hatfield-McCoy vendetta over in Logan County. Ed fanned himself with the paper he'd bought but not yet looked at. He was too busy looking up and down the street for the pretty woman he'd ogled.

"There she is," he almost yelled.

"There who is?" asked Dewey McDougal.

"The gal George had a man shoot me fer lookin' at," answered Ed. He left the others snickering as he hurried after her. Up close she looked even better than before. Her eyes were ice blue and her light brown hair was piled in a waterfall of curls. She wore a gray cashmere dress with fashionable loopings and trimmings that molded to her sensational figure. It turned out she wasn't married to the man she'd been with or any other man for that matter, he was her brother. The girl's name was Daphne and she lived with her mother above a dry goods store.

Ed invited her to dinner and she accepted. He wore a new lightweight felt derby and collar he'd bought, stuck a large white gardenia into his lapel, put extra pomade on his hair and parted it neatly on the side. He rented a hansom. Wheeling's crushed rock streets were far from smooth and Ed was glad this cab had rubber wheels. When he picked up Daphne she was wearing a dress of rich brocade that had no tucker and it sloped downward. As he helped her into the hansom it revealed a lot more shoulder and

The Only Del

bosom than Ed was accustomed to seeing. The cabbie, who wore a lupine smile, gulped and gave Ed a wink.

"The McClure," Ed told him.

"Good choice," whispered the driver. "I'll warrant her other beaus haven't taken her anywhere *that* fine."

When the maitre d' ushered them to a candle-lit table for two in the alcove of a tall window Ed grinned at the way everyone stared at Daphne the very same way he had when he'd first seen her on the street. She was easily the best looking woman in the room and she carried herself with understated aplomb. She ordered Canard à l'Orange and then sherbet for dessert and ate daintily. Ed ordered a steak, a small one in light of the steep prices.

"How's the duck?" Ed asked after Daphne had gently placed a third forkful into her pretty mouth. "I mean the canard."

"Quite delicious," she answered. She hesitated a moment. "Do you think we could have some wine with our dinner?"

Ed's face turned white and Daphne knew she'd said something wrong. She'd passed the McLure a thousand times but had never eaten here. She guessed that wine would be very expensive.

"I suppose ..." Ed started.

"Wait. I've changed my mind."

"You have?"

"I have. It's a woman's prerogative to change her mind and I have just decided that I would like ice water instead."

Ed breathed a sigh of relief. He'd known he would have to write a check if dinner included wine. He had exactly $4.13 cents in his bank account. The bottle of wine alone might be close to that.

"Are you sure?" he asked Daphne.

"I am quite sure. But you are going to have to promise to take me for an ice cream float this weekend."

the greatest batsman in the land

"Ball games aren't allowed on Sundays. We could go after church. Which one do you and your mother go to?"

"Twin Oaks Presbyterian," Daphne told him. "And you?"

"Sacred Heart," answered Ed.

"Oh dear."

"What's wrong?"

"I should have thought."

"Thought what?"

"You're Catholic."

"Of course I'm Catholic. The whole part uv town I grew up in is Catholic. What uv it?"

"It's just that my mother would not be pleased if she knew I was seeing a Catholic boy."

Ed got a worried look and then the check came and he had something else to worry about. Thankfully it came to just over five dollars and he had that much in his wallet. He had no idea how much a man should leave as a tip in a nice restaurant but he figured that two bits would be plenty. He decided to go big and left thirty cents.

After dinner Ed took Daphne for a ride in the hansom through Hornsbrook's Park whose grounds couples came from miles away to stroll.

Daphne put a gloved hand on Ed's forearm. "I need to apologize," she told him.

"Apologize? Fer what?"

"For going along with that awful trick your friends played on you."

"Don't give it another thought. We're always pullin' stunts like that. You wouldn't feel like part uv the gang if the lads weren't hazin' ya."

"But I had no idea my brother was going to shoot you. Even with blanks. It must have given you an awful fright."

"It did shiver me timbers a might."

"How can I make it up to you?"

The Only Del

Ed hesitated. He knew exactly what he wanted her to do. He thought it might be too bold but he went ahead anyway. "I'd like to kiss you when I take you home tonight."

Daphne answered right away. I'm sorry, but you may not."

Ed was crestfallen. He was sure Daphne was beginning to like him. "I shouldn't uv asked. It was …"

"You may not kiss me when you take me home," she repeated. "My mother might be watching."

"I understand," sighed Ed.

"You'll have to kiss me here instead."

Chapter Five

"No team's ever paid that Kind of Money."

The two became an item, the handsomest couple in town. Ed took Daphne for long rides on the new chain driven safety bicycles that were all the rage. When he was a little boy he'd ridden a velocipede. Everyone called them bone-shakers because they had wooden wheels and iron tires and riding them on cobblestone streets was sheer torture. Since the pedals were mounted on the front wheel and the bigger the wheel the farther you could travel with each revolution, front wheels had grown bigger and bigger.

No girl would even consider riding a high-wheeler, they were the reserve of daring young men, but the safety bicycles people were calling rovers were much more stable. Their wheels were the same size and the pedals were set in between them. With the center of gravity lower, the odds of taking a header over the front handlebars were greatly reduced. No lady could bear such an indignity.

Daphne could get her bicycle up to a pretty fair speed. Ed thought she must have strong legs and wondered how shapely they were. Of course he'd never see them unless he and Daphne were married.

"My mother isn't sure it's lady-like to ride a bicycle, but lots of girls *are*," Daphne told Ed one evening as they rode through town attracting stares and some whinnies from the horses they passed.

"Oive started seeing men riding them to work," said Ed. "As much as I like horses, you have to admit bicycles go where they're pointed, don't need to be fed, and best of all, don't leave droppings in the street." Ed remembered teaching Daphne how to maintain her balance on a bicycle, walking slow, then faster, and then running alongside her. He'd loved

The Only Del

having an excuse to have his arm around her. Then he thought again about what Daphne's legs might look like and nearly ran into a tree.

The two sometimes rode out into the country on Rambler bikes for a picnic. Daphne brought cheese and crackers, grapes, cherries, pickles, strawberries, and iced tea. Ed brought beer and ham sandwiches he asked the cook at the hotel to make for them.

"Do you think you could ever earn a living from playing baseball, Edward?" Daphne asked one evening as they sat under an elm tree. "Every time I go to the market or the post office you're all anyone is talking about."

Ed swatted a fly away from her hair. "I certainly mean to."

"My mother thinks baseball players are hooligans."

"Some of us ... I mean some of them are."

"Does that mean a girl shouldn't be alone with one?"

"It probably wouldn't be very safe."

"What might happen to her?" asked Daphne.

"Something terrible, like this." He pulled her into his arms.

"That wasn't so terrible."

"What about this?" He kissed her.

Daphne closed her eyes and savored the feel of Ed's lips on hers. "That wasn't terrible either," she said when she opened her eyes and saw Ed staring into hers.

"Are you sure?"

"No. I'm not sure. I think you'd better do it again so I *can* be."

Daphne had never been to a baseball game but she loved going to Ed's. She beamed when the Nailers' boosters cheered her beau's long hits and daring base running.

"That Delahanty lad can hit a ball harder and further than any player I've ever seen," said a man a few rows behind Daphne.

"Ed Delahanty is *so* handsome," a teenage girl told a friend.

the greatest batsman in the land

"Do you see that lovely girl in the lilac dress and bonnet in the second row?" an older lady asked the woman beside her.

"The one with no gloves or parasol?" asked another female voice.

"Yes."

"What about her?"

"I saw her with the big new Irish player the other day. They were playing croquet in the park."

"I saw them coming out of the opera house. They looked absolutely adorable together."

The first time Daphne saw Ed bat she almost fainted. She watched in horror as the first pitch headed straight for his head. For some reason he didn't leap out of the ball's way. He didn't even flinch. In fact, he smiled! She gasped and went to cover her eyes. Then the ball swerved away from Ed and out over the plate. He stepped into the pitch and drove it over the shortstop's head into centerfield as Daphne recovered her breath.

"There's another one," Al Buckenberger told George England a month into the season. The two were watching Ed take batting practice.

"Another *what?*" asked England.

"Another scout to see Ed. Yesterday Gunner McGinnigle the Brooklyn Bridegrooms' skipper was here to watch him. The day before Billy Barnie from the Orioles was here to look him over."

Both managers were in desperate need of a good second baseman. Jack Burdock, was batting a robust .122 for the Bridegrooms and no kind of glove would have improved *his* inept fielding. Baltimore's Bill Greenwood was batting below .200 and his fielding average was less than .900. The Philadelphia Quakers had been set at second base at the end of the '87 season. Their second baseman, twenty-five-year old Charlie Ferguson, was one of the best players in the National League.

Al Reach, the owner of the Quakers, was born in England, but he grew up in Brooklyn, the hotbed of New York baseball in the 1860's with twenty of the fifty-nine National Association of Base Ball Players Nines, and he

The Only Del

led the Eckford club to a championship. Most of the clubs were made up of men of a certain occupation. The Eckford players were shipbuilders named after Henry Eckford, who'd designed ships for the United States Navy during the War of 1812. The Manhattans were New York policemen, the Mutuals were firemen of Mutual Hook and Ladder Company No. 1, and the Metropolitans were schoolteachers.

Rosters were devastated by the Civil War and teams were desperate for talent. They began offering players gifts, generally jobs in their business. Reach, a gifted left-handed second baseman, let word get out that he was open to offers and became the first professional baseball player when he agreed to play for the Philadelphia Athletics for $25 a week "for expenses."

Reach led the Athletics to a National Association championship in '71 and then opened a cigar store on Chestnut Street to cash in on his notoriety. It became a magnet for Philadelphia sportsmen. Reach decided to turn it into a sporting goods store and took in a partner named Ben Shibe, a leatherworker who specialized in whips. The two began turning out the increasingly popular baseball gloves, including "heavily-padded mittens" for catchers which would compete with the Decker Safety Catching Mitt, and balls with a two-piece cover and cork center. They took over a five-story factory at Palmer and Tulip in a part of Philadelphia that Charles Dickens had nicknamed Fishtown because of the stench from its markets and used an assembly line to crank out balls by the hundreds.

When Lee Richmond, their ace twirler, finished with a 14-33 record and only six rooters showed up for their second last game of the 1882 season the Worcester Ruby Legs opted to fold up their tent at the Driving Park and Agricultural Fairgrounds. A.G. Mills, the president of the six-year old National League, saw a new baseball magazine at a newspaper stand soon after learning of the club's demise. It was called "Reach's Official Baseball Guide." He'd been disappointed when Beadle had stopped issuing his "Dime Baseball Guide" - which called games "matches" and put outs "hands lost" - the year before and was intrigued.

Mills made it his business to find out about Reach and he got excited when he learned that he had a baseball equipment factory in Philadelphia. Mills was anxious to get a National League club in the City of Brotherly Love to compete with Henry Pennypacker's successful Athletics of the

the greatest batsman in the land

American Association. Mills met with Reach and invited him to buy the Worcester team. Reach didn't need very much coaxing, but he did need a partner.

He found one in John Rogers, a prominent, imperious, self-promoting Philadelphia lawyer. Active in the state militia, Rogers had served in a contingent that quelled the Pittsburghh labor riots of 1877 during which twenty workers were killed. Rogers had been appointed Judge Advocate General of the Pennsylvania National Guard with the rank of colonel and Colonel Rogers was what he liked to be called. The two men bought Recreation Park, leveled the grounds, re-sodded the playing field, and built a three-section wooden grandstand with a press box on top. The Quakers racked up seventeen wins and eighty-one losses in their first season while the Athletics won the American Association pennant. Al Reach knew he needed a player who could boost his team's fortunes.

Charlie Ferguson from the University of Virginia had pitched well enough to attract the attention of Henry Boachen, a leather merchant from Richmond who ran a club in the Eastern League. Charlie caught and pitched for Richmond and he led them to a championship. Boachen was one of Reach and Shibe's suppliers and when he bragged about his young new star's overpowering arm, skill with the bat, impressive fielding, and speed on the basepaths Reach offered to buy Charlie.

Ferguson was a work-horse for the Quakers. He played the outfield when he wasn't pitching and batted .309 in his second year. The next year he won thirty games and posted a 1.98 ERA. In '87, his fourth year, Ferguson was even better. With about a month left in the season, the Quakers were ten games out of first place, but still within reach of second. White-bearded, gentlemanly Harry Wright, the Quakers' manager, knew the team couldn't move up in the standings without more offensive production so he installed Ferguson at second base. In 264 at bats, Ferguson hit .337, led the team with 85 RBI, and scored 67 runs. In their last seventeen games, the Quakers won sixteen and tied one. They finished 75-48, clinching second place and ending up just three games behind the champion Detroit Wolverines. As good as Ferguson was with a bat he was even more impressive at second base. Charlie was going to be a full-time second baseman from now on and he was likely to be the best in baseball.

The Only Del

During training camp in March of '88 Charlie told people he was feeling poorly and began complaining of headaches and muscle pains. His teammates didn't pay much attention, Charlie was always claiming to have *some* malady or other. He'd often told Harry Wright he was too sick to play and when prevailed upon he pitched brilliantly. Charlie carried enough tonics and elixirs to fill a convoy of traveling salesman's wagons. The team did start to be somewhat concerned when Charlie, who thought he must have eaten tainted food, completely lost his appetite. When the team got him a cake for his twenty-fifth birthday party he couldn't eat a bite of it. He grew steadily weaker and then took to bed. When his wife arrived to nurse him she was horrified to discover red spots on his chest, a tell-tale sign of typhoid fever.

Philadelphia's marvelous new second baseman never played another game. He died nine days into the '88 season. Black crepe was hung above the bench and his disheartened teammates wore black armbands. Barney McGlaughlin, who'd played second base before Ferguson was installed there, took back the position. He earned his release after registering a .220 batting average and a dismal .879 fielding average. Wright decided to try Charlie Bastian, even though he'd batted just .218 in '87. He did even worse.

The Quakers believed that Ferguson's death had placed a hoodoo on the team. As a particularly bleak April drew to a close they were mired in last place. When a shoe salesman visited the team and tried to interest them in some spatterdashers and patent leather boots he heard the players grumbling about how badly they needed a new second baseman.

"You should send someone to look at a kid I saw in Wheeling," he told Harry Wright. "An Irish kid named Dela something. He's smooth as silk at second and there isn't a baseball park in the world big enough to hold *his* wallops."

Wright wasted no time in dispatching James Randall, a Quaker scout, detective, and all-round trouble-shooter, to see the prospect. When Randall arrived at the Wheeling field the first thing he learned was that the kid, whose name he found out was Delahanty, had been 'Chicagoed' only twice in twenty-one games and was batting over .400. Ed smacked three home runs that afternoon and Randall placed a call through the hotel switchboard to Harry Wright as soon as he got back from the game. After

the greatest batsman in the land

Randall enthused about the Irish kid's home runs Reach asked, "Can he *place* his hits?"

"Place 'em?" asked Randall. "This lad doesn't *have* to place them. If an infielder's dumb enough to get in front of one of his drives the ball knocks the legs right out from under him."

"You'd better not let this fellow get away," Wright told Reach as soon as he got off the telephone.

Reach got on a train to Wheeling the next morning. When he arrived he learned that there were agents for other major league teams sniffing around about Delahanty. They were more than interested, but the price the Wheeling club was asking for him was astronomical. Reach almost choked on his turtle soup when he dined with the club's directors at the Howell House that night.

"Twenty-five hundred dollars! No team has ever paid that kind of money for a prospect." He offered $1,500 and the directors wiped their mouths and asked for the check.

"Seventeen fifty," Reach suggested.

"Twenty-two fifty," a bespectacled director countered.

"Two thousand and we have a deal," said Reach. The directors smiled at one another and shook Reach's hand.

The Nailers were in Kalamazoo for a two-game series. When James Randall caught up to them and told Al Buckenberger that his star player had been sold he was livid. Randall met with Ed at the Kalamazoo House before the first game with the Kazoos.

"How would you like to play in the major league?" Randall asked Ed.

Ed thought for a moment. "Oid want two hundred ... no, wait two hundred and twenty-five a month."

"What would you say to two hundred and fifty?"

"Oid say that you've got yourself a ball player," Ed told Randall, reaching out and shaking his hand. "But I want to play the two games *here* before

The Only Del

joinin' the Quakers."

"Not a problem," said Randall. He pulled out a contract for Ed to sign. He'd never seen a major league contract before.

"What's this then?" asked Ed, pointing to a clause at the bottom stating that it carried over into the next season.

"It's called a *reserve* clause," Randall explained. "The league's putting it into every player's contract now."

Ed shrugged and signed on the dotted line.

Wheeling won the first game 16-5 with a smiling Ed Delahanty rapping two hits. In his final game with the Nailers Ed went three-for-four and stole three bases. He took off his spikes, handed his uniform to a somber Al Buckenberger, and boarded a train for Indianapolis to join the Quakers. The Nailers plummeted in the standings without Ed. People said his departure had taken the heart out of them. But the *Wheeling Register* hailed Ed's good fortune and splendid play and remarked on his "gentlemanly manners."

When Ed's father read the letter their oldest son had written him on the train ride to Indianapolis he couldn't help but smile.

"No pick-and-shovel jobs for Edward," Mr. Delahanty told his wife. "Our boy's gointa be a major leaguer."

Chapter Six

It's a Whole Lot Safer There

After arriving at the brand new Union Station in Indianapolis, Ed walked the six blocks to the Pyle House, the modest hotel where the Quakers were staying. The cleaner and more modern Enterprise catered to families, so ball players weren't welcome. The newly-furnished Capitol House charged $1.50 a night and the first class Brunswick was completely out of the question at $2 a night. The Pyle House cost a dollar.

He got his black flannel uniform from Billy Shettsline, the rotund club secretary and "travel nurse". Shettsline had pudgy cheeks, a thin, sandy mustache, and a perennial smile. He liked his work and the players liked him. Ed paid him for the uniform and then put it on in the room he was to share with Will Schriver, another rookie hoping to make the team. Schriver had already left for the game. Ed threw his spikes over his shoulder, went down to the street, and asked a policeman for directions.

"I know it's on Seventh Street," Ed told him, "cuz it's called Seventh Street Park."

When Ed reached the ball grounds Harry Wright told him he would be playing second base and batting ninth. The pitcher, another rookie named Ben Sanders, played the outfield or first base when he wasn't pitching and was considered too good a hitter to bat last. Wright had been the Quakers' pilot since 1884. He grew up playing cricket and baseball. He'd trained as a jeweler and applied the precision of the craft to his managing. After seasons with the Knickerbockers and Gothams as a twirler and outfielder Wright moved to Cincinnati in '69 to manage the Red Stockings. He scouted and signed players, adopted the knee-length knickerbockers that would become an accepted part of a baseball uniform, and organized their famous cross-country tour. The strongest drink the Red Stockings were allowed to imbibe was egg lemonade. The players called it "Harry's Punch."

The Only Del

Although his code of sportsmanship and genteel conduct seemed anachronistic now, his teams were models of efficiency and discipline. He was the first manager to have his nine take batting practice before a game and the first to hit fungos to his outfielders. Players, fans, and owners affectionately referred to him as Uncle Harry and the Philadelphia press, who were hardly known for civility, showed respect for the father of the game, calling the team Harry's Ponies. His players were always the best drilled in the league. He pushed them hard but no one complained. The Quakers appreciated that Wright stood up to management and protected them as best he could from Reach and, more important, from Rogers.

The plate at which Ed stood for his first turn at the bat in the third inning was the new five-sided model that had been mandated by the National League the previous winter. In the early days of baseball the home base had been a circular cast iron metal plate, though on many diamonds it was made of stone, white marble, or wood if nothing else was at hand. They'd been replaced by 12-inch square ones hammered into the ground with one point facing the twirler and the opposite one facing the catcher. They were made of rubber to reduce the possibility of injury when players slid across them. Ed sported nasty welts on his shins and ankles thanks to the iron plates he'd slid over. The trouble was that the square shape made it difficult for the umpire - especially if he was stationed near second base - to pinpoint the strike zone. With the new five-sided plates the league was confident there would be no more arguments about whether a pitch was a strike or a ball.

The Hoosiers' twirler, Long John "Egyptian" Healy from Cairo, Illinois, delivered two pitches that were in the dirt and then a soggy one just outside. Ed socked it to the fence in left field and elatedly took off for what he was sure would be an easy double. He was unprepared however for the line of deadfalls that awaited him. The minor league infielders had stepped out of Ed's way, giving him all the room he desired. Jumbo Schoeneck, the six-foot-two, 220-pound Hoosier first baseman, stood with his heels along the line, apparently completely absorbed by the flight of the ball. But when Ed reached first Schoeneck stooped as if to tie his shoe and then stepped right into Ed's path. The rookie caromed like a billiard ball off the giant's form and landed on his face in the dirt. He had to scramble like a crab to get back to the bag in time.

the greatest batsman in the land

A moment later Harry Wright gave Ed the steal sign, a left-eyed wink, and he took off for second as though he'd been shot from a cannon. Ed had enjoyed a reputation as a master stealer in Wheeling. He slid headfirst as usual and the second baseman, Charley Bassett, fired a pound of dirt and pebbles into his eyes and then tried his level best to stuff the baseball down Ed's throat. The shortstop, Pebbly Jack Glasscock, came over and stomped on Ed's arm with his spikes. Glasscock took a lot of ribbing about his surname. He got his nickname from his habit of scrutinizing the infield for small stones and pocketing them, a practice that helped him to avoid the bad-hop ground balls that plagued other diamond denizens.

Two innings later Ed drove a ball to left-center and this time he deftly side-stepped Schoeneck. He tore off for second and when he arrived he put his shoulder down and knocked Bassett over with such force the man bounced twice when he hit the ground. But as he attempted to carry on to third he found that his feet didn't work. He looked down at them and then behind him. Pebbly Jack had a firm grip on Ed's belt. Ed elbowed Glasscock in the ribs and scrambled to third.

The next batter hit a pop fly to shallow right and Harry Wright yelled at Ed to run home. Ed waited until the ball had lodged in the right fielder's hands and went to take off. He couldn't. Jerry Denny, the third baseman, was standing on his left foot. Ed took a swing at Denny but he jumped back out of the way and grinned at the rookie. Ed raced home and was out by ten feet.

"Did you see what Denny did?" Ed demanded of the umpire.

"Didn't see a thing, busher," snarled the ump.

After the game Ed went to Smith's Hotel and ordered the special - soup, liver and onions, pie, and coffee - which set him back thirty cents - and then went next door to Smith's saloon and had two beers. When he got back to the Pyle House he wrote a letter to one of his former teammates he knew had aspirations to play in the major league. "Don't hanker for the big time, stay put in Wheeling," he wrote. "It's a whole lot safer there."

The Only Del

The Quakers headed to Chicago for three games. When they reached town Ed and the other players piled into the tally-ho that would take them to West Side Park. There were seats for twelve passengers on the bottom level and room for fourteen on the top. Finding the lower level full, Ed climbed the circular staircase and looked around. When he found an empty seat a grim-faced Jack Clements told him not to sit there.

"Why not?" asked Ed.

"That's where Charlie Ferguson liked to sit," Clements grunted. He pointed to a spot on the bench at the front. "Sit up there," he said. "But watch out for fruit. That's why most of us sit below."

"Fruit?" asked Ed.

"Ya, fruit. Some of the hooligans along the route have good enough aim to turn pro. Buffinton got hit square in the kisser with a tomato last time we were here."

When they reached Chicago's bathtub-shaped park Ed saw the White Stockings' championship flags fluttering in the breeze above a giant advertisement for Beake's Stacholine Moustache Wax. The White Stockings took the field in their sleeveless jerseys with CHICAGO across their chests. There was a special section in the grandstand for the fairer sex. The ladies were clad in their spring millinery - silks and satins, bustle skirts, tapered dresses with billowy cotton sleeves, and grand hats purchased for the Easter parade. Ed had never seen private boxes before but West Side Grounds had lots of them - for team officials, newspapermen, and visiting dignitaries. The most expensive ones had armchairs and curtains to shield their wealthy occupants from the sun. One had wires running in and out of it and a ticker inside.

"Pony" Jim Ryan, the red-headed Chicago centerfielder, came over when he saw Ed looking at the Western Union gear. "Good to have anuther bog trotter in the ranks," said Ryan as he shook Ed's hand.

"Thanks, Jimmy, I hope I can do as well as you are."

"You see that telegraph?"

"Oim guessin' they get the scores from the other parks and post um there?" said Ed, pointing to the out-of-town scoreboard. "The Cleveland

the greatest batsman in the land

park doesn't have telegraph lines yet. I hear they're still usin' carrier pigeons ta send reports uv the games."

"That's not what *I* use the telegraph for," said Ryan conspiratorially.

"What do *you* use it for?"

"I get them to tell me the results of the first two races at Hawthorne and Garfield. Anson'll bet on *anything*, especially the ponies. I hint around about who he likes in the first or second race and bet him that a nag that wasn't expected to do a thing but actually ended up among the leaders is gointa beat his favorite. I get the old geezer every time."

"Yer a sly one, Jimmy. Watch out though. I hear your man Anson's got quite the temper. He ever finds out yer trickin' him you'll be in mighty hot water."

"D'ya see that?" asked Ryan, pointing to team president Al Spalding's private box. Spalding was holding something to his ear. "The man has a telephone in his box," explained Jimmy with a sneer, "so he can send orders to his team without leavin' his seat. We're not to utter profanity or spit tobacco juice on the infield grass and we're ta have our shirts tucked in at all times."

At first base for the White Stockings was their player/manager, 220-pound Cap Anson. He ruled his team with an iron hand, disciplining his players for drinking, missing curfews, or being overweight, which won him few friends. He used his foghorn voice and belligerent manner to rile opponents and intimidate umpires. His outbursts had earned him the title "King of the Kickers."

Anson was an innovator. He was the first manager to use the hit-and-run and a pitching rotation. He also initiated spring training, taking his teams south to take advantage of the warmer weather, and he oversaw a diversified workout routine that included swinging Indian clubs, skipping rope - good for the ankles, legs, and wind, he claimed - punching a heavy bag, and playing handball.

The Chicago manager had used his influence to drive minority players out of baseball. An 1883 exhibition game in Toledo between the local

The Only Del

team and the White Stockings nearly ended before it began when Anson angrily refused to take the field because the Toledo Nine had a colored catcher named Moses Fleetwood Walker. Faced with the loss of gate receipts Anson relented, but his bellicose attitude made him the leader of the forces that strove to keep colored players and Indians out of the game.

Under Anson, their cleanup hitter, Chicago was the highest-scoring team in baseball and he was the game's leading run-producer. The *Chicago Tribune* even introduced a new statistic in 1880 labeled "runs batted in" and reported that Anson led the league in this category by a healthy margin. They soon dropped the statistic, baseball bugs complained that it discriminated against the batters at the top of the order. At 35 years old, Anson won the batting title in '87 with a career-best .421 in a year in which walks counted as hits. The league wasn't doing that anymore.

Most of the players on both sides wore gloves now - except twirlers of course. It had been impractical in the early days of baseball to play double headers since no catcher could be expected to play two games in one day due to the number of times his hands would be struck by the ball. Now most catchers wore a kid glove on each hand. Silver Flint, the Chicago catcher, aware that a team could make just one substitution, wore a mask, a quilted pad on his chest, a mitt on his left hand that looked like a small pillow, and a thinner glove with the fingers cut out on his right hand that rendered accurate throwing feasible. Ed wished he'd had all that protection when he'd been a catcher. Emboldened by his gear, Flint crouched close to the plate, closer than any catcher Ed had seen.

When the umpire tore the red cover off a brand new baseball Ed knew he was not playing on a sandlot anymore. The first pitch to Ed was two inches outside. He laid off it.

"Ball one," called the umpire, bearded Billy McLean, whom Ed was surprised to see was wearing a chest protector too. McLean had been the umpire in the first National League game. He was so highly regarded that he was paid an unheard of $5 a game. A former boxer, McLean refused to tolerate the abuse other umpires endured. When a mob approached him after a close call had ended a game he threw a bat into their midst.

The National League had given umpires the authority to fine a player

the greatest batsman in the land

for unruly behavior, but umpiring in the major leagues was a stressful and sometimes dangerous occupation. Frequent revisions in the rules made their job exceedingly difficult and they needed to be track stars to cover all four bases. Umpires were routinely spiked, kicked, cursed, and spat upon. Cranks hurled vile epithets and all manner of debris at them. Mobbing and physical assaults were frequent, so much so that umpires stationed themselves well behind the plate so they could beat a hasty retreat if there was no police escort on site.

The transformation of the umpire from esteemed arbitrator to despised villain was largely deliberate. As club owners and league officials recognized that umpire-baiting boosted gate receipts, they refused to support the umpires' decisions and paid abusive players' fines. They did little to curb rowdiness and even joined sportswriters in depicting umpires as scoundrels and scapegoats. Occasionally umpires retaliated by hurling objects back into the stands or by punching players.

"That was a horseshit call, McLean," thundered Anson.

"Watch yer lip er I'll make it a fat one," McLean called back. "And you'll be ten dollars light inta the bargain," he added for good measure. That shut Anson up for a while.

"So much fer nobody arguin' over balls and strikes with the new plates," McLean muttered to himself. He had something in his hand Ed had never seen before. When he thumbed the thing it made a clicking sound.

"What's that?" Ed asked McLean.

McLean showed him the small wooden object with dials and numbers. "We just started usin' them. We're callin' them indicators. They're to help us keep track of the count and the number of outs. With all the hooliganism that goes on and everything but kitchen sinks being thrown at us it's easy to lose track."

Ed tried his best to pull the next pitch into left field but he ended up hitting an easy ground ball to Ned Williamson, the Chicago shortstop. He scooped it up in his bare hands and fired to first. Anson caught it and snarled at Ed as he reached first too late. "Nice hit, busher. You were out by a country mile."

Ed went 0-for-4 and misplayed two balls at second. But the next day he recorded his first major league hit, a single off George Borchers, a 19-year-old right-hander from Sacramento.

When the Quakers boarded a train for their next series Ed took a different one back to Wheeling. He'd been given permission to go and retrieve his belongings and say goodbye to his former teammates. More than anything he wanted to see Daphne.

"I'll come and see you whenever we play in Pittsburghh," Ed told her when they went for a walk along the riverfront. They found a secluded spot and spooned more amorously than they ever had. Tears welled in Ed's eyes the next morning when she saw him off at the train station. He knew a girl as beautiful as Daphne might have a lot of gentleman callers while he was trying to make his way in baseball. He was afraid some of them might not be gentlemen at all.

Ed traveled to Boston to rejoin the Quakers for a series with the Beaneaters. He arrived just in time for the Friday afternoon game, which was the debut of the Grand Pavilion, Boston's glorious new ball park. The Beaneaters had started the season with an extended road trip and their home opener on May 25th was a noteworthy and celebrated occasion. Boston's upper crust and dignitaries from all over New England attended in their choicest finery. The Beaneaters, who had a red-haired, cross-eyed boy named George Washington Decker as their mascot, elected to bat first to get first cracks at the new baseball before it got soft and soggy and the Quakers retired them in order. Boston catcher Tom O'Rourke greeted Ed when he went up to bat in the bottom of the inning. "I wouldn't be diggin' in too hard with Clarkson in the box," O'Rourke warned Ed. "The fella's bin known to put a man on his arse if he's lookin' too cocky."

John Clarkson, who had penetrating eyes and a jet black mustache he'd just had trimmed at the barbershop, always wore a white silk kerchief when he pitched and many ladies waved their kerchiefs adoringly at him over the course of a game. He'd been let go by the Worcester Ruby Legs after his major league debut because they thought he was too skinny. It was one of the stupidest decisions ever, for Clarkson might have been able to save the

the greatest batsman in the land

franchise from ruin. He signed with the White Stockings and won fifty-three games for them in '85.

His specialty was the drop curve, which he delivered from a variety of angles, but he threw a lot of swift pitches that rose. Part-time player and former drinker Billy Sunday, who'd found God and seen the error of his ways, said Clarkson "could put more turns and twists into a ball than any twirler I ever saw." He was a master at pitching to a hitter's weakness and he quickly realized that Ed was trying to pull the ball. He threw drop curves and high fast ones on the outside corner and Ed meekly grounded out to the first baseman Mike "King" Kelly. Ed could hardly believe he was on the same ball diamond as his hero.

Kelly was a handsome man with a full mustache and thick red hair. With his good looks and chicanery he'd quickly became a favorite of Chicago rooters and baseball's first big drawing card. Kelly was the first catcher to use finger signals. When he tried to pick a runner off first he'd sometimes intentionally throw wide. But he would have signaled the right fielder to creep in and when the runner jogged to second he was an easy out. Ed and his Irish friends always loved to trade King Kelly stories over beers at the fire hall. Now he could boast that he'd played against his hero.

On the base paths Kelly deceived base defenders that he was coming in from one approach and then used a hook slide from a different angle. His steals were so crowd-pleasing that when he got on first a chant would erupt from the stands: "Slide, Kelly, Slide! Slide, Kelly, Slide!" King was superstitious, he often brought his lucky parrot to games. He spent his winters in Hyde Park, N.Y., where his next door neighbors were a family named Roosevelt who had a cute baby boy named Franklin.

The White Stockings won the pennant in '86. On Valentine's Day 1887 they stunned the baseball world by selling King Kelly to Boston for an astounding $10,000. Ed remembered being told the incredible news by Sean Murphy over foamy beers. Kelly was immediately dubbed the Ten Thousand Dollar Beauty. The Beaneaters believed their new star would attract the city's large and still growing Irish population and were willing to pay the extraordinary sum to purchase his contract.

The Only Del

Perhaps taking the rookie a bit too easily in Ed's last time up, Clarkson threw him a curve closer to the middle. Ed smashed it into the gap for a double, giving the Quakers an unexpected 4-1 win and sending the big crowd home disappointed. In front of a smaller crowd the next day Ed faced Old Hoss Radbourne. With the Providence Grays he'd racked up records of 48-25 in '83 and 59-12 in 679 innings in '84. He may have worn himself out because he'd gone 28-21 and then 27-31 for Boston. Old Hoss was thirty-three now. Ed managed a hit off him too.

When the Quakers arrived back home after the Boston series Ed decided to spend some of his first pay check on some new clothes. The "elegant gentleman" with his monocle, gloves, and gold-headed cane had all but disappeared, ridiculed now as foppish, effeminate, and un-American. The formal suit all respectable men wore in public had been largely replaced by a casual-looking sack suit. It dropped the pleated "skirt" of the frock coat and was streamlined, with masculine detailing. Men wore softer shirts and lower collars under unadorned suit jackets that had narrow lapels. Worn with a vest, a bow tie, and a bowler hat, the sack suit had quickly become the standard costume for middle-class, white-collar men.

Ed was impressed with the park he would be playing half his games in. Huntington Street Grounds in North Philadelphia was built on an oddly-shaped dump bounded by Broad and Fifteenth Streets and Lehigh Avenue and Huntingdon Street. Cohosksink Creek ran through it and it had taken 100,000 wagon-loads of dirt to fill in the gullies. When it opened it was regarded as a magnificent showplace and the finest baseball facility in the country. Built of brick instead of wood, it featured 23-row pavilions topped on each end by 75-foot turrets. The main entrance featured a massive 175-foot turret. Paneled brick with ornamental moldings enclosed the playing field. Sheds for fifty-five horse-drawn carriages were located under the stands along with ones for the three sheep that groundskeeper Sam Payne employed to keep the grass short. There were no seats around the outfield, but the ones around the infield were close enough to the diamond that the players had no trouble hearing catcalls and even some of the cranks' conversations and could smell the peanuts the boosters munched away on during the proceedings.

the greatest batsman in the land

There was a quarter-mile track for bicycle racing around the edge of the field. It was fifteen feet wide and had banked turns that outfielders were forced to run up to chase flyballs. The park's dimensions were 400 feet in left and 408 to straightaway center, but just 300 feet to the ugly black 40-foot high right field wall. Balls hit over it often landed on the Reading Railroad tracks or in the laps of passengers in horse-drawn omnibuses. The tracks paralleled the park across Broad Street and a train tunnel ran under centerfield, making it ten feet higher than home plate. The uneven ground was nicknamed "The Hump" and outfielders occasionally felt the rumblings of trains passing beneath them. Locomotives often billowed smoke and sprayed sparks onto the grandstands, sometimes starting small fires on the wooden seats and floorboards.

Ed began to struggle at the plate. Catchers like Washington's Cornelius McGillicuddy tipped his bat when the umpire was stationed near second base and couldn't see. Twirlers took advantage of his inexperience and his anxiousness to show what he could do. They changed speeds and kept the ball away, sensing correctly that the fledgling was trying to pull every pitch. The *Sporting News* reported that "Delehanty is too free in his swinging and is being tempted into going for balls that curve around his neck." Writers started referring to him as a shine and a flash in the pan. There was even speculation that the Quakers would give up on him. Tellingly, Harry Wright still had him batting ninth. Ed responded by fuming and cussing and scolding himself and he even wrote Daphne that he was so frustrated he was thinking about quitting baseball. He'd never had trouble hitting before. Harry Wright knew the big lad had talent but he clearly needed to be coached. He put him under the tutelage of small, dapper Art "Sandy" Irwin, the Quakers' veteran shortstop and team captain.

Irwin had originated what people were calling "the squeeze play" and he'd come up with the idea of putting fingers in his baseball mitt to protect two of his that had been broken. Ed couldn't have had a better mentor. Irwin was a contact hitter and he could see how twirlers were taking advantage of Ed. "Be less impetuous and hasty, Edward, "he counseled him. "Modify your speech and calm yourself. Strong words won't make you be a better ball player."

The Only Del

"I know that, damn it," Ed told Irwin. "But what the hell are you supposed to do if you can't hit the ball to suit you."

"You need to wait for pitches you like and then stroke them to all fields instead of trying to pull every blasted ball you see," Irwin calmly explained.

"But I'm a right-handed batter and I can't hit them anywhere but to left," moaned Ed.

"And every twirler in the league knows that," Irwin told the brooding rookie.

Ed promised to come to the ballpark every morning and work on curbing his big swing and practice hitting the ball the other way. Irwin nodded and then told Wright to fine Ed five dollars every time he *did* try to pull the ball.

On June 2nd the Quakers were home to the Chicagos. Like most reporters outside Pennsylvania, Joe Murphy of the *Chicago Daily Tribune* was still spelling Ed's last name with an e in the middle instead of an a and it bothered Ed. Murphy wrote,

> *"Delehanty played a fine game at second but was unfortunate in his batting. He was caught out three times on long hits to the outfield. The crowd went wild with delight and yelled like a band of Comanche Indians breaking into a post-trader camp when the Philadelphia nine defeated the Chicago team."*

But by June 6th, two weeks after Ed's arrival, the Quakers were a disappointing 14-18 and in fifth place, 9½ games behind the league-leading Brooklyn Bridegrooms, so-named because five of their players had married in the same off-season. The Quakers went on a tear and won seventeen out of their next twenty, but it didn't make much of an impression at the turnstiles. Desperate for bigger crowds, Reach and Rogers reduced ticket prices from fifty cents to a quarter. It worked, attendance jumped from 1,200 a game to more than 4,000.

On June 13th against Indianapolis Ed's infield work was "the great feature of the game." One of his plays was deemed "worthy of a gold frame." He singled in a seven-run second inning and homered in a five-run outburst in the sixth. Little did he know it would be his only home run of the year.

the greatest batsman in the land

The next day Ed made two errors that opened the way for the Hosiers to score four unearned runs in a 9-4 win over Philadelphia. He would have made more if earnest Sid Farrar, who was a sure-handed fielder but a slouch at the bat, hadn't dug two of his throws out of the dirt with his enormous meathooks. On the 21st, after the first of what would become seven losses in a row, Ed fumbled a grounder with the bases loaded and two runs crossed the plate in a 6-5 loss.

The next day the Quakers were home to the men from Gotham. The bleaching boards were full a half hour before game time. The Giants' fire-boy mascot irritated the Quakers by heaving balls at them while they were trying to warm up. The Philadelphias presented their pony pitcher Ben Sanders and he booked Clements to receive his curves. Clements, a left-handed receiver, was death to base stealers with his strong throwing arm. Usually when a manager got a left-hander with a good arm he made him a pitcher, but Clements liked to be behind the plate every game instead of in the twirler's box two or three times a week. Sanders, by far the best hitting twirler the Quakers had, was hitting in the leadoff spot. Ed batted fifth for a change. He fumbled a ball at second but robbed Buck Ewing of a hit later on. At the plate he was no match for Smiling Mickey Welch's array of benders, slow ones, and screwballs. He lashed away the whole afternoon and couldn't get a ball out of the infield.

On the way back to the Quaker City after a road trip in which they'd gone 2-and-7 Harry Wright called his players to the back of their Pullman car. Wright stroked his beard and held up a piece of paper. He adjusted his tiny spectacles while he waited for everyone to settle. Sid Farrar was complaining to the teammates around him about King Kelly. With darkness enveloping the park in extra innings, Farrar had hit a liner over the King's head. Kelly leapt into the air and seemed to catch the ball. The crowd roared its approval. Their hero had saved the day again. Actually, their hero had pulled the spare ball he kept for such occasions out of his pocket and held it up for the umpire to see - if he could make it out in the failing light. Asked later where the ball was hit Kelly replied, "How the hell should I know? 'Twas a mile over me head."

The Only Del

"If you are done recounting Kelly's infamy for the fifteenth time I would like to begin, Mister Farrar," said Wright. Sid nodded an apology for making his manager wait. "I am now going to let you gentlemen know how you fared on our travels. Mister Sanders batted for an even four hundred average. Mister Clements, you were second best with a three seventy-one mark. I am afraid you are the only two men with admirable records. Mister Andrews was third with a two forty-three average. Mister Bastian hit two thirty-three, Mister Schriver two twenty-two, Mister Buffinton an even two hundred. Almost everyone else batted in the *one* hundreds."

There was a loud groan. "One man did not even accomplish that mark. Mister Delahanty with his wild swings at every ball he saw batted zero sixty-seven. No stolen bases in eight games. No runs scored. Fine work, Edward."

On July 20 at home to the Giants Ed fumbled a grounder in the ninth and allowed New York to tie the game up. The Giants won it in the tenth. Ed went out alone that night to drown his sorrows. The errors kept on coming, two in a 14-5 loss to Washington on the 24th of July and another pair in a 14-2 loss to the Giants on the 26th. The fact that he was playing with a sore hand didn't help. Handsome, clean-shaven Bill Hallman often played second base instead of Ed. He was a much more sure-handed infielder than Ed but he wasn't impressing Sandy Irwin with his hitting either.

The Quakers lost eight straight and were glad the papers were full of news other than baseball. Art Irwin, Joe Mulvey, the Quakers' excitable third baseman, Ed, and tall, long-nosed Charlie Buffinton ate dinner at their hotel after a 7-0 loss to Washington. Charlie had been hit hard. His arm had never really gotten over hurling sinkerballs for 587 innings as a 23-year-old in '84. He'd had the droopy-eyed waiter bring him a bucket of ice water, which the waiter had thought an unusual request since no ball player ever ordered champagne, and was soaking his throbbing right arm in it. Irwin finished eating before the rest and picked up the newspaper he'd bought on the way to the hotel.

"That's seven now," Art told the others.

the greatest batsman in the land

"Seven what?" asked Ed.

"Seven murders in Whitechapel in the East End of London," Irwin replied. "Polly Nichols was killed on Friday. She's different from the others though."

"How's that?" asked Buffinton. "She wasn't a prostitute?"

"No, the police are pretty sure she was."

"So what was different about her?" asked Ed.

"She's the only victim that hasn't been horribly mutilated," Irwin explained. "She had her throat slashed like the others, but her lady parts weren't cut out."

"And Scotland Yard hasn't got a clue who's doin' the foul deeds?" asked Joe.

"No idea," said Irwin. "The murderer seizes the women by their throats and strangles them until they're unconscious. Then he lowers his victims to the ground, cuts their throats, and makes his other mutilations. No sign of intercourse has been detected - nor does the man masturbate over the bodies. The surgeons who examined the bodies think the killer must have some degree of anatomical knowledge to do what he does and almost certainly has had experience using a knife."

"What is it they're callin' him?" asked Ed.

"The police have been calling him the Whitechapel Murderer?" said Art. "The newspapers call him Jack the Ripper."

"Where'd they get that from?" asked Buffinton.

"It's the name some lunatic who sent a confession to the Times called himself," Irwin explained. "Nobody thinks he was serious. I'm sure glad the fella isn't slicing up women over here. I'd be afraid to go on the road and leave my wife alone."

"Why, Sandy?" asked Joe. "Is she still workin' the streets?"

Art fired his uneaten dinner roll at Joe. He ducked and it hit a plump, florid man behind him square in the forehead.

The Only Del

In late September the Quakers mounted a late-season winning streak to slip ahead of Boston and Detroit and managed a third-place finish, 14½ games behind the Giants. With Charlie Ferguson gone the Quakers' offense had sputtered. Young Delahanty had managed only a pair of triples and a lone home run and he had almost as many strikeouts as RBIs. His average was a paltry .228 and he'd committed 47 errors in 73 games. Ed wouldn't have much to boast about when he got back to the fire hall.

Chapter Seven

Mighty Fine Words

Ed went to see Daphne on his way home to Cleveland. She was happy he had, but as he crossed the platform she could see that a dark cloud loomed over him. When he set down his valise and reached to embrace her she kissed him hard on the lips. People stared in shock but Daphne didn't care.

"You're even fairer than I remember," Ed told her.

"I imagine there are a lot of pretty girls in Philadelphia, and New York, and Chicago," she said.

"None prettier than you, I'm afraid."

"Edward Delahanty!" she huffed. She was glad his glum mood was lifting.

"I suppose I'll just have to do then."

"I suppose," Ed shrugged before ducking out of the way of Daphne's handbag.

Ed took Daphne to Wheeling's new roller skating rink that night. Roller skates were all the rage now that someone had been clever enough to install ball bearings on them and every town was building a rink. Ed and Daphne sped around the oval at high speed and he bought sarsaparillas and popcorn when they finally stopped for a rest. They spent three wonderful days together. Ed could only wish there had been nights together as well.

"Has yer muther accepted that oim Catholic?" Ed asked as they strolled along Wheeling Creek.

"I fibbed and told her your parents were Presbyterians from Northern Ireland," said Daphne.

"Clever girl," Ed told her. "I knew it wasn't yer looks that sent me heart aflutter."

The Only Del

"Just for that you may never again kiss me," she pretended to pout.

He pulled her close. "Not even once. Lord knows I'm already a God-fearin', church-goin' Catholic. I might just as well become a monk."

"Perhaps just one kiss then, but just a quick peck on the cheek. Pretend that I'm your sister."

"I'd rather pretend you were me wife." He went to kiss her on the offered cheek. She moved her head so his lips landed squarely on hers.

Bridget Delahanty cooked a huge dinner in honor of her oldest boy's return for the winter. In spite of her resentment of baseball she beamed when a large crowd from the neighborhood greeted Ed at the train station. She celebrated Ed's homecoming by cooking her specialty, the corned beef and cabbage that he called Irish turkey.

"Did you know about Thompson?" Sean Murphy asked Ed the next morning as he read his newspaper at the firehall. Murph was smoking one of the cigars Ed had brought for the men, a Birmingham Lime Kiln Brand that Jimmy Ryan had recommended.

"*Sam* Thompson?" asked Ed, flicking a cigar ash from his lap and getting up to put a log into the woodstove.

"Yes. Sam Thompson."

"He plays for the Wolverines. What about him?"

"Al Reach just announced the Quakers have bought him from Detroit. He said they hope he'll be the big bat they need to replace Charlie Ferguson."

Ed thought to himself that *his* had been the bat the club had hoped would fill the gap left by Ferguson's sudden death. If only he hadn't had such a dreadful season.

Murphy read his thoughts. "Don't fret, young Delahanty. I'm sure you'll do better next year."

"Oid better," moaned Ed. "Else oill be workin' on the docks the rest uv me life."

the greatest batsman in the land

"Ya think so, do ya? Well then listen to *this*." He read from his paper. "Some reporter asked Arthur Irwin, who I expect would know about such things, what he thought of Ed Delahanty. He said you're already one of the best handlers of thrown balls in the business and you're completely undaunted by base runners who try to intimidate you. He said Delahanty is always there when the ball arrives and knows just how to touch them up."

Ed chuckled. "Oill be a munkey's uncle, all he ever said to me was 'Don't put your hand on the knob uv that bat - that's no way to hit - and stop pulling the damn ball.'"

"There's more," said Murphy. "Irwin said you are a great batsman and base runner, you can fire the ball like a rifle and you are going to make one of greatest players in the country."

"Lord luv a duck, them's mighty fine words."

"I'd say so," agreed Murphy. "No docks for *you*. Not yet anyway. Maybe we should show ya how ta work the hook and ladder though just in case."

"Gimme back that stogie."

Del spent a lot of his time working out with three other young Irish players at Wood's Gymnasium on Sheriff Street in downtown Cleveland. They exercised, skipped ropes, ran windsprints, and lifted weights. Mostly they chewed the fat. One of them was Ed "Mac" McKean, who had dark eyes and an arching pencil-thin mustache. He played for the Cleveland Blues, who had moved into the Cedar Avenue Driving Park and suffered through a 41-90 season. McKean, who sometimes packed on as much as fifty pounds in the off-season, had made ninety-nine errors and was being ribbed mercilessly about it. The cause of some of his errors was his disturbing habit of pouting after misplaying a groundball. He would refuse to pick up the ball he'd bobbled and by the time a fellow infielder had retrieved it the batter stood safely on first.

"You couldn't bobble one more and make it an even hundred?" teased Rowdy Jack O'Donnell. Jack was clean-shaven and parted his hair in the middle. When he'd played ball as a teenager in St. Louis his manager had dubbed him a real peach and now people called him Peach Pie. He was a part-time catcher and outfielder for the Cincinnati Red Stockings.

The Only Del

O'Donnell liked to drink and he liked to fight, so the others weren't about to tease him about the fact that he'd played only thirty-six games the past season and batted just .204.

Deacon McGuire, a big catcher the Blues had released after he'd struggled with the bat and a new mitt, was the other Irish ball player at the gymnasium. He had a finely-groomed mustache and greased back hair. Deacon never drank nor used tobacco and he rarely cussed. McGuire began the '85 season with the Quakers, but he'd batted a meager .198 and Jack Clements was given his job.

"How did it feel ta play against King Kelly?" McKean asked Del.

"'Twas really somethin'," puffed Del, who was doing pull-ups on the horizontal bar. "I kept lookin' ta see if he still had a flask in his hip pocket, oid heard plenty uv stories."

O'Donnell chuckled. "I heard one about a game in Chicago on a blazin' hot afternoon in July. Kelly was playin' right field. He'd bin out 'til all hours the night before. He was tired and thirsty, so he brought a mug uv beer with him to the outfield. He decided to take a sip just as Larry Corcoran messed up and threw a ball right over the middle uv the plate and the hitter ripped a screamer ta right. Without missin' a beat, Kelly - mug in hand and all - ran full tilt and made a one-handed catch. Didn't spill so much as a drop."

"I heard one time Cap Anson sent a detective out to tail Kelly and he came back with a report that he had seen old Kel drinkin' lemonade at three in the morning," said Deacon. "When Anson confronted him, Kelly snapped, 'Bah, 'twas straight whiskey! Oive never drunk lemonade at that hour in me life!'"

"All right, lads, dat's enuff," declared Peach Pie, tossing the weights he'd been using to do curls to the gymnasium floor.

"High time we hoisted a couple er three jars. People won't believe we're Irish," said Ed, wiping sweat from his brow.

"What's it to be?" asked Mac. "Whiskey er suds?"

"We'll start with one and move to the uther," Del told him. "Deacon can have his usual - warm milk and a little ginger snap for excitement."

the greatest batsman in the land

When Ed got to his bedroom that night he had to tell the furniture to stop moving. When he got up in the morning and opened his bedroom window he was convinced that the birds chirping on the new telephone lines were Satan's pets.

Across the globe another group of players were part of a world-wide tour Albert Spalding had organized to promote the game of baseball. Several Chicago White Stockings and a group of all-stars were heading through the Indian Ocean to Egypt where they'd hit balls at the Sphinx before journeying to France to play under the half-finished Eiffel Tower and then to England to play for Prince Edward. Spalding was unaware that each night after he went to bed some of the players huddled over brandy and cigars in the cool breeze of the ship's deck.

"The reserve clause is the bain of our existence," blond, blue-eyed John Montgomery Ward told the others at one of their hushed get-togethers. Ward was learned and erudite if somewhat aloof. When he spoke others listened. "There has been a complete departure from its original intent - to empower each club to protect its five most valuable players - and in consequence abuse after abuse has been fastened upon it. The clause is akin to a fugitive slave law and a violation of the Thirteenth Amendment," he intoned. "Players have been bought, sold, and exchanged as though they were sheep instead of American citizens."

"What was the use uv formin' the Professional Base Ball Players Brotherhood if not to allay our grievances?" moaned Jimmy Ryan. "We're shackled to one club for perpetuity and forced to collect tickets, sweep the aisles after games, and buy and clean our own uniforms. It's a wonder we don't have ta shine the owners' shoes."

The *Boston Globe* heralded Spalding's expeditionary mission an idea that exceeded anything ever attempted in the world of sports. What they didn't know was that Spalding had a hidden agenda. It was no coincidence that the leadership of the Professional Base Ball Players Brotherhood and the most influential players in baseball were across the world when National League owners were meeting to finalize a new salary structure. Players were now to be judged on their "performance, special qualifications, earnestness, habits, and adherence to team rules" and paid accordingly.

The Only Del

There would be five rungs on the new ladder with an increase of $250 for each rung. The highest salary was to be $2,500. When they returned to the States and heard about it, Ward and the others were livid. Ed Delahanty, a rising star, would be among the players affected most.

Chapter Eight

Attracting Attention

Ed traveled to New York in March and joined his teammates on a Clyde Line steamer to training camp in Jacksonville. Speedy San Franciscan Jim Fogarty who had stolen 102 bases in '87 wasn't with them. He was still traveling the globe with Spalding. Sid Farrar wasn't with them either. He was holding out for more than the $2,000 Reach had offered him according to the classification system, high marks for conduct off the field, mediocre ones for performance on it.

The Quakers would be staying at the just-finished Sunnyside Hotel. The concierge grimaced as he watched the husky players climb down from their coach. They whacked one another up and down to get rid of the layer of dirt that covered each of them. None of Jacksonville's streets were paved. At least these players were well-mannered enough not to spit tobacco juice on the wooden sidewalk thought the doorman.

"Finer digs than oid expected," said Deacon McGuire, whom the Quakers were giving another shot, looking up at the three stories of wood and pink brick. Massive oak trees on either side of the hotel lent the place a stately air it really didn't merit.

Harry Wright had his players up at six o'clock each morning for a mile and a half run. When they weren't eating, sleeping, or working out at the ball park they played tennis on the hotel's coquina courts or threw horseshoes in the backyard. Ed won two dollars when he threw six ringers in a row in a match with Joe Mulvey. At a more elegant hotel they would have had to stick to croquet or shuffleboard. Ed took his fellow horseshoe chuckers out for beer with his winnings.

The next morning the players trudged up and down through the dunes for the required half hour. They went down to the shore and doused one

The Only Del

another with buckets of sea water and then it was off to the practice field for dumbbell-lifting, batting, fielding, and sliding drills, and a scrimmage.

Ed did well at training camp, but not well enough to guarantee himself a starting position. Harry Wright thought he was trying too hard at second base. Wright liked the way Ed swung a bat but he was still rough around the edges. "Keep working with the lad," Wright told Art Irwin. Ed would swing at anything, even wild pitches. Sometimes a twirler would put the ball well outside the strike zone and then watch in disbelief as Delahanty stepped across the plate and drove it deep, as if he was picking cherries off the farthest branches. With runners on first and second one game Harry Wright signaled for him to bunt. Ed huffed and stepped back into the box.

"The old man doesn't know what I can do," Ed muttered to himself.

On the very next pitch Ed swung with all his might and hit the ball over the left field fence. He had a big smile on his face when he got back to the bench. Wright stormed up to Ed as the other players stood watching to see what would happen to the rookie and announced, "That stunt you just pulled will cost you twenty-five dollars."

"But I hit the damn ball out of the park," Ed implored.

"I don't care if you hit it to the moon, your next pay will be twenty-five dollars short. And don't do anything like that again. You hear?"

Wright wanted to teach the young man lessons about life, not just baseball. He'd noticed Ed was wearing more expensive clothes than he did and smoking better tobacco as well. Ed's next pay was $26.25 cents short. He'd been docked $1.25 for throwing an old ball he presumed wouldn't be used again to a kid in the stands. Colonel Rogers had watched him do it.

The Quakers left Florida on March 25 and played three games against the Orioles in Baltimore.

"Shite!" yelled Ed as he walked through the dressing room the team was using. He'd stepped on something sharp. He sat down on a bench and looked at the bottom of his throbbing left foot. Blood oozed from a small cut. He looked at the floorboards he'd just walked on and saw a rusty nail sticking up. Mike Scanlon, the trainer who had accompanied the team on their trip, bandaged Ed up as best he could. The cut wasn't especially deep, but the foot became badly infected and his leg was soon swollen all the way up to his knee. Ed had to sit out exhibition games for a week.

Jack Clements, Joe Mulvey, Bill Hallman, and Ed decided to go out on the town their first night back in Philadelphia. Ed had teased Joe that morning by pointing out an advertisement in the newspaper for "Dr. Sander's Electric Belt and Suspensory for all Personal Weaknesses of Men."

"It's for men debilitated by indiscretions," Ed told Mulvey. "It gives a mild, continuous flow of electricity through all weak parts restoring them to vigorous energy. It's for lame backs, rheumatism, and kidney ailments too."

"I may soon be debilitated by indiscretions," said Joe, "but I don't need me weak parts gettin' any more vigorous energy. The wife's complaining the little fella's too energetic as it is."

The four headed to Billy McGonegal's establishment on Chestnut Street, a favorite tippling spot for journalists and sporting types. A sign in the front window advertised five-cent beer, ten-cent whiskey, and free lunches. Inside, a Negro pounded away on a piano, trying his best to drown out a sot who was singing another tune that was completely unrecognizable. Green lamps hung over the bar and light sputtered from brass sconces. The walls were papered with theatrical posters and daguerreotypes of actors and actresses.

Ed looked around and saw a man with a pock-marked face, a hooked nose, and a thick red neck whose name he guessed had appeared on more than a few police blotters. Clements saw who he was eying. The man tipped his bowler to Clements. Jack gave him a thin smile but didn't return the pleasantry. "Steer clear of *that* scoundrel, Edward," warned Clements. "He's always on the lookout for players to put the fix in."

The man went and sat down in a booth and played dice with two other disreputable characters. Clements waved to a waitress with creamy skin and glistening black hair. "We're looking to get oiled tonight, hun," Jack told her when she arrived.

She bent down to wipe the table in front of Ed and her low-cut blouse unveiled a gentle curve as her bosom disappeared into a truffle. "Two

The Only Del

pitchers uv beer," he told her, eying her chest.

The waitress winked and said, "Anything your heart desires, luv," before ambling to get them, her hips swaying provocatively.

Mulvey watched her leave. "Did ya see the diddies on that wench?"

"Nature's been very been kind to her," sighed Hallman.

Clements rolled a cigar between his callused hands, struck a match on the leg of his chair, grinned, and said, "I think the lass has takin' a shine to young Edward."

"It's that baby face uv his," said Mulvey. "They want ta let him have a nibble."

"She's liable to smother the poor lad with those cushions," said Hallman.

"Del's too busy pinin' away for his precious Daphne," teased Joe.

It was true. Ed thought about her all the time. He'd written her just that morning to ask if she could come to Philadelphia to watch him play. The waitress returned with the pitchers of beer.

"Nice pair uv jugs," Joe muttered.

"I beg your pardon," said the girl.

"I'd beware uv thugs," said Joe. "I heard there's a gang of pickpockets workin' the neighborhood."

The others stifled a laugh. The waitress handed Ed a slip of paper and left.

"What's that then?" asked Clements.

Ed read the note.

Joe grabbed it from him and read it out loud. "My name is Jasmine I'm done at one. I live around the corner over the millinery shop."

The others hooted. "Sounds like young Ed'll be breakin' curfew his first night in town," said Hallman.

"Don't worry, oill cover for ya, Del," Joe told Ed. "Oill put a dummy inta the bed in case Wright checks the rooms. You wouldn't want to pass up a bit uv crumpet as fine as that."

Ed had promised Daphne that he wouldn't so much as look at another

the greatest batsman in the land

girl, but this offer was going to be hard to resist. He thought a minute and said, "No need, Joe, I'll not be takin' a chance like that."

"Good thinking," said Clements. "No need to go risking your career before it even gets started. There'll be plenty of girls more fetching than her when you're a big star."

Clements was right. There would be.

Del's infection still bothered him so he sat out all of the exhibitions until the middle of the month. Bill Hallman took over at second and excelled. Del spent his time on the sidelines watching six foot two, 28-year-old, handlebar mustached Sam Thompson. In his four years with the Wolverines, "Big Sam" had averaged .304. Thompson was a terrific clutch hitter. He ran the bases well and had the best arm in baseball, regularly leading the National League in assists. But Sam had hurt his arm in '87 and was something of a question mark in the outfield now.

Del had plenty of time during his convalescence to listen to the grievances of the older players. Among other things they were steamed about Rogers interfering with Harry Wright's handling of the team. Del was optimistic about his chances of doing better in his sophomore year. In his first game back on April 13 against the Athletics he singled and made a hit for three bases that scored two runs. He made an error too though. Bill Hallman hadn't botched many while he'd played second base but he had a habit of making lazy throws to first - in sharp contrast to Del's often too powerful ones. Hallman took meticulous care of his fingernails. He guarded his nail file and scissors the way most people protected their life savings. Teammates got a kick out of snatching them from his locker and hiding them in the trainer's room or Harry Wright's office.

At the jam-packed West Side Grounds in Wilkes-Barre the next day Del drove in two runs in the ninth and made a nifty one-handed leaping catch of a line drive. In a rematch two days later Del fumbled an easy chance. The *Wilkes-Barre Record* commented that, "Delahanty makes his error every game but he makes up for it with the willow and is now an assured fixture at second for the Quakers."

On Thursday, April 24 just before noon the Quakers, or at least the

The Only Del

thirteen men Irwin chose to make the trip, arrived in Washington for the 4 p.m. season opener. They joined the Senators for the trip to Swampdoodle Grounds in six open carriages accompanied by a band wagon. Tiber Creek ran past the park, creating the swampy ground from which the park and surrounding mostly Irish neighborhood got their names. A grizzled vendor shuffled through the grandstand with a pail of oysters and a cruet of vinegar and salt. Many of the 3,500 cranks stood along the outfield foul lines, there were no bleacher benches. The dome of the capitol building loomed in the distance over the right field fence beyond the large "McDowell & Sons Steam Elevators" sign.

The *Washington Critic* reported that "Buffinton and Delahanty were the heroes of the games for the visitors. Delahanty played a good game at second base and batted like a demon, crushing a two-bagger and a three-bagger to right field and causing four runs to cross the dish."

Del went without a hit or an error in the Quakers' chilly and lackluster home opener five days later, an 8-3 win for Boston. Sales of hot cider dwarfed those of root beer. In warmer temperatures and in front of three times as big a crowd the next day they got revenge with a 7-6 win over the Beaneaters. In the first inning Del hit a ball so hard it ricocheted off the second baseman into deep left field. He scored a minute later when third baseman Billy Nash's attempt to gun him down at the plate hit him square in the back.

Batting second now, Del contributed only a single to his team's sixteen-hit 10-8 win over the Hubites on Wednesday but he played error-free ball. He decided to head out on the town with Joe Mulvey and Dan Casey, whose parents had fled Ireland like Del's and Joe's. As they left the park in a hired rig, a newspaper headline at a kiosk they passed announced that a new railway bridge, the Buffalo/Fort Erie International Bridge, had been built at Niagara Falls to replace the one that had been destroyed by a storm in January. Del made no notice of it.

The three hit Bob Steel's Saloon & Eatery first. On its dark walls hung lithographs of Wolfe Tone, the Dunlavin Green executions, and British redcoats torching farms and leading chained and bedraggled prisoners

the greatest batsman in the land

along country lanes. Steel's was like a tomb on a Tuesday night so Del, Joe, and Dan moved on to Finelli's place on Tenth above Chestnut. The décor was decidedly cheerier, with leprechauns and overflowing pots of gold everywhere, but it wasn't much livelier than Steel's. Finelli, who looked and sounded as though he had been sampling his own booze all day, suggested the three try his other bar on Chestnut east of Broad. They went to Dooner's Tavern instead.

"Isn't this where the swells hang out?" asked Dan as they went through the richly-appointed entranceway.

"They're called bon vivants," Del corrected him.

"Whatever they are, they're sure dressed to the nines," said Dan. "And they've all got their noses in the air."

Joe and Dan drank whiskey, Joe neat, Dan with ice. Del stuck to beer.

"It's a shame we're always at training camp on Saint Patty's Day," said Joe as he dug into a bowl of peanuts.

"Aye, 'tis," said Dan.

"An awful shame," agreed Del.

"I suppose we could celebrate it now," suggested Joe.

"That's a fine idea," Del congratulated him. "Barkeep. It's anuther round uv these we'll be havin' when you can manage."

"On their way," said the bartender, a stout man with a day's growth of whiskers.

A man in a bowler hat who looked to be three or four sheets to the wind approached the bar. He was cleaning his teeth with a thin gold pick. He carried a fancy walking stick which he smacked on the bar. "Inn keeper, I require more sherry," he growled at the bartender in a clipped English accent. "And I require it to be something better than the swill you served me the last time."

The bartender brought a bottle and filled a glass. The Englishmen took a drink. "I suppose this will suffice," he grunted. "Leave the bottle." He drank what was left of what the bartender had poured and filled his glass again.

The Only Del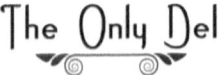

The players' drinks arrived and they did their best to ignore the snoot.

"Do you know the poem DeWolf Hopper is reciting on the vaudeville circuit?" Dan asked the others.

"What? Casey at the Bat?" asked Del.

"That's the very one," said Dan.

"King Kelly's recitin' it now too," said Joe.

"So I'm told," said Dan.

"What uv it?" asked Del.

"It's based on me."

"How in the name uv Pete do ya figure that?" asked Joe.

"I didn't know that you'd played fer the Mudville Nine," teased Del. "Sam Thompson said you were with the Wilmington Quicksteps."

"I was. But before that I went to high school with Ernest Thayer, the …"

"The poet who penned Casey at the Bat," interrupted a foppishly-dressed young man with delicate features and long, wavy hair sitting next to them at the bar. The players turned to see who'd been listening in on them.

"And who might *you* be?" asked Joe.

"Quincy Jones, at your service," the little man replied. "I'm with the Quaker City Players."

"We're Quakers ourselves," said Del.

"You are?" asked Quincy with a puzzled expression. "You mean your faith is Quaker?"

The three laughed.

"It's Papists we are," said Dan. "And our ancestors were nearly drawn and quartered for it."

"Oim guessing yer an actor, not a ball player like us," said Del.

"Quite right," said Quincy. "And you three men I now realize must play for the Philadelphia base ball team called the Quakers."

"Right ya be," said Joe, pounding the little man on the back and almost

the greatest batsman in the land

knocking him off his barstool. "Oim Joe Mulvey and me drinkin' mates are Daniel Casey and Edward Delahanty."

"I am dreadfully sorry to have interrupted," the actor said, turning to Dan. "You were saying something about Casey at the Bat. It's a rather wonderful poem. I'm just now learning it. Our director is always looking for fillers in the event that something goes wrong and we need to entertain the audience while the trouble is seen to. Let me think a moment." He hesitated and then with a flourish he lowered his voice and intoned, "Oh, somewhere in this favored land the sun is shining bright; the band is playing somewhere, and somewhere hearts are light. Somewhere men are laughing, and somewhere children shout; but there is no joy in Mudville, mighty Casey has struck out."

Some men at a nearby table applauded, others laughed. The drunken Englishman sneered and guzzled more sherry.

"Bravo," said Del. "Now, Dan, what was it you were saying about you bein' Casey?"

"I was saying that I went to high school with Ernest Thayer. I pitched for the school team and he reported on our games for the journal. I don't recall what the rag was called. At any rate, I had a bad outing this one time, got knocked about pretty hard, and Thayer wrote a scathing article about it. Everyone started askin' me if I'd read what he wrote and I finally got so mad I threatened to knock a few of his pointy teeth loose if he ever wrote another foul word about me. He wrote Casey at the Bat right after he heard about me striking out in the ninth inning with the bases loaded against the Giants last year."

"I remember that game," said Joe. "I was on third base when you struck out."

"That's an compelling tale," said the wide-eyed actor. "I can hardly wait to relate it to the rest of our ensemble."

"Speakin' uv tall tales, did you hear the one about the Irishman who finds a lamp on the Balbriggan beach?" Del asked Joe and Dan.

"Oive not," said Joe.

"Nor have I," said Dan, glad to have the focus shift from his strikeout.

"Well, a young lad from Dublin is walkin' along the Balbriggan beach

The Only Del

lookin' fer whatever mightuv drifted ashore when he comes across a dirty old lamp. He picks it up and rubs the sand off the thing and lo and behold a genie pops out. The genie tells the lad that he'll grant him three wishes. 'Oid like a glass uv beer that's always full,' says the lad. He looks in his hand and sure enough there's a full glass uv beer in it. He drinks it down and the thing fills right back up. He smiles and drinks it down and doesn't the thing fill right to the top again. 'What are your other two wishes?' asks the genie. 'Oill have two more uv these,' says the lad."

The other two burst out laughing. Beer suds spurted through Dan's nose and Joe and Del had to pound him on the back to get him breathing again.

"I hope you are all right," the small actor said to Dan. "You told that story very well," he told Del. "You'd make a fine thespian."

"He'd make a fine what?" asked Joe.

"A fine actor," explained the little man.

"I have one," the drunken Englishman bellowed.

"A what?" asked Joe.

"An Irish joke, you fool," said the man. "What are you blokes, anyway? You're well-dressed enough to work in an office but you are clearly coal crackers and those hands of yours make it rather obvious you work on the docks or in the railyards. I thought this place catered to a better clientele."

"We're ball players," said Joe.

"No surprise there. That's what a lot of your kind go into, isn't it? Baseball or boxing."

The players glared at the rude Englishmen, who emptied his glass and poured himself another.

"Playing b...b...baseball is the only job you can hold down?" the Englishmen sputtered contemptuously.

"At least we can hold our *liquor*," said Del.

The man spilled some of his drink down his starched shirtfront and launched into his joke without invitation. "Muldoon lived alone in the Irish countryside with only a pet dog for company. One day the dog died and Muldoon went to the parish priest and asked, 'Father, could ya be saying a mass for the poor creature?' Father Patrick replied, 'I'm afraid not; we cannot have services for an animal in the church. But there are some Baptists down the lane, and there's no tellin' what they believe. Maybe they'll do something for the dog.' Muldoon said, 'I'll go right away Father. Is a thousand pounds enough to give them for the service?' Father Patrick exclaimed, 'Sweet Mary and Joseph. Why didn't ya tell me your dog was Catholic?'"

The buffoon laughed at his own joke. The players looked at him with stone cold faces.

"That was uv mighty questionable taste, sir," said Del. "We're proud ta be Catholic we are."

"Is that so?"

"It's one thing for these fellows to have fun at their own expense," the actor told the Englishman, "it's quite another for you to ridicule them."

The drunk walked over and pulled the actor off his stool and then waved his stick in his face threateningly. "Why don't you mind your own business, pipsqueak?" he stormed.

Del spun the Englishman around to face him. "Why don't ya try pickin' on someone your own size, you besotted limey."

"Maybe I will, bog trotter."

He took a swing at Del, who easily ducked out of the way and pushed the drunk away. The man's face flushed crimson and his eyes blazed like hot coals. Del took a closer look at the cane in the Englishman's hand and recognized it as a Malacca walking stick, a Malay cane made from rattan palms. He knew what was inside it. The man cracked it open to reveal a thin sword.

He lunged at Del, who moved back - away and to the side. As the sword passed by his left ear he grabbed the arm that held it and pulled as hard as he could, propelling the drunk forward with his own momentum. He crashed hard against the mahogany bar. Joe grabbed a bucket full of ice and jammed it over the drunk's head and the three players stood over him laughing at how ridiculous the recently full-of-himself popinjay looked. The barkeep came out from behind the bar, pulled the dazed Englishman

The Only Del

up by the arm, dragged him to the door, and threw him into the street.

"Don't even think about setting foot in this place again, " he yelled as the man stumbled out of the way of a passing trolley in the nick of time. "Your drinks are on me," the bartender told the players.

The actor thanked Ed for sticking up for him, handed him some passes to the theater, and hurried out. Ed, Joe, and Dan picked up their refilled glasses. "Who are we drinkin' to now?" asked Del.

"Saint Patty, remember," said Dan.

"And ta sendin' the English back where they came from," said Joe.

On May 2, a day after Charlie Bastian was sold to the Chicago White Stockings, Del made an error but it didn't cost his team this time. Art Irwin made two and they led to three runs in the Quakers' 5-4 loss to the Beaneaters. The next day "Farrar, Mulvey, and Delahanty led in the field work" in an 11-2 victory. On May 6th at home to New York Del played error-free ball and stroked two singles as part of a 6-4 win that moved the Quakers into a share of first place. Del and Billy Hallman were praised for their infield work in the Quakers' 6-0 win over the Senators in Washington two days later. The pair had turned some slick double plays in support of Buffinton's four-hit effort and Ed's hard-hit double in the fourth accounted for two of the half dozen runs. The next day he singled and tripled against Washington.

Del's tally in a 14-1 romp on Saturday the 11th was six trips to the plate, three runs scored, three singles, a triple, five runners sent home, an unassisted double play, and no errors. People were beginning to sit up and take notice of the handsome, free-swinging 22-year-old with the sunny disposition.

Chapter Nine

Secret Meetings

On May 17th the Philadelphias were home to the Indianapolis Hoosiers. They were clad in their drab gray road uniforms instead of the gaudy yellow and blue ones they wore at home. Ed's double over the head of Pebbly Jack Glasscock and his drive to deep center that got past Jack McGeachey accounted for half of the runs in the Quakers' 6-5 win. He "gave general satisfaction" at second base with four assists and three putouts, one a "sharp trick" in which he caught Sullivan taking too big a lead, one example of the visitors' "stupid base-running" in the hour and thirty-five minute contest.

On May 22nd, a year to the day after Del had made his major league debut, the Quakers hosted the Cleveland Spiders - the former Cleveland Blues - for the start of a four-game series. The Spiders, who got their name from the unusual web design of their uniforms, had won seven out of nine games before a four-game losing streak had brought them back down to earth. The Quakers were tied atop the National League standings with the Boston Beaneaters and excitement filled the air of the Philadelphia Baseball Grounds. Del fumbled a hot grounder and made a wild throw, but he had two hits and scored the winning run in the ninth. He scored both runs in a 5-2 Quaker loss in the second game and fielded well, but was a bust at the plate in the third game, a 4-3 loss.

In the final game of the series Skinny Cinders O'Brien strode to the pitching box for the Spiders. He had a walrus mustache and a habit of facing center field throughout his windup. The batter had no clue where the pitch might end up. Cinders had a wicked curve but he hit a lot of opponents. In his first at bat, Del let a pitch on the inside corner go by. Though the umpire, Wally Fessenden, declared it a strike Art Irwin nodded approvingly. "Wait for one you like, Del," he called out.

The Only Del

The next pitch was low and outside. Del watched that one go by as well.

"He'll have to give you something sooner or later," yelled Harry Wright.

The next pitch was a change of pace. O'Brien obviously believed that Delahanty was anxious for something he could lay into and would swing wild and early. He didn't. Del waited until the last split-second and when he swung, the ball shot off his bat toward the left fielder, Jimmy McAleer. He stood in his tracks mesmerized by the speed at which the gray sphere was racing toward him. McAleer didn't even lift his arms to protect himself and for a second it looked as though the blurring rocket would decapitate him. The ball struck McAleer in the middle of his chest and he fell like a stone.

Paul Radford, the center fielder, raced over and picked up the ball. He threw it to Cub Stricker at second base. He caught it with his bare hands and then braced himself. Del crashed into Stricker, knocking him for a loop.

Stricker sat up and looked daggers at Ed. "You fuckin' Mackerel Snapper! You nearly killed McAleer and then you tried to lay me out."

"You were blockin' the bag," Del explained innocently.

Del ripped a single to center his next time up. From first base he studied Cinders O'Brien's unorthodox delivery. It looked just as strange from this angle. When O'Brien finally turned to face the plate Del took off for second. The catcher, Chief Zimmer, didn't wear a mask so he had a clear view of Del's attempted larceny. He fired a chest-high bullet to Stricker. Del slid head first into second. Stricker had braced himself better this time. He was short but stocky and had a low center of gravity. Del wondered if Stricker had held onto the ball. Then he didn't care. He felt a searing pain in the shoulder that had jammed into Stricker's knee and lay on the ground moaning. The team doctor ran down from the stands. He and Mike Scanlon helped Del into the dressing room under the third base pavilion.

The doctor delivered the bad news the next day. Del's collarbone was fractured. The bone was set and Del's arm was bound tightly to his side. He was told that his arm would be in a sling for a month. Del cursed his

the greatest batsman in the land

bad luck and took the train home to Cleveland the next morning.

He'd committed thirteen errors in a month of play, mostly on wild throws, but he'd batted .344. He had nothing to be ashamed about when he got home this time. He worked out as best he could to keep in shape. The bone had to be reset and his return to the lineup would have to wait. He enjoyed his mother's cooking, got reacquainted with his brothers, and hung around with his Irish friends. He played checkers and drank beer at the fire hall too, but he was soon frustrated and bored.

When the Quakers came to town they were amused to see that Del was one of the ticket takers. He went out with Deacon McGuire, Joe Mulvey, and Jack Clements before they left town. Over milk for Deacon and beer and shots of whiskey for the other three they talked about the secret plans the Professional Base Ball Players Brotherhood were making.

"We're startin' up a league uv our own," Mulvey whispered conspiratorially. "We've had it up to our ears with the new salary classification system, money bein' held back fer no good reason, and the fuckin' reserve clause."

"It's bad enough we've gotta pay for our uniforms. Now the owners are charging us fifty cents a day for meal money," said Deacon McGuire. "They're makin' us go inta the stands to retrieve foul balls and fining players for missing games on account uv bein' hurt. The Washington owner fined a man fer missin' a game on his wedding day!"

"I heard about that, but how the blazes are we gointa get up our own league?" Del asked louder than he should have.

"John Montgomery Ward's bin meetin' with some rich fellas he's hopin'll back us," explained Joe. "Ned Hanlon's found a trolley operator in Cleveland that's real interested. Name's Al Johnson. Whenever we're in Cleveland our Brotherhood reps - Irwin, Huffinton, and Fogarty - meet with Johnson at the Hollenden." He looked around to see if anyone was listening. "It's all hush-hush. We post lookouts in the hotel and bribe the police not to report us goin' in and out."

Twenty-six year old Johnson was a wealthy streetcar magnate. He'd made a pile of money investing in Beeman's Pepsin Gum. His brother Tom, who

The Only Del

had made his own fortune via the invention of a see-through fare box, was a co-investor. Al Johnson was a huge baseball booster. He loved drinking, playing cards, and swapping stories with Mike Kelly, Ned Hanlon, and Dandelion Pfeffer, whose mustache so closely resembled a broom that an umpire had once asked him if he could borrow it to brush off home plate.

Al loved to watch Pfeffer play second base. He had a lot of tricks up his sleeve. He was the first infielder to cut off the catcher's throw to second and throw home on an attempted double steal. If there was a runner on first and a soft line drive was hit to him, Pfeffer would purposely drop the ball, pick it up, step on second, and throw to first for an easy double play. Del had seen him do it and couldn't wait to pull the stunt himself.

One time when Johnson was playing poker with King Kelly and George Gore of the New York Giants in Johnson's sixth floor hotel room Gore consumed five or six large glasses of whiskey. Half-primed, when he found himself down close to fifty dollars he climbed out the window. Johnson ran to it and looked down to the street in horror. He saw nothing but a couple of carriages passing by. Hanging by his fingertips from the ledge was Gore. It took all of his might but Johnson grabbed Gore by the wrists, pulled the 195-pounder back up onto the ledge, and told the terrified man to forget about the fifty dollars.

Through the smoke from four-bit cigars Al Johnson told the players how his uncle Richard had killed Tecumseh, the great Shawnee Chief, during the War of 1812 and how the Union Army had burned the plantation of his father, a Kentucky colonel, to the ground. Johnson also told the players how he wanted to put a ballpark on one of his trolley lines.

Ed finally returned to the lineup on August 2nd. He was sad that his mentor Sandy Irwin was gone. Infuriated by his Brotherhood activities, ardent anti-unionist Rogers had sold him to Washington. There wasn't much protest from the Philly cranks. They'd been on him for his feeble hitting and ragged infield work. Del found his position occupied. Fed up with Del's infield play, Reach had purchased Al "Cod" Myers from the financially-challenged Washington Nationals to play second. Harry Wright had decided that Del's speed and strong arm could be put to better use in the outfield.

the greatest batsman in the land

Leading off and playing left field on August 27, Ed made a terrific catch of a line drive, socked two doubles and knocked in three runs. He played left again in the first game of a Labor Day doubleheader at home to Cap Anson's Chicagos. It was a great opportunity for him to prove he deserved to be a regular, but only one ball came his way the whole game and he mishandled it. Luckily the gaff didn't lead to a run in the ten-inning 2-1 loss. Ed managed only a bloop single in five appearances at the bat. He was 1-for-5 again when he got to play in the last game of the Chicago series. When the Spiders came to town the next day he was in his familiar position - beside the water bucket.

Ed was back in the lineup on September 9 and the *Pittsburghh Daily Post* raved that,

> *"The crowd cheered themselves hoarse and Delahanty was their especial favorite. Five times he batted and each time he sent the ball into fair ground and out of the fielders' reach. He played left field to perfection and two of his catches were deserving of the applause that greeted them."*

In the middle of October the league posted the National League batting and fielding averages for the '89 season. Del had finished fifteenth in hitting at .291, second only to Sam Thompson's .300 among Philadelphia batsmen. He ranked a disappointing tenth among second basemen in fielding but he was third among outfielders with just three errors. He was an established major leaguer now, but would he be in the major league?

The Only Del

Chapter Ten

A League of Their Own

The National League owners all scoffed at Ward's plan to start a new league. Albert Spalding went so far as to label it a dangerous experiment by a handful of hot-headed anarchists. They considered it nothing more than an idle threat and they refused to negotiate better terms with the Brotherhood. But the owners had underestimated Ward by failing to recognize that in addition to his strong influence among the players he had connections in the business community. On November 4, 1889 he announced the formation of the Players League of Professional Base Ball Clubs. Over the winter, fifty-six of the best players in baseball defected to it. The new league would have a profit-sharing system for the players and no reserve clause or salary classification plan. The players would sign one-year contracts with a two-year option to renew, after which they would be free agents. Trading players without their agreement was prohibited.

The Players League would include the Buffalo Bisons, King Kelly's Boston Reds, Charlie Comiskey's Chicago Pirates, the Brooklyn Ward's Wonders, the New York Giants, the Philadelphia Athletics, the Cleveland Infants, and Ned Hanlon's Pittsburghh Burghers. Only Jack Clements, Will Schriver, Cod Myers, Kid Gleason, and Sam Thompson decided to stay with the Philadelphia club that would now be known as the Phillies. Charlie Buffinton and Jimmy Fogarty, who'd be managing the Athletics, told the club's backers Earl Wagner and Ben Hilt, the owner of the Hilton Hotel, that they should steal young Ed Delahanty from the Phillies. But Al Johnson badly wanted Del for his Infants. Hilt went to Cleveland in November to persuade Del to play for the Athletics with an offer of a $2,800 salary and a $1,000 bonus. Del liked the sound of all that money, but he listened to Colonel Rogers when he warned him that the Players League might never play a game.

The Only Del

Then things got complicated. Ben Hilt assured Del that whatever happened he would get his money. Then he put the lie to it by never actually sending Del the bonus money he'd promised. A month after agreeing to play for the Athletics Del signed a new contract with the Phillies and accepted $500 in bonus money. But then he started to think that he'd been bullied into signing with the Phillies by Colonel Rogers' strong arm tactics and began listening to offers from Al Johnson. The lure of playing before his family and friends and a home town crowd was strong so he told Johnson he'd play for less than what Ben Hilt had promised him. Johnson, who could be very persuasive, convinced Hilt to give up the territorial claim to Del that the Players League directors had given the Athletics.

By now it was time for Del to report to the Phillies' training camp. He half-heartedly headed to Jacksonville and spent much of his time whispering with roommate Jack Clements about what he should do. His former roommate Joe Mulvey had snored loud enough to wake the dead, Clements was a bed hog. Del and Jack were wakened by a soft rapping on their door the fourth morning in Jacksonville. Del, who was jammed up against the wall, hauled himself out of bed, wiped the sleep from his eyes, and stumbled to the door. A teenage bellhop whose efforts to grow a mustache like the ball players sported had thus far resulted only in peach fuzz handed him a telegram.

"I'm very sorry if I woke you, Mister Delahanty," said the boy.

Del grabbed a nickel from the nightstand and handed it to the porter. He'd hoped for a dime but was fine with the nickel, some guests gave him a penny.

"Another plea from Johnson?" Jack asked groggily.

"I expect so," Del replied. He tore open the envelope and sat down on the bed. The message read, "The Cleveland boosters would be thrilled to see their home-grown hero belting baseballs at Brotherhood Park this summer. STOP. Please reconsider staying in Philadelphia. END."

"You were right," Ed told Clements. "Johnson again."

"What are you going to tell him this time?"

"Oive no idea," said Del. "The Brotherhood's mighty steamed I said I'd play for the Athletics and then signed back on with the Phillies."

"Well you're gonna have to make up your mind soon."

The next night, after yet another telegram from Johnson offering even more money, Del packed his trunk and headed down to the lobby. Harry Wright was there, reading a newspaper. A cloud of smoke from his meerschaum surrounded him.

"Where are you off to?" he asked.

"Nowhere," said Del like a kid who'd been caught with his hand in the cookie jar. He turned and headed back up the stairs.

When Del got back to the Sunnyside after an afternoon intra-squad game three days later there was an envelope waiting for him at the front desk. It contained a guaranteed, three-year contract from Al Johnson for Del to play for the Cleveland Infants of the Players League. He would be paid $3,500 for his services as a baseball player. There was also a note from Johnson saying to come to see him at the Pavilion Hotel in Charleston, South Carolina where the Infants were training to work out the final details, the promised bonus check for $1,000, and fifty dollars cash for train fare and "sandwich money". Del smiled. This time he was leaving whether he ran into Harry Wright on his way out or not. He boarded a Savannah & Charleston Railroad train that night.

When he got off the train in Charleston Del noticed that the station and buildings around it looked brand new. Everywhere around there was construction going on. He remembered reading that the city had been nearly reduced to rubble by an earthquake in '86. A hundred people had been killed and the city had been isolated after the telegraph poles were downed and the railway tracks ripped up. Fourteen thousand chimneys were turned into heaps of sooty bricks.

Del took a black extension-top phaeton to the Pavilion. He stopped on his way in to read a plaque just inside the front doors. It read, "While stationed at Fort Moultrie Edgar Allan Poe spent weekends at the Pavilion

The Only Del

and it was under this roof that he wrote The Gold Bug."

"Ed? Ed Delahanty, is that you?" boomed a baritone voice.

Del turned around to see a large man in an expensive suit smiling at him. His collar was fastened to his shirt with pearl studs. "I'm Al Johnson. It's good to see you, Del. Come join me in the bar."

Del left his trunk with the desk clerk and followed Johnson into the Pavilion's lobby bar.

"Cognac all right with you?" asked Johnson after the two men had sat down.

"Sure nuf. Truth be told oive never tasted the stuff."

"I'm sure you'll like it," said Johnson, signaling the bartender to bring two more of the same.

"How is it yer club's called the Infants?" Del asked Johnson.

"The newspapers gave us the name because we signed Willie McGill to pitch for us," Johnson explained. "He's only sixteen."

"I guess it's been pretty tough to find enough players, what with the three leagues runnin' now," said Del.

"It's a lot worse for the American Association. I imagine *they'll* be looking for players at carnivals and circuses. Did you have much trouble getting away from the Phillies?"

"'Twasn't easy."

"I can imagine."

"Oive got a confession ta make, Mister Johnson," he said sheepishly. "I took bonus money fer signin' on with the Phillies."

"I see," said Johnson. "How much?"

"Five hundred."

Johnson thought for a moment. "I tell you what. If they want it back, *I'll* give it to them. I have no intention of losing you now."

Del smiled. The pallid waiter arrived with the drinks. Johnson handed Del one of the crystal glasses and picked up the other. "Here's to a bright future in Cleveland," he toasted.

"It's gointa be a pleasure workin' for ya, Mister Johnson," said Del. He took a gulp. The cognac burned on the way down but tasted smooth. Del shook Johnson's hand. His new boss took a fat cigar out of a humidor on the bar and handed it to Del. He admired it and thought to himself that he could get used to this kind of life.

"Now *you* can afford cigars like these," chuckled Johnson.

The Phillies threatened legal action to get back their deserters. Del was one of the players they most wanted back. On March 28 Al Johnson stated matter-of-factly that Ed Delahanty would be playing for Cleveland's Brotherhood team and "there will be no trouble about it."

When he joined up with his new team Del found the hodgepodge of talent he'd expected. There were a few familiar faces; he knew the second baseman Cub Stricker all too well, and Patsy Tebeau, the third baseman and captain, Jimmy McAleer, the left fielder, and centerfielder Paul Radford. They'd come across town from the Spiders.

Everybody knew Big Pete Browning, the good-natured, hard-drinking right fielder. The Louisville club had once required him to swear an oath of abstinence before a judge before signing him to a new contract. Browning, who had a high-bridged nose and penetrating eyes he called his lamps or peepers, had led the American Association with a .402 average, 103 stolen bases, and 118 runs batted in '87, but Del could see that some effects of 'the drink' were already beginning to show on the 29-year-old slugger. Browning was the only Infant making more money than Del. He had a habit of referring to himself in the third person. "Old Pete has the best lamps in the world, but he has to take special care of them," he would say. "He goes outside at ten o'clock every morning and looks straight up into the sun for five minutes. That opens his peepers up real good and come game time, Old Pete can line 'em out just fine."

Al Johnson had talked 30-year-old Henry Larkin, the Infants' manager and first baseman, into playing Del at shortstop. He thought that was where a team's biggest attraction should play. Larkin thought it was a mistake. Del wasn't as agile as he had been. He'd bulked up and was downright clumsy in the middle infield now. Besides, his strong arm seemed much

The Only Del

better suited to the outfield. Del was anxious to play shortstop; he wanted to prove he was every bit as good as his pal Ed McKean. But Del was slow getting to the lively Keefe-Becannon baseballs the Players League was using in hopes of adding offense and excitement to their games. When he did reach the ball and handled it cleanly he often threw it a mile over the first baseman's head.

The fact that the best years of several of the Infants twirlers' careers were behind them was evident from the get-go in Cleveland's first regular season game, a chilly April 19th contest at Buffalo's Olympic Park. Del, clad in his dark blue uniform, was surprised to see umpire Wally Fessenden, who'd come over from the National League, starting the game behind twirler Henry Gruber. He was just as surprised to see that he was dressed in white.

"That's a luvly get-up'," Del told Fessenden. "Are ya fixin' ta deliver milk after the game? And what the blazes are you doin' out here? Shouldn't you be startin' behind the plate?"

"There's another man there," replied Fessenden. Del took a look and sure enough there was another umpire standing behind the catcher. Players League games would be officiated by two umpires.

With a Bison runner on first in the third inning, Del caught a softly-hit flyball. Fessenden raised his arm and was about to signal the out when Del grinned and dropped the ball. The runner coming from first stopped in his tracks, unsure what to do. Del picked up the ball, jogged to second, and put his foot on the bag. He was about to fire the ball to first when Fessenden said, "Not so fast, the batter is out." He looked at the runner. "And you can go back to first."

"Fer the luva God, what are you doin'?" Del yelled at Fessenden.

"It's a new rule to stop infielders from pulling what you just did. The base runner doesn't have a fair chance."

"Have ya got a *name* for this new-fangled rule?" demanded Del.

"The infield fly rule," Fessenden told him. "Umpires have been talking about the need for it ever since Dandelion Pfeffer started making easy double plays dropping balls on purpose."

"This new league is sure full uv surprises," said Del. "A pair uv umpires

the greatest batsman in the land

in white uniforms, a lively baseball, and now this infield whatever ya call it. At least we're allowed ta overrun first base like they started lettin' us do in the National League last year. It was a pain in the arse ta fly down the line, slam on your brakes, and hang onta the bag."

This pair of umpires had lots to do today. Del thought he was watching a track meet as one runner after another raced by him. The Bisons scored twenty-three times. In the next three games the Infants' staff gave up another fifty-two runs in 15-8, 19-2, and 18-15 drubbings. At least they fared better than Bert Cunningham, the Bison starter in the get-away game. He threw five wild pitches in one inning, a record Del thought was likely to stand.

The Infants traveled to Pittsburghh, where a hundred and fifty shivering rooters huddled together in the freezing cold, and won their first game against Ned Hanlon's Burghers 9-8. Kid McGill got roughed up in the second game, a 15-10 loss, but the Infants took the series with a 7-6 win in the third game. Del, who played error-free ball and had four hits on the day, was happy to drive in the winning run off Pud Galvin.

There was a parade before the Infants' home opener on Wednesday, April 30. A smiling Al Johnson watched rooters stream off his electric trains and into his beautiful new Brotherhood Park. He invited Ohio gubernatorial candidate William McKinley, an avid baseball fan, to sit with him in his box. McKinley waved his top hat to the crowd and settled in to focus on the game instead of the campaign. Del went over and shook McKinley's hand and wished him luck. "Oive got a hundred down on ya ta win," he told him.

Then Del held court in front of the Infants' bench. Well-wishers, proud relatives, and anxious reporters looking for an angle crowded around, competing for his attention. Del had never felt so special and adored. A stout dowager more than a bit past her prime, feathers sprouting from her bonnet, presented Del with a huge bouquet of flowers. A teenage girl in a clean gingham dress with white china buttons and a round straw hat winked to her friends and then planted a kiss on Del's cheek. Fergus Maloney, Shaymus Finnegan, and Logan O'Shea sat high up in the grandstand.

The Only Del

"Ya know the kids on the sandlots copy everything Mush does," Fergus told the others. "Just like his brothers always have - the way he saunters up to the plate, adjusts his cap, hunches his shoulders, all uv it."

Del pointed his bat at Silver King, the Chicago pitcher. The dowager sat in the fifth row, clapping her white gloves fervently. Del fouled a pitch just over her head, nearly ripping one of the feathers from her bonnet. King's next pitch was right over the heart of the plate. Del swung as hard as he could. He knew how hard he'd hit the ball the instant he made contact. It climbed into the cloudless sky and disappeared over the Beattie & Sons Jewelry Emporium sign on the left field fence, to the chagrin of Chicago first baseman and manager Charlie Comiskey and the uproarious delight of the hometown crowd.

It didn't take Del very long to get onto the Cleveland social scene. He was a frequent attender at Marcus Hanna's Opera House on the corner of Euclid and Sheriff Street in the heart of the theater district. Hanna was one of the swells Del hobnobbed with at the theater. One night, when Richard Mansfield was on stage as Beau Brummell, Hanna told Del how he'd gotten to know John D. Rockefeller when they went to high school together in Cleveland and how he'd been expelled from college.

"Best thing that ever happened to me, Del," Hanna chuckled as he took a puff on his huge cigar. "I became a coal and oil monger and I was millionaire by the time I was forty." He paused and then laughed. "Of course my wife's money had a lot to do with that," he chortled, his belly rippling so hard he almost spilled his brandy.

Del always had an attractive woman on his arm at the opera, which led to murderous stares from Jeffrey Forrester, Thomas Spencer, and Charles Bolton. In the lobby they puffed on cheroots, sipped champagne, and gossiped. Each wore a topcoat. Not Del. He'd picked up the latest in men's fashions at Brooks Brothers when the Quakers were in New York. It was a short, black jacket with satin lapels that was modeled on the English smoking jacket. It had been worn by tobacco heir Riswold Lorillard at the '86 Autumn Ball at the Tuxedo Park Country Club in Tuxedo, New

the greatest batsman in the land

York. Invariably, whenever Del's lovely escorts saw bejeweled but homely Mrs. Thomas Spencer, frumpy Mrs. Charles Bolton who was addicted to Belgian chocolate, or dowdy Mrs. Jeffrey Forrester they would say, "It's not hard to tell *he* married for money."

Two women in a third level box looked admiringly at Del. One peered through her opera glasses at him as Emma Eames took center stage. "Who is that ruggedly handsome man in the short suit coat?" she whispered to the other woman softly enough that their husbands couldn't hear.

"I believe that is Ed Delahanty, the baseballist," said the other.

"Isn't Delahanty *Irish*?" said the woman with the glasses.

"I don't care if he's Irish or Mongolian. He can loosen my corset any time he likes."

Before an Infants' home game Cinders O'Brien told Del a funny story. "Twas my turn ta take the tickets today," said O'Brien. "This fella comes up to the gate and says, 'Lemme in, oim Ed Delahanty's bruther.' Well he looked just like you, only younger and smaller, so I let him in. Right behind him is anuther lad, a little younger and smaller but lookin' just like you as well and he says, 'Lemme in, I'm Ed Delahanty's bruther.' So I let him in too. Then comes anuther one. Same thing, little younger and smaller but the spittin' image uv you as well and he says, 'Can ya let me in, I'm Ed Delahanty's bruther?' So I let him in too. Right behind him is another fella, even younger and smaller but lookin' just like you as well and he says, 'Lemme in, I'm Ed Delahanty's little bruther.' So I let him in too. I was shocked when the fella behind him was a big blond fella and not anuther bluddy Delahanty."

His brothers were in seventh heaven. Del gave one of the vendors a dollar so they could get sodas, peanuts, and hot pretzels. The Infants lost 14-10 to the Brooklyn Ward's Wonders. Del was frustrated by his infield work and by how the losses were piling up. The club had fallen to sixth place.

"Ed Delahanty is one of the hardest losers on the Cleveland team. He plays to win and snaps his fingers at records. He is disappointed that some of his

The Only Del

teammates do not give it the college try day in and day out. Patsy Tebeau says that Del is close to tears after a game if he didn't get two hits and drive in at least one run."

Del was hitting, but his play at shortstop was so poor the Cleveland bugs turned their attention to Pete Browning. Browning was facetiously called "the Gladiator" because he seemed to be in mortal combat with every flyball hit his way. He had an odd, one-legged defensive posture and many a time Del had to retrieve balls that had bounced off his glove or his chest. But Pete was a terrific hitter. He gave Del a lot of welcome advice about how to wait on a pitch and drop his shoulders so he could deliver the barrel of the bat to the ball more effectively and how to take better advantage of his powerful lower body.

Pete took special pride in his bats, which he retired when they'd reached their quota of hits. In '84 he'd been mired in a slump when a seventeen-year-old named Bud Hillerich snuck away from making porch columns, stair railings, and wooden bowling balls at his father's woodworking shop to see his idol play for the Louisville Eclipse. Ambidextrous Tony Mullane was firing strikes, some left-handed, some right, and Browning was swinging at air the whole afternoon. When he finally did made contact, Pete broke his bat.

Bud sought out the disconsolate slugger after the game. Browning pulled his wad of chewing tobacco out of his mouth and fired it at a wall. "I'm hitting bad enough as it is and that was my favorite bat," Browning told the teenager.

"Come to my father's shop. I'll make you a new one," said Bud.

An hour later young Hillerich, with Browning at his side lending advice, lathed a perfectly-formed bat from white ash. Pete got three hits the next day and he was hooked. He had Bud make all of his bats from then on and told everybody he ran into how grand Bud Hillerich's bats were.

"We make butter churns, bedposts, and balusters," Bud's father told him when his son asked if they could concentrate on making baseball bats.

Every time a visiting team came to town another player who'd listened to

the greatest batsman in the land

Browning rave showed up at the shop to have Bud craft bats for him. He'd fashioned a centering device for his lathe and an automatic sander and he called his bats Falls City Sluggers. Because of his tremendous hitting, Browning became known as the Louisville Slugger and Bud adopted the name for his creations. They sold so well Bud's father gave up making butter churns and renamed his shop "J.F. Hillerich and Son, Batsmakers."

Del borrowed one of Pete's bats for a game at South Side Park in Chicago on June 2 and hit two doubles, a triple, and three singles in six at bats off Fido Baldwin. Now Del was hooked too. He traveled to Louisville and had ten bats made. He was fussier than Bud's other visitors. "Me lumber's just like me hat," he told him. "It's got to fit or it don't go." Del called his new bats his wagon tongues and he took special care of them, carefully rubbing a bottle along them before each game to keep them from splintering. He guarded them as if they were the Crown Jewels.

The other Infants called Browning "Red Light Pete" because of his propensity to frequent establishments in the seedy parts of whatever town he was in. He had plenty of great stories to share when the Infants got together at his hotel, the Hawley House.

"Fanny was her name," Pete said of a buxom woman in Detroit who knew every way there was to drive a man to distraction. "She's got a face that'd drive a dog from a butcher shop, but a body that'll make your dick as stiff as a bat. She's real partial to *my* Louisville Slugger if you catch my drift. And there's a gal named Thelma in St. Louis that plays a pecker like a piccolo," he told his riveted teammates, "and a little honey called Heidi in Richmond who ... well, you lads are too wet behind the ears to hear what *she* does to a fella."

The Infants looked to turn things around when the Quakers came to Cleveland for a soggy Fourth of July double header - a term borrowed from the railroads for two locomotives being coupled together to pull a heavy load. Del was glad to renew acquaintances with Bill Hallman, Joe Mulvey, Jim Fogarty, and Sid Farrar. Al Johnson hoped attendance would be higher and more rooters would be riding his trains than on Wednesday,

The Only Del

when just 250 people had shown up. It should have been a surprise to no one that three baseball leagues were too many. Ed went hitless and made four errors in the morning game and slugged a triple and committed *five* errors in the afternoon game, a 15-6 loss. He made another two errors the next day against his old team. By now he was afraid to show his face around town. When his friends ran into him they talked about the weather.

"I made ten wild throws and drove more people out uv the stands behind first than the rain," he told reporters later.

"What do you suppose is the matter?" one asked.

"It's me arm," Del told him. "It's too bluddy strong fer the infield it is."

Del finally had a solid outing a week later in Philadelphia. The *Times* made note that "Delahanty put up a great game at short that has seldom been surpassed, his two put-outs and eight assists being made on the hardest of chances."

A crowd - if 762 could be considered one - turned up at the Polo Grounds to see the visitors from the Forest City take on the Giants on July 14th. The *World* said,

> "Delehanty is either possessed by the devil or has wings on his feet. He stroked a safe hit in each of the first four innings and was hit by a pitched ball in the fifth. In the sixth he was hit on the nose by a liner off the bat of Roger Connor. He had to leave the game and will not appear in society for several days.

Del was back for the next game, his nose a bit the worse for wear, and made three hits and three errors. On July 19 in Brooklyn he singled, doubled, and scored three times in another 14-10 loss to Ward's Wonders. On July 26 at home to the Giants Del clouted a double and a triple and played error-free shortstop in a double header sweep. On the 29th in front of 1,213 rooters, many of them ladies since they were admitted free, Del stroked four singles and scored two of his team's seventeen runs. On the 31st he singled, tripled, and doubled in two runs, all to no avail as the Infants lost to the Quakers 12-10 and fell 13½ games out of the lead. Tebeau replaced frustrated Henry Larkin as captain. The move had little

the greatest batsman in the land

effect, the Infants kept right on losing.

The Cleveland papers still raved about how great it was to have the former teenage sensation back on his home turf. They wrote about Del's long hits and daring-do on the basepaths, not his errors. On August 12th Stricker and Del each made a pair of them. It wasn't just the middle infielders that were botching plays. The day before the Infants had allowed Pittsburghh twenty runs. Eighteen were unearned.

On the 22nd Del made another three errors at short. After he made two more early in a game four days later in New York Tebeau took him out. The new captain had decided enough was enough. He moved Radford to shortstop and Del to centerfield. Del wished the switch had come three months sooner.

On September 8 in Pittsburghh Del hit a double that would have been a home run and a triple that would have been one too if not for the fact that he was limping badly. With great effort he reached three long flies. Banged up or not, it was a relief not to be playing the infield any more. On the 18th at home to Pittsburghh, Del slapped three singles in the Infants' fourth straight win. It hardly mattered, they were now an embarrassing 27 games from the lead.

Del ended up being overshadowed by Pete Browning, who had the second best average in the league at .376. Ed finished the year with a solid .296. His thirteen triples showed that Pete's advice had helped him hit for more power, but Del was far from satisfied; he'd wanted to do much better. He'd have a hard time forgetting the 94 errors he'd committed. At least he hadn't been the *clumsiest* shortstop in the league. The Quakers' Billy Shindle had made 122.

The Only Del

Chapter Eleven

Havin' a Wee Peek

Even with their paltry attendance figures the Players League had drawn larger crowds than the National League, partly due to all the runs that were scored, mostly because that's where the lion's share of the best players were. All three baseball leagues lost money in 1890, but the Players League, which was supported by the trade unions, lost the least. But its owners had no idea how much money the National League was losing and naively thought it was in a stronger position.

The Players League owners began meeting secretly with NL representatives, who offered them hefty bribes to fold their teams. They accepted. The Brooklyn, New York, Chicago and Pittsburghh franchises were merged into the National League, the rest disappeared. The players had been unhappy with their salaries before jumping to the Players League. Now they would be paid even less. And they'd be bound to their team not just for one year beyond the term, but for two or even three.

Al Reach, Harry Wright, and Colonel Rogers met after the season ended to discuss the prospects for '91. Rogers was dead-set against re-signing any of the players who'd deserted the Phillies.

"I'm going to be desperately short of twirlers," Wright told Reach and Rogers. "We should get Charlie Buffinton back."

"Over my dead body," snarled Rogers. "Without him there might not have been a Players League team here."

"What about Jim Fogarty?" asked Wright. "He had as big a part in the league as Buffinton."

"I know Fogarty got off to a great start last year," said Al Reach, "but

The Only Del

I didn't read much about him after that." He took out his own *Guide* and flipped through to the Players League statistics. "That's odd. He ended up batting .239."

"You didn't hear?" asked Harry Wright.

"Hear what?" asked Reach.

"The man is dying," said Wright.

"Dying?" asked Rogers. "Of what?"

"He has tuberculosis," Wright told the owners. "He's not expected to last six months."

Reach thought for a minute. "I'd like to at least put him on the roster," he said. "Even if the man doesn't play another game. At least he'd be around old friends."

"Fine," grumbled said Rogers. "But we're not a charity here."

"No one'd ever mistake us for one of *those*," Wright mumbled under his breath.

When he went to attend the wake/post-mortem for the Players League in New York in January, Del met with Colonel Rogers in the glass-roofed Palm Room of the Endicott Hotel that had just opened for business on the Upper West Side. The Endicott boasted steam heating and its own power plant. Rogers' sumptuous suite cost $65 a month.

The sour-faced owner grimaced when Del drained his glass of single malt Scotch at a single draught. "I'm none too happy to take back any jumpers, but I am prepared to make an exception in your case, Mister Delahanty," he told Ed. His furry eyebrows arched. "But don't expect to be paid what you were last year." Remembering something, he hesitated. "And you still owe me ninety-four dollars for your hotel room and train fares from the Spring before you cut and ran off to Cleveland." He slid a contract across the mahogany table. It called for a 33% cut - to $2,100.

Del gulped and pointed to his glass. "I think oim gointa need another one uv these," he told Rogers.

the greatest batsman in the land

The Phillies would have an interesting mix of players for '91. The new first baseman, six-foot-two Bill Brown, was from San Francisco. Everyone called him California Bill. He showed up in March as brown as a berry. Second baseman Cod Myers had made 96 errors in '89 but he'd cleaned up his defensive work and stolen 44 bases in '90 so his job looked secure. The Phillies had signed Billy Shindle to play third base on the strength of his .324 batting average and league-leading 282 total bases in '90 in spite of all his errors.

"Crikey, Bill, I thought *oid* had a bad go uv it last year," Del told Shindle, one of the few Phillies who was bare-faced like Del. "Oive got a feelin' your record's gointa stand fer a while."

Del was happy to see that big-eared Bob Allen, his teammate in Mansfield, would be twirling the ends of his mustache at shortstop. Jack Clements, who'd had by far his best season yet with a .315 average and a team-high seven home runs, was back behind the plate. Gloves for left-handed catchers were as rare as hen's teeth so Clements had designed his own. The thing had no pocket; its face was as flat as a shingle and instead of catching with the mitt he used it to ricochet the ball into his other hand. It allowed him to send a throw to second faster than any other catcher in the game.

Charlie Bennett of the Detroit Wolverines, who wore an ordinary kid glove with the fingers and thumb cut off, had been the first catcher to wear chest protection. His new bride was alarmed by her husband's bruises and fashioned a shield by sewing strips of thick cork between bed-ticking material. He wore it underneath his jersey so the cranks wouldn't think him chicken-hearted. Then William Gray, a Hartford inventor who would later be responsible for the pay telephone, used the same principle employed in the recently patented pneumatic tire to design a rubber protector that shielded a catcher's chest - and his groin as well - without hindering his movement.

Giants' outfielder Jim O'Rourke was called upon to catch the odd time and he was not fond of being hit by foul tips. He saw an advertisement for the Gray's Patent Body Protector in the '84 *Reach's Guide* and hurried to Spalding's store to get one. To demonstrate its effectiveness he encouraged

The Only Del

his teammates to punch him in the gut and he got Mickey Welch and Tim Keefe to throw shoots at his chest from a few feet away and then laughed as they bounced off him. When Clements saw him doing it he got one himself. He'd blow it up just before the umpire yelled "Play" and deflate it when the game was over. The Philly cranks gave him a hard time about it for a while. He ignored them.

Catchers had always needed to be as agile as a cat to get out of the way of deadly foul tips, but that wasn't necessary anymore. They became bigger and slower. When Columbus Solons catcher Rudy Kemmler said he felt more like a backstop than a ball player with all the gear he was now wearing reporters picked up on the term and some catchers began feeling inferior to their teammates, especially when they were referred to as "a mere backstop."

Del couldn't help but be impressed with Billy Hamilton, the Phillies' speedy new outfielder. Though he was only five-foot-six he was head and shoulders above the rest of the players the Phillies had picked up to augment their devastated lineup. Reach had scooped him up from the Kansas City Cowboys for whom he'd stolen 111 bases and scored 144 runs in '89. Hamilton was mediocre in the field, but he could fly on the basepaths. He was able to take a huge lead because he was so adept at scrambling back to the bag. He'd mastered the head-first slide and the Philadelphia rooters called him "Sliding Billy." His only drawback was that enemy runners routinely took extra bases on his feeble throwing arm.

Off the field, Hamilton was a religious family man. Notoriously thrifty, he saved his money and invested in real estate. It enabled him and his wife Rebecca to live comfortably. Billy didn't smoke or drink and was not a night clubber. He was usually in bed by nine. Hamilton had little or no power but he hit a lot of singles and because of his tremendous patience at the plate he drew plenty of bases on balls. Harry Wright had quickly installed him in the leadoff spot and Hamilton scored 133 runs and swiped a league-best 102 bases in '90. He was often on base when Sam Thompson came to bat. With the addition of Del in the third outfield slot Harry Wright figured his lineup would stack up pretty well against the other rebuilt National League teams, but he worried about his pitching.

the greatest batsman in the land

Kid Gleason had been the surprise of the Phillies' 1890 season. He'd pitched 506 innings and racked up thirty-eight wins. Wright wasn't prepared to use him as much this year though. Left-hander Duke Esper, who had thick eyebrows and a scrupulously-waxed mustache, had won eight and lost nine in his rookie season with the Athletics, relying too heavily on the slowball he'd mastered.

Al Reach had wanted to send the team down south for Spring Training. Penny-pincher Rogers talked him into using Sea Isle City in Cape May County, New Jersey instead. Rogers had a summer home there so he'd be able to keep tabs on his players. He knew he didn't need to worry about Sam Thompson. He wasn't the type to go looking for mischief and couldn't have if he'd wanted to. Sam's wife Ida went to Cape May with him. Billy Hamilton wouldn't be up to any mischief either. About the rest Rogers wasn't so sure.

The team met at the passenger station on the corner of 12th and Market Streets above the Reading Terminal Market in early March. The open-air Butchers and Farmers Markets had been in operation since 1853. The team walked through the stands of fruits and vegetables, mutton, veal, pork, and poultry and went upstairs. They boarded the Atlantic City Railroad and then switched to the West Jersey Seashore Railroad. They reached Sea Isle City early on a wind-chilled morning.

"Those men don't look like shoobies, they don't have lunch boxes," Del heard a woman tell her husband as the players unloaded their luggage from the train.

Del turned to Harry Wright. "What in the world is a shooby?"

"It's what they call day-trippers who get a boxed lunch packed in a shoe box included with their ticket when they take the train to the beach for the day. The shoobies aren't very welcome. They deprive the local businesses of the revenue tourists would normally spend on food."

"I wonder how welcome *we'll* be?" Del muttered to Bob Allen.

"About as welcome as a skunk at a garden party," answered Bob, pinching and twisting an end of his mustache.

The Only Del

A stiff ocean breeze blew as the team entered the five-story Continental Hotel at the base of 25th Street. It was on the shore but some distance from the other more popular resort hotels. It had steam elevators that took guests to the expensive top floors that provided a grand view of the Atlantic. The Phillies' rooms were on the ground floor between the kitchen and the employees' rooms.

"Look at that," Bob Allen told Del. Their room was next to one shared by two young maids. Bob had just finished wedging two loose wallboards apart to provide a peek next door. A shapely blonde was bending over to unlace a shoe. She was wearing bloomers and a corset. Across the room a lovely brunette had just taken off her nainsook chemise and crinoline and wore nothing but her petticoats.

"Yer a bluddy genius," said wide-eyed Del. He went and knocked on the opposite wall. Bill Brown and Cod Myers were on the other side.

"What do you want?" a voice answered.

"Come in here, quick," whispered Del.

Seconds later Brown and Myers came in, each half-dressed. Del pointed them to where Allen had his face shoved against the wall.

"What the hell is *he* doing?" asked Brown.

"Havin' a wee peek is what he is doin'," Del explained.

Bill looked puzzled but went over to stare into the wall himself. "And here you lads were complaining about all the noise from the kitchen," he told Del.

Cod went over and shoved Bill out of the way. "Look at the knockers on that girl!" he shouted.

The maids could hear him as clear as a bell. They shrieked and grabbed for their clothes.

Thanks to Cod's vociferous admiration of the maid's breasts, the Phillies were asked to leave the Continental. Billy Shettsline had a hard time finding

the greatest batsman in the land

a hotel at a price Rogers would allow him to pay. The Great Fire of '78 had destroyed half of Cape May's hotels including the Knickerbocker, the Congress Hall where presidents and their cabinets had met, and the Columbia, which had burned to the ground in ten minutes. He tried the Stockton, the Windsor, the Bellevue, and the Excursion House. None was prepared to accommodate the team. The Devon catered to families. Sam and Ida took a room there. The other players were always polite to her, but Ida was happy to be in a different hotel. She enjoyed sitting on the beach watching children play in the sand. Surf-canoes were the latest rage and there were generally half a dozen running the waves.

Shetts finally managed to get the players into the Aldine. The rooms were on the ground floor again, but when Bob Allen chiseled a hole in the wall *this* time he and Del were treated to a view of the hairy backs of two fishermen.

Del was still writing to Daphne, but she was noticeably slower to write back lately. He wondered if she'd found someone else. He got his answer the next day.

This letter wasn't perfumed. Del scanned it and was disappointed to see it wasn't signed "Your darling Daphne" as the others had been. Something was wrong. Daphne's mother already disapproved of her daughter stepping out with a ball player. Now she'd learned that Del was indeed Catholic. Daphne was forbidden to see him again.

Wanting to make a good impression, Del had reported in peek condition at 175 pounds. One reporter wrote that he was "as strong as an ox and as spry as an antelope." The Phillies opened at home against the Bridegrooms. Like most teams they had a sizable contingent of Irish players including Tom Daly, Bill Joyce, Darby O'Brien, Mike Griffin, and hard-hitting Oyster Burns. Their player/manager John Montgomery Ward was said to be depressed over his divorce from the busty, self-promoting Helen Dauvray, who had put up the money for the trophy she'd had named after herself.

Del liked the look of the Phillies' new jerseys. They had dark red flange around the collar and wrists, dark red lacing down the middle instead of the short ties the Grooms wore, and a large Gothic *P* on the left breast.

The Only Del

Their pillbox caps were unchanged, with two wide stripes around the top. Del had finally discarded the calf-skin Spalding Chicago Club shoes that had set him back six dollars. Now he wore the all-kangaroo leather shoes Spalding made. They were durable and comfortable but they cost seven dollars. And that didn't include the $1.50 he had to pay for his spikes.

The Phillies lost their home opener but beat the Brooklyns in each of the next three games. They split a series in Boston and then dropped three out of four in New York, the only bright spot for Del being the three hits he managed off the Giants' red-haired, flame-throwing Amos Rusie, "the Hoosier Thunderbolt". His blazing swift balls seemed to travel the fifty-five feet, six inches to the plate in the wink of an eye. They were so hard on his battery mates' hands they stuffed cotton batting, grass, and even strips of meat into their gloves. Del wasn't intimidated by Rusie even though anyone who'd been hit by one of his shoots said it was like being hit with a rock.

In Brooklyn, the *Eagle* said the home side was bent on getting square for their three straight losses in "the overgrown village." Extra cars had been added on both of the city's noisy elevated railroads. There was no need to dodge trolley cars on the way to Eastern Park, the Bridegrooms' new home in Brownsville; no trolley lines ran there yet. Many of Brownsville's predominantly Jewish homeowners rented their yards to serve as stables for game-goers' horses.

The tally-ho from the Phillies' flea-bag hotel was surrounded by other tally-hos that brimmed with Brooklyn boosters. Leading the procession was one carrying thirty members of the Young Men's Democratic Club and their blaring trumpets and sundry other noisemakers. The Grooms delighted the crowd in the first game with a 15-5 pounding of the overgrown village dwellers. The Phillies came back to win the next day but lost the last two in Brooklyn.

They headed to Cleveland on the New York Central for a four-game series without Jimmy Fogarty, who said he didn't feel up to the long train ride. The others knew he was glum, having to watch every day as Billy Hamilton played his old position. Del didn't know what kind of reception he'd receive in Cleveland. But as he was on his way to the plate in the

the greatest batsman in the land

first inning two well-dressed men came out of the stands and presented him with what the newspapers called a "gay horseshoe of roses and other flowers." Del responded by slashing a ball to the left field wall. He raced around the bases and slid safely into third to a large round of applause. As he got up and dusted himself off he heard a familiar voice coming from a few rows up in the crowd.

"'Twas a fine belt, Mush," yelled Shaymus Finnegan.

"Well if it isn't Shaymus Finnegan," Ed yelled back. "How the devil did you find two bits fer a seat?"

"From doin' an *honest* day's work, not like sum lucky stiffs that get ta play in the sun and get paid fer it."

"Wait fer me after the game, we'll go hoist a couple uv jars."

Del got another hit his next time up and he made a fine running catch near the fence in the eighth that preserved a 5-3 win. Shaymus met him outside. Well-wishers were shaking Del's hand and patting him on the back. There was a pretty girl with Shaymus.

"And who might this sweet thing be, Shaymus?"

"This is Moira McFingle," he told Del.

"Davey's wee sister?"

"The very one."

"All grown up now and a lovely woman. Are Davey's pastries still fresh out uv yer muther's oven at five this mornin'?"

"They are," said Moira with a smile.

"What's this gal doin' with the likes uv you then?" Del asked Shaymus.

"Oive asked her to be Missus Finnegan."

Del winked at Moira. "I hope you've not said yes."

"She *has*," said Shaymus.

"Has she then? Well congratulations to the both uv yas."

Moira beamed.

"What about you, Mush?" asked Shaymus. "Are you and Daphne gointa get hitched?"

The Only Del

"Her muther's put an end to any thoughts uv that. Seems she won't have the Pope tellin' her grandchildren what they can and can't do. Say, can I buy the two uv yas a nice dinner?"

"That ud be grand, Mush, but Moira's mum wants us to meet some people from the parish."

"Well meet me at the hotel for breakfast. I'll get you a pass and you can watch me play for free tomorrow."

"Free's me favorite price. Oive gotta save me pennies ta buy a ring fer me bride-ta-be."

"I told you I can wait," Moira told Shaymus.

Shaymus shook his head. "Oill not hear uv it, girl. Oive already picked one out."

She smiled and squeezed his arm.

"Tomorrow it is then," said Del as he headed off to join his teammates.

Shaymus met Del for breakfast at the team's hotel at nine o'clock the next day.

"Hop aboard," he told him when the team's tally-ho pulled up at ten to take the Phillies to the park.

"What do you think you're doing?" asked Harry Wright.

"What's the problem, Pops?" asked Del.

"Only players ride for free," said Wright.

"This fella's an old friend uv mine."

"It doesn't matter who he is, he can't come with us."

"There's *plenty* uv room."

"That's not the point," Wright explained in his usual patient manner. "If I let *you* bring a guest how can I tell the rest they can't give whoever they want a free ride?"

"If he can't go, I'm not either," huffed Del.

"What do you mean?" asked Wright. "How are you going to get to the

the greatest batsman in the land

game?"

"I'm not going to the damn game."

"You are so," said Wright, his face reddening.

"I am not," said Del. He grabbed Shaymus' arm and led him back inside the hotel. "C'mon. Let's go see if they serve beer at this hour uv the day."

That night someone slid an envelope under Del's door. Inside it was a telegram that read, "The Philadelphia Base Ball club has fined player Edward Delahanty one hundred dollars for insubordination and refusal to participate in the May 12 game in Cleveland. A. Reach, President."

Del marched across the hall to Harry Wright's room and banged on the door.

"What do you want?" asked Wright when he opened it.

"Whose idea was *this*?" Del demanded, waving the telegram in the air.

"If that contains news of your one hundred dollar fine, the answer is me."

"*You* fined me a hundred dollars? I thought it was the damn owners."

"It's time you stopped being a hot-head and grew up. I won't go to bat for you with the owners if you're going to put yourself ahead of the team. We need you in the lineup, not off somewhere sulking."

Del took Wright's words to heart and never pulled another stunt like that. When he got his next pay check he discovered that Harry had reduced the fine to $25. The Phillies headed to Pittsburghh. Their team's owners had signed highly regarded second baseman Lou Bierbauer, who was the property of the American Association's Philadelphia Athletics. They'd failed to include him on their reserve list and Pittsburghh grabbed him. The plunder led to loud protests by the Athletics and an official complaint. An AA official claimed the club's actions were piratical. Pittsburghh made sport of being denounced for being piratical and named themselves the Pirates, though it would be years before the name appeared on the team's uniforms.

The Only Del

The Pirates had assembled a strong club. Besides Lou Bierbauer they had Cornelius McGillicuddy, who now went by Connie Mack, behind the plate, manager Ned Hanlon at shortstop, and Pete Browning, who was batting cleanup. Like most managers, Hanlon was going with three starting pitchers now instead of two. Del managed hits off each of Hanlon's starters, Fido Baldwin, Silver King, and old Pud Galvin, including a triple in his first game back to go along with a game-saving catch.

After the Saturday, May 16 game Del went for dinner with Pete Browning at the Priory Hotel. After gobbling down steaks and having three or four whiskeys they lit cigars and talked about their new teams and, of course, their bats.

"How many have you got *now*, Gladiator?" asked Del, speaking as loudly as he could in a restaurant. Pete was almost deaf.

"Close to seven hundred," Browning told Del.

"Have you still got your favorite? The one with Eighty-Seven at St. Louis printed on it?"

"I do," said Pete, his eyes lighting up. "It was the ninth inning. The sacks were drunk and so was Pete. Old Red-Eye can't hit the ball until he hits the bottle. Old Pete put a dent in the centerfield fence and made himself a home run." He paused for dramatic effect. "That four-base bingle won the game."

Del chuckled and blew a perfect smoke ring into the air. "Your ear still devilin' ya, Pete?"

"Worse than ever, Mush."

"What is it you've got?"

"The doctors call it mastoiditis. It's an infection that runs from the ear to the air cells in your brain. I'm up half the night with the fever. I suppose I'm lucky though, they say it *kills* a lot of wee ones."

"What do you take for it?"

"Ear drops and plenty of this stuff," he said, indicating his drink. "They

the greatest batsman in the land

don't call me Distillery Pete for nothing."

The two players had another drink and then another. Pete asked the languid waiter, who had a ship's prow of a nose, to bring them a bottle of the hotel's best whiskey, which he did somewhat reluctantly. Their conversation became more and more animated to the point that the manager came over and asked them to take their bottle somewhere where they could talk more freely.

"That's a fine way to treat a guest of the hotel," boomed Pete.

"Don't worry yourself then, Pete," said Del. "Oive bin thrown out uv better places than this."

Pete grabbed the bottle and thrust a five-dollar bill on the table peremptorily. "Kindly inform the proprietor that I will be looking for other accommodations," he told the manager with as much dignity as he could muster.

They went to a park and shared their bottle with a couple of men. When they asked their new friends where they lived they looked around the park and shrugged, "Here."

After the series in Pittsburghh, the Phillies headed to Chicago on the Baltimore, Pittsburghh, and Chicago Railway. Cheapskate John Rogers was sending his team around the circuit on the least expensive, most dangerous railways he and Billy Shettsline could find and putting them up in shabby hotels as well. The players called them whistle stop hotels because they were often miles from the downtown stations. Even Sam Thompson was complaining about the cheese-paring management. "The owners make a barrel of money but they grind the players into the dirt," said the usually Silent Sam. Colonel Rogers shot back that Thompson expected to be sent around the circuit in parlor cars and stay in $5 a night hotels.

Before the first game in the Windy City, Harry Wright called a team meeting. It was a rare thing for the team to meet before a game. When Billy Shettsline had finally managed to get everyone to be quiet, Wright took off his top hat and cleared his throat.

"Must be sumthin' pretty serious," Del whispered to Bill Allen.

The Only Del

"You're right about that," agreed Bill, who could see that tears were welling up in the manager's eyes.

"Jimmy's gone," Wright struggled to say. Fogarty had died the night before.

"What!" gasped Del. "So soon?"

There was silence until Kid Gleason asked if they would be back in Philadelphia in time for the funeral for their stricken twenty-seven-year-old teammate.

"I'm afraid not."

The Phillies, wearing black armbands, lost the game. The score was 8-6 but no one cared much. A lot of the players were remembering what Charlie Ferguson's death had done to the team's spirit in '88. The Phillies lost again the next day but won the Saturday game before boarding a CC&L train to Cincinnati. The Reds were struggling. Tony Mullane was having the worst season of his career and now at thirty-six Old Hoss Radbourne really *was* old.

Baby-faced Bug Holliday, the Reds' centerfielder, was the club's only bright spot. He was leading the league with four home runs and batting .300. Ed watched the way Bug played groundballs and line drives, noting which ones he charged in for and which ones he let fall and come to him. Del wanted to be a lot better in the outfield than he'd been at second base and shortstop. Slowly but surely he was learning how to harness his strong arm and he was starting to throw out more and more baserunners. He was usually the first player at the park in the morning and he would coax whoever showed up next to hit him flies and grounders.

He was getting more patient at the plate but still striking out more than he and Harry Wright would have liked. The Reds started Buster Pearl Rhines, a left-hander who threw sidearm, in the first game. Del had never seen him pitch before. Rhines threw a baffling pitch that curved up instead of down. Del flailed away and struck out in each of his first three at bats. He finally made contact his last time up in the ninth, bouncing a dribbler to Rhines. Disgusted with himself, he turned on his heel and trudged to the bench. Rhines could pitch, but he was a terrible fielder. He bobbled the

the greatest batsman in the land

ball and Del would have been safe at first. The usually calm and forgiving Wright was livid. He chewed Del out and told him he had better not do that again. He never did.

California Brown got injured and Del had to play first base. Then Cod Myers got hurt and Del had to move to his old spot at second, where he was awful. It got so bad it affected his hitting. He started trying too hard and swung at bad pitches. Del finally resorted to bunting once or twice every game. He was moving runners over but the newspapers wondered if that was what a man in the heart of the order should be worrying about.

He finally broke out of his slump on June 2 with two doubles, a single, and three runs scored against Chicago. The next day he singled, doubled, and tripled in an 8-0 rollick. He jumped into the air and caught Cap Anson's ninth inning line drive to right in his bare hand to end the game. Anson was steamed. Before every game he and teammate Walt Wilmot bet two dollars on who would get the most hits that day. Del homered to left in a 9-2 drubbing of the Pittsburghs the next day. General John Forbes had named Pittsburgh to honor Prime Minister Pitt the Elder and had spelled its suffix the same way the one in Edinburgh was. In 1891 the United States Geographic Board corrected the spelling to the German suffix burg as one of its thirteen general principles to be used in standardizing place names. It would be another twenty years before Pittsburgh would get its h back.

Del homered again the day after in a 7-4 loss. The Phillies dropped six straight to fall to sixth place, nine games behind the Giants. They swept Brooklyn and Boston at home at the end of June to close the gap to five and a half but couldn't gain an inch of ground in July, winning seven out of eight and then losing seven of eight. Even though he was playing the game hard, Del was hoping to get through the season without serious injury, but in August he ran into the cross-piece of the center field fence in Pittsburgh and two innings later he tore after a ball hit by the Pirates' Fred Carroll and ran straight into the brick wall in right. He spent a week in Pennsylvania Hospital. He was lucky he was too dizzy to read the Boston papers. They were calling him "a pretty good utility man who had not done

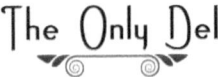
The Only Del

much brilliant work this year."

When he returned to the lineup he had an awful time bending over for groundballs. Two of them got "through the wickets" on him in Pittsburgh and five runs crossed the plate. Luckily for Del his misplays weren't the big story. As the *Pittsburgh Chronicle Telegraph* reported,

> "a mob in the grandstand grossly insulted umpire Tim Hurst and pelted him with rotten eggs. Tim knocked down one crank and precipitated a general row. Police escorted him out but a block away a man hit Hurst in the back of the head. The umpire sent his assailant to the sidewalk but the mob closed in. Breaking through, Hurst jumped on a trolley car and took the first train out of town."

When the new "Spalding's Official Baseball Guide", which had praised Del for his "courage, pluck, endurance, and physical activity," published the team and player records for '91 under a story about the demise of the American Association they reported that Del had played in 128 of the Phillies' 137 games. Billy Hamilton was clearly the team's top performer with 141 runs to Ed's 92, 102 free passes to first to Del's 32, and 111 stolen bases. Hamilton hit .340, Del just .243.

Del was just four behind Sam Thompson in runs batted in but Sam hit .294 and led the Phillies in triples and home runs. The only department in which Del had led the team was strikeouts with a disappointing fifty. At least he felt better than the Phillies' pitchers. They'd given up five and a half runs a game.

Chapter Twelve

In Need of a Wagon of Empty Barrels

Representatives from the National League and the American Association, which had been fatally weakened by the Players League, met in Indianapolis in December 1891 and agreed to consolidate. The Association's Baltimore, Louisville, St. Louis, and Washington franchises were absorbed by the National League. The rest - Toledo, Rochester, and Syracuse - were bought out. *Sporting Life* editor Francis Richter coined a term that would stick when he called the new twelve team amalgamation the "big league." In order to accommodate more teams the directors decided to expand the 140-game season to 154 games and created a split-season format. Hoping that a different team would win each season, the directors planned a post-season "world championship series."

The Phillies were holding spring training in Gainesville this time. They assembled at the Broad Street Station at the end of February and complained to one another about their salaries. Del was in terrific shape, he'd spent a lot of time at the gymnasium. He'd used breast bars to improve his flexibility, pummeled a punching bag relentlessly, and worked out on a body and wrist machine. He'd played a lot of handball and rackets too and there wasn't an ounce of fat on him. He told everyone he hadn't touched a drop all winter.

The players spent much of the forty-hour train ride to Gainesville playing pinochle - at which Del was invariably the winner - and getting to know one another. There were a lot of new faces. Switch-hitting Charlie Reilly, a journeyman infielder who was called "Princeton Charlie" not because he had graduated from Princeton but because he was born in Princeton, New Jersey, would play third base. He'd batted .219 for the Pirates in '91, struck

The Only Del

out twice as often as he walked, and made sixty errors. Del liked him, but he could understand why he'd been let go. On April 29 he would become the first player in baseball history to record a hit as a pinch-hitter, though the feat would not be remarked upon. The *Chicago Tribune* misidentified Reilly as Kelly and the *Philadelphia Inquirer* didn't even include Charlie in the box score.

The Phillies had lost one kid and gained another. Kid Gleason had jumped to the St. Louis Browns and been replaced by 19-year-old, 140-pound Wilfred "Kid" Carsey, who'd racked up a 14-37 record for the American Association's Washington Statesmen, giving up a league-leading 512 hits in the process. He struggled to find the plate with his sidearm, cross-fire delivery. He walked a lot of batters and threw a lot of wild pitches too. The other players teased him because he was having a devil of a time growing a mustache. Skinny "Rubber-Winged Gus" Weyhing had won thirty games for Ward's Wonders in '90 and another thirty for the Athletics in '91. Harry Wright was hoping to get fifty games or more out of his wing.

Four of the new additions had played together with the Athletics. Carsey could only dream he'd ever grow a mustache like the Phillies' new first baseman, Roger Connor, who was three months away from his thirty-fifth birthday. He'd started out with the Troy Trojans and then starred for the New York Gothams, who had been renamed Giants primarily because of him. Connors had batted .371 in '85 and knocked in 130 runs in 130 games in '89. Connor could still strike fear in a pitcher's heart and he could still steal a base now and then. He slid feet first and, as he landed, he would bob up like a jack-in-the-box. Del was glad the Phillies had acquired Connor. Now he wouldn't be called upon to play first base.

Billy Hallman was hoping to take over Cod Myers' spot. "I sure hope Harry likes you at second," Del told Bill as their train chugged through the Florida flatlands. "I sure as hell don't want ta go back there." Big-nosed Lafayette Cross, whom everyone called Lave, was an unconventional third baseman. He'd started out as a catcher and loved his catcher's mitt so much he used it at the hot corner, where he was a wizard. Cross played shallow, daring the batter to hit one by him. He was notorious for knocking down bullets struck from the bats of big stick wielders and using his tremendous throwing arm to gun them down at first.

the greatest batsman in the land

When the Phillies arrived at the Gainesville station the depot was being remodeled to provide two passenger waiting rooms.

"Why do ya need two uv um?' Del asked the man in the ticket booth. "One for men and the uther for ladies?"

The man gave him a strange look and drawled, "One's for whites. The other's for darkies."

The Phillies could feel the tension in the air as tangibly as the heat. The front page story in the *Gainesville Sun* told how leaders of enemy gangs had been taken from the jail and lynched. The newspaper berated the city for having only a single police officer who could hardly be expected to deal with all the violence. The *Sun* was calling for the city council to authorize a posse to round up thugs and called for the pillory, the lash, and even public executions.

"You had better watch what you say down here, fellows," Harry Wright told the players. "We want you swinging a bat, not swinging from a rope."

The players checked into the Alachua Hotel which sat on Main Street between the Baird Theater and the magnificent red brick courthouse. There wasn't much drinking or going out on the town - not that there was much in the way of entertainment anyway. Even though several of the players, especially Jack Clements, needed to sweat off a few pounds Harry Wright had scheduled the workouts to start at eight in the morning in an effort to beat the heat. The Phillies played a series of exhibition games with the Brooklyn Grooms who were training in Tallahassee. The crowds were small, a lot of folks were afraid to leave their homes especially when the lone police officer was off duty. When Billy Shettsline wired Al Reach that the team had lost $469.69 on the trip Reach wired back that they should head home.

Beck's Band played lively airs from 3 to 4 p.m. in the center field pavilion of the Broad and Huntington Grounds before the season opener. Harry Diddlebock, the head sports writer for the *Philadelphia Times* and the highest paid baseball writer at a princely $50 a week, reported that at half

The Only Del

past three the players of both teams entered at the left field terrace and with captains Clements and Ewing leading the way they marched in single file to home plate, where they separated and immediately commenced their preliminary practice work.

Before the game Harry Wright had told reporters that he adored Ed Delahanty's hitting in Florida and said Del was playing with more enthusiasm than he'd seen since his collision with Cub Stricker two years ago. Ed swatted a ball to the left field fence in the sixth inning. He tore around first and reached second just ahead of the throw from Jim O'Rourke. But in an effort to keep his foot on the bag he tore his ankle and had to be helped off the field.

Ed was on crutches for two weeks. Though he'd looked forward to getting off to a good start, this time he didn't bemoan his bad luck. "Think of how strong me arms are gointa be after haulin' meself around town on these sticks," he told his teammates.

He went back to Cleveland for a few days. He stayed with his parents but he went out a lot. He enjoyed it when he went out for dinner - first on his crutches and after a while using a cane - and pretty waitresses made a fuss over the handsome invalid. Lave Cross took his place in center and did so well that the *Times* said "when Delehanty recovers he should be used for utility service." That hurt more than the ankle.

On May the 2nd the Phillies came to Cleveland and Del asked Shaymus if he'd like to go to a game.

"Oid be happy to," said Shaymus. "Ya won't get inta trouble will ya? Remember what happened the last time?"

"It'll be fine," Del chuckled. "Oim not playin' and we're not taken the tally-ho."

"Could Moira and her friend come too?"

"Sure nuff, I can afford a couple uv extra tickets, I didn't think I would, but I'm still gettin' paid even though oim not playin'."

Del rented a three-quarter brougham from the Detroit Street Stable and he and Shaymus went to pick up Moira and her friend. The brougham, a

the greatest batsman in the land

four-wheel like most now, struggled through the congestion of carriages, omnibuses, and bicycles. They would have been better off in a hansom but a brougham was a lot showier.

When Shaymus finally pointed to Moira waiting out in front of her house, Del groped in the darkness of the carriage for the bell that signaled orders to the coachman. He rang twice to indicate they wanted to stop. The carriage drew up to the curbstone and Shaymus got out. Del grabbed his cane and followed him out the door.

The girl with Moira was beautiful. She had a heart-shaped face, sculptured cheekbones, and coral sea eyes. Golden champagne curls cascaded from her temples. She was tall, Del guessed close to five-foot-nine, slender, and immaculately dressed.

"Good morning, Edward," said Moira. "This is my friend Reagan Byrne. She works at Halle Brothers, the new department store."

Del stepped up and kissed the woman's gloved hand with all the gallantry he could muster, never having done so before. Shaymus stifled a guffaw.

"Edward Delahanty at your serice, Miss Byrne. What is it they have ya do down at the store?"

Reagan hesitated a second. "She's a model," said Moira.

"Oim not surprised," said Del.

"I understand you are a baseballist, Mister Delahanty," purred Reagan. "And a rather good one from everything I hear."

"Oid do better at *hurlin'* with this thing," said Del, indicating his cane.

"What?"

"Never mind." He took his expensive watch out of his coat and flipped it open. "We'd better get a move on. First pitch is in a half hour."

Shaymus handed Moira and Reagan into the back bench of the brougham so they'd be farther away from the sweaty horses.

"*Finally*. A man who's taller than I am," whispered Reagan. Moira laughed.

"What is it, me luv?" asked Shaymus.

"Nothing, Shaymus, just girl talk is all."

The Only Del

"Is Ed McKean gointa be playin' fer the Spiders today, Mush?" Shaymus asked Del as they handed Denton Young their passes at the gate a few minutes later. Denton, who preferred to be called Cyclone, wasn't pitching today so he was serving as a ticket-taker.

"Why wouldn't he be?" asked Del.

"Didn't ya hear? It's been all over the papers. The darn fool went and shot himself the uther day."

"Where?" asked Ed.

"In the finger, he was cleanin' his revolver."

Del was glad when the Phillies beat the Spiders 3-2. Billy Hamilton drove the Spiders so crazy with his larceny on the basepaths that after he crossed the plate for the third time Chief Zimmer, the 190-pound catcher Cleveland catcher who bicycled to and from all of his team's home games, picked the little speedster up, carried him to the stands, and dumped him into the first row of seats. Del spent most of the game trying not to stare at Reagan. He finally screwed up his courage and asked her to go to dinner with him the next night.

"I'm working tomorrow night," she told him. Del frowned.

"But not the night after."

Del brightened. "Wednesday night it is then. Oill pick you up at seven."

Del planned to take Reagan to the Hollenden Hotel, which boasted a lavish interior of paneled walls, redwood and mahogany fittings, and crystal chandeliers. On Tuesday morning he went to study the menu of its lavish dining room so he could sound refined when he ordered his meal. He sneaked back to the kitchen and waited until the chef had a minute to talk. The man was busy but, unlike most of the Hollenden staff, he was a huge baseball fan. He recognized Del.

"Ed Delahanty," he said, setting down a tray of pastries. "The Spiders could sure use you. It's a shame you had to go back to Philadelphia."

"There's a certain lady I want to impress," Del told the chef.

the greatest batsman in the land

The man thought it rather charming that a muscular baseball player would go to such an effort to make a good impression. "You'll want to order soup and wine and an appetizer first. Then a salad and an entrée and finally dessert." The chef told Del which sauces, garnishes, and appetizers were Hollenden specialties.

Del picked up Reagan in a rented landau. The young driver was almost drooling over her. She wore a figure-fitting beaded Jet Bolero dress and had her hair arranged in the latest style. On the way they passed a building that had just burned to the ground.

"What used to be there?" Reagan asked Del.

"Applegate's Place of Flying Animals," he told her. "I guess they won't be havin' bats in their belfry anymore," he chuckled.

Del's talk with the chef paid off. He ordered pinot blanc, lobster bisque, panzanella, steak tartare, coffee with brandy, and cherries jubilee. Reagan couldn't help but be impressed. While they ate she told Del that her parents had died in a ship wreck and she'd inherited the small house she lived in and enough money to pay some bills - as long as she worked enough to make ends meet. Del told her how his mother had disapproved of him and his brothers playing baseball instead of getting real jobs, but that she had a somewhat higher opinion of his profession now.

"What about your brothers?" Reagan asked. "Are they still pursuing careers in baseball?"

Del hesitated for a moment. "They're are. Oive had better luck than they have though," he told her modestly.

After dinner they went to the Lyceum Theatre to see young Sarah Bernhardt in "Cleopatra." Del chuckled the next morning when he read a review written by a critic who had been less that impressed with the performance. "Miss Sarah Bernhardt came down the Nile on a barge last evening ... and sank."

The game was rained out the next day so Del took Reagan shopping at the new Arcade on East 4th Street between Euclid and Superior. She wanted to help him pick out a new cologne and she needed a new hat.

The Only Del

Apparently all of the ones at Halle Brothers were gauche. Del had no idea what that meant but he figured it must be bad.

The Arcade had been built for a staggering $875,000 by Stephen Harkness, the president of the Euclid Avenue Bank, Charles Brush, whose arch lights lit not only the Arcade but Wanamaker's in Philadelphia and most of Broadway as well, John D. Rockefeller, and Marcus Hanna, Rockefeller's old high school buddy. They'd had the Arcade designed to resemble Milan's Galleria Vittorio Emanuele.

As Del and Reagan walked from one fashionable boutique to another they saw Clevelanders and tourists gawking skywards in amazement at the iron balconies, ornate embellishments, and stunning glass ceiling. The models in the Arcade's haberdasheries and clothing stores couldn't hold a candle to Reagan. The handsome couple got almost as many stares as the Arcade's remarkable accoutrements.

Del bought some fifty cent collars, Balbriggan and Madras shirts, cuffs, several pairs of Balbriggan hose, and three hemmed handkerchiefs at Schuneman & Evans Gents' Finishing Goods. Reagan bought mascara, a lacy tricora corset, and French perfume. Some of the Arcade's stores for ladies featured the latest in French fashion. Reagan wondered if the styles would ever be carried in her store.

The Phillies' record stood at 11-14 when Del returned to their lineup after a 25-game absence on Tuesday, May 17 for the first game of a three-game series against Washington. He batted sixth behind Billy Hamilton, Roger Connor, Billy Hallman, Sam Thompson, and Jack Clements and went hitless in five trips to the plate. Duke Esper lost 7-6. Del moaned as he watched Esper surrender thirteen hits to the Senators, whose new manager was Arthur Irwin. Del had wanted to show Irwin that he was a better hitter than he'd been when Sandy was tutoring him.

After the game Del invited his friend Deacon McGuire, the Senators' catcher who'd been delighted when the Washington club had been absorbed into the National League, and Patsy Donovan, Washington's right fielder, to join him for dinner at the Divine Lorraine.

the greatest batsman in the land

"Your ankle doesn't seem ta be botherin' you much, Mush," said Deacon as he dropped his napkin onto his lap and picked up his menu.

"I don't know as oill be stealing bases fer a bit," said Del, "but oim gettin' around the outfield better than I'd thought I might. What part uv Ireland are ya from?" he asked Donovan.

"Queenstown," answered Patsy.

"I *thought* you sounded like a Northerner," said Del. "A County Cork lad at that."

"Guilty as charged," chuckled Donovan.

"Speakin' uv guilty, isn't that the place where the convicts got transported to New South Wales from?"

"Aye, 'tis, they stopped when I was a wee lad, right around the time me family emigrated to America. Dad got work in a cotton mill. I was lucky I could play ball er I'd be there meself."

"All uv us bog trotters'd be in a mill or a mine or working on a dock if we couldn't play ball," said Deacon.

"Oill say one thing, yer fleet uv foot, Patsy Donovan," said Del. "I was sure as could be I had ya dead ta rights at third in the ninth and it wasn't even close."

"Did you lot git yer pay cut like we did?" Deacon asked Del.

"We sure nuff did," answered Del. "The National League's the only game in town now and the owners are milkin' us dry."

"Anuther few years uv cuts like the last one and oill be making the same as me dad," chuckled Donovan.

Kid Carsey had pinpoint control and the Philly bats were booming in the last game of the series. Del hit two doubles and a triple in an 11-0 rout. He'd stuck to beer after dinner. Deacon McGuire went hitless in spite of foregoing spirits. Patsy Donovan looked like the wrath of God. He'd sampled the hotel's whiskey and found it much to his liking.

The Orioles came to town for a single game and the Phillies triumphed 5-0, a rare shutout for Gus Weyhing. Del hit a ball over the head of left

The Only Del

fielder Piggy Ward in the fourth for a two-run double and singled, stole second, and scored on a long fly from Sam Thompson in the eighth.

Big Sam battled the right field sun all afternoon and was outraged when he read that O.P. Caylor, a *Sporting Life* writer, had taken him to task for it. Oliver Hazard Perry Caylor was well-known for his sarcasm, with which he cut friends and foes alike. "Sam Thompson fought the sun this afternoon and lost," wrote Caylor.

> "The big right fielder has misplayed many a leisurely struck flyball this season and last and has cost his side many a run. He is not a man to abide mention of his misdeeds however. Big Sam is more sensitive to newspaper criticism than any man in the National League. An unfriendly sentence by a baseball writer will throw him into a spasm and a paragraph will cause him to sulk for a month."

Sam'd had enough. He went to the Sporting Life offices and stormed up to the city editor's desk, demanding to know where Caylor's office was.

"D...D...Down the hall," the man answered nervously. "Second door on your left."

Sam marched to the door, straightened his collar, lifted the wings of his enormous mustache, and knocked hard on the door.

"Come in," squeaked a thin, piping voice.

"Sounds like a woman," growled Sam. He pushed the door open and marched to Caylor's desk. He eyed the man perched over a typewriter from head-to-toe and was taken aback by the tiny, wizened fifty-year-old who could not have weighed more than 110 pounds peering at him through soda bottle spectacles.

"Are you Caylor?" Sam demanded in his deep bass.

"I am. What can I do for you?"

The gigantic ball player towered over the writer. He inflated his lungs and blew a huge puff of air into Caylor's face, fogging his glasses. He turned on his heel and strode to the door. He jammed his derby back on his head and turned back to face Caylor again. "That settles it," he announced. "You're dead."

When Caylor told the story on himself, as he did on many occasions, his audience was always startled that Sam Thompson, who had never fought or argued on a ball field and had never been thrown out of a game, would have stormed into Caylor's office. The writer apologized to Thompson and never wrote another bad word about him.

After a second straight shutout, this one by Carsey, the two clubs hustled to the 24th Street Station and boarded the Baltimore and Philadelphia Railroad. They arrived at Camden Station, the turreted brick terminus of the B & O Railway, late Sunday night. The next day the Philly subs spread out across their bench, looked up into the stands, and wondered if any of the cranks would fire bottles or hard-boiled eggs at them as Baltimore boosters were known to do. It would be several years before players would enjoy the protection of a dugout. There was no protection in the field of course. Del was nearly beaned with a beer glass in the third inning and again in the ninth.

Thomas J. Murphy, the Orioles' groundskeeper, had been hard at work implementing "Foxy Ned" Hanlon's orders to tailor-make the field to give the home side an edge. He graded the baselines to ensure bunts stayed fair, laid hardened clay in front of home plate to help the "Baltimore chops" bound over the heads of infielders, and mixed soap shavings into the dirt around the pitching box to make it hard for visiting twirlers to grip the ball after they rubbed the dirt into their hands.

Egyptian Healy started for Baltimore in the first game. He threw swift shoots but he and his catcher Wilbert Robinson weren't always sure where they were headed. Del and the other Philly batsmen were ducking all afternoon. Billy Hamilton and Sam Thompson had two hits each and Del managed not to get beaned and drove in three runs in an 8-5 win.

Only a small crowd showed up for the second game. A lot of rooters who might have paid two bits to watch the game in person went to the opera house instead. The invention of the telegraph had been a godsend for baseball fanatics who couldn't bear to wait until the morning newspaper to see how their heroes had fared. In 1884 three savvy telegraph operators had come up with a plan. They painted a ball field onto a large poster which they placed in a theater in Nashville. One operator went to Chattanooga

The Only Del

where the Nashville Nine were playing and telegraphed the play-by-play back to the theater, where the second operator read the wires and instructed the third man as he moved cards with the players' names on them around the poster. The theater sold out, so they moved the operation to a larger opera house. In Atlanta, DeGive's Opera House hired young boys, dressed them in team uniforms, and had them run around a ball field on the stage, recreating the plays. Meanwhile, the Nashville system expanded to Chicago, Cincinnati, and Detroit.

Newspapers got into the act two years later, starting with Joseph Pulitzer's *The World* in New York. They erected a ball-field diagram with holes in it for numbered and colored pins that represented the players. It attracted a crowd of six thousand people, who created a traffic jam on the just-built Brooklyn Bridge. Then came electricity. In 1891 a former Edison employee named Samuel Mott obtained a patent for a system involving light bulbs and motors. He named it the Compton Electric Base Ball Game Impersonator.

Now hundreds of boosters huddled under the magnificent chandeliers of the Baltimore opera house to watch the Impersonator recreate the action taking place at Oriole Park. As the Western Union telegraph operator at the ball field clicked away, bells of varying tones on the theater stage signaled hits, walks, errors, and runs and movable figures on the ingeniously constructed curtain ran the bases and chased down flyballs.

The Phillies scored five runs again in the second game, and like the day before Del knocked in three of them. Unfortunately, Kid Carsey got roughed up for eight. Part of the problem was the defense behind him. It wasn't that they lacked talent; the Phillies weren't sure where to play. Harry Wright would tell them how to play the batters before the game and captain Jack Clements would say the exact opposite when the game got underway. Sometimes Clements would tell the fielders to play in and then change his mind and tell them to play deep. Often they'd still be on the move when Jack signaled for the twirler to go ahead and pitch.

Sadie McMahon pitched the Thursday game for the Orioles. Sadie was a drinker and a carouser. He often missed a game and then cursed out the manager when he was taken to task for it. McMahon had an accent twice as thick as Del's. Sadie was sober today and he held the Phillies to four runs. Del managed only a single in a 6-4 loss.

The Phillies returned home disappointed. The Reds were already there, in town for a three-game series. Their catcher Morgan Murphy was twenty-five and another player from the Emerald Isle. Thirty-two year old Charlie Comiskey, the "Old Roman" who believed that all was fair in war and baseball, was at first. Still gloveless Bid McPhee tended second base. In an interview with the *Cincinnati Enquirer*, McPhee stated, "No, I don't use a glove on either hand. I have never seen the necessity of wearing one; besides, I cannot hold a thrown ball if there is anything on my hands. The glove business has gone a little too far. It's wrong to suppose that your hands will get battered out of shape if you don't use gloves. Hot-hit balls do sting a little at the opening of the season, but after you get used to it there is no trouble on that score."

Tony Mullane pitched for the Reds. He still sported the bruise from where his wife had hit him with a potato roller. She'd recently described to a packed courtroom how her husband had cut her with a knife and smashed a water pitcher over her head. After the game Mullane grabbed two teammates and went out and got drunk to celebrate his 4-3 win.

Edwin "Ice Box" Chamberlain was the Reds' twirler in the second game. Chamberlain was cool on the ball field and hot-headed off it. He was fond of bars and of fighting in them. He knocked out a teammate with a mallet in one saloon. Like Mullane, he was ambidextrous, so he could throw to a base with either hand. Baserunners could never tell which one he'd use and he picked off a lot of them. Chamberlain gave up ten hits, three to Del, but held on for an 8-6 victory. The Phillies had now lost four in a row and sat ten back of Boston in tenth place. They were searching the skies for a white pigeon and the streets for a wagon loaded with empty barrels - sure signs of a change in fortune.

The Only Del

Chapter Thirteen

Juicy Fruit, Aunt Jemima, & Pabst Blue Ribbon

Baseball playing on Sundays was verboten in Philadelphia. On Monday, the light-hitting Louisville Colonels took the field for a double header. The Phillies struggled in the morning game but put a halt to their losing skid with a 7-6 victory in the second one. It didn't end until almost six o'clock and stomachs were rumbling. Del made a crowd-pleasing over-the-shoulder catch in the ninth and sent the Philly rooters home hungry but happy when he led off the fourteenth with a triple and scored the winning run minutes later.

Del was feeling good. *The Sporting Life* had reported that "Delahanty's fielding was brilliant and his batting hard and timely." He'd been booed a lot more than cheered up until now except in Cleveland and he soaked in the affection. Kids started waiting for him outside the park after games and often followed him on his walk through the neighborhood to the house he'd rented a few blocks away. Men started tipping their trilbies when they passed him on the street. Women had always found Ed attractive, but now, helped by expensive, neatly-trimmed clothes and the best barber in town, and his skin bronzed by afternoons spent in sunny outfields, his appearance was positively striking.

The Phillies swept the Colonels and then did the same to Cap Anson's youthful Chicago "Colts". They reeled off nine straight wins, the most impressive a 12-3 rout of the Chicagos in which Del sandwiched a pair of doubles around being hit by a pitch. The game featured a lighter moment that further enhanced Del's new popularity with the Philly bugs. With two

The Only Del

teammates on base and his team trailing by two runs, Anson smashed a line drive to right center. The ball whizzed straight for the Stars and Stripes flying from a pole next to an equipment shed where the scoreboard boys kept their number cards. Del raced up the terraced slope and looked up. The ball struck the flag and got entangled in its folds. Del watched in frustration as the ball dropped to the ground behind the shed. He looked over his shoulder and saw the runners tearing around the bases. He threw himself onto the sloped roof of the shed but couldn't get over it. Then he got down on his knees, tried to crawl into the small doorway of the shed, and got stuck.

Delahanty, "waving his can and his feet in the air" as Frank Hough of the *Philadelphia Press* reported, finally reached the ball. He stood up and and held it in the air as Anson crossed the plate with a bizarre inside-the-park home run. "The rooters roared with laughter and then broke into merry applause to express their approval of Del's mighty but fruitless struggle and his gallant effort."

The Phillies took two out three from the Browns and then dropped a pair to the Spiders - one to Nig Cuppy, the other to Cyclone Young, the 25-year-old darling of Cleveland boosters. After going 27-22 in his first full season he was mowing down batsmen on his way to 36 wins. With Ed Delahanty leading the way with his bat and glove the Phillies swept Pittsburgh and two games in Boston and then came back home and swept Brooklyn and Baltimore in three-game sets. They went to New York and swept three from the Giants to finish off a sixteen-game win streak. There was a lot of talk they'd be the champions of the first half of the split season.

After two tough losses, one close the other a 7-2 defeat in which Del drove in both runs with a homer, the Phillies went on a tear and won seven of their next eight. Unfortunately, Boston was getting outstanding work from Happy Jack Stivetts and Kid Nichols, their impressive young twirlers, and in spite of their great play the Phillies couldn't chip away at the Beaneaters' lead. Frustration finally set in. The Phillies dropped five out of six to start the month of July and Boston won the first half by six.

the greatest batsman in the land

The *Sporting News* reported that Ed Delahanty had played in 53 games and batted .303, with twenty-two doubles, five triples, and three home runs. They put his picture on their front cover along with an article describing him as a brilliant center fielder. Delahanty, they raved,

> *"is very muscular and unusually active for a man of his robust build and he always plays to win. You look at his batting and say, well that chap is valuable if he couldn't catch the measles, and then you look at his fielding and conclude that it wouldn't pay to let him go if he couldn't hit a bat bag. Delahanty shows great vim and dash on the basepaths and has become a great favorite with the Philadelphia baseball enthusiasts."*

In a July 26th devastation of the Reds Del collected five hits and tallied five of his team's twenty-six runs. He'd developed such bat control that he could foul off pitches that weren't to his liking, driving pitchers and catchers around the bend as he did. He'd heard talk that the league was considering counting fouls as strikes though. Apart from finally joining the .300 club the numbers that Del was proudest of were his strikeout total of just eight - a far cry from his swing at anything first seasons - and his error total, only three. Seemingly overnight, Ed Delahanty was being referred to as one of the best players in the game.

When the Reds came to town on August 18 Del stole three bases and preserved a shutout for Gus Weyhing when he took off with "a magnificent spurt" to rob Bug Holliday of an extra-base hit. Del was belting vicious line drives. In St. Louis he hit a shot with such force it tore off third baseman George Pinkney's shoe and broke his ankle. In Cincinnati he feasted off Billy Rhimes' upcurves, going 5-for-5 with two doubles and a triple to raise his average to .355. After the game he went to the Oakley Racetrack with Bill Hallman and Jack Clements. The track was known as the Gentlemen's Full Mile Racing Park. He made $85 on a tip from a baseball booster who recognized him. To celebrate, he took Bill and Jack to see Maggie Cline, McIntryre and Heath, E.H. Sothern, and the lovely Julia Marlowe perform at Pike's Opera House.

The Only Del

In Cleveland Del amazed Shaymus and Moira and more importantly Reagan with his new-found power. The Spiders' pitcher was Cyclone Young. Del came to the plate with two out in the bottom of the ninth and the winning run on second base. Chief Zimmer signaled for an intentional pass. Young nodded. His first pitch sailed two feet outside of the plate. Del stepped right across the plate and swung. Young could hardly believe his eyes. Even though the pitch had been that far outside Del had somehow managed to pull it. The ball climbed and climbed and finally exited the park over the left field fence 415 feet from home plate. No one had ever done that.

"I told you to let him walk," Zimmer shouted at Young as Del circled the bases.

"I know you did," Young yelled back. "But I had to put the ball somewhere. I thought it was gonna be a wild pitch until I saw it leave the park!"

Del, whom all his teammates were now calling Mush just as his friends had on the sandlots, took Reagan, Shaymus, and Moira out to dinner to celebrate - at an Irish pub, not the Hollenden this time. When he'd taken Reagan there the bill had come to almost nine dollars. When Del took Reagan home she invited him inside. When they reached the sitting room she took Del's jacket, got a spill from the brass bucket beside the hearth, and lit a fire. She lit Del's cigar with it too and they sat together in the front window listening to the clopping of hooves on the cobblestones outside.

"There is something I need to tell you," said Reagan after Del got his cigar going. "I mean that I want to tell you."

Del looked at Reagan, puzzled. Her beautiful eyes glistened in the firelight. "I know it's not all that serious between us just yet, but I am very fond of you and before things go any farther ..."

"What is it, Reagan?"

"I had mumps when I was a little girl, soon after my parents died."

"What does that ..."

"Let me finish, Del. I'm barren."

"You mean you can't ..."

"That's right, I can't have children."

"Well that's a relief," said Del.

"What do you mean?" asked Daphne, bewildered.

"I was afraid you were going to tell me you were dying."

"No. I'm perfectly healthy now. I just can never have children."

"Well, to be honest, as fond as I am uv you, I'm not quite ready to settle down just yet. I'm still learnin' how ta be a better player and I feel like I've got a few wild oats left ta sow."

"I'll tell you what then, let's just enjoy one another's company."

"And how do you suggest we do that?"

She put a hand on his arm. "You can take me to the opera tomorrow night for one thing."

"And the other?"

"You can kiss me."

September 8 was a dark and drizzly day. Del was forced to leave the game when he was hit by a pitch he never saw. The dingy gray, tobacco-stained ball came out of the gloom and right at him. "The ball struck him in the stomach," said the reporters. In truth it had hit him in the groin. Del was batting .347 at the time. He missed eight games and when he came back his timing was a bit off. His average fell dramatically and he finished the season with a .312 average, 92 runs batted in, and a league-best 21 triples and .495 Slugging Average.

Del hung around Philadelphia for a while hoping for a better contract and advance money, neither of which arrived. The owners had decided not to offer any contracts until they'd agreed upon a new salary cap. Rogers went around telling anyone who would listen that the club had lost two hundred dollars a day the last month of the season and that substantial salary cuts were inevitable. Rogers had lost $15,000 over the season, or so he claimed.

Del laid down some bets. He won two new suits, three hats, and $95 betting on Grover Cleveland to be returned to office, but he and Cub

The Only Del

Stricker lost a fortune at a gambling resort in Gloucester. Stricker was glad to be out of jail. He'd served some time after going into a jeering crowd and pretending to throw a ball at them. He'd accidentally let go of the ball and it had bounced off the ground and broken a boy's nose. Then Del headed back to Cleveland to see his parents, his brothers, his pals, and Reagan. When he saw her she told him that he was more handsome than ever and teased him about the women she'd heard who hung around ball players looking for a good time. Del said nothing.

In October, the National League owners used the ten-day notice clause to release all of their players. It was quite a change from two years before when they wouldn't have dared to pull such a stunt. The releases meant they didn't have to issue the players their final checks of the season. They made some changes to the rule book over brandy and dollar cigars as well. The rule that had allowed batters to use a flat-sided bat was done away with. One that exempted a hitter from a time at bat on a sacrifice was brought in. That was sure to help Ed, who in spite of his power still unselfishly laid down bunts to move runners over.

The pitching box was eliminated and replaced with a rubber slab twelve inches by four inches. A twirler would be required to place his foot up against it. No longer could he run from the back of the box toward the plate during his windup. Baltimore groundskeeper Murphy built up the ground beneath the rubber so the twirler could stride downhill. He adjusted it each game to suit that day's pitcher, a lot of dirt for five foot nine Sadie McMahon, not so much for five foot eleven Duke Esper. Of course there was no restriction on how high he could raise the rubber.

But it wasn't the composition of the pitching area that caught everyone's attention. It was the new distance. John Clarkson, Amos Rusie, Cyclone Young, and Kid Nichols were having their way with batters and it was time for a change. The owners had voted to move the pitchers back five feet, to sixty feet, six inches. No one knew just how big an impact that would have. Del was one of the few to realize right away that it would not just be that a batter would have a split-second more time to get around on a shoot, he'd be able to pick up the spin and curve on the ball more easily now too.

the greatest batsman in the land

Del finally received his contract from Rogers in February. Instead of the raise he'd anticipated, hopefully to the new maximum of $2,400 he was to take a $300 cut. Billy Hallman threatened to keep doing his song-and-dance act on stage rather than accept his cut. Roger Connor told Billy Shettsline he had no desire to stay in Philadelphia. He got his wish. He was traded back to the Giants for New York's first baseman, six-foot-four, 195-pound "Honest Jack" Boyle. He was handy with the glove and a big target for the other infielders, but he'd batted .183 in '92.

At the end of March, Del wrote Harry Wright that he had been working hard at the gymnasium and was tipping the scale at less than his usual playing weight. He warmed up for the season with four hits in a game against the University of Pennsylvania on April 20. The Phillies hosted the Brooklyns on Friday, April 28 in the first game of the '93 season.

Harry Diddlebock, the *Philadelphia Times* scribe, wrote that,

> *"outside the park the scene was extreme agitation as boys hawked scorecards and vendors sold peanuts, dyspeptic-looking cakes, and other indigestible delicacies. Inside a crowd of 8,142 was a representative American gathering and embraced all classes of society, from street urchins to those standing high in the learned professions who had come in all manner of conveyances by train, streetcar, omnibus, and private carriage. In the box seats were many ladies, gay in their spring wraps and bonnets giving a pleasant touch of color to the assembly."*

Half way through the game a cushion fight broke out in the right field stands. They flew through the air and when they landed they discharged a spray of sawdust on their targets and everyone around them. The Phillies batted first to take advantage of the crisp new baseball and the strategy worked as they plated five runs. Del received a generous round of applause, bare-handed from the gentlemen and white-gloved from the ladies, when he came to bat with one on in the first. He blasted Ed Stein's second pitch to the wall to drive home Sam Thompson and scored himself a minute later. Boyle was a big hit in his debut, scoring three of his new team's runs in a rare home opener win.

The Only Del

Thompson had struggled in left field and Harry Wright decided it was time to move him to right and put Del in left. He quickly became a huge favorite of the spirited boosters in the left field grandstand and bleachers with the hustling style of play that helped him to reach balls which lesser outfielders like Thompson allowed to drop in for base hits. When Del made a running catch over his head or against the wall the rhymers among the cranks would call out "Don't ever sell Del" or "Nuff said, that's our Ed."

His teammates were surprised that Del was still using a glove that was half the size of the ones they were using. He'd made it himself when he was a rookie and now it was held together with stitches and tacks. The thing looked awful. "You might just as well go back to playing bare-handed as use that wretched thing," Sam Thompson told him.

The Phillies lost six of their next five games but then reeled off seven wins in their next nine. On May 2 Del singled, homered, and swiped two bases in a 13-7 win over Boston. The *Philadelphia Times* had high praise.

> *"Delahanty's playing was gilt-edged, he making two hits, including a home run, stealing two bases, and capturing three flies. He was the principal factor in a sensational double play made in the fifth inning when with Merritt on second he, by hard sprinting, made a circus catch of Long's short fly ball to left center, taking the ball a few inches from the ground."*

Del contributed two home runs, one inside the park the other outside, in a 16-1 shellacking of the Colts on June 1st. When the Phillies lost the final game of the series 11-5 Harry Wright decided he needed more pitching. He talked Rogers into getting cantankerous "Brewery Jack" Taylor, a former Staten Island league star. Taylor had a drinking problem but told everyone that his gray visage was the result of malaria. The move paid off, the Phillies went on another seven-of-nine tear. Del was seeing the ball better than ever, hitting vicious line drives and spraying the ball to all fields. Enemy nines had no idea where to play him, though the infielders were certain they wanted to be as far from the plate as they were allowed.

The fourth page of the June 6 *Philadelphia Sunday Herald* contained an advertisement for W. Speare Undertaker and Embalmer: Telephone 240, and a notice that Mr. E. P. Mertz, Druggist, has taken the agency for Jule's

the greatest batsman in the land

Famous Toilet Powders. The Elks' Excursion to Indian Head would stop at Marshall Hall. The boats would be leaving at 6:30 and 6:45. Beneath that was news that Ed Delahanty, who was batting .390 and leading the league in home runs, had gone the first two months of the season without striking out. The paper claimed that he was "smashing the ball in a manner that delights all lovers of savage batting."

A small, odd-looking man with iron gray hair found out where Del was staying and approached him as he was on his way out for breakfast one morning. The man, who had tiny spectacles perched on the end of his nose, introduced himself as Waldo Claflin. He said he had a plant that manufactured women's footwear and handed Del his card. It featured a picture of a pair of dainty, high-heeled shoes.

Del gave him a blank stare. "What is it that I can do for you?" he asked the man impatiently.

"I've invented a new baseball shoe."

"I see. What's new about your shoe, Mister Claflin?"

"The spikes are attached to the bottom."

"They are? Good for you. But what …"

"I would like you to endorse it."

"Endorse it?"

"Yes, endorse it and allow me to use your name and picture to advertise it. If you find the shoe and design to your liking that is."

"I see. No one's ever asked me to do anything like that before."

"I may be the first, but I expect I shan't be the last."

"Well the shoes and spikes I'm wearin' now look as though they've marched to Tipperary and back, so I might as well give yours a try."

"What size are you?" asked Claflin?"

"Eleven," said Del.

"Fine then, I will have a pair that size made and bring them to you next week."

The Only Del

"Mister Claflin."

"Yes, Mister Delahanty?"

"Would I be *paid* for doing this?"

Claflin laughed. "Of course you would. One hundred dollars. *Two* hundred next year if sales are brisk and you tell other major leaguers about them."

Del tried the shoes and liked them. They were comfortable and they held up well to the elements. He found he could run faster than ever in them. Two months later he saw the ad. It said that "Ed Delahanty of the Philadephias wears and likes Claflin's Standard Baseball Shoes." A few weeks later he saw a pair in the window of Marshall E. Smith & Bros. sports equipment store on South Eighth Street. And the shoe man had been right. There would soon be other companies who wanted Del's name and face on their posters.

The Phillies found themselves in a dead heat for first as they took the field for a Fourth of July double header in Cincinnati. They won the morning game, a 15-14 slugfest that was interrupted several times by boys in the stands letting off fire crackers. They had no fireworks left for the late afternoon game and had to settle for pelting one another with peanuts. The Phillies won again, 6-5 this time.

On July 12th in the third game in St. Louis Del's home run was the margin of victory in a 4-3 decision. Two days later in Louisville the Phillies were seeking revenge for a 9-5 loss to the Colonels the day before. Del's three-run homer in the eighth was "the centerpiece" of a 9-5 win.

The Phillies came home to face the Senators on July 20 in good spirits, having clobbered them 14-3 in Washington the day before. They'd been in first place for two weeks and boasted a 44-24 record. The cranks were positively euphoric when Del came to bat in the first inning. The umpire called time when a group of dignitaries led by Marcus Hanna and Charles Brush came onto the field. Brush handed Del a package. The crowd quieted as he unwrapped it. The regulation size silver bat he uncovered glittered in the sun as the boosters roared their approval. The inscription on the bat, which Del would cherish for the rest of his life, read "Ed

the greatest batsman in the land

Delahanty, master batsman of the Philadelphias." Hanna gave Del a small box which he opened slowly. Inside was a silver baseball. Del held it above his head for the crowd to see. They roared again. Del lashed a pair of singles and Brewery Jack beat the Senators 8-1. The Phillies lambasted the Washingtons the next day 20-4. Del had three hits and was robbed of a fourth on a jumping catch by Washington shortstop Joe Sullivan.

Then the fun stopped. Jack Clements got hurt and Lave Cross had to give up his spot in the infield to don the mask. Then Billy Hallman was injured and Del had to take his position. Harry Wright put five-foot-six, 155-pound rookie George 'Tuck' Turner in Del's place. The Phillies won just three of their next eleven games and fell out of first. Turner wasn't the problem. His highest level of ball had been with the New York State Asylum team in Middletown, New York but he assured his new teammates that the patients had not been allowed to play. Tuck was the same age as Del, but he claimed he was only twenty. Del thought Turner looked closer to thirty. Unlike Del when he'd hit the big league, Turner started hitting immediately. He'd end the year with an average of .323, almost a hundred points better than Del had batted as a busher.

On Thursday, August 3rd the Senators came into Philadelphia for a three-game series and immediately wished they hadn't. The home team blasted them 22-7, 14-7, and 21-8. Del singled, doubled, homered and scored each time up in the Saturday game and made two terrific running catches for good measure. Unfortunately for the Phillies there was no chance they'd be regaining the lead any time soon. Led by Kid Nichols and Hank Gastright the Bostons were in the midst of a 21-2 stretch. Just when it appeared as though things couldn't get any worse for the Phillies, Billy Hamilton - the last regular standing in their outfield - came down with a severe cold that turned into a nearly fatal bout of typhoid fever.

By the middle of August the Phillies had fallen to third place and trailed the high-flying Beaneaters by twelve games. Reach and Rogers were fed up with Harry Wright. They believed their club needed more "ginger" in their play. On Friday, August 25 the Colonels came to the Huntingdon Street Grounds. Del made a great catch in foul territory, stroked four singles, scored three times, and was robbed off a certain three-bagger on a long running catch by Tom Brown, the Louisville centerfielder. The Colonels

The Only Del

rallied in the ninth to beat the home side 9-8, another nail in Harry Wright's coffin.

A week later, in the first inning of a Saturday game at home to the Reds, a groundball ricocheted off a pebble and struck shortstop and now captain Bob Allen in the right cheekbone. It had been a cruel month for Philadelphia. As the long-faced players cleared out their lockers Harry Wright told them he didn't expect to be back. There were tears in Del's eyes as Pops went into his office and closed the door behind him. He'd learned a lot from the old gentleman.

The Phillies ended their 20 game home stand with a disappointing 7-1 loss to the Reds. They'd won six of their previous seven though and the fact that they were taking the Exposition Flyer to Chicago was cause for excitement. The Flyer had been built to take wealthy passengers to the Columbia Exposition the papers were calling the World Fair. Reach and Rogers hoped that the luxury treatment would make the players feel like kings and incite them to push for the championship. They'd booked it before the team had dropped their last two games.

The players were mesmerized when they saw the Flyer's interior. There was an ornately-appointed washroom, a barber shop, and a library. They played cards in an upholstered sitting room trimmed with mahogany and lit by gaslight chandeliers. As much as they were sick and tired of train rides by this time of the year, they were almost sad when this one ended.

Del was in a good mood after the Phillies took two out of three from the Colts. With their train for Cincinnati - a less expensive one this time - not pulling out until late Sunday afternoon, Del went to the Exposition with Bill Hallman and Charlie Reilly after attending the eight o'clock service at St. Michael's.

They could see the place long before their cab arrived. Across the street William Cody had set up his enormous Wild West Show tent to compete with the Exposition. Its organizers had decided that Buffalo Bill's show would detract from the other exhibits. Now Cody was contemptuously siphoning off a lot of their business. Del saw Little Annie Oakley outside the tent smoking a cigarette with a cowboy and an Indian he guessed must be Sitting Bull.

the greatest batsman in the land

The Exposition's 265-feet tall wheel, which was named after its inventor George Washington Ferris, towered above buildings designed in French neoclassical architecture and the MIDWAY PLAISSANCE, a long strip of rides and booths. The three gawked at a suspension bridge made of soap, a map of the United States made with pickles, the Liberty Bell that Philadelphia had sent, and Virginia's contribution to the Exposition - a replica of George Washington's Mount Vernon estate.

Sunlight sparkled off a massive stained-glass display assembled by Louis Comfort Tiffany. On the water's edge floated a replica of a Viking ship that Norway had sent. Alongside it were replicas of the Nina, Pinta, and Santa Maria, which was only fitting because all this was a celebration of the arrival of Columbus four hundred years ago.

The three Phillies hadn't had time for breakfast so they had some of the new Cream of Wheat at a booth on the MIDWAY PLAISSANCE and then watched as a woman made them pancakes using a mix she poured out of a box they'd never seen before. Del looked at the picture of a colored woman on the box and asked the others, "Doesn't that look like the vaudeville performer?"

"You mean Aunt Jemima?" asked Bill.

"It sure does," said Charlie.

The three ate a lot of the delicious flapjacks. They were lucky there was no game this afternoon. They watched in amazement as the cook placed their dirty dishes into a large metal box. They heard hissing inside and the sound of water whirling around.

"What in tarnation is that?" asked Charlie.

"It was patented in Eighty-Five by Josephine Conrad," said the cook. "It's a machine that washes dishes."

"The little woman'd sure love one of those contraptions."

"You can't afford one on a ball player's wages," Bill told Charlie.

They tried some new chewing gum that a well-dressed man in his early thirties who introduced himself as William Wrigley was giving away. He told them he made baking soda and had started attaching free samples of his new gum to the boxes. He was getting ten times as many requests for

The Only Del

the gum as he was for his baking soda. Del thought the one called Juicy Fruit was delicious.

Even better - though they had to spit out their gum - was the beer from the Pabst Brewing Company called "Pabst Best Select." The pretty *fräulein* with honey blonde braided pigtails that was serving the beer in large mugs made a point of holding them up in front of her impressive cleavage. With a sparkle in her eyes, she said, "Zis beer has von blue ribbons at four State Fairs zis summer. If it vins one here too I zink they are goink to change za name from Best Select to Pabst Blue Ribbon."

The players snacked on Cracker Jacks, sipped the Pabst, admired the *fräulein*, and then ate sausages a Bavarian vendor who introduced himself as Anton Feuchtwanger was serving. Del thought it odd that he was putting the sausages inside rolls.

"I vas giving za customers vite gluffs to keep za zosages from burning zer hands. But za people ver keeping zem for *zouvenirs*. So my frau told me I should put zem inside uff rolls instead," Feuchtwanger explained.

As they wolfed down the delicious sausages in buns Del noticed a small, rather creepy-looking man in his early thirties with dark eyes and a thin mustache talking to a plain-looking woman at a nearby table.

"If you haven't found a place for the night I know of a hotel nearby where a lot of fair-goers are staying," Del heard the man tell her.

As Del and the others left the Exposition an hour later he noticed the woman getting into a carriage with the man.

The Boston Beaneaters won their second straight championship, but they were hardly popular in doing so. They were mocked by writers for playing a "sissified bunting game" in an age when rooters wanted manly slugging. On their way back to the hotel in their tally-ho after their last game in Pittsburgh they were pelted with stones. On-looking policemen ignored their cries for help.

the greatest batsman in the land

Reach's Guide told the story of Ed's terrific season.

Runs Scored	145 - *third*
Doubles	35 - *second*
Batting Avg.	.368 - *third*
Total Bases	347 - *first*
Hits	219 - *second*
Slugging	.583 - *first*
Home Runs	19 - *first*
Runs Batted In *unofficial*	146 - *first*

The Phillies had led the league in attendance and were thought to have netted some forty thousand dollars, which was not information the owners planned to share with anyone, especially the players. For the first time in his career Del had played in each of his team's games. In spite of needing to man first or second base several times, he'd led all left fielders in putouts, assists, and fielding percentage. Now he was clearly one of the dominant players in baseball. He wondered if he would ever be paid like one.

The Only Del

Chapter Fourteen

Run For Your Cloths

Treasurer Rogers summed up ownership's feelings about Manager Wright. "Harry has been in the game too long. He goes back to the Cincinnati Nines of the Sixties. We're playing a different kind of baseball in the Nineties." On November 21 Rogers made it official. The old gentleman was relieved of his duties.

As sad as he was at Wright's departure, Del could not have been happier with his replacement, his former mentor, Arthur Irwin. Sandy had managed the Boston Reds to the American Association championship in '91. He'd just married a Philadelphia woman thirteen years his junior. She was blissfully unaware that her new husband already had a perfectly healthy wife and four children as well in Boston. Both wives thought Arthur was a kind and devoted husband.

Sandy was more tolerant of booze than his predecessor had been, though he wouldn't tolerate players showing up for a game "as corned as a goat." As long as they got to the park early enough that he could sweat the beer out of them he was fine with it. He knew that his team badly needed pitching and looked into getting Sadie McMahon, who'd won thirty-five games for the Orioles in '92. Irwin wired Ned Hanlon and offered him Sam Thompson in exchange for McMahon. Hanlon telegraphed John Rogers and said he would be happy to send him McMahon … in return for Ed Delahanty. Rogers telephoned Hanlon and told him to go fly a kite - if he let Delahanty go he'd have to leave Philadelphia *himself* - on the next train.

The Phillies had a new look when they took the field in '94. Their tunics had PHILA printed in an arc in bright red letters across the breast and the stripes on their caps had disappeared. They were plain white now, though

The Only Del

they still had the same conductor hat shape. Red belts added color to the outfits. The team split their first two games of the season in Washington then won their Saturday, April 21st home opener against the Senators 10-2 in front of a far more than capacity crowd of 17,500 and, after the mandated Quaker day of rest, beat them again on Monday 8-4.

The next day, in the first of three in Brooklyn, the Phillies were up against lean, blond, illiterate "Roaring Bill" Kennedy, who got his name from the way he vociferously attacked umpires and, on occasion, teammates as well. He was also called Brickyard because he worked in one during the off season. The Phillies bunted a lot on Kennedy, taking advantage of the fact that he had never seen the need to cover first base, an invention of Charlie Comiskey. The Brooklyn catcher Cornelius Daly or the Grooms' first baseman/manager Dave Foultz, would field the ball, but when they went to throw to first Kennedy would never be there. "That's not my job," he would call out to his exasperated teammates. "I'm a twirler, not a god damn infielder. If I was, I'd be wearing a glove wouldn't I?"

Kennedy walked eight batters and hit two. Lave Cross, who was catching, hit for the cycle, got a pat on the back from Del, and then took a seat. Mike Grady took over behind the plate for his major league debut. The Phillies waltzed to a 22-5 victory, their fourth in their first five games. It helped that Arthur Irwin had put in place a communication system between the bench, the baserunners, and the coaches - something Harry Wright had never bothered to do.

Gus Weyhing was the Phillies' designated twirler on April 26 in Brooklyn. With his team in the middle of a big rally in the first inning, Irwin sent hard-hitting Jack Taylor up to hit for Weyhing. Minutes later, after the Phillies had tallied three runs, Weyhing went out to the pitching slab. The umpire Billy Stage, whom Del recognized as a former Cleveland university track star, was working his first game. He thought nothing of Weyhing going out to pitch. Amazingly, no boosters or reporters seemed to notice either. The line score after the game simply read, "*Taylor batted in Weyhing's place in first inning." Gus held the Brooklyns to six hits and won the game 13-3.

But Dave Foutz was well aware of what Irwin had done and he knew the substitution rule. Before '89 substitutions had been allowed only in

the greatest batsman in the land

the event of injury. Then they were permitted for any reason, but only at the end of an inning. Rule 28, Section 2 now read, "Any player may be substituted at any time by either club, but no players retired shall thereafter participate in the game." Foutz said nothing. The day after the loss he filed a protest and the win was taken away from Philadelphia.

Del had been forced to leave the game after hurting his ankle sliding into second. He sat out the first two matches when the Phillies returned home to play the Beaneaters. After dropping two out of three to Boston the Phillies took the first of a three-game set in New York. Del lofted "a cloud-kisser" to deep center his first chance at the bat. He hit "a heartbreaker" down the third base line in the fourth and then a "neat but gaudy fly" to right in the seventh. With two aboard, Del slammed "a peach of a sailer" to center to drive home both runners and a minute later he scored the winning run on a knock to left by Sam Thompson.

Del was interviewed about his batting style after the game and told reporters, "Say, if I could only hold meself back like that old crab Cap Anson I'd bat better than he ever did. But I can't, if a ball comes in that's to me liking oive just gotta belt it. I don't care whether it comes past me eyes or across me bootlaces, I'll either hit or miss it. And if I miss, God knows I'll likely miss it by enuff." For public consumption the reporters translated his words into the King's English.

On May 8 Mike Grady got his first major league hit in an 18-5 trouncing of Brooklyn. Mike had light green eyes, a long nose, and like Del stood out because he was clean-shaven. Grady was tall at five-foot-eleven and a muscular 190 pounds. He wore a mask and a chest protector behind the plate but no shin protection. Mike was a local boy from Kennett Square and he ice skated on its frozen ponds every winter to keep in shape. His father still worked for the Baltimore Central Railroad as he had ever since emigrating from Ireland. His older twin brothers Thomas and Timothy played for the Mohican Baseball Club of Kennett Square with teammate Theodore Pennock, who often brought his son Herb to games.

"Take a look at this advertisement in the newspaper," said Mike Grady, who was a lavish spender like Ed. They sat waiting for the rain to let up. "Duffy's Pure Malt Whiskey is as pure as ocean air and of rare medicinal

The Only Del

virtue. If you annoy people at church or the theater with your cough you can profit by taking a swig or two of this extraordinary elixir. It wards off pneumonia and bronchitis and can nip a cold in the bud. Available from druggists and grocers."

"Are there any advertisements in there for nose plugs?" asked Del.

"Why would you have need uv *nose plug*s?" asked Grady.

"You probably can't smell anything behind home plate unless the batter has gas, but out in the field if the wind's blowing from the northeast we get a nasty whiff uv Gunner's Run."

Grady chuckled. "Let me think now. How would the Duffy Whiskey people describe Gunner's Run?"

"An intoxicating blend uv industrial sewage and human waste," said Del.

After the rain let up Del doubled in a run in the first inning, singled home Grady and another runner in the seventh, and singled and scored in the ninth. The Bridegrooms' third baseman, Del's former teammate Billy Shindle, told reporters after the game that "when Mush begins to shell our corner of the diamond we third base guarders get a sick sensation in our guts. Ed is not one to boast of his batting talents, the man doesn't have a vain hair on his head, but have you noticed where he hits the ball? If we're in a park where the left field fence is closer to home than the one in right he hits to left field. If the right field fence is closer he damn well hits 'em there."

The Phillies hosted the Giants for three games and won them all to improve their record to 14-and-7. After the last tilt, a 10-1 triumph, they received news that the Beaneaters, who were en route to Philadelphia, had lost their ball park. The South End Grounds, constructed on Columbus Avenue and Walpole Street across from the New York, New Haven and Hartford Railroad tracks in Boston's Roxbury district in 1888 at a cost of $35,000, had been considered one of the most beautiful ballparks of its day, with striking twin spires rising from each corner of the Grand Pavilion.

the greatest batsman in the land

On Tuesday, when the Beaneaters' Tommy "Foghorn" Tucker slid into third, the Orioles' John McGraw had kicked him in the face. The umpire broke up the ensuing brawl and Tucker nursed his sore jaw and waited for a chance to exact revenge. The opportunity hadn't come. With the Orioles at bat the next inning, Boston right fielder James "Foxy" Bannon spotted a fire under the right-field bleachers. He rushed over to the stands and tried to stamp out the flames with his feet. At first, most fans ignored the small fire, preferring to watch Tucker in anticipation that he might find a chance to get back at McGraw. The conflagration swept swiftly around the outfield fence to the left-field bleachers, then up the line to the grandstand, setting the beautiful pavilion ablaze and shooting flames up to its highest tower. The fire destroyed the Grounds in less than forty-five minutes and quickly spread to houses on Berlin, Tremont, Walpole, Cunard, Burke and Coventry.

One of the homes destroyed belonged to groundskeeper John Haggerty, who led fans to safety and then ran to the nearest fire house. The nine-alarm fire caused no fatalities, but burned more than twelve acres and destroyed two hundred buildings. Close to two thousand Bostonians were left homeless. Haggerty worked all night to get the Congress Street Grounds, the home of Boston's former American Association team, in reasonable shape for the game the next day. There were no seats, so Haggerty had to borrow hundreds of chairs from organizations around the city. Haggerty reoriented the field more to the west and in the process greatly shortened the distance from home plate to the left field fence. A *Baltimore Sun* description of the Congress Street Grounds said, "The left field fence in Boston is so close that any long fly to left sails over it."

During the 27 games played at the Congress Street Grounds in May and June, 86 home runs were batted out; the league hit only 629 homers in 400 games during the entire season. Little Bobby Lowe, who'd averaged six home runs a season, smacked twelve at the Congress Street Grounds in twenty-nine games. In the second game of a Decoration Day doubleheader Lowe hit four to enter the record books as the first major leaguer to hit four homers in one game though they would likely have been flyball outs in any other park.

The Only Del

On Tuesday, May 29 the Colts came to town and the Phillies ran their record to 17-8. They were winning at home, but not 'abroad.' Pittsburgh was in first place a half a game ahead of Cleveland. The Pirates were managed by Al Buckenberger, Del's old skipper in Wheeling. They would fall to fifth place within a month and when they slid all the way to seventh in September their 31-year-old catcher and captain, Connie Mack, would take over Buckenberger's job.

On June 2 at home to Louisville the Phillies won 11-0. It was a rough outing for Colonels' starter Gus Weyhing, who had never adjusted to the new overhand curve delivery and had been driven out of Philadelphia by the demanding and unforgiving cranks. Del threw out Buck "Farmer" Weaver, who'd just married his fourteen-year-old girlfriend in Wood County, West Virginia, when he tried to stretch a single into a double in the fifth.

On June 5 Del doubled, tripled, walked, and stole a base in a 7-3 loss to the Browns. The Phillies were in the middle of an 8-2 run. On the 13th they lost 8-6 even though Kid Nichols walked twelve and gave up ten hits. Del popped up to 36-year old shortstop Pebbly Jack Glasscock who caught it in his bare hands. He and Jerry Denny of the Louisville Colonels and Bid McPhee were now the only position players fielding without a glove, though twirlers were still bare-handed.

On Friday, June 15 the Phillies were at home to Cincinnati. Tuck Turner hit his head against the right field fence going after a flyball in the first. He staggered around dazed for a while but was able to stay in the game. "I lost it in the sun," he explained, groaning and holding a block of ice to his head between innings."

Three people - two ladies and one gentleman - fainted minutes later at the eerie sound when Bob Allen was hit in the cheek with an inside shoot from Ice Box Chamberlain. It sounded as though the air had been drained from the park. All of the Phillies rushed to see what they could do.

"Back," instructed Del. "Give the man some air." He and Lave Cross picked Allen up and carried him to the bench where the team doctor shone a light in his eyes and shook his head. Del and Lave looked at one another gravely. Del put a ball out of the park with two teammates on base in the seventh to put the game out of reach. The home team, still rattled over what had happened to Allen, made four errors in the ninth but held on for a 21-8 win.

"'Tis damned lucky they moved the pitcher back five feet. That could've been even worse," Del mused after the game.

He and some of Bob's other teammates went to visit him in the hospital that night but they weren't allowed in to see him. An examination revealed that Bob's jawbone had been fractured. Two operations were needed to remove bone fragments from his brain.

The injuries were starting to pile up. The Philly newspapers had taken to calling the team "our cripples." Del was filling in everywhere now. When Tuck Turner continued to battle the sun Del moved to right field. He threw out even more runners from there than he had from left. Jules Jurgensen of the *Inquirer* wrote, "Would that we had a whole team of Dels. The Phillies could challenge any nine in the land."

An overflow crowd turned up for the Saturday game. In the fifth inning Bug Holliday hit a ball to the fence. Del turned and ran back for it. He had to shove and elbow his way through the boosters massed in front of the fence.

"Excuse me, madam," he said when he determined that the ball had rolled under the bustle of the woman's billowing dress.

She gave him a queer look and stepped out of the way. Del tipped his cap, picked up the ball, whirled and fired it on a perfect line toward home. It bounced a few feet in front of Mike Grady. Holliday was trying to take advantage of the ball rolling into the spectators and was going for an inside-the-park home run. As he slid toward the plate Grady smiled and applied the tag. The umpire, Tim Hurst, gave the out signal.

"That was a grand throw, Del," said the husband of the woman whose billowing dress had obscured the ball.

At the bat Del scorched a single up the middle in the first, part of a five-run opening salvo. In the second he hit a ball off the top of the centerfield fence for a two-bagger. He singled home Turner in the third, singled again in the fifth, and singled his last time up in the seventh. Del, who was on a

The Only Del

14-game hitting spree and led the league with a .447 average, did just about everything a batter *could* do in the Phillies' game with the Reds on Friday, June 15. He was hit by a pitch, singled, tripled, homered, and scored four runs in a 21-8 mauling of the Cincinnatis. The Philly Faithful hissed at "Ice Box" Chamberlain when he gave Del an intentional pass.

On Saturday he had six hits and scored four times. On Monday Del proved he had power to both fields when he drove a ball over the head of the Giants' right fielder for a grand slam home run that moved his team within 3½ games of the lead. But then the Phillies lost 9-5, 18-14, and 18-11 in Brooklyn to fall to 6½ back of Baltimore.

Wherever Del played he attracted attention. After he registered three hits, three runs, and three spectacular catches in the 18-14 loss, word reached town that stockbroker Eddie Talcott, one of the owners of the New York Giants, was after him. He'd seen how fond the Gotham cranks were of Delahanty. "He might as well ask for the Liberty Bell," said Frank Hough in the *Inquirer*.

The last week of June was an absolute disaster for the Phillies. Their depleted lineup just couldn't win on the road. Of course it was an unmentioned but well-known fact that umpires unwilling to risk the wrath of the cranks tended to give close calls to the home team. The Phillies lost eight in a row and fell all the way to seventh place, eight games out of the lead.

After a rare 11-10 win in their first game in St. Louis, Del, Jack Taylor, Lave Cross, and Mike Grady went out to celebrate. They went to Chestnut Valley, the "sporting district." They started out at a boisterous place that had a picture of a tiger stamped on its window to advertise that a game of faro could be had inside. There were already several punters and the Phillies had to use their elbows to get seats at the table. It was covered with green baize and there was a board on top of it with a suit of spades from ace to king pasted to it and a cut-out for the banker. She was a beautiful Creole woman with flashing oval eyes and puffy, sensuous lips. She asked the punters how many checks they wanted.

the greatest batsman in the land

"Each one's fifty cents," she announced. "The plain limit'll be a dawlar, the *running* limit'll be four."

Lave and Mike took ten each. Brewery Jack hadn't sat down yet. "The dealing box is probably gaffed in a place like this," he grunted before heading to the bar. The others looked around, hoping they wouldn't be asked to leave after Taylor's accusation. Luckily, the owner and the huge Negro beside him had been preoccupied.

"Oill have twenty, darlin'," Del told the beauty. She smiled at him as she shuffled the cards, cut them, and put them in the shoe. She waited until all of the punters had placed checks on their chosen numbers and then burned off the first card - the soda. She dealt a card for herself and placed it to her right and then dealt another for the first player and placed it on the soda.

Del was glad there was a casekeep with a spindle for each card denomination and four counters on each spindle to aid the punters and prevent the dealer from counting cards. He put his chip on the 9 of spades and set a copper on top of it. The first card the dealer turned was the 5 of spades. Since Del - by coppering - had bet on the nine of spades to lose, the dealer paid him. The others barred their bets or halved them. Del kept parleying his and won big.

When the players joined Jack at the bar Del deftly swatted Taylor's hand away as he went to grab the ass of a passing waitress. "Did you see the size uv that bouncer," he asked, indicating the huge black man cutty-eying them.

Taylor grunted and emptied his glass. When he tried to fondle another girl a few minutes later Del tossed a bill on the bar and pulled Taylor out the door. The foursome had a few nickel shots of booze in a barrel house and then the group went to a gambling house and played chuck-a-luck. The others bet big, small, or the field. Del bet triples and won twice even though the odds against it were thirty to one.

The Phillies took the field at Robson Park the next day in a good mood, though Del and his friends were a bit the worse for wear, especially Jack

The Only Del

Taylor. Del had ordered bacon, sausages, black pudding, mushrooms, soda bread, baked beans, and tea for breakfast to soak up the booze. Taylor had chewed on a piece of dry bread and had a raw egg in a tall glass of beer.

The ten runs they'd given up in their first game in the Mound City proved to be an omen. They trudged off the field two hours later after a 17-8 loss. The Phillies' pitching staff was in disarray. In their next five games - all losses - they allowed eighty runs. The press suggested that Art Irwin might as well look for new twirlers in playgrounds. Scorekeepers complained they couldn't fit all the action onto their cards. Del and the other outfielders were losing five pounds a game chasing batted balls all over the yard and the games often lasted more than two hours.

In Cleveland the Quaker crew lost the series opener 20-10. Reagan was in the crowd for the Friday afternoon game. She looked as beautiful as ever. Del saw several bugs pointing to her and then at him. The Phillies did only a bit better than they had in the first game, losing 16-8 this time. After it was over Del took Reagan for dinner and then they took a side-bar buggy out to Beyerle Park. He rented a punt at the boathouse and they rowed around the lake that had been created by the damming of Burke Brook, enjoying the cool breeze. They took in a couple of innings of a game some semi-pros were playing at the ballpark that was interrupted when some of the players realized that Ed Delahanty was among the spectators and made a big fuss over him.

Then he and Reagan watched kids riding the merry-go-round. Tears welled in her eyes and Del wondered how much it bothered her that she could never have children of her own. He wanted to go bowling but Reagan wasn't dressed for it. He didn't mind, he took her dancing under the lanterns of the pavilion instead. When he took her home she invited him in. She played one of the songs they'd just danced to on the phonograph and then poured drinks.

"It was awfully warm under those lanterns," she said, handing Del a bourbon and branch water. "Not even a hint of a breeze. I was thinking of taking a cool bath."

Del looked at his drink, confused. "Should I be goin', then?" he asked.

"No silly," she purred. "I need you to wring a cold cloth down my back."

the greatest batsman in the land

Del smiled. "I suppose I could do that."

"I'll probably think of something else too," said Reagan.

The Saturday game, a 14-7 loss, was another disappointment, though Del was glad to hit a home run for Reagan. After it was over he took her to see Fannie Batch Elder in "Cordelia's Aspirations" at the Lyceum. When he took her home she checked Del's body for bruises and showed him a couple of beauty marks she thought he might have missed under all of the soap suds the night before.

On Monday, July 16 back in Philadelphia Del ripped three hits and scored three runs in a 9-2 win over Boston. The next day it rained off and on. The *Wilkes-Barre Sunday Leader* told the story of what happened after the Beaneaters had taken a 2-1 lead.

> *"After the Quakers opened up their Wanamaker bargain counter of base hits against Boston the men from the commonwealth began playing the game as a mule race is run in hopes that the contest would be brought to a halt before it became an official game. Boston's Tommy Foghorn Tucker, who has a voice like the lead bass in a frog pond and a mouth that works on a double hinge, engaged in a heated argument with the 8,000 boosters present and bestowed a vicious tongue-lashing on the spectators. The angry crowd surged on Tucker when the umpire forfeited the affair to Philadelphia, who possessed a 12-2 advantage. Just as things looked blackest for Tucker, Ed Delahanty came to his rescue. Del threw his arms around the Boston first baseman and succeeded in getting the object of the crowd's wrath to the safety of the clubhouse. Delahanty comes nearest to being the greatest all around baseball player now living."*

The Phillies journeyed to Brooklyn, where they dropped three out of four, and then it was off to Washington, where they coughed up two out of three. Their already beleaguered pitching staff was down a man. Arthur Irwin had delivered a strong warning when Jack Taylor had missed a game without offering a reasonable excuse for his behavior and when he missed another one Irwin fined him $25. Taylor cussed out his manager and went home to Staten Island.

The Only Del

The dispirited Phillies, now ten games behind Boston, went home and lost twice in three tries to the Giants to fall to twelve back. The Phillies and Orioles played a rare Friday double header. The home side won the early afternoon game convincingly, 14-4, but got pounded 16-3 in the late afternoon tilt. The Phillies improved their record to 43-38 in Saturday's game. Al Burris, Art Irwin's latest find, gave up ten runs in five innings in his only major league appearance, but the Phillies rallied for a 19-12 win.

The teams spent a leisurely Sunday and went to the park on Monday morning for the get-away game. At 10:40, as the Phillies were finishing batting practice, Ed heard the roar of a locomotive passing the field. Sparks flew over the outfield wall and into the grandstand that ran along 15th Street. He didn't take much notice; it happened all the time. He called out to Sam Thompson to see if he wanted to play long catch. Then he saw it.

Someone had left a pile of scorecards in the seats. Ed motioned to Sam to wait a minute and then looked back at them. Their edges were burning. As he watched, the tiny flames spread to empty some Cracker Jack cartons and wrappers.

"Fire!" yelled Ed. "Fire! Get every pail you can find." He raced to the bench and got the water bucket. Luckily it was full. He ran up to where the scorecards, cartons, and wrappers were burning. In a matter of seconds the flames had spread throughout the entire section.

"We're gointa need a lot more buckets," said Mike Grady as he arrived with one he'd found in the storage shed. Charlie Reilly and Lave Cross appeared with other pails, water sloshing out of them everywhere but onto the flames. It didn't take the players long to realize they were fighting a losing battle. Fanned by a steady breeze, the fire spread rapidly through the dry wooden stands and up the walls to the turrets of the grand pavilion.

"Run for your clothes!" yelled Sam Thompson. As the players sprinted for the dressing rooms the rest of the park was engulfed in flames. Street clothes in hand, they ran through the smoke for the exits. Charlie Reilly shrieked as his shirt caught fire and he madly tore it off his body. One of the players realized he'd forgotten the pocket watch his grandfather had given him and ran back to the dressing room. He was trapped by flames and had to jump out a window to safety. Ed lost his new suit but was relieved to save his bats.

the greatest batsman in the land

The city's fire companies arrived much too late. The magnificent building and its fixtures were destroyed. Al Reach estimated the damage at $80,000. Only the center field fence and the brick wall on Huntington Street remained. The rest was a sodden heap of charred timbers and twisted iron. Even the field had been scorched. The fire had spread to the adjoining properties and consumed several stores and the Omnibus Company and its stables for 350 horses. In an incredible feat of engineering and workmanship, three shifts of crews worked day and night for twelve days to discard the cooling debris and prop up an interim facility with 9,000 seats. The team was playing in their new park by the third week of August. Fans were seated in temporary stands for home games during the rest of the 1894 season.

The day after the fire the players packed what was left of their charred equipment and headed to Boston. The Beaneaters wore the same style of tunics as the Phillies, with lacing running down from the neck. The letters BOSTON were emblazoned across their chests and they wore bright red belts and stockings. One of their smallest players was their gifted centerfielder Hugh Duffy, who looked more like a library clerk than a ball player. He took full advantage of playing at the Congress Street Grounds. Duffy had hit five home runs in '92 and six in '93. He had fifteen this year, several of them fly balls that had fallen among the borrowed chairs in the left field grandstand. Del wished the Phillies could play there more. He'd only visited the place to take in hurley matches between teams from Boston's Irish neighborhoods.

Duffy had just opened up a billiard room and cafe in downtown Boston. Del and Mike Grady went there after the first game, a 19-8 win for the Beaneaters, to play some pool and drown their sorrows. They laid down some wagers while they were there, betting five different patrons five dollars each that the Phillies would beat the Beaneaters the next day. The National League allowed players to bet on their team to win the pennant or even a particular game, so long as they didn't associate with gamblers. Of course players and managers were never permitted to wager that their club would lose a game.

The Only Del

Grady got into a fracas with a couple of rowdies when they said the Phillies were a bunch of gutless wonders. The rowdies ended up getting the worst of it and Duffy had to replace a cue Grady had broken over the head of a drunk who'd gone at him hammer and tongs. The Phillies won 18-10 the next day with Del ripping three hits. He went and collected his winnings that night but lost some of it shooting pool.

Irwin's men played their home games at Franklin Field on the University of Philadelphia campus while the park was rebuilt. It was built for football and track meets, not baseball. Del groaned when he saw the layout but he made the most of it, batting .483 during the Phillies' stay at the campus.

On Saturday, August 18 the Phillies resumed work at their hastily rebuilt park against Cleveland. They took the opener 11-6. On Monday they faced Cyclone Young, now just Cy Young, who was struggling this year.

"His shoots aren't quite so explosive from five feet further back," Del told Charlie Reilly after smashing a double his first time up. He hit another two-bagger his next at bat, then singled, then homered into the new seats and finished off with a hard-hit single that tore Ed McKean's glove off the hand that was short part of a finger. Patsy Tebeau offered to take Young out but Cy said he wouldn't hear of it. The Phillies pounded the burly 26-year-old for sixteen runs. His ERA wouldn't be under 2.00 *this* season. It would be barely less than 4.00.

Pitching for the Spiders in the third game was swarthy Nig Cuppy, who was doing a lot better with the new distance than Young. Cuppy threw a rising shoot he called a jump ball. He astounded everyone when he went to the pitching rubber. He had something on his left hand.

"What the hell is that?" asked Jack Clements.

"I could be wrong, but I think it's a glove," Del told Clements.

"Twirlers don't wear gloves," said Jack.

Del looked again. "Well *he* is."

the greatest batsman in the land

In Del's second at bat he leaned into an inside shoot, hoping to drive it to left field. The ball struck him in the chest, just below his heart. He felt the air knocked out of his lungs and fell to the dirt. Sam Thompson rushed from the on-deck circle and he and Lave Cross helped Del off the diamond. He missed the next nine games with chest pains.

Between August 15 and 27 the Phillies reeled off ten straight wins - at home of course - to climb to fourth place. Though Del was out for most of them the pitchers had finally stopped giving up boatloads of runs. Arthur Irwin knew they had to keep it up. He'd looked ahead and knew his team would play their last seventeen games on the road. His potent offense was averaging close to nine runs a game but his team still couldn't gain any ground on the Bostons and Baltimores.

After 13-6 and 15-11 losses to the Colts, the Phillies hosted the Senators for a double header the last day of August. Del was back in the lineup and he was cheered boisterously every time he went to the plate. He could hardly believe it when Wake Forest grad Bill Wynne, who had already drilled Lave Cross, hit him with a swift pitch in almost the same place he'd been hit two weeks ago. He had to leave the field again and he was out for five games this time. As for Wynne, he never returned. This would be the only game of his major league career.

Umpire Tim Hurst had been hit with several foul tips in the first game and the teams agreed that Charlie Reilly and Washington's regular catcher Deacon McGuire should officiate the second game. Billy Hamilton went to town against McGuire's replacement, Dan Dugdale, of whom his manager had said "as a catcher, Dugdale makes a good third baseman." Hamilton stole a major league record seven bases.

"Are ya gointa celebrate tonight?" Del asked Billy after the game, pressing an ice pack to his tender ribs.

"No, Mush. Rebecca will have dinner waiting for me."

"What about after that? Why don't you join me and Brady? We're gointa go and hoist a few. You could buy a round to celebrate gettin' inta the record books."

"We all know that you're as good a spender as a batter but I don't see why

The Only Del

I should throw away my earnings just to prove I'm a good fellow."

"That's our Billy," chuckled Del, "speedy on the basepaths but tighter than bark to a tree."

"I sure wish I could play tomorrow," Del told Hamilton.

"Why's that?" asked Billy.

"Gleason's pitchin' for the Browns. "He can't get used to the extra five feet to the plate and he's getting hit sumthin' awful."

Del was right. Gleason, clad in the Browns' new dark blue uniform with crimson trim and brown stockings, gave up nineteen hits in a 19-9 loss. The Browns' manager Doggie Miller believed that rifle shooting improved eyesight and the players spent an hour every morning at a local range.

"I guess you boys needed to take a few more shots," Del told brainy Tommy Dowd, the Browns' long-nosed left fielder after the game. Dowd had attended Brown, Georgetown, and Holy Cross before his playing days.

"I suppose," said Dowd, who was fiddling with a button on his sleeve.

"Didn't you have *short* sleeves at the start uv the game, Tommy?" asked Del.

"Aye, we did. They're detachable they are." He showed Del the holes on his jersey where the buttons on the sleeves attached.

"Lord love a duck, what'll they think uv next?"

"Maybe dark-lensed glasses for a fella ta wear when he plays the sun field," offered Dowd.

"Sam Thompson'd give you a hundred bucks for a pair uv those if there ever was such a thing," chuckled Del.

Del stayed in the lineup, but he felt stabbing pains in his chest whenever he swung a bat. He went 20-for-76 in September and watched with chagrin as the newspapers traced the steady decline in his once heady batting average. In a September 6 doubleheader at home to Cincinnati he made three outstanding catches, two on the run in foul territory in front of the open seats along the left field fence and the other a shoestring catch of a dying quail behind the shortstop. At least he could still be a force with his glove.

the greatest batsman in the land

On September 17 the Phillies - minus a few players who needed to give nagging injuries a day to heal - played an exhibition game in Mansfield. It seemed odd to Del that he was back at the St. James Hotel where he'd stayed seven years ago. The owner served him coffee and whiskey in one of the 1887 Mansfield Baseball coffee mugs with his picture on it and gave him a handful of Hautzenroeder's cigars. Del showed the delighted townsfolk that he still carried the gold watch they'd given him.

The game was a dull affair but the bugs cheered Del's every move. Before his first at bat a delegation that included the mayor and his daughter Mildred, now nineteen and a child no more, presented Del with a diamond ring. Mildred slid it slowly onto Del's finger and grasped his big hand for an extra beat before whispering to him that she was free to have dinner after the game. Del was visibly moved by the expensive token of the town's affection but had to tell Mildred that the team's train was leaving right after the game.

The Phillies finished the season in Cleveland. They lost the first two 26-4 and 8-6. Bill Hallman hurt his hand in the second game and Del asked Irwin if his brother Tom could fill in for him.

"Come on, Art," Del pleaded, "Tommy hit close to three hundred for the Peoria Distillers this year."

To humor his star Irwin capitulated. Bridget Delahanty had finally agreed to get a telephone so Del called home and told Tommy the big news. In front of 1,500 boosters, most of whom Del figured Tommy had invited, his brother managed a single in four times up and made just one error. His famous brother made three, he'd been out reveling with Fergus Maloney and Shaymus Finnegan until two in the morning. When Del finally went to bed he spent much of the night having erotic dreams about Mildred.

The Phillies ended up in fourth place. The newspapers were debating who would be the champion batsman of the '94 season. They lamented that it was impossible to say. There was no way to get the official figures from President Young. He never computed the averages until the season closed. When Young finally released them they showed that the Phillies' outfield had posted remarkable numbers. Sam Thompson had batted .415 and Del had hit .404. Billy Hamilton batted .403 with an on-base-

The Only Del

percentage of .521 in 702 trips to the plate, stole a hundred bases, and scored a never-to-be-equaled 198 runs. Del had knocked him in many of those times. Part-time outfielder Tuck Turner batted .418. Del's season had been one of the best a player had ever put together. He was proud of the fact that he'd gone down on strikes just sixteen times in 497 at bats.

The October 3rd newspapers featured a reminder that a reception for Ed Delahanty would be held to-night at the Hanover Hotel. The festivities at the reception were described as "a sumptuous dinner and a spontaneous tribute with an absence of all restraint and oppressive formality." Del, his tailored tuxedo unbuttoned, his bow tie hanging over his flapping collar and a cigar dangling from his lips, got rip-roaring drunk along with Charlie Reilly, Mike Grady, and Art Irwin. Del was wobbling a little when he was presented with a large, inscribed gold watch charm. With champagne dribbling down his chin he thanked everyone in attendance. He'd been voted Philadelphia's most popular player in a poll conducted by the *Philadelphia Press*. "Hurray for Delahanty, the best player in the world!" trumpeted the *Press*.

A month later came the sad news that King Kelly had died. It was known that meat over-stimulated the gut - as did alcohol, tobacco, and coffee - and Mike loved them all. Though cigarettes were considered effeminate, King smoked one after the other in hopes they would keep his weight down. Everyone knew that spices, butter, sugar, and white bread caused dyspepsia and Kelly had suffered from it for years. He'd traveled to Boston to perform "Casey at the Bat" at the Palace Theater on November 4 and a snowstorm had hit the city. When he got off the boat he saw a man shivering in the cold and gave him his overcoat. When Mike reached his hotel he was running a fever. He soon had trouble breathing and the next day a doctor diagnosed him with pneumonia.

When he was taken to Emergency Hospital he slid off the stretcher and rasped, "This is my last slide." King Kelly, whose lifestyle Del had aspired to when he was a boy, was dead at the age of 36, penniless in spite of the $90,000 he'd earned playing baseball. He left behind an infant child and a wife saddled with debts. "Money had no charms for the King unless he could make it talk and make his friends merry," one obituary noted. "His money went like the mist before a noon day sun. It came easy and he thought that it would last forever."

Chapter Fifteen

Use a Different Stable

While he was having breakfast on November 17 Del read in the *Philadelphia Inquirer* that Herman Webster Mudgett, a.k.a. Dr. Henry Holmes, had been arrested in Boston after being tracked there from Philadelphia by the Pinkertons and that his murder spree was at an end. Del was about to move on to the sports page when he glanced at the photograph of Holmes. Coffee exploded from Del's nose as he stared at the picture in disbelief.

"It's the man from the Exposition!" he yelled. Everyone turned to stare. "The one who took that homely woman he'd just met away in a carriage," he said - to himself this time.

Del read on with fascination. Holmes had purchased an empty lot on West 63rd Street across from the Chicago drugstore where he worked and built a three-story, block-long building. He called it the World's Fair Hotel and opened it as a hostelry for Exposition goers. Inside, there were doorways opening to brick walls, stairways leading nowhere, oddly-angled hallways, and doors that could only be opened from the outside.

The ground floor contained shops. The top floor contained Holmes' office, bed chamber, and a labyrinth of rooms in which he tortured his victims. Del's eyes widened as he read that the third-floor rooms had gas lines that enabled Holmes to slowly asphyxiate his victims. On the second floor was a "secret hanging chamber." There were trap doors and a chute that led to the basement, where he stretched bodies on a rack, stripped off their flesh, dissected them, crafted them into skeletons to be sold to medical schools, or burned them in one of two enormous furnaces.

Holmes had told the *Inquirer* that he'd committed thirty murders. Del was disgusted to read that the Hearst newspapers had paid him the ungodly

The Only Del

sum of $7,500 for the lurid details of his infamy. Holmes gave various contradictory accounts of his life, initially claiming innocence and later stating that he was possessed by Satan. The number of his victims was being estimated at anywhere from fifty to two hundred based upon missing persons reports and the testimony of Holmes' neighbors, who recalled seeing him guide many unidentified young women into his hotel, women they never saw leave. Del gulped, realizing that he'd seen one of them with his own eyes and he tried not to think about what had happened to her. Many girls had gone to Chicago to see the World's Fair but, for one reason or another, never returned home. Now their horrified families knew why.

Over the winter Del was busy helping to organize the Philadelphia lodge of the newly-established Knights of Equity, a fraternal organization of Irish Catholics. Its articles stated that its intent was the creation of "a spirit of mutual helpfulness among its members; to advance them intellectually and socially and by cooperation to promote their material interests." Del was more interested in the Knights' other aims - to fight bigotry and discrimination, help Irish boys interested in the priesthood, and - of greatest importance to Del - to provide aid for impoverished families, orphans, and the elderly. Del was a founding member of the Cleveland lodge and whenever he was in St. Louis he helped other Knights distribute funds and boxes of food to urchins in the Patch. He handed out something else the children loved and didn't get from any of the other Knights - tickets to baseball games and balls for the stickball games that provided an alternative to petty theft and gang wars.

"Prices are levellin' off since the Panic," Bridget Delahanty told her husband. She was looking at the advertisement for the A & P store on the back of the section of the paper James was reading in the parlor. "Flour's twelve cents for five pounds, sugar's twenty-six cents for the same, eggs are twenty-one cents a dozen, butter's twenty-five cents a pound, and potatoes are ten pounds for fourteen cents."

"No time to be a common laborer making nine dollars a week," James remarked. "Our boys'd do well to learn themselves a trade so they're not paupers when they finish their ball playin'." He set his paper down. "Say, why does Edward never bring that girl uv his around ta meet us?"

"Moira McFingle told me Reagan might not want to meet us."

"Not wanta? Why not? There's nothing wrong with us."

"Moira says she might be too embarrassed in light uv ..."

"In light uv what?"

"I wasn't supposed ta say anything."

"Anything about *what*?"

"She had mumps when she was a wee girl."

"What in the name uv all that's holy does that have to do with anything?"

"She's barren, James."

"Oh. The poor thing."

"Moira believes we won't think she's a match for Ed because uv it."

"She's bein' a bit hard on herself. It's not like she can do anything about it."

The 1895 schedule called for a lot more travel than previous ones had. There would be no more month-long home stands. The league had tinkered with the rule book again over the winter again too. They'd rescinded the rule that had forbidden twirlers from intentionally discoloring the baseball. They'd be able to soil it to their heart's delight. The sacrifice rule had been amended as well, limiting it to bunts, and for the first time not counting sacrifices as times-at-bat. That was bound to help Del, who sacrificed as much as anyone in spite of his heavy hitting.

On February 6, a child was born to a German-American couple at 216 Emory Street in a Baltimore neighborhood called Pigtown. The infant's name was George Herman Ruth, Jr. A week later nine inches of snow fell in New Orleans. The next day the *Inquirer* reported that Chris Von der Ahe, the dictatorial, half-mad owner of the St. Louis Browns, had contacted Billy Shettsline and offered a staggering $30,000 for Ed Delahanty, Sam Thompson, Billy Hamilton, Jack Clements, and Kid Carsey.

The Only Del

"We might just as well sell you the whole club," had been Shettsline's response.

Few people who knew anything about Von der Ahe believed a word of it. He didn't have that kind of dough and if he had he certainly wouldn't have spent it on his ball team - his brewery or his race track maybe, but not his team. *The Sunday Item* said, "Think of no Del in left to plow up the sod and cut off long hits which look as though they are good for anywhere from four to forty bases!"

To get in shape Del was playing handball every morning at the Quaker City Athletic Club with Jack Clements, Billy Hallman, and Charlie Reilly. In the afternoon Clements, Hallman, and Reilly went to use the batting cage at the University of Pennsylvania. They'd expected Del to join them. He didn't. He went to Ursinus College to teach the theology students instead.

The college was an hour carriage ride away in woodlands adjacent to Freeland Cemetery. Ursinus had been established so that "young men could be liberally educated under the benign influence of Christianity." It was not supposed that Del could teach them much about divinity, but he could teach their new baseball team a thing or two about lifting a ball heavenward. Del was startled to see that there were young women on the campus. They'd been admitted after the closing of the Pennsylvania Female College. Del figured they were there to test the boys' commitment to abstinence from the pleasures of the flesh. He struggled not to be tempted himself.

After the August fire, Alfred Reach had been thinking about building a more permanent and fire-resistant ballpark. His interest led him to John Allen, a local architect who specialized in theaters and "fire-proof work." Allen suggested a steel-and-concrete structure previously untried in baseball and drew up a double-deck design with a cantilever process that eliminated the need for the supporting posts which typically obscured the views of field-level fans. Huntington Street Grounds II was built out of steel and brick, with no wood apart from the floors and grandstand seats. The new park, which would later come to be called Baker Bowl, had a seating capacity of 18,800. The main entrance behind home plate was constructed in the shape of a castle topped with turrets; all it needed was

the greatest batsman in the land

a drawbridge, knights at the door, and lit torches. There was a tin-over-brick wall in right field, long racks for boosters to store their bicycles, and a swimming pool in the basement of the centerfield clubhouse.

The Phillies disappointed their rooters by losing the first two games in their new home. Irwin, who coached third when the Phillies batted, had base runners scratching their heads - going when they had no chance to advance and staying put when they could easily have made it to the next base. He trotted one "can't miss" prospect after another out to the pitching rubber with similarly awful results.

The Phillies trailed New York 8-3 in the final game of the series but mounted a comeback in the ninth against a tired Amos Rusie. Michael Grady had already sent two runners scampering home when Del, who'd made a two-base hit in the third, came to bat "looking as stern as a defeated politician the day after the election." Rusie thought to himself that Delahanty was the only batter apart from Dan Brouthers who didn't look the least bit nervous when he came to bat against him. Del just smiled and dug in. To the consternation of the anxious crowd he sent several of Rusie's offerings foul into the seats. The last one couldn't be found and umpire Campbell had no choice but to put a brand new ball into play even though he was loath to this late in the contest. To add to the drama, Del sauntered to the bench and got a drink from the oaken water bucket.

"I'm gointa wait until he gives me one to me liking," he told Art Irwin as he wiped his mouth on his sleeve. He returned to the plate and hammered a shoot that Rusie had thrown right down the middle in frustration all the way to the centerfield wall. The runs Del knocked in were among the seven the Phillies scored in the inning. The Giants scored one of their own in the bottom of the ninth but Del chased down a long drive by Shorty Fuller to end it and sent the cranks home hoarse but giddy. Sam Payne and his crew would not be getting home on time for dinner; the exuberant cranks had showered the field with their seat cushions after Del's climactic catch.

A week later the Phillies were in St. Louis. Toeing the pitching rubber, which had been expanded from 12 by 4 inches to 24 by 6, was the Browns' ace Ted Brietenstein. He'd been hit in the knee by a wicked line drive the

The Only Del

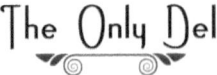

previous season but had stayed in the lineup in fear that his pay would be suspended. Brietenstein remembered that when Del had broken George Pinkney's ankle with a line drive, Chris Von der Ahe had fined Pinkney $25. Von der Ahe had a cadre of nefarious low-lifes follow the Browns around to see if they were drinking. In order to keep their jobs, if they couldn't catch any players in a saloon the spies had to invent stories. Von der Ahe fined a man two dollars if his spies reported he'd been seen drinking beer, five dollars if it was whiskey, and a ludicrous fifty dollars if the man was seen consuming gin.

When Brietenstein had been exhausted after pitching 34 innings over a five-day span and refused to pitch in relief the next day the owner had charged onto the field and, in front of Brietenstein's embarrassed and disgusted teammates, fined his ace $100 and told him he was suspended. Von der Ahe had been in a particularly foul mood. The night before he'd rented a horse and carriage to take him and his mistress for a midnight ride and had made the mistake of going to his usual stable. Von der Ahe and his mistress had started carrying on as though they were still in their hotel room and Von der Ahe hadn't noticed where the horse was taking them. Out of habit, the nag clip-clopped its way to Von der Ahe's quiet street. His wife had been awakened by the sound and she was none too pleased when she looked out the window. Von der Ahe tried desperately to get the horse to hightail it out of there but couldn't. Mrs. Von der Ahe stormed out of the house, grabbed the lash, and horsewhipped the two of them.

In the third inning Del singled in Billy Hamilton with a vicious liner up the middle that nearly decapitated Brietenstein, stole second, and scored when Sam Thompson doubled to right. In the sixth, with Philadelphia ahead by two and Browns on first and second, Tommy Dowd lined what J.P. Sheridan of the *St. Louis Post-Dispatch* called "one of Kid Carsey's pet balls" toward the left field fence. Del was off with the crack of the bat. He sprinted back, caught the ball over his head, reeled around, and fired to Billy Hallman, who stepped on third to get the lead runner and then threw to second to complete a triple play.

In the eighth Ed "hit a beauty down the left field fence and made a circuit of the bases." The Phillies led 4-2 going into the ninth when the Browns staged a comeback. With a run in and two men on base Brietenstein lined a sure base hit to left and the runners took off. It looked as though the overworked hurler would get the victory but Del charged in, caught the ball just before it hit the grass, and fired to second to double off the runner and save the game.

The Phillies won the first of three when they went to Cleveland but faltered late in the second and lost 8-7. None of Del's friends or relatives were at the game because of the weather. Neither was Reagan. It snowed throughout the afternoon and Del had to run out through the centerfield gate a couple of times to warm his hands over a bonfire some hobos had burning. He gave them a dollar so they could get something to warm their insides.

Rookie Bobby Wallace started for Cleveland in the finale. Del blasted a ball over the distant left field fence - an unheard of accomplishment - to propel his team to a 9-7 win. Reagan had been at the game this time and Del took her to the Hollendon House after getting pats on the back from his teammates for his hefty belt. The Hollendon staff was in a tizzy over the up-coming Republican National Convention. Marcus Hanna was there overseeing arrangements. He told Del he was sure McKinley was going to get his party's nomination.

Reagan was unusually quiet all through dinner. It seemed to Del as if she wanted to tell him something but couldn't manage it. She finally pushed her plate away and put her hand on Del's arm. He set down his whiskey glass and looked into Reagan's eyes.

"I'm leaving Cleveland," she blurted.

"*Leaving*? Why? Where are you going?"

"Some men from one of the big fashion houses in Paris came to the store a few weeks ago. They showed an unusual amount of interest in me when the owner had me try on the dresses they wanted us to carry. I'm accustomed to men staring at me, I know I'm attractive, but it was more than that. They kept talking about me and they didn't care that I heard them. They were speaking French so I couldn't understand very much of what they were saying."

The Only Del

"But now you've found out what it was about?"

Reagan took a long sip of her wine. "I got a telegram from them the other day. They want me to come to Paris and model in their store."

Ed stared at her.

"You know I love you, Del, but how can I turn up a chance like this? I was hoping some day I might find a job in fashion or modeling in New York, but Paris is the *center* of the fashion world. I think it would be stupid of me ..."

"It'd be insane uv you to pass up an opportunity like that, Reagan," said Del, trying to be happy for her but not managing very well. "At least you aren't leaving me for another man, that's what I've worried about ever since we started seeing one another."

"I'm not going there to meet charming young Frenchmen, I'm going for the exposure and the opportunities. And if it doesn't work out I'll hurry right back here into your arms."

"As much as I would love that, I hope it works out for you. I'm sure you'll amaze the French just like you have everyone here."

She excused herself and hurried to the powder room where she burst into tears. She hadn't been able to tell Ed that what she wanted more than any job in Paris was to marry the man she loved and give him children. But since she knew she could never do that, she'd unselfishly decided to let Ed go. It was breaking her heart.

Chapter Sixteen

Supernaturally Blue Eyes

Still shaken by the news that Reagan was going to Paris, Del boarded the team train for Chicago. He hoped the upcoming series would help take his mind off her. Chicago wasn't much warmer than Cleveland, but at least there was no snow.

Mike Grady put his arm around Del on their way into the park. "Yer lookin' mighty glum, Mush. What's happened to ya?"

"It's me own fault," said Del.

"What's yer own fault?"

"It's me own fault fer steppin' out with a model."

"What's *that* supposed to mean?"

"Reagan's goin' ta Paris to show off clothes for rich madams and mademoiselles."

"Yer right, ya damned fool. You should be with a washerwoman who looks like the back end of a turnip wagon."

"Thanks, Mike. That's the kind uv girl I'll look for."

An hour later Del loped to his spot in left field. Grady ran beside him.

"Where the hell do ya think yer goin'?" asked Del.

"Right here," said Mike, stopping at third.

"Irwin has you playin' *third*? No offense, but has the man taken leave uv his senses?"

"I'm guessing he meant Reilly, but I wasn't about to argue with him."

Del shrugged and continued out to left.

The second batter hit a grounder that Mike caught, dropped, picked up

The Only Del

and threw twenty feet wide of first. He looked out at Del, who was trying hard not to laugh. "Oive never thrown a ball from here," he shouted.

The next batter struck out. The one after him lofted a soft pop toward Mike. He ran forward, then back, then covered his head. The ball bounced off his right shoulder.

"Delahanty. Play third," yelled Irwin. "Turner, take left," he told Tuck.

Grady's errors were among thirteen the Phillies made that afternoon. Kid Carsey, who made two of his own, was so disgusted he took to lobbing the ball to the plate so the Colts could fatten their batting averages.

Referring to his .400 managing record in Washington, the *Washington Evening Star* commented,

> "Irwin is as great a failure as a manager in Philadelphia as he was here. Today he lost his head and put Grady at third instead of Reilly, creating a comedy of errors. Sixteen unearned runs were scored in a 24-6 loss."

On May 29 the Phillies went to New York for a single game and beat the Giants 11-10. That night Del, who'd doubled, tripled, and scored three runs, went to dinner with Mike Grady. It was a warm evening so they sat beside an open window. They had big steaks with all the trimmings and cleaned their plates. The diners beside them left a lot on theirs. Before the busboy arrived, a pair of dirty hands reached through the window and snatched the uneaten food. Del walked over and looked out. An unshaven middle-aged man in a threadbare suit sat greedily wolfing down what he'd purloined. Del could see that the fellow was no ordinary beggar. The unfortunate soul looked up guiltily. "I haven't eaten in a week," he explained.

Del reached into his pocket and got out his wallet. When he handed the man a ten-dollar bill he thought he was going to cry.

Mike, whose turn it had been to pay for dinner, saw what Del had done. "That was mighty nice uv you, Mush," he said.

"There are thousands uv New Yorkers who've still not recovered from the Panic uv Ninety-Three," said Del. "That fella could've been a bank manager or God knows what. I can't imagine goin' from havin' the world by the tail and endin' up like that."

the greatest batsman in the land

"What are all uv those people lining up for?" asked Grady, indicating a lengthy queue across the street.

"Oive no idea," said Del. "Let's go see."

The name above the storefront read "Black Maria Movie Studio."

"I know what a *studio* is. It's where you have pictures taken. But what the hell's a movie?" asked Grady.

"I haven't the foggiest," said Del.

He tapped a tall man in a flat tweed suit on the shoulder. "Are you folks lookin' ta get yer picture taken?"

"No," the man answered. "They have pictures that move in there."

Del and Mike looked at one another.

"Whad'ya mean?" asked Mike. "Somebody carries them around?"

"No. I can't really explain it, but there's a string of them and they move somehow."

Del and Mike joined the lineup. They paid the two cent admission price and went inside. It was so dark they could hardly find their way to empty chairs. After a few minutes a white light shot out of a square hole in the wall and shone on the blank wall opposite it. All of a sudden numbers popped up, one after another. Then everyone jumped as the grainy image of an attractive teenage harem girl flickered. The audience stared in amazement.

"That's Annabelle Whitford, the vaudeville performer," shouted the man Del had talked to outside. The woman with him shot him a disapproving look.

The image continued to flicker as the girl on the wall did a serpentine dance.

"Well oill be damned," Grady whispered to Del. "Imagine havin' a sexy girl dancin' on yer wall. If this is what *movies* are like, they might just catch on."

That night Del attended a smoker - a bachelor party - at the Opera Club with some rich swells who were baseball enthusiasts in addition to being patrons of the arts. The invitation he'd been handed by a thirty-something

The Only Del

man in a fifty-dollar suit who'd introduced himself as Nigel Farnsworth the Third said the affair was discreet and to wear tails.

The smoker began at ten sharp with a sumptuous dinner of pheasant, lobster, and broiled steak. All of it was consumed without benefit of forks or knives. Del thought prominent members of the 400 Club holding a tankard of ale in one hand and gripping an enormous steak with the other a rather bizarre sight. A silver medal was presented to the obese man who devoured the most meat. The medieval supper was followed by dollar cigars and brandy in crystal snifters. There were some toasts and then two dancers, twin sisters, took the stage in short, fluffy skirts and pranced around, their toes kicking high toward the ceiling to give the men a full view of their shapely legs and bottoms. Del noticed some other girls, even more scantily-clad, in a hallway along the side of the stage. Some of the men, with lecherous looks on their faces, joined them and led them into an anteroom. Del guessed they weren't going to discuss the stock market.

The next morning the Quaker crew returned to Philadelphia for a twenty-game home stand. They began with a rare Thursday double header against Cincinnati. The crowd for the morning game, a 9-1 Philly win thanks to a seven-run third, numbered 9,500, but 18,000 cranks turned out for the afternoon contest. Del drove home the winning run in the eleventh inning of the three hour long game with a fence-rattling double.

The Phillies beat the Reds again the next day and leapfrogged into a tie for second place, a mere two games off the lead. A week later, after six straight losses, they found themselves in eighth. Del was hardly to blame. Despite playing on a badly sprained ankle he'd hit safely in 33 of his club's 35 games and was batting .416. Part of the club's dilemma was that Joe Sullivan and Lave Cross had come down with mysterious maladies. Another factor was that Arthur Irwin was taking his frustrations out on Billy Hamilton.

"Why does Irwin have me batting cleanup?" Billy asked Del during batting practice.

"Makes no sense to me," said Del. He lowered his voice. "Oive got a feelin' he's tryin' to embarrass you. You're the best leadoff hitter in the

the greatest batsman in the land

bluddy league and he knows it."

"Did you hear what he said to reporters the other day, Mush? He said I was guilty of indifferent play and that I was on bad terms with everybody on the club."

"Well, you aren't the most *popular* fella in the room, Billy, but everybody appreciates what you bring to the table, or the way you *set* the table if yer leadin' off."

No one was shocked when Irwin benched Hamilton for a series against Louisville but the move said a lot more about the manager than the player.

In a June 14 double header against the Colonels Del hit a ball a foot below the top of the right field wall. The two boys who hung the numbers onto the scoreboard leapt from their stools in alarm. Tuck Turner laughed at them as he jogged home. Del singled his next time up and moved a runner along with a sacrifice his last time at bat. He ended up crossing the plate four times in the Phillies' 17-6 win. In the late game Del went 4-for-4 in a 14-6 victory.

On June 19 the Phillies hosted Baltimore for the first game of the final series in their long home stand. John McGraw, who was nursing a sore knee, was sitting in the front row behind the Orioles' bench. In front of him against the railing was a bat. Del recognized it and went over to Mugsy. "Where d'ya get that bat, McGraw. I've seen it before and you weren't the man using it. You're too small ta swing a big one like that."

"The Gladiator gave it to me."

"I knew it had ta be one uv Pete's."

"Like you said, I can't use the fucking thing. It's way too heavy for me. I'd still be swinging it when the catcher threw the ball back to the twirler."

"You could give it ta Keeler," suggested Del.

They burst out laughing. Keeler employed the smallest bat in the big league. It was only thirty inches long and two and a half inches thick. In Del's hands it would have looked like a toothpick.

"Can I have it?" asked Del.

The Only Del

McGraw thought for a minute. "I suppose. But don't use it when you play us."

Del took the bat and went ahead and used it anyway. He slammed a double with his new favorite wagon tongue in a five-run Philly fifth and a triple in a five-run sixth to lead his side to an 11-5 win. McGraw cursed him both times.

At the beginning of July the Phillies took three straight from Boston, knocking the Beaneaters out of first place in the process and sending them on a downward spiral that would drop them into sixth. But in an all too familiar story, Arthur Irwin tried another new twirler the next day in Washington, Henry Lampe this time, and although Del hit a home run and made two terrific catches the Phillies lost 11-10.

Jack Taylor was doing the only solid pitching for the Phillies. They returned home the next day to face the Senators and he won his sixth straight. Del played shortstop. Art Irwin had despaired off Joe Sullivan. He was batting just over .300 but his .880 fielding percentage was among the worst in the league. Scoring runs wasn't the Phillies' problem; they needed to stop giving up so many. When Del made four errors that led to four unearned runs Irwin reluctantly put an end to the experiment and sent Del back to left field.

"Oim no shortstop," Del told Irwin. "I think I proved that in Cleveland."

Del was ten-for-ten in outfield chances in the next series. The left field bleachers were becoming known as "Delahantytown." In the last ten games of August Del set a major league record with twenty-five hits in ten games, seven doubles and four home runs among them. He crossed the plate eighteen times during the stretch. With Carsey and Taylor pitching better than ever, Al Orth, a burly six-footer with pinpoint control but no speed the Phillies had picked up from the Lynchburg Hill Climbers, winning almost every start thanks to his teammates scoring an average of eleven runs a game for him, and the addition of Con Lucid from Dublin the Phillies went on a tear. They swept the Senators in the middle of September to improve their record to an impressive 77-48, the best in franchise history.

the greatest batsman in the land

But Del had something other than the team's fortunes on his mind now. In early September he was walking to the park one morning when a group of neighborhood boys spotted him.

"Hey, Del, can we walk with you?" asked a dirty-faced lad who seemed to be the leader of the pack.

"Sure, why not?" said Del.

"Are you gonna hit a long one today?" asked the smallest of the bunch.

Del smiled and ruffled the kid's already messy blond hair, "You never know, me sun? I might just hit a couple."

As he reached the players' entrance he saw three girls huddled together. He was accustomed to seeing girls outside the park in their frills and finery. He thought he'd seen two of the three before. But not the third.

They were talking loud enough to be overheard. "Jack Boyle sure is big," a tall, plain-looking girl told the others.

"Bill Hallman is the best-looking player on the team, hands down," declared another girl, a freckle-faced redhead who was twirling a parasol above her head.

The third girl, the one Del had never seen before, had her back to him. She was short and had long, wavy chestnut brown hair. She said, "I remember the team picture you showed me. I'd say Ed Delahanty's the most dashing and virile man on the team."

"*Virile* is he?" said the plain girl.

"It sounds as though Norine has the vapors for Ed Delahanty," said the redhead.

Del smiled and turned to head inside the park. On his way he looked back to see what the girl who'd praised him looked like. He stopped dead in his tracks. She had an oval face, supernaturally blue eyes that seemed to sparkle and dance, a cute little, slightly upturned nose, full lips, and high, perfectly rouged cheekbones. Her hair was arranged in clusters of curls, like bunches of grapes. The girl could not have been any more than eighteen or nineteen, but she looked mature, very mature, in part because

The Only Del

of the eye-catching décolletage that the tight bodice of her dress displayed. A small black pearl that hung from a thin silver necklace sat wedged in the middle of her ample cleavage, contrasting with the paleness of her skin.

She had a Spanish blonde shawl around her shoulders but was careful not to clasp it tightly enough that it hid her most prominent assets. She wore a lavender dress with a pale green ribbon about the waist and black top button silk boots with heels designed to add four inches to her height, which Del guessed could not have been more than five-foot-two.

He turned and walked back to the girls. "Are you young ladies here to see the game?" he asked, looking at the other two to disguise his interest in the short one.

"We are," said the tallest girl.

"Aren't you Ed Delahanty?" asked the redhead with the parasol.

"He most certainly is," said the beautiful girl with the impossibly blue eyes. They were even brighter up close. She sounded somewhat refined, though Del couldn't detect an accent.

The tallest one said, "Norine here was just ..."

Norine stopped her. "Never mind what I was just saying, Elaine."

Del tried not to chuckle. And he tried not to look down at the girl's breasts. Her mascara-highlighted eyes were enough of a treat.

"Norine has never been to a game even though she lives just a few blocks from here," said Elaine.

"I'm Fanny," said the girl with the parasol. "Elaine and I come all the time, but Norine reads the society page, not the sports page. She always says she hasn't much interest in baseball."

"I might now," said Norine, gazing flirtatiously into Del's eyes.

The other girls looked at one another and stifled giggles.

"It's Norine's birthday," said Fanny. "She just turned ..."

"Eighteen," Norine finished for her. Her friends looked at one another. Norine shot them a minatory glare.

"Well happy birthday it is to you, Norine," said Del as Art Irwin walked by.

the greatest batsman in the land

"Get a move on, Delahanty," he said. "You can tell those girls about your long hits some other time. We have a ball game to get ready for."

Del ignored him. "Do you have tickets then?" he asked Elaine.

"We do. For the bleacher benches."

"Would yas rather box seats?"

"Where is it that *you* play, Mister Delahanty?" asked Norine.

"In the outfield."

"Isn't that near the bleachers?"

"Aye, 'tis."

"Then the bleacher benches will be just fine."

The other girls giggled again.

"Could I treat you ladies to a soda after the game?" asked Del.

"You certainly could. If you bring Billy Hallman with you," answered Fanny.

"Oill see what Bill says," Del told her. "And oill see if one uv the other fellas'd like ta come along as well."

Elaine smiled. Norine blinked her long eyelashes at Del. "Have a good game, Mister Delahanty. I'll be rooting for you."

Del tipped his hat. "Yer tickets'll be waitin' for yas at Gate Three," he said, pausing a beat to soak in Norine's curves again and hoping he'd be able to focus on the game.

Del singled, stole second, and scored in the first and lashed a double to deep right-center in the fourth. In the sixth inning he fired a strike to Mike Grady to nab a runner who'd tagged up at third presuming he could easily score on the deep flyball. Del turned and smiled up at Norine who was clapping her white gloves together in appreciation. She may not have been a baseball booster but she could tell from the roar of the crowd that it had been a terrific play.

After the game Del, Billy Hallman, and Mike Grady met the girls outside. Hallman and Grady went along for sodas for their friend's sake. They

The Only Del

could tell Ed had an eye for the youngest of the three. Neither was much interested in her friends and they drained their glasses and took off in pursuit of something stronger to wet their whistles. Del walked the girls home and made a note of Norine's address. He had a hard time thinking about anything but her the next few weeks. He looked for her every time he neared the ballpark and if it was just a band of boys anxious to meet their hero he was disappointed that she and her friends weren't among them.

When he finally did see Norine he gave her tickets to the game - her friends as well - he didn't want to be too obvious. "I hope you ladies enjoy the game," he said, looking at not just Norine but her friends too. She could see though that he really had eyes only for her and couldn't have cared less if her friends came along.

The Phillies were five games behind Baltimore, the club against whom they were about to play a four-game series. If they overtook second-place Cleveland they'd compete for the Dauvray Cup against the Orioles. Their hopes was quickly shattered. The series was a nightmare. Billy Hamilton was on the sidelines with an unspecified ailment and the Phillies badly missed his ability to get on base, rattle the pitcher, and generate runs. They got pounded 12-4 in the first game in Baltimore, had the second one called due to darkness with the score tied at sevens in the second, and lost the final two 7-1 and 10-1. Most of the Phillies' hits came with no one on base. Del's only hits were cheap singles. He tried every wagon tongue he had, each with the same result.

Completely demoralized, the Phillies went home and lost three straight to Brooklyn. They had played so badly in the final two series rumors circulated in the press that the Philadelphias had thrown the games. Del went 5-for-5 against Brickyard Kennedy in the meaningless last game of the season, a 10-9 win. The Phillies finished third, a disappointing ten games behind Baltimore.

Del began to realize that he was completely smitten with Norine and he suspected she knew that he was. He'd been with other women before and after Reagan, some very experienced in the art of pleasing a man, but none held the charms of this nubile coquette. He sent her flowers and letters and a Theodore Watts-Dunton's poem he'd found called "The Coming of Love."

Then he dropped by her house with more flowers for her and chocolates and flattering words for her mother, who decided Del was quite charming. He brought Cuban cigars for Norine's father, who thought Del was a man's man, even if he was acting the infatuated swain at the moment. Del could see that Norine's father, a carpenter from Scotland, doted on his baby girl.

"I'm just a tradesman, I'm nae able to provide my wee girl with the fineries of life she craves," he told Del one night when Norine had gone to the powder room to freshen her makeup.

"She does have an eye for fashion, frills, and jewelery," said Norine's mother. "She reads Collier's and Scribners and stares at Charles Gibson's illustrations of wealthy women in Harper's Weekly every chance she gets. The man she marries will need to be able to draw on a sizable bank account." She paused and said, "You do know she's only seventeen."

"I thought she'd just turned *eighteen*," said Del.

"Is that what she told you? I imagine she didn't want to scare you off. Norine is clever and charming, but she knows how to get her way. She certainly has her *father* wrapped around her little finger."

Norine's mother was a fine-looking woman who seemed much more sophisticated than her Scottish husband. She explained to Del that she was a Hutchinson from one of the first families of Virginia. Sir Thomas Hutchinson had been a Member of Parliament. William Hutchinson had landed in Boston aboard the Griffin in 1634, the same year his brother Joseph arrived in Salem. William was a prominent merchant and a judge in the Massachusetts Bay Colony and a founder of Rhode Island. Norine's forebears had been officers in the French-Indian Wars and had established counties in Virginia. Norine didn't exactly think she was royalty but she did feel that she was entitled to a higher station in society.

Del took her to see an open air concert and a vaudeville show at the Bijou and for rides in the expensive calash he'd just bought. They drove through Fairmount Park on Sundays and he took her to the beer garden

The Only Del

at Lemon Hill, where Norine sipped tea and smiled as scores of baseball boosters made a fuss over her handsome beau.

Sometimes they would just go for a walk, Norine loved being a pretty adornment on the arm of a celebrated ball player and he loved showing her off. Of an evening they played dominoes, or backgammon, or checkers, or looked at pictures on the family's stereopticon. Del finally screwed up the courage to ask Norine's father for her hand in marriage. His approval was important, he would have to sign a parental consent form since Norine was not of age.

"I assure you that my intentions have been honorable, sir," said Del.

In the next room Norine was telling her mother that her handsome and famous but much older beau had not done anything untoward. She didn't tell her mother that she rather wished he had.

Chapter Seventeen

Until Death Do Us Part

Del had missed fifteen of his team's games in '95 due to a strained throwing arm and other assorted injuries but he still led the league with 49 doubles and a .500 On Base Percentage and finished second in slugging and total bases. His .404 batting average was second only to Jesse Burkett's .405. Between an advertisement for Laird's Fine Calf Shoes and an enormous plug for Battle Ax Plug, which was hailed as the largest piece of good tobacco ever sold, the *Press* reported on October 6 that Ed Delahanty had signed for next season. They did not relate what salary he'd be paid but Del figured it was just enough to support a wife.

He and Norine took an evening stroll in the chilly fall air in late October. When they reached a spot on the sidewalk illuminated by the street lamp above Del stopped and gently spun Norine around to face him. Her dazzling eyes shimmered. Del reached into his pocket and took out a small box. He opened it and the ring inside sparkled in the light. Though he had thought of several clever ways to ask, now all he said was, "Will you marry me?"

"It's about time you asked," said Norine.

On November 1 the *New York Times* reported that Andrew Freedman, an arrogant Tammany Hall back room fixer who would eventually engage in fist fights with a retired umpire, two sportswriters, a political columnist, and three fellow owners, and had bought controlling interest in the Giants for $53,000, had taken his check book to Philadelphia and invited Al Reach to name his price for Ed Delahanty. Reach told Freedman that Delahanty was not for sale at *any* price. The Phillies had set a record for attendance, having drawn close to half a million cranks to Huntington Grounds II.

The Only Del

But in spite of his team having led the league in batting for a third straight year Irwin had failed to win a championship. During the season cryptic O.P. Caylor had wondered whether Irwin could manage the front end of an ice wagon.

At the annual meeting of National League managers in November the Beaneaters made room for Jimmy Collins, their talented new third baseman, by trading the incumbent third baseman Billy Nash to the Phillies. To the shock of baseball boosters around the league the player Philadelphia sent Boston in return was Billy Hamilton. Nash was among the best third baseman in the league but Reach and Rogers had not obtained him for his fielding prowess; they needed him to captain their team. Del thought the Phillies had been stupid to trade Hamilton. He was sure to have several good years ahead of him, especially the way he took care of himself.

Del took Norine to Cleveland to meet his parents. He was more than a little nervous. He remembered his mother's words of advice about choosing a wife. "Do not be blinded by a girl's charms and choose one that is fond of society, vain, artificial, and showy in dress. You don't want a doll or a coquette for a partner. Choose instead a sweet, modest, sensible girl who has learned to deny herself." They were a little taken aback by how young Norine was, but she was charming and they could tell she loved Ed. They weren't impressed that she was Protestant, but she promised them she would raise her children as Catholics so they gave their blessings.

Unwilling to wait, the young couple were married in a private ceremony at St. Charles Borromeo, a small church in South Philadelphia, by a priest who was so old Del thought he might have heard Jesus preach. Ed's brother Frank and Norine's sister Nettie served as witnesses. Norine looked absolutely gorgeous in her white satin wedding dress. Frank wished the practice of kissing the bride after the ceremony hadn't gone out of style.

The ceremony went off without a hitch - except for one troubling moment. Just as Ed was saying "Until death do us part" the young organist accidentally fell forward on his bench and to avoid landing face-first on the keyboard he put his hand on it and the notes that resulted struck an ominous chord. Everyone looked at one another and sniggered uneasily at the dreadful timing. After they signed the register Ed and Norine took Frank and Nettie to lunch. Norine hoped some sparks would fly between them, but none did.

Del took his bride to Atlantic City for their honeymoon. She wouldn't let him touch her on the train.

"Come on then, Missus Delahanty," Del begged, staring at Norine's breasts. "Just a wee feel? They're so amazing."

"You've waited this long, you can wait a few more hours," teased Norine, stroking the diamond ring Del had picked out for her at McCully & Company.

"It's gointa seem like *years*," groaned Del.

Norine took a book out of her valise. It had a lengthy title. "Instruction and Advice for the Young Bride by Ruth Smythers, beloved wife of The Reverend L.D. Smythers, Pastor of the Arcadian Methodist Church, published in the year of our Lord 1894 on the Conduct and Procedure of the Intimate and Personal Relationships of the Marriage State for the Greater Spiritual Sanctity of this Blessed Sacrament and the Glory of God."

Norine read a section she'd bookmarked to Del. "To the sensitive young woman who has had the benefits of proper upbringing the wedding day is, ironically, both the happiest and most terrifying day of her life. On the positive side, there is the wedding itself, in which the bride is the central attraction in a beautiful and inspiring ceremony symbolizing her triumph in securing a male to provide for all her needs for the rest of her life. On the negative side, there is the wedding night, during which the bride must pay the piper, so to speak, by facing for the first time the terrible experience of sex."

She paused while Del handed the conductor their tickets to be punched and then resumed. "At this point, dear reader, let me concede one shocking truth. Some young women actually anticipate the wedding night ordeal with curiosity and pleasure! Beware such an attitude! A selfish and sensual husband can easily take advantage of such a bride. One cardinal rule of marriage should never be forgotten: give little, give seldom, and above all,

The Only Del

give grudgingly. Otherwise what could have been a proper marriage could become an orgy of sexual lust."

A middle-aged dowager across the aisle from Del and Norine had been listening in and she nodded approvingly. Norine glared at her and she turned away. Norine went back to reading to Del. "On the other hand, the bride's terror need not be extreme. While sex is at best revolting and at worse rather painful, it must be endured, has been by women since the beginning of time, and is compensated for by the children produced through it. Most men, if not denied, would demand sex almost every day. The wise bride will permit a maximum of two brief sexual experiences weekly during the first months of marriage. As time goes by she should make every effort to reduce this frequency. Feigned illness, sleepiness, and headaches are among the wife's best friends in this matter. Arguments, nagging, scolding, and bickering also prove very effective if used an hour before the husband would normally commence his seduction. A wise bride will make it her goal never to allow her husband to see her unclothed body."

Del looked at his shapely young wife and groaned.

Norine went on, "Sex, when it cannot be prevented, should be practiced only in total darkness. Many women find it useful to have thick cotton nightgowns for themselves and pajamas for their husbands. These should be donned in separate rooms. They need not be removed during the sex act. Once the bride has donned her gown and turned off all the lights, she should lie quietly upon the bed and await her groom. When he comes groping into the room she should make no sound to guide him in her direction, lest he take it as a sign of encouragement. She should let him grope around in the dark. There is always the hope that he will stumble and incur some slight injury which she can use as an excuse to deny him sexual access. When he finds her, the wife should lie as still as possible. Bodily motion on her part could be interpreted as sexual excitement by the optimistic husband. The wise wife will allow him to pull her nightgown up no farther than the waist, and only permit him to open the front of his pajamas to thus make connection. She should be absolutely silent or babble about her housework while he is huffing and puffing away. Above all, she should lie perfectly still and never under any circumstances grunt or groan while the act is in progress."

Norine closed the book and looked at Del, who had a look of horror on his face. He gulped, "How much uv that advice are ya plannin' ta follow?"

She hesitated for a long beat and then smiled. "Not a single word of it. In fact, I shall probably do the exact *opposite*." She stared over at the appalled dowager across the aisle and kissed Del hard on the mouth. Then she added, "And you can be a selfish and sensual husband and take advantage of your bride whenever and wherever you desire."

They checked into the Algonquin at the corner of Atlantic and Pennsylvania. It had just been rebuilt with lavishly appointed parlors illuminated by frosted incandescent light. Norine liked that it was located in the midst of Atlantic City's finest shops. After eating in the Algonquin's richly furnished dining room, a meal Del couldn't eat fast enough, he and Norine sat on the hotel's veranda for a while holding hands. The other guests admired the handsome couple and some of the men whispered to their wives that the man looked just like pictures they'd seen of Ed Delahanty, the Phillies' star outfielder. All they usually got in response was, "That's nice, where are you taking me tomorrow?"

"It's getting dark, me luv," said Del impatiently after a few minutes. He was dying to get his bride alone. "Shouldn't we be getting to bed? It's been a long day."

"Are you tired?" Norine chided him.

When they got back to their room Del undressed quickly and jumped into bed. Norine went to change in the bathroom. He hoped she wouldn't come out in some shapeless flannel nightgown like the one recommended in the book she had read to him on the train. Then he thought of something and went to the closet. He got a towel to put over the sheets. Del was sure that in spite of all her feminine wiles and worldliness Norine was a virgin. There was bound to be blood. She seemed to be in the bathroom forever, but when she finally came out Del saw that it had been well worth the wait. His eyes lit up. His young bride wore nothing but high heels and a French

The Only Del

Coutel silk corset that struggled unsuccessfully to contain her breasts. The corset was the same color as her eyes. Del gulped at the vision of Norine's diaphanous figure and said, "I feel like a leprechaun. I'm lyin' here countin' me lucky stars."

Norine smiled and climbed into bed. Del lay behind her and ran his hands across her shoulders. Then he began stroking her beautiful hair. He splayed the long fingers of his right hand across the base of her neck and then slowly pushed up, gathering strands of hair between his fingers like a rake, then pulling back toward himself. Norine cooed each time he did it.

He slowly unclasped the sties of the corset and pulled it off. His member began to throb and Norine pushed up against him and whimpered. She took Del's hand and put it over her bosom. He had to steel himself not to try pushing inside. As anxious as he was he didn't want to rush things.

"Rub it up and down against me," said Norine breathlessly.

Del obliged and felt himself grow harder than he'd ever been.

"It so big, Del."

Del rubbed himself slowly up and down against his bride's little bottom, trying his best to concentrate on stroking her hair but breathing heavily.

"That feels wonderful. Absolutely wonderful."

"It certainly does. You have an incredible body if I might be so bold."

"If *I* might be so bold ... could I touch it?"

"My wee night stick?"

"I've never seen or felt one before, but that is *anything* but wee."

Norine reached behind and took Del's erection in her hand. She rubbed it up and down for a minute and then pushed inside her. They both groaned, him in delight, Norine in pain. Del knew it hurt. He took it slow, but he still lasted only a minute or so.

"I'm sorry, me luv, I usually last a lot longer than that."

Norine gave him a dirty look.

"Not that I've done it that many times. But you're so beautiful. And you're so tight inside."

"I hope it won't hurt so much the next time," said Norine. "At least there wasn't as much blood as I thought there might be," she said, picking up the towel Del had thought to put under them.

They got up and had a bath together. Del was glad he'd paid the $2.50 so they could have a room with a tub. He squeezed in behind Norine and cupped her breasts in his big hands. They barely fit.

"Is that what you wanted to do on the train?" purred Norine.

"Aye, 'twas. Do you think it might uv alarmed the other passengers?"

"Possibly." She hesitated and said, "Del, your night stick seems to be swelling. Does that mean he wants to go inside again?"

"I thought you'd never ask. Truth be told, he'd like to have done *that* on the train as well."

"If there's a bath on the next train we take he can. Now hurry up, it's not just my *skin* that's gotten wet."

After they'd made love twice more in the morning and then had breakfast Del took Norine to the revolving observation tower on the boardwalk on New York Avenue. Its thirty-five tons of machinery was a triumph of mechanical engineering. The clerk at the hotel desk had said that the view from its height of 125 feet was sensational.

"This is magnificent, Del," Norine told her husband when they reached the top. Then she realized that Del wasn't beside her. He'd been foolish to expect that he could go to the top of the tower. As soon as he'd stepped off the steam elevator the nightmare had returned and he'd seen himself falling headfirst into the churling water. He'd stepped right back into the car and ridden back down to the street.

"Why have you not told me you have acrophobia, darling?" Norine asked when she rode back down the elevator and found Del waiting for her with a sheepish look on his handsome face. "It's nothing to be ashamed of."

"It isn't acrophobia, me pet, it's the damned nightmares oive bin havin'."

The Only Del

"Well I have a solution for that," said Norine with a beguiling look.

"A solution?" asked Del.

"Yes. Whenever you have one of those nightmares I'll wake you up and we'll make love."

A big smile swept across Del's face. "You know what?"

"What?"

"Now oim gointa look forward ta having them."

Norine rapped his arm with her parasol. "You are a rascal, Edward Delahanty. Just for that you are going to have to take me to the most expensive store on the boardwalk and buy me something nice."

Del took Norine to three stores and bought her each of the pretty things she picked out. He didn't mind the cost, he knew she'd look marvelous in anything she wore. Then they went for a walk along the boardwalk and watched people frolicking in the Atlantic. Swimming costumes had shrunken to positively scandalous proportions, short-sleeve or tanks tops and shorts that didn't even extend to the knee. It had been alarming to see women's ankles in the 80's, now to see their calves was almost too much to fathom.

When it started to rain they hurried back to their room and took turns reading "When the Kissing had to Stop" to each other in the nude. He stroked her back and legs and rubbed her little feet while she read. She played with the hair on Del's chest and slowly and teasingly stroked his member while he read. He kept losing his place and they had to stop a couple of times for amorous intermissions. When they got dressed, Norine took a small box out of her trunk. She sat down at the writing table and opened it. She'd read in "The Boudoir Chat" column of one of the Sunday papers a couple of weeks after she and Del had begun stepping out that the smartest women were using the new pigeon-blood notepaper. She'd ordered some of it and some white ink for her fountain pen.

As she began writing to her sister, Del looked at the letters *ND* she'd had monogrammed in silver in the top left corner. "When did you order that writing paper, me luv?" he asked.

the greatest batsman in the land

"A couple of weeks after we started seeing one other," Norine said matter-of-factly.

"A *couple uv weeks*? How could you possibly have known I would ask you to marry me?"

"A girl just knows."

Del shook his head. "What gave me away?"

"When that handsome man at the Bijou was ogling me. I thought your blood was going to boil. I could tell you weren't about to let any other man have me."

―――

There would now be a lot less need to chase kids down the street if they refused to throw balls back onto the field and made off with them. The home team was now required to have a dozen new baseballs on hand for each game. The umpire, not the home team captain, would decide when and if play should be resumed after a rain delay and umpires now had free reign in ejecting rowdy players and fining those who kicked unduly at their decisions or engaged in "villainously filthy language." Because so many of them had quit in disgust over abuse, the league had been forced to employ fifty-nine different umpires in '95 and Tim Murnan - no stranger to hooliganism in his own playing days - opined that, "The time will soon come when no one above the rank of garrotter will be secured to officiate."

In June, the *Brooklyn Eagle* would remark, "If President Young continues to agree not to send umpires to each city that protests, there will not be enough men to go around. Washington objects to Tom Lynch, Stage and Tim Hurst, St. Louis objects to Ed Swartwood, Boston and Brooklyn draw the line at Jim O'Rourke, New York is down on Stage and Louisville can't stand John McQuaid. The season is only a month old."

Instead of getting the first-rate pitcher the team so desperately needed, the Phillies chose to pay $500 for badly over-the-hill, 38-year-old Dan Brouthers. It was the very same thing they'd done when they'd picked up Roger Connor at the end of *his* great career. Brouthers, whose name was pronounced broothers, had a luxurious mustache, the ends of which he kept exquisitely pomaded He always had his Irish setter Kelly with him.

The Only Del

No one minded, Kelly was very well-behaved. Del taught him how to fetch bats, gloves, and the team's water pail. Dan hated to be called Jumbo as some cranks did, referring to P.T. Barnum's famous elephant. Brouthers had added a few pounds to his already bulky frame. Del remembered hearing as a child that Brouthers had run into a catcher in his first year of baseball while playing against the Harlem Clippers in '77. Dan's shoulder had collided with the catcher's temple and the man had passed out and later died. Brouthers was so grief-stricken he'd quit the game for two years.

The Phillies lost their first game of the season as usual but won their next six. Del singled, doubled, tripled, and drove in three in a 14-12 win over the Giants. He went hitless the next day but his mates still managed to tally nineteen runs against the demoralized New Yorkers. They used four different pitchers.

"Oive been around a while now and oive never seen the likes uv this," Del told Joe Sullivan when the fourth Giant twirler took the mound.

Sully was showing signs of consumption and Del was worried about him. Joe was coughing something awful, sometimes for minutes on end. He'd started to lose weight too. Del felt powerless to do anything for him but he did offer to pay his doctor's bills.

On May 7 Henry Holmes was hanged at Moyamensing Prison. Until the moment of his death he remained calm and amiable, showing no sign of fear, anxiety, depression, or remorse. He asked for his coffin to be buried in cement ten feet deep. He was concerned that grave robbers would steal his body and dissect it. Holmes' neck wouldn't snap; he was strangled to death slowly, twitching for more than a quarter of an hour.

Tuck Turner was supposed to take Billy Hamilton's spot in the outfield but the Phillies had soured on him. He'd thrown out only five runners and made seventeen errors in '95 even though he'd kept his batting average high. This year he was hitting .219. The Phillies sent Turner and Joe Sullivan to the Browns for Duff Cooley, who sprang from Leavenworth, Kansas. He'd led the Browns in hits, runs, and total bases but the competition wasn't very stiff.

the greatest batsman in the land

On May 23rd O.P. Caylor wrote a piece about the Phillies, who he said were playing terrific ball in the spring for the first time in recent memory.

> *"Delehanty, Thompson, Brouthers, Clements, and Cross when lined up before a pitcher cause him to feel that life is a very serious matter after all. That big fellow Delehanty I consider the best batsman in the country. While he has never led the league, he hovers around the top every year and twice has fetched up second. Delehanty is a model athlete and an ideal player in all points of the game. Should any club be offered its pick of all the outfielders in the league every one of them would take Del."*

Del was pleased when he read the tribute from the generally critical writer but he wished that after all this time people would spell his name right. The Phillies lost eight straight games on the road and then came home and won six straight.

On Friday, June 5th at home to the Pirates, Dan Brouthers fumbled a ball and made a wild throw with two out in the third and Pittsburgh scored six runs to take the lead. Still misspelling Del's name like O.P. Caylor did the *Pittsburgh Press* reporter wrote, "It was Delehanty's day. Ed was responsible for four of the Phillies' runs and he denied four Pirates the pleasure of crossing the plate by his performances in left field. Del hit a solo home run in the eighth and a two-run homer in the ninth to retake the lead and win the game."

It rained the next day so Ed and Norine went shopping, after which Ed decided to take his beautiful young wife to the opera. He loved showing her off and "Don Quixote" was in the final week of its run. They went home and changed into evening clothes. She wore a low-cut gown, blue sapphire drop earrings, and a string-of-pearls necklace. Their seats were in a box they shared with two well-dressed couples who looked to be in their early forties. The way they were talking about the opera it seemed as though they'd seen it several times. The men didn't seem pleased to be seeing it yet again. Ed guessed the women had dragged them along just so they could show off their jewelry. The woman beside Ed peered at her program through a tortoise-shell eye-glass adorned with diamonds that hung from a long chain.

The Only Del

Midway through the second act one of the men began to cough - quietly at first, and then louder and with greater frequency. Ed suspected it was an excuse to leave. The women seemed to share his suspicion but eventually had no choice but to get him out of the theater before he ruined things for the entire audience. Ed and Norine had the box to themselves.

They watched in silence for a few minutes and then Norine whispered in Ed's ear, "Do you remember how I told your mother we would raise our children as Catholics?"

"I remember. Why? Have you changed your mind?"

"Not at all, it's just that …"

"Just that what?"

"It's just that we can't do that unless we actually *have* children to raise."

Ed gave her a look of puzzlement. Then he felt something. Norine was unbuttoning his fly.

"Norine!" he whispered.

"No one can see," Norine whispered back.

She struggled and then pulled out his already excited member. She stroked it slowly, then stopped. Ed shuttered. She took off her glove and started stroking again.

"We need to go someplace," whispered Ed. "*Fast!*"

"Where?"

"I'll find a place."

With great difficulty he stuffed his manhood back inside his trousers and buttoned up his fly. He grabbed Norine by the hand and led her up the stairs and through the curtain at the back into the deserted hallway. He looked up and down it. "There," he said.

He led her to a door that said "STORAGE" and tried the knob. The door was locked. Norine frowned. "Where else can we go?"

"This'll be fine," said Del.

He reached into his vest pocket and pulled out a nail file. "I learned this trick at Cleveland High School," he explained. He didn't add that he'd used a nail file to unlock the janitor's office door so he could be alone with Colleen between classes. Either this lock was sturdier than the custodian's or this file was more brittle. It snapped.

"Damn!" groaned Del.

"Try this," said Norine, pulling a pin from her hair.

"You did it!" she whispered after Del had jimmied the lock open. He led her inside, closed the door behind them, and fumbled for the light. Norine hurriedly unbuttoned her blouse and then unbuttoned Del's fly again. He admired her breasts for a moment and then grabbed Norine by the shoulders.

"Del, what are you ...?"

"Makin' a baby." He spun her around and pulled up her dress and petticoats. He was glad bustles were a lot smaller than they had been. She pushed her bloomers down to her knees and then sighed as Del's erection slid slowly up and down against her behind.

"You don't need to wait, I'm ready! I've been ready since those people got up and left."

He pushed inside her and she groaned in delight. Del pulled back out again.

"Don't you dare tease, Edward Delahanty!" she almost yelled.

Del pushed back inside and thrust rapidly again and again. Norine shuttered violently, once and then twice more. Del could feel her insides tighten around him. He grabbed her breasts and came like he'd never done before.

As they returned to their seats a man who'd taken one of the seats vacated by the two couples asked if they were feeling all right.

"I'm fine *now*," said Del. "I just had a bit of swelling is all. My wife took care of it."

Norine giggled and punched Del's arm.

The Only Del

On the way out of the Metropolitan the theater manager was at the open door to the street. He recognized Del and asked, "Did you enjoy the performance?"

Norine answered for her husband. "It was very satisfying, he never disappoints. It was quite … penetrating."

"He is a marvelous tenor, is he not?"

The theater manager scratched his head as they walked away and Norine said over her shoulder, "Really? It seemed a lot *deeper* than that."

The next afternoon Delahanty played like he'd had a hard night. The *Times* remarked that "during his wakeful moments in left field he pulled in two flies that earned applause but missed out in doubling up a runner when he made a very Nancy Mackintosh throw." Blurry-eyed or not, Ed singled to right and drove a ball up the middle that rolled all the way to the distant center field fence. The Phillies moved into a three-way tie for second, a mere half game back of Baltimore.

On Monday, June 22 Ed went to Wilkes-Barre to see his brother Tommy play for the Toronto Maple Leafs against the Coal Barons. Tom had batted .409 in sixteen games with Detroit in the Western League in '95 and had high hopes of making it to the big league. Ed was one of the six hundred on hand to see his kid brother lead off and play shortstop. Everyone kept looking at Ed and then Tommy and then back at Ed, remarking to one another that they could be twins except that Ed was a lot bigger. Tom helped the Toronto club beat the home side with two hits, two runs, and a well-turned rally-ending double play. Ed took Tom out for a big meal and a few jars after the game. He was excited for his little brother when Shaymus wrote a few months later to say that the Spiders had signed Tommy. He was absolutely awful in his major league debut though, making eleven errors in sixteen games and batting .232.

In the customary Fourth of July double header the Philly cranks amused themselves by setting off firecrackers every time their heroes hit the ball- even fouls and pop flies. Colonel Rogers called the team in to the clubhouse

the greatest batsman in the land

for a meeting after the second game. The players were about to head west on a sixteen-game road trip and just wanted to pack up their gear and head to the Broad Street Station. They thought this very strange and wondered what the owner could possibly have to tell them.

"I imagine he's gointa say we've got to bring our own baseballs ta battin' practice from here on and make sandwiches to take on the train," Del whispered to Sam Thompson. Sam was afraid to voice an opinion on the topic. Instead he asked Del where Dan Brouthers was.

"Oive no idea," said Del, looking around the room for the big man and not seeing him. In the first inning of the first game Brouthers had missed a routine grounder, dropped a pickoff throw, and muffed an easy pop fly

"That was pretty bad the way he cost us all those runs. Maybe he's taken off ta drown his sorrows."

"Dan Brouthers has been given ten days' notice of his release as required in his contract," Rogers announced in a somber tone. Everyone looked at one another anxiously.

"Poor bugger, I hope *I* don't go out that way," Del said to Sam.

"Brouthers told me he's stashed away thirty thousand from his baseball salaries and is set for life."

"Is that so?" said Del, who hadn't put away a cent.

"On a happier note," said Rogers, "I am taking my wife on a trip to England at the end of the season and the team will pay the way for any player who wishes to bring his wife and join us."

"Begorrah!" yelled Ed, who could scarcely believe his ears.

All the others looked at him and laughed. He didn't care. He knew his bride would be thrilled.

"For he's a jolly fine fellow, for he's a jolly fine fellow," Ed began to sing only half mockingly. Mike Grady, who was in fine spirits after hitting a home run with the bases full to win the afternoon game, grinned and joined in and then the others did too. They had no way of knowing that Dan Brouthers' unceremonial release had opened a door for the team's next star player, one who would become Del's best friend.

The Only Del

Del had been right. Norine was beside herself when she heard the news of the trip to England. "How wonderful it will be to show off my handsome, successful, and famous husband when we visit our relatives in England," she told her sister Nettie. "Our cousins will be *so* jealous. I can't wait to write cousin Gladys. She's always writing me that she's seeing a Shakespearean actor or the son of an earl."

No game was scheduled for the next day so Del took Norine shopping on Market and Chestnut Streets. The Gimbels had bought the Granville Haines store at Ninth and Market that had closed soon after it opened, a victim of the Panic of 1893. Over the front window was a sign that read "Nobody but *Nobody* undersells Gimbels." The Gimbels had been the first store to set fixed prices on items. There was no haggling here, which Del found refreshing. They put the prices on little pieces of cardboard they attached to their wares.

Del bought a fifteen dollar blue suit for $8.50 and three striped shirts with Bishop sleeves, as well as four collars and a tie-pin. Norine bought embroidered Muslin drawers, corset clasps, silk garters, and a black and white striped taffeta bonnet trimmed with Persian ribbon and American beauty roses. At Leary's Bookstore Norine bought "Tess of the Dubervilles" and Rosa Carey's "Wooed and Married." Del finally decided on "The Prisoner of Zenda." Then they visited Whitman's Chocolates and Confections. Norine bought perfume at Strawbridge & Clothier's Dry Goods, a 5-story brick building with large skylights and an open atria on the corner of Market and 8th Streets that had once been Thomas Jefferson's office. It featured domestic goods but the latest Paris fashions as well, which is what interested Norine.

"I wonder what Reagan is doing right now," Del thought to himself as he broused. "Oive certainly got nuthin' to kick about though," he said aloud, looking at his young bride trying on high-heeled shoes.

They finished their spree at Lit Brothers, whose mottos were "Hats Trimmed Free of Charge" and "A Great Store in a Great City." Del was relieved that the prices were reasonable here, he'd spent enough already. All he bought was a shaving kit with a razor, a strop, a pure gray badger bristle brush, a cup, and soap that was on sale for 75 cents. At Snellenbergs, "the Thrifty Store for Thrifty People", they browsed the giant jewelry counter and looked at a $950 diamond solitaire ring before choosing a four dollar rhinestone pendant.

Despite Del's strong play, the ball club didn't improve its standing. When they arrived in Chicago in the middle of July they were 0-for-6 on their road trip, including three losses to last-place Louisville. The Colonels were so bad that when a group of their most loyal boosters went with them on the road they traveled in a hearse. Chicago had just hosted the Democratic Party convention that nominated William Jennings Bryan for president and they gave little thought to a Monday afternoon midsummer ballgame. A heat wave that caused 133 deaths the day of the game also kept rooters away and only 1,100 turned out at West Side Park. The huge *Waltham Watches* thermometer on the grandstand read in the triple digits by 11 a.m.

Toeing the pitching slab for the Chicagos was William "Adonis" Terry. The handsome right-hander's specialty was benders. He'd used them to rack up twenty-one wins in '95. Del had done fairly well against Terry, but he'd never hit a home run off him. West Side Park's left and right field foul poles were 340 feet from the plate. The on-field clubhouses in center were more than 450 feet from home. The right-field wall was forty feet high with a scoreboard and a canvas screen fastened to telephone poles to block the view of rooftop spectators. It was an unlikely setting for the greatest hitting performance of the 19th century.

The Phillies began the game with Dick Cooley drawing a walk and being sacrificed to second. With two outs, "Delahanty, batting fourth in Dan Brouthers' former spot, caught the first pitched ball, a swift upslanter, with an easy swing and floated it over the rightfield wall."

In the third inning Del hit a vicious line drive toward short that knocked over Bill "Bullhead" Dahlen and went into left field for a single. Del's third at bat came with two runners on base. This time he smashed the bruised and dented sphere over the bulletin board and canvas-topped right-field wall. It landed across the road amidst a disgruntled flock of chickens. A young boy picked up the ball and ran several blocks with a panting

The Only Del

policeman on his heels, giving Del the record for the longest home run ever made.

Del came to the plate in the seventh inning with his team trailing 9-6. He found a straight shoot to his liking and propelled the pitch through the air waves and over the head of Billy Lange, the fleet-footed Chicago center fielder. The ball rolled against the door of the distant clubhouses. Someone opened the door to see what had happened and quickly closed it again. Del circled the bases for his third home run.

When Del came to bat in the ninth inning, most of the bugs had forgotten all about the heat or the score and were just cheering for another home run. When some cranks got up to leave a man said to them, "Wait till Del makes another one." The sweaty man beside him yelled, "Line another one out, Del."

Chicago manager Anson threatened to fine his whole team the price of three meals - at Columbian Exposition prices - if any Philadelphia player was put on base before Delahanty, who was due to hit third, got his last at bat. After the first two batters were retired Lange yelled to Adonis to hold on a minute and retreated to the farthest part of the grounds - the uncut grass in front of the centerfield clubhouses. Del, in his soaking-wet woolen uniform, laughed at the spectacle of the retreating center fielder.

"I can hardly see ya, Bill. Can you see *me*?" Del yelled to Lange.

Lange didn't answer. He was much too far away to hear.

Many bugs were standing on their seats when Del fooled everyone by bunting the first pitch. He chuckled as it rolled foul. His action brought shouts of protest from the grandstands. Del enjoyed his little stunt and waited on Terry's next pitch, a slow, outside curve. The bat impacted with the sound of a rifle shot. Del had hit it on a line, ten feet above the ground. It flew over 450 feet, past Lange - though that had hardly seemed possible - and bounced off the roof of one of the centerfield clubhouses. It fell to the ground and while Lange scrambled to get it Del "circumnavigated the diamond" for his fourth home run. Lange hid the ball under the clubhouse to save as a souvenir.

As he crossed the plate, Terry was waiting to shake his hand. The sweaty cranks stood on their seats cheering wildly for a full ten minutes. After the game, spectators followed Del to the omnibus and gave him congratulatory claps on his back. The twirler-deprived Phillies lost the game, 9-8, their seventh setback in a row. Del had five of their nine hits. He'd knocked in seven runs and batted for seventeen total bases.

That evening, back at the hotel, a lot of people commiserated with Del. They told him it was a tough loss after the spectacular way he'd batted.

Del sighed and said, "I did the best I could. I couldn't hit any more." Queried about "Adonis" Terry, Del confessed that he'd never hit hard against him, "but today they came in just right. Tomorrow I probably won't hit a damn thing."

"Why is it that you offer at the first pitch so often?" asked a reporter who'd read a colleague's article about Del. It said that, "the champion heavy-weight timber wielder is not a subscriber of the theory that a batsman should overlook the first pitched ball."

"What difference does it make if it's the first ball delivered or the last?" asked Del. "If I think I can do business with it I swing. Oive bin makin' a pretty fair showin' in the battin' department these past few years and I didn't do it by watchin' juicy ones the twirler has sent amidships over the plate sail by."

In recognition of his amazing achievement, before the game the next day William Wrigley presented Del with a box of his popular gum for each of his home runs. When Del got back to the bench he tossed the boxes of gum to Mike Scanlon. "Give um ta yer kids, Mike. I only chew tobacco." He turned to Sam Thompson and said, "I should uv hit them in St. Louis. Busch might uv showed up with four cases uv beer."

Del disappointed the cranks who came to see if he'd hit any more home runs off Chicago ace Clark Griffith on Tuesday.

"It turns out you're a mere mortal after all, Edward Delahanty," Jimmy Ryan chided him after the game. "Just two lousy doubles to the fence and a three-bagger past poor Bill Lange."

The Phillies limped home from their road trip with a 4-and-16 record. One of the few bright spots was a ninth inning single by Del that ended Cy Young's bid for a no-hitter. Billy Nash headed to New England to look

The Only Del

for talent. He was interested in a speedy little infielder playing for the Falls River Indians, a club in the Class B New England League, by the name of Billy Geier. But when he got there he was a lot more impressed by a much bigger player of French extraction with sad brown eyes and a lantern jaw named Napoleon Lajoie.

Lajoie's father Jean, who had moved to Woonsocket, Rhode Island from Quebec, had worked as a teamster, but his premature death in 1881 had forced his children to find employment as soon as they were physically able. After attending school for less than a year, Napoleon was obliged to forsake his education and followed in his father's footsteps as a teamster. He drove a hack for the Consolidated Livery Stable. On his days off he played for semi-pro teams, first for two dollars a game, then three, then five, under the nickname "The Slugging Cabby." At six-feet tall, he was always the biggest player on the field. Soon he was making more money on the side than he was delivering lumber, straw, hay, and coal, and occasionally donning a suit and top hat to drive people to weddings and funerals.

Lajoie joined the Falls River Indians when they offered him $500 for the season. He was making $7.50 a week as a cabby and his words of acceptance were, "I'm out for the stuff." He recorded 163 hits in 80 games and led the team in doubles, triples, and home runs. He played first base, second base, and center field, and he was fearless behind the bat. Lajoie was widely regarded as an outstanding prospect. The first offer for him was $500 from the Pirates. Indians' owner Charlie Marston turned them down flat. More and more mention was being made in the newspapers of this kid who was tearing up the New England League with a batting average over .400 and a "total" or Slugging Average over .700. Lajoie was being scouted by Boston and Brooklyn too.

Nash liked what he saw in Billy Geier, but he was amazed by Lajoie. He telephoned Colonel Rogers from his hotel room after he had seen the big young man play. "Lajaway glides toward the ball and gathers it in like he's picking fruit," Nash yelled into the phone, even though Rogers could hear him just fine. "He's an excellent bunter and he can hit the ball to all fields. But he's the least disciplined batter I've ever seen. He goes after pitches down at his ankles or up at his eyebrows."

the greatest batsman in the land

"Go ahead and offer Marston twenty-five hundred for Geier and the French kid," Rogers told Nash. "And by the way, you've no need to shout into a telephone, Mister Nash, you aren't yelling out a window."

Marston accepted the offer and on August 7 Lajoie debuted at first base against Washington and played well. Del threw out a runner at home and led the way at bat with a double and a single while Jack Taylor shut out the Senators on ten hits.

The Phillies were down by three runs in the ninth the next day when Del started a rally by nearly tearing off the right foot of Duke Farrell with a vicious line drive. He and Sam Thompson and Bill Hallman scored to tie things. Del singled home the winning run in the twelfth. On August 19th in Louisville, Del walked, singled twice, and homered in a 15-0 rollick over the Colonels and then headed to Hillerich's to order some more of the bats that were working so well for him. On August 26th the Spiders came to town. Lajoie jogged to first after ramming a ball to the outfield. When he realized too late that the fielder was not going to reach it he dug in but it was too late and what should have been an inside-the-park home run ended up a triple.

"How about you try running as soon as you hit the ball next time, Lajaway," snarled Billy Nash, who was coaching third.

Del, who had one hit on the day, did everything he could to keep foul-mouthed "Crab" Burkett, with whom he was having "a warm fight" for league batting honors, off base. He charged in to trap two short flies and "made a ringer" on another, but re-injured his shoulder on the play. It got so bad that he was hospitalized and missed eight games. He hated spending days away from the ball field and nights away from his amorous young wife.

One night Del had been asleep for about an hour when a nurse came into his room. He was a bit surprised, it was almost midnight. The nurse didn't turn on the light as she closed the door behind her. Del rubbed the sleep from his eyes but still didn't recognize the nurse. She appeared to be young and she was shorter than any of the nurses that worked the ward.

The Only Del

Del thought she must be new and had probably been stuck with the night shift because of it.

"I've come to relieve the swelling," said the nurse.

Del couldn't see her face but her voice sounded very familiar.

"Swelling?" asked Del. "Oive no swellin' in me shoulder."

"Not your *shoulder*, Mister Delahanty. The large swelling you often get down here," said the nurse. With that she pulled up the covers and put her hand on Del's groin.

In an instant he recognized that the 'nurse' was Norine and in another instant he was as hard as a rock.

"There," said Norine. "*That's* the large swelling I was talking about. The swelling I've been missing."

When the Phillies headed off on their next road trip, Del was back with them and he batted safely in 27 out of 28 games. He wasn't just excelling with his Louisville bats either. The *Wilkes-Barre Record* reported that Ed Delahanty had gone thirty straight games without an error. The *Sporting News* said Delahanty is now "the king of outfielders."

"What does Lajoie mean?" Del asked Napoleon one day as they waited for their turns in batting practice.

"The joy. It's French. That's what we spoke when I was growing up."

"Why does everybody call you La ja way then?"

"I have no idea."

"What did the people back home call you? Your friends."

"You mean what was my nickname? It was Sandy."

"But your hair's jet black."

"My mother hated baseball. She thought it was a waste of time and she'd tan my hide for playing it all day long. So instead of calling out Napoleon or Nap when my pals and I played they'd yell Sandy and my mother wouldn't know I was in the game."

the greatest batsman in the land

"That was clever. Sandy it is then. I'm glad you're with us."

"Why's that?"

"With you playin' first base, I can stay in the outfield."

Sam Thompson was still making contact but as the season progressed fielders started reaching his flies more easily. When his average fell below .300, Sam told everyone he was just having an off year. Jack Clements was stricken with typhoid fever on a hot August day in Baltimore and missed the rest of the season. Team morale sank and the players began openly disobeying Nash's orders, many of which they knew he was getting straight from Rogers. Reporters berated the team for indifferent and sloppy play, though Del was never mentioned. The team lost six of its last eight games including three straight in Baltimore. When the baseball press suggested the Phillies' play against the Orioles was so bad it called for a league investigation no one could blame Del. He'd racked up a single, three doubles, a triple, and three home runs in his thirteen at bats in Baltimore.

"Oive got some bad news, darlin'," Del told Norine the night the dismal season ended. "The trip to England's been canceled."

"Why?" groaned Norine.

"They've decided the only time we could go is the summer and the cricket pitches we were gointa use aren't fit fer baseball."

Del was disappointed about the canceled trip but more than satisfied with how well he'd done in '96. He'd finished among the top four in all of the important batting statistics.

On Base %	.472 - *second*
Hits	198 - *fourth*
Doubles	44 - *first*
Home Runs	13 - *first*
Batting Avg.	.397 - *third*
Runs Batted In	126 - *first*
Total Bases	315 - *second*
Slugging	.631 - *first*

The Only Del

But the Phillies' twirlers had yielded the second most runs in the league. Billy Nash had batted a measly .247. Billy Hamilton, the man he'd been traded for, led off every one of Boston's games, hit .365, scored 152 runs, and led the league with 110 walks and 83 stolen bases. *Sporting Life* had awful things to say about the Phillies' performance in '96 but had nothing but praise for Del. "Amid the train wreck of this year the play of Delahanty shines out luminously and marks him indeed the star of the team."

Chapter Eighteen

A Miserable Manager

The Phillies named Atlanta-born George Stallings their new manager while Del, who'd just returned from a hunting trip with Ed McKean and Deacon McGuire, was in Cleveland reading about how the Giants and the Colts were trying hard to get him. Norine said she would love to move to New York. The Colts had offered Rogers three front-line players and Norine told Del she'd be fine with Chicago too. There was talk the Giants would give Philadelphia their ace Amos Rusie, who'd sat out the entire '96 season in a contract dispute with Andrew Freedman, and the Spiders were seriously considering trading the popular Jesse Burkett for Del.

Stallings, who was the same age as Del, had a puffy nose, dark, arched eyebrows, and a pronounced widow's peak. He'd made a brief appearance in the Bridegrooms' lineup in 1890, but was released after going hitless in eleven at bats. The next year he played outfield for San Jose and led the California League in stolen bases. He was back east in '93, managing his hometown team in the Southern League. Stallings took over the Nashville Tigers the next year and led them to a pennant. He was managing Detroit in the Western League when Rogers decided to hire him. Stallings was fastidious, demanding, and high-strung.

A reporter asked Del what the new manager had said of himself when he was introduced to the team. Del chuckled. "'Twas quite a speech he gave. He said 'I don't like to throw violets and roses at myself but facts are facts and I take a pardonable pride in my success as a minor league manager. Now you all know what a manager of a baseball team must do to make a hit with the owners. He must be a hammer and do a little rubber shoe work around the hotel corridors around eleven at night. He must be an all-round highbinder so to speak.'"

The Only Del

The reporter raised his eyebrows as he scribbled. Del chuckled again. "Then Stallings, who's got a voice sharp enough to fillet a herring at forty paces, said, 'So if I dock any of you for throwing joy juice into your face or failing to report every morning at nine you can't blame anyone but yourself.'"

"What did the players think of that?" asked the reporter.

"Is this gointa be on the record?" asked Del.

The reporter put his pencil in his pocket. "*Off* the record, Del."

"We were none too fuckin' impressed."

Stallings, his wife Bell, and his new charges departed for Augusta aboard the *City of Macon* at 4 p.m., March 14. Del had taken Norine to the Grand Opera the night before to see Tim Murphy, the eminent Irish comedian, perform his hit sketches "Old Innocence", "Sir Henry Hypnotized", and "A Texas Steer." She enjoyed the show but made a bit of a scene when Del dared to look at another woman, a former acquaintance of his, during the intermission. She calmed down and smiled when Del told her, "I was just comparin' her ta you, me luv. And you won hands down."

Smiling Al Orth and Willie Brandt, who'd won twenty-six games for the Portsmouth Truckers in '96, were the only two players to get seasick on the ocean trip to Charleston. Kid Carsey and Jack Taylor climbed the rigging on a dare from Del and they made it all the way to the top and back down without mishap. Del had wanted to race them, he was sure he could win. But the memory of his nightmares of falling from a high height came back to him in a rush and he decided against it. The players passed the time on board running the decks in thick sweaters and taking turns on the new Whitely exercisers.

The team arrived on March 17. In honor of St. Patrick, Mike Grady and Del, with a tiny harp pinned to his lapel, hoisted a few when the team arrived at the Partridge Inn. Stallings split up the former roommates and matched veterans up with rookies. Del asked for and got Nap Lajoie as his.

The players were a sorry site on the practice field the next morning. It took them a half hour to limber up. Brandt was the latest hope to emerge as a talented twirler. He'd be a starter for the Yannigans, a Gaelic term

the greatest batsman in the land

that meant "easily beaten", along with Tully Sparks, George Wheeler, and Davey Dungle.

In the first intra-squad game Billy Geier made a great impression at shortstop for the Yannigans. Del had two hits but muffed two flies. Clements and Del were the role models for the younger players during the calisthenics and practices. No one worked harder or took getting into condition more seriously. Unfortunately Stallings wanted them to be just as serious during their free time. He took the team on a three-mile run after the seven inning game was over. Their uniforms were drenched in sweat.

"I'm almost too tired to drink tonight," Nap panted to Del. "Almost."

The next day a reporter from the *Pittsburgh Press* wrote about Stallings' diligent monitoring of his men. "Stallings has a stop watch on the movements of the ball players off the practice field. This 'hey Rube' minor league method is certain not to wash with seasoned players such as Clements, Hallman, Thompson, and Delehanty."

The men practiced and did fifty-yard runs in the morning on March 30 and then got drenched by a sudden storm while they were playing a friendly game of football. In the afternoon they did a seven-mile run around the track and then ran back to their hotel. Everyone kept up the pace except Jack Clements, who was nearly lame, and Sam Thompson, who had his usual spring Charley Horse. At the weigh-in the next morning. Clements had lost seventeen pounds, Del had lost six.

The next morning Del, Clements, Orth, Lajoie, Grady, and manager Stallings went for a long bicycle ride in the country. Del, Jack, Napoleon, and Mike rented Columbia models. Stallings had brought his cycle with him. Orth, a bicycle fiend, had his wheel, an expensive Wolf American model, shipped in from Lynchburg. The five players returned to the hotel covered in dirt and sweat. Stallings was covered in mud. Nap had run his bike into Del's and it had knocked Stallings into a ditch that had two inches of water in it. When he got back to the hotel he was quite a site. He strode through the lobby with as much dignity as he could muster, trying his best to ignore the snickers.

The Only Del

On April 3rd Del "played a sensational field." Four of his catches were phenomenal. That night Del, Hallman, Orth, and Grady took Nap Lajoie snipe hunting. A coon hunting expedition three nights earlier had been rained out.

"The snipe are delicious and this is the best time uv year to get um," Del told Lajoie.

They tramped through the woods for miles then stopped, for no apparent reason, far from any landmarks.

"This is a perfect spot," Del told Lajoie. "Take these." He handed Napoleon a lantern and a canvas bag and pointed off into the gloom. "We'll go out there and scare the snipe toward you. All you have to do is catch um in the bag. It's like shootin' fish in a barrel."

Lajoie looked at Del doubtfully. Then he looked down at the canvas bag and shrugged. "If you say so, Mush."

Del and the rest of the party left. Instead of attempting to chase the non-existent snipe out of the pitch-black woods they scampered back to the hotel, laughing all the way. They got very sour looks from Lajoie at breakfast the next morning.

"How many did ya bag, Sandy?" asked Del, trying hard not to giggle.

"I'll get you for that, Delahanty," snarled Lajoie.

The team boarded a Southern Railroad train that afternoon to head back home, with stops for games in Athens, Greensville, Charlotte, Richmond, Norfolk, and Portsmouth. On April 18 they played the Athletics at Broad and Huntington. Del ripped three doubles and a single as the Phillies won the exhibition 10-9. On the 21st the Phillies went to play in Falls River. Del was the star of the game even though everyone was pulling for Lajoie.

Twenty thousand cranks had streamed into the park for the home opener against the black and gray clad Giants by the time the starting bell was rung and Mayor Warwick threw out the first ball from his box in the upper pavilion. Lajoie made brilliant catches on ugly twisting flies over first and Geier threw ringers from deep shortstop. Cooley was a little at sea on line

the greatest batsman in the land

drives but showed two hundredfold improvement over last year. Clements saved several wild pitches from Taylor on wide balls. Del was given a grand ovation when he came to the plate. He walked and stole second and then singled in the seventh. The crowd went home happy after a 5-1 win.

On Tuesday Al Orth's curves floated to the plate like balloons and the Beaneaters rapped out seventeen hits. But the Phillies inflicted far worse damage on the Boston hurler. Billy Nash managed only one hit against his former mates, but Lajoie had three, as did Cooley and Geier. Del had four hits "on shyly pitched balls" and scored three times as the Phillies won their fifth straight. To cap off the day, Del ran to the left centerfield fence to catch Fred Tenney's long drive to the cheers of the the bleacherites and carried the ball right into the clubhouse. After the game he took Napoleon and Al Orth out to celebrate the win.

"Isn't the little woman going to mind?" asked Napoleon.

"Oill make it up to her," Del told him. "She's had her eye on a piece uv jewelry and oive bin tellin' her we can't afford it. Oive got it right here in me pocket." He took a small box out and opened it up. There was a shiny bracelet inside.

"How much did that set you back?" asked Orth.

"Don't ask," said Del. "Rogers'd cut me pay if he knew."

They had supper and then went to Billy McLean's. Orth lost five dollars playing dice and Lajoie lost twelve playing billiards after drinking so many beers Al and Del lost count. Del won twenty playing stud poker, just enough to pay off what was left on the bracelet he'd bought Norine. Napoleon made a pass at a barmaid old enough to be his mother. The woman was shy a few teeth and had a growth of dark hair over her upper lip. Del and Orth decided it was time to leave. They had to help Nap to the hack and it was no easy chore, he weighed a ton. He was singing, "Frere Jacques, Frere Jacques, dormez-vous, dormez-vous?" loud enough to wake the dead.

"I used to drive one of these," he announced when they threw him into the hack. Then he hiccupped. "Where are we going now, fellas?" he asked.

"We're takin' ya snipe hunting," said Del, winking at Al. Lajoie didn't get mad. He hadn't heard Del. He was sprawled out on the seat, fast asleep.

The Only Del

Del got home just before two. He took off his shoes and tiptoed into the bedroom. He pulled off his clothes and snuck into bed. He felt around and frowned. Norine's side was empty.

She turned up the gas on the lamp and the room slowly filled with light. She was sitting in a chair in the corner in her powder blue sheer nightie. She was frowning and had her arms folded in a fit of pique. The gaslight flickered in her fiery blue eyes.

"What do you think you are doing coming home at this hour of the morning, Edward Delahanty?"

"Come to bed, me pet," said Del. He lifted up the covers.

She hesitated a moment, pouting. "I sat here by myself the whole night." Then she went over and climbed into bed with a huff.

"I've got a wee somethin' for you, Missus Delahanty."

Norine looked down at her husband's groin. She could see that he was aroused. "It's certainly not wee and it's the same thing you usually have for me."

"Not *that*. This," said Del, holding up the little box.

Her eyes widened. She grabbed the box and opened it. "It's the *bracelet*! The one I was looking at last week at Gimbels. You said we couldn't afford it."

"Maybe we can, maybe we can't, I bought it for you anyway."

She let him put it around her wrist and held her arm up so the flickering light would catch it.

"I'm the luckiest girl in the world."

"And I'm the luckiest man," said Del.

"You're about to be," said Norine as she jumped on top of her husband.

At home to Boston on the 28th Del slammed a two-bagger and a three-bagger to knock in three runs. Jack Boyle was subbing for Lajoie, who was out with a split finger. Boyle's two errors led to three Boston tallies. The result was the Phillies' first loss of '97. Del reached on a fumble by the third baseman, walked, singled, and doubled home Hallman the next day

the greatest batsman in the land

as the Phillies eked out a 12-11 win. The team headed to Boston in good spirits but returned home with dampened ones after two tough losses. Their moods and those of their boosters weren't helped when the Orioles came to town and won all three games. On May 8 Jack Taylor pitched a six-hitter against Boston and Del ripped a single and a run-scoring double. But Geier, who had been terrific so far, misplayed two ground balls at short and the Phillies went down to their sixth straight loss and sank to seventh place.

After the game they grabbed their valises and trudged past the tall new downtown buildings - the nine-story YMCA building on Arch Street, the Betz Building at South Penn Square east of Broad, and City Hall, which it appeared might never be finished - to the train station and headed to St. Louis.

Del, who was being walked and pitched around a lot, banged two singles in a 13-1 win over the struggling Browns in the first game. But the big Frenchman was the star with two home runs, a double, and a single. The papers were predicting that Lajoie would challenge Delahanty for the team batting honors.

The two sat in their room at the Lafayette Park Hotel on the corner of Park and Mississippi on Tuesday and looked out the window at the marble statue of George Washington in Lafayette Square getting pelted with rain. The day's game had been washed out.

"I suppose George is glad the pigeon shite's gettin' washed off," chuckled Del.

"I imagine the tornado they had last year gave him a scare though," said Nap. He looked at some uprooted trees and an empty space where buildings had stood. "What was there?" he asked. He'd joined the team after its last western swing in his rookie year.

"When we came here in May there was a bandstand, gazebos, pavilions, and big, beautiful trees in the square. When we came back at the end of July they were all gone. The tornado - the people here called it the The Great Cyclone - took down more than three hundred buildings. It took the roof off the Females Hospital and just missed the insane asylum. It

The Only Del

sucked one patient out the window of his second floor room at the City Hospital. The fella landed upright on his feet somehow and ran right back into the building! Another patient got sucked out of the fourth floor and flew a hundred and fifty yards through the air. All he had were scrapes and bruises. Not a single broken bone."

"Sacre bleu!" said Nap.

"It wiped out a lot of homes, factories, and saloons too. Mind you I saw in the Post-Dispatch that there were twenty-one hundred saloons so I suppose they had a few ta spare."

"It's still sad," said Nap. "So what are we going to do? Our train doesn't leave until noon tomorrow."

"Some of the waterin' holes may be gone but let's see what we can find."

They hopped on board one of the Lindell Railway's Blue Line electrified trains and headed to the Jewel Billiard Parlor at 4th and Pine. They shot some pool and had a couple of the Michelob beers St. Louis was now brewing and then headed for Kerry Patch, the Irish neighborhood northwest of downtown. The Patch was rough. A guide book warned that its residents' chief amusement was "punching each other's eyes out."

Del and Nap could see that the tornado had taken its toll on the neighborhood's ramshackle dwellings. A lot of families were living in the street. The smell of steaming cabbage filled the air. Del and Nap remembered seeing "No Irish Need Apply" signs downtown and put dollar bills into several beggars' cups along their way.

A gang of dirty-faced boys ran up to them. Napoleon figured his wallet was a goner. Del had told him how the Hogan Gang, Egan's Rats, the Green Ones, and the Ashley Street Bunch gathered at Bollman's Brickyard on nearby 19th Street to roast potatoes in the kiln ashes, swim in the clay-wetting pond, and steal bricks for gang fights. But the boys stopped and their leader turned to his minions and said, "It's big Ed Delahanty, fellas, he's come to see us again."

"I told yuz I would, Jimmy. What shenanigans have you lot bin up to today?"

"Nuthin' out uv the ordinary, just redistributin' the wealth a little is all.

the greatest batsman in the land

Rich folks don't need alluv that money they carry around and there's a lot uv folks starvin' round here."

"Well here's a little help fer the cause," said Del, handing Jimmy a five-dollar bill.

"Thanks Del, who's yer new friend?"

"Napoleon Lajoie."

"That don't sound Irish to me," said Jimmy.

"'Taint. It's French."

"What's a *Frenchman* doin' in this part uv town?"

"Getting an education," said Nap.

"And now we need to learn about the effects of alcohol on the human body. Which uv the saloons still have a roof and four walls?"

"Hennessey's, Gill's, and Keogh's are all that's left. Hennessey's has got the cockfights tonight though so it'll be tough ta get in."

"Kinsky's Grocer and Saloon's opened up again," said one of the other boys.

"That's right, I forgot about Kinksy's," said Jimmy. "That's yer best bet. The rats stick to the grocery and leave the bar alone. Old man Kinsky's still pretty banged up from the Saint Paddy's Day parade though. He's bin eatin' his meals through a straw."

"Kinky's 'tis then. See ya next time, Jimmy. Be good, me sun."

"Always, Del," said Jimmy over his shoulder as the gang tore off in search of its next victim.

The beer was warm and the whiskey diluted at Kinsky's. The bartender sounded as if he'd just stepped off the boat from Ulster. "Evenin', 'tis a bit chilly out the night," he said. "You gents fancy a jar?"

As usual, Del sipped at his glass and Nap downed his. Del worried about getting his big friend back on the electric train. Some men in the back who were well into their cups lustily belted out "Bridget O'Malley."

The Only Del

"The day is approachin' when we're to be married
And I'd rather die than live only to grieve
Meet me my darlin' where the sun sets on the barley
And I'll take ye on the road to Drumslieve."

Del was called upon to sing and decided he would see if he could remember the words to a song he'd heard in an Irish pub in Cleveland. He thought a moment and then sang,

"I've loved the young women of every land,
That always came easy to me;
Just barrin' the belles of the Black-a-moor brandies
And the chocolate shapes of Feegee.
But that sort uv love, 'tis moonshiny stuff
And never will addle me brain,
Fer the bells'll be ringin' in Ballyjamesduff
Fer me and my Rosie Kilrain."

The place erupted in cheers and applause. Several of the sots wanted to buy Del drinks but he knew he could afford them a lot better than they could.

The Phillies played a double header against the Browns back home in Philadelphia on the 12th. Del singled and scored the winning run in the morning game and led the way with four hits in the afternoon match. The pair of one-run victories pushed the club all the way up to second place. In the middle of May the league records showed that the Phillies stood second in runs scored. Cooley ranked tenth in batting with a .390 mark. Del was eleventh at .370 while Lajoie was fourteenth with an average of .366. Del, who led the team in stolen bases and the league in runs scored, thought Cooley and Lajoie's performance at the bat was impressive considering how much the two of them were drinking.

Del did some drinking himself. He got into a heated argument with the Giants' obnoxious president Andrew Freedman in the dining car on the

the greatest batsman in the land

way to Louisville. Del considered himself a snappy dresser, but Freedman's get-up was first order. He wore a pin-striped cut-away with a 2¼ inch starched linen collar, a white vest, gray striped pants, a black neck-tie, and a silk hat. In his entourage Freedman had a physician, a chef, a barber, a manicurist, and a valet who brushed away his dandruff and opened his newspaper to the financial page.

"Do you spend as much on yer players as you do on yer *servants?*" Del asked Freedman after his third glass of the railway's excellent whiskey.

"I pay them what they are worth and not a penny more," snorted Freedman. "Luckily they have more ability than your club."

"We could run circles around yer bunch," Del retorted a bit louder than he should have. He didn't want to risk being thrown off the train.

"Even your own manager hates your team," Freedman taunted. "What does that tell you?"

"Without Rusie your club can't beat the Ladies' Auxiliary," Del snapped. "Oill bet you every cent oive got we'll win the season series with your lot and finish ahead uv them in the standings inta the bargain."

Luckily, Freedman didn't accept. Del would have lost on both counts. But Del *had* made a bet with Freedman on the Kentucky Derby. The Phillies would reach Louisville the day after it was run. Freedman bet on Doctor Shepard which finished fourth. Del bet on Ornament, who finished second by a nose.

The Phillies won the first two in Louisville. Del and Nap were happy when the Saturday game was called due to a wet field. "Let's head over ta Churchill Downs," Del suggested. Nap nodded and grabbed his hat.

As they waited for a cab to take them to the track Del couldn't help noticing how many people were staring up at the cloudy sky. Even Nap, who was preoccupied with looking for Southern belles, noticed. "What's everybody rubber-necking about?" he asked.

"Airships," said Del.

"Airships?"

The Only Del

"Don't you ever read anything but the sports page? The sightings started last fall and they're back again. Flying ships of unknown origin they're sayin'. Some people have even claimed to see alien beings operating them."

"I hope you're just pulling my leg."

"I'm doing no such thing. The first sighting was in Sacramento last November. People reported a huge oblong craft passing across the sky faster than a high-speed train. At first the folks who claimed to uv seen the things were thought to be out of their skulls, but then respectable people - engineers, businessmen, and even professors - said they'd seen the things and the newspapers started to run their stories."

"And one of them was spotted here in Kentucky?"

"'Twas. Last week. This airship was about forty feet long and fifteen feet wide and it had flashing red and green lights. The piece I read said cats and dogs were runnin' fer cover, cows were bellowin', and horses were kickin' their stalls inta splinters. One fellow, an umbrella mender, said he saw what looked like a man standing at the front of the thing directing its course. A lad that works as a groom at Churchill Downs was driving one of the ticket girls home in his buggy and the road was nearly pitch black. Then all of a sudden it was lit up like daytime. He heard a whirring sound and looked up and this huge airship dipped and shone a powerful searchlight on them and then tore off like a comet. Scared the bejezzus out uv him and the girl too."

At Churchill Downs Nap drank whiskey sours and flirted with comely girls whose fathers made sure they did not reciprocate his attention. Ed stuck to Hood's Sarsaparilla so he could focus on the odds and he won big. The rest of the crowd stared into the sky whenever there was no action on the track and sometimes even when there was if their horse was running last.

While Nap was chatting with a couple of girls who'd eluded their fathers Ed went down onto the infield. A middle-age Negro who was as thin as a reed was walking one of the horses that had run in the last race.

"That's a fine lookin' gelding," said Del.

"It's one of Mister Schreiber's biggest winners," said the man.

the greatest batsman in the land

"Are you the trainer?"

"I am. Felix Carr."

"*Felix Carr?* I see your name all the time. You were one uv the best jockeys in the land."

"I don't know about that. Say, are you Ed Delahanty?"

"I am. Do you ever pick horses for gamin' men, Felix?"

Carr looked around to see if anyone was listening. "I handicap the odd time, if the gentleman makes it worth my while."

"How could I reach you ... if I happened to be lookin' for a tip?"

"You couldn't. I live in boarding houses. They don't have telephones and the places that do don't cater to my kind. I could send you wires from time to time if there are ponies you might want to place a wager on. Who would I send them to?"

"Mike Scanlon, Huntington Grounds, Philadelphia. He'll make sure I get them."

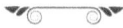

Del got to spend Sunday with his parents when the Phillies arrived in Cleveland. They wanted to know how married life was treating him.

"You don't look to have gained any weight, Edward. As a matter uv fact you look as though you've lost some," said Bridget Delahanty.

"I'm afraid Norine is no great shakes in the kitchen," said Del. "Her big sister always did the cooking."

"Our Ed has got himself a pretty bauble instead uv a proper wife," Bridget whispered to her husband.

"A wife with a pair uv very *large* baubles," he mumbled.

"What did you say?"

"Nothing, dear. What's for dinner?"

In the first game in Cleveland Del singled twice and was stranded each time. Each hit should have been a double, but his ankle still hurt from a

The Only Del

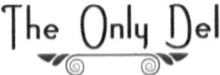

nasty slide in Louisville. Jack Taylor gave up six straight hits in the ninth and the Spiders won 9-8. The Phillies were down 6-2 in the eighth in the second game but scored seven runs to take the lead. The Spiders scored four in the ninth to win 10-9.

Del was in a foul mood because he'd heard that Stallings had said he was covering as much ground as a manhole cover. The only consolation was that he was saying even worse things about other players. At least Billy Shettsline had stuck up for Del. He said that Stallings' remarks were unfair and brought a tear to his eye when he thought of everything Del did for the team. It was no fault of *his* that the Phillies kept losing.

On May 27th in Chicago the team faced Herbert Theodore Briggs, who was on his way to a 4-17 season. One of his handful of wins would be this day as he served the visitors up a feast of goose eggs. Jimmy Ryan took Del out after the game and bought him a few beers to console him. The next day Del smashed a three-bagger, a long sacrifice fly, and a bases-clearing home run to left centerfield. When the game ended in an 11-7 win for the Phillies and their ten-game losing streak was over they joined hands and danced around home plate in glee. The Phillies scored three in the seventh and three in the eighth in the finale of their road trip. They didn't need to bat in the ninth. The home team had elected to bat first and failed to score in the final frame.

"Two in a row!" hollered Del. "We're on fire, boys."

Chapter Nineteen

The Staggering Stallingites

The cranks came out to scoff when the Phillies returned to Huntingdon Grounds to host the Colonels in a May 31st double bill. Norine had kept Del up most of the night.

"The girl is absolutely *insatiable*," he told Napoleon when they were getting into their home whites for the first time in more than three weeks.

"Maybe you shouldn't have married such a young one," said Lajoie. "Would you like me to help satisfy her desires? I mean what are friends for if they can't go to bat for an older fellow who can't keep up to his wife in the boudoir?"

"Keep yer bat in yer pants, Romeo. I'm doin' just fine in the luvin' department."

Del drew a base on balls in the first inning of the morning game. He took a lead, yawned, and got picked off. Lajoie at second almost fell over he was laughing so hard. Del singled and scored in the ninth but was stranded when the game ended 4-2 Louisville. Taylor was mightily jeered when he toed the rubber for the late game. Del had grabbed a sandwich between games and felt a bit more energetic. With one out in the eighth Taylor singled, Boyle walked, and Lajoie took a bender that never curved square on the shoulder.

"Have you got enough strength left to swing that thing?" Napoleon called to Del as he toted his latest Louisville Slugger to the plate. He was hitless after four journeys to the box against William Cicero "Still Bill" Hill from Chattanooga. Del grimaced and then laughed when Hill threw over to first and nearly caught Napoleon off the bag.

The Only Del

"You attend to your work and oill attend to mine," Del yelled at Lajoie. He hit the next pitch, a swift shoot, onto the hump beyond the centerfield fence and Napoleon waited for him at the plate. "I guess there's still some wind in your sails after all," he told his friend. Jack Taylor won the cranks over and shut out the Colonels 14-0.

The next morning Del and Nap met for breakfast at a greasy spoon near the park. Norine had burned the toast and eggs again. After they ate, they hurried to Parker, Bridget & Company on Seventh Street where the ten and twelve dollar summer suits were on sale for $6.50. They had Fine English Men's Striped and Mixed Cheviot trousers on for $2.50 as well. Then Napoleon stopped in at Jos. Fleming & Son on Market Street to get a couple of quarts of their Old Export Whiskey.

"A dollar a quart," said Nap. "You can't pass up a bargain like that."

"You're gointa drink yerself out uv the game if you don't start easin' up on that stuff," said Del.

Nap shrugged his shoulders and opened one of the bottles. He took a swig and offered it to Del. He shook his head and headed out to the street.

"Where are you going?" asked Nap.

The Phillies beat Louisville 7-2 the next day, but the atmosphere was one of gloom. Three of them had fallen victim to the club's awful road trip. Kid Carsey and Del's friend Mike Grady had been traded to St. Louis for Ed McFarland, a talented 23-year-old catcher, and Bill Hallman was off to the Browns in exchange for "Buttermilk" Tommy Dowd.

Grady and Hallman were apoplectic. "I know I'm having a bum year," groaned Bill in the somber clubhouse as he stripped off his uniform, "but of all the places I could have been sent it has to be *Saint Louis*."

Del put an arm around Hallman's shoulders. "At least you'll have all those Southern belles ta spoon with," he consoled him. Bill perked up a little, but not much.

"The women are hot but the ballpark's hotter," said Hallman.

the greatest batsman in the land

"It cools down to ninety in September," offered Del.

"In the shade," said Kid Carsey. "I weigh a hundred and forty. A few hours on the rubber there every week and I'll be lucky to weigh a hundred. I'm not going."

"What d'ya mean?" asked Del.

"I *mean* I'm not going."

It would be a week before Carsey would show up in St. Louis. He only pitched when his new teammates begged him to and when he took the field he showed how thrilled he was to be in St. Louis by wearing his Philadelphia uniform.

Ed McFarland was a steal for Reach and Rogers. He had a great glove and a strong, accurate arm. He'd led all catchers in assists in '96. McFarland could hit too. *Sporting Life* said, "As a catcher Eddie McFarland is a peach. All pitchers look alike to him and he catches them all with equal style and grace." Like pretty well every other Brown, he'd badly wanted out of St. Louis. He'd even threatened to quit baseball and go back to Cleveland to work in his father's shoe store.

As for Tommy Dowd, he was positively thrilled to be away from Von der Ahe. Little did he know he'd be traded back to St. Louis at the end of the season. Buttermilk, who had a receding hairline and an angular face, was an outfielder who played second base sometimes. Like Del, he was great in the outfield, not so good at second. He could run like a colt and he stole a lot of bases.

"You *managed* for a while in St. Louis didn't you, Buttermilk?" Del asked Dowd as he was putting on his new uniform the next day.

"Twenty-eight games. Lost twenty-two of them."

"Mighty tough ta win in Saint Louis. What was it like managing for Von der Ahe?"

"Don't ask, Del. Don't ask."

The Only Del

It was old home week for many of the Browns when they arrived in Philadelphia on June 16. They had six former Phillies in their lineup. Del had two hits, two runs, and drove in three in an 8-7 win in the first game. His ankle was better now and his bat was on fire. The forecast called for steady rain the next day so Del had Bill Hallman and Mike Grady over for dinner and drinks. He wisely had Amy, their plain but hard-working eighteen-year-old housegirl, do the cooking. Norine served the drinks.

"That's quite the looker yuv got there, Mush," said Mike. "How old is she?"

"Eighteen," Del told him.

"Wait a minute," said Bill. "That's the girl we went for sodas with. I *thought* I recognized her. Doesn't she like to cook?"

"Trust me, Bill. You wouldn't want her to."

The Phillies lost both of the next two games to St. Louis. They went to Washington and got swept by the Senators. With only a pair of wins in their last eleven games, finger-pointing had begun. O.P. Caylor wrote, "The Quakers are as weak as kittens in every department and the story going around balldom is that the players are laying down on Stallings with the purpose of forcing him out."

Del was determined to show that *he* had no intention of lying down on the job. When the Phillies returned from Brooklyn he "soaked the ball on the stitches" for five hits, bruised his old teammate Charlie Reilly with a line drive, and made a terrific grab in foul territory in the first game against Washington on the 28th of June, a 7-6 triumph. He racked up four hits and scored twice in a 10-9 win over the Senators the next day and won a hat and tie from Parker, Bridget & Company for hitting a ball off their sign in deep left behind the bleacher benches in Delahantyville.

Before the game Del had gone for a swim. Colonel Rogers had told Pete the janitor to keep the players from using the swimming pool before games. When the team had traveled to Atlantic City for an exhibition game they'd hopped off the train and right into their bathing costumes. They frolicked in the waves for hours and were so enervated they could hardly

the greatest batsman in the land

play. Sam Thompson nodded off while leaning against the pole in right field. He only woke up when a flyball hit him. When Pete told Del that he had orders not to let any players swim in the pool, Del grabbed him around the waist and leapt in with him. Pete didn't say another word to Del about using the pool.

That night Del stayed in. Norine tried her hand at cooking, with predictable results. The carrots weren't properly peeled, the potatoes were rocks, the soup tasted like dishwater, and the meat had a funny smell. "It's lucky you're beautiful," Del told Norine when he pushed his plate away. Amy cleared away the dishes, shaking her head at the gruesome fare the lady of the house had prepared.

"You know I was born to have servants and dine at the finest restaurants," Norine told Del only half kiddingly. "Besides, I have other skills you seem to appreciate."

"You're a grand *shopper*," Del teased.

Norine swatted him with the newspaper she'd brought him. Del lit a pipe and sat down in his favorite armchair to read.

"Oh dear," he said a few minutes later.

"What is it?" asked Norine, who was trying her best to thread a needle.

"It's me bruther. Tom."

"What's happened to him?"

"He got called up to play for Louisville."

"They aren't much of a team but at least he's in the big league like he's always wanted to be."

"No he's not."

Norine put down her sewing. "But you just said …"

"He only lasted one game. They sent him back to the minors after it. The Colonels lost thirty-six to seven! To the Colts of all teams. They're playing worse than the Colonels. The box score says Tom played second base and got one hit in four times at the bat. How's that grounds fer being released? Oh. Wait. He made two errors."

The Only Del

"Well I hope he gets another chance," said Norine.

Tom never did.

"Just a minute," said Del. "There's a piece here on yours truly."

"What are they saying about you, darling?" asked Norine.

Del read, "Delahanty is the greatest batter in the world. His average is an honest one, the Philadelphia scorekeepers don't pad the records. Another thing that emphasizes his place at the top of the list is that none of his hits are weak ones. His record is made on good, clean line drives."

"That's wonderful!" exclaimed Norine, jumping onto Del's lap. "I could *kiss* that reporter. But I think I'll kiss the greatest batter in the world instead."

When the Phillies had last been in Cincinnati, Red Ehret had asked Del if he knew his average.

"I'm not one of those fellas that keeps his record on his shirt cuff."

"Well I know a lot that do," Red told Del. "Some know their average the minute they reach first base."

"The only time I kept track was on a road trip last year," said Del. "A friend uv mine bet me a suit of clothes from Becker's I wouldn't get thirty-five hits on an eighteen game road swing. Well, we got rained out once and only played seventeen. I got thirty-four hits and missed out on a new set of togs."

In a Tuesday double header in Louisville the next day "Delahanty's batting was the feature of the day's play." The writers were finally spelling his name with an a. He hit four singles and scored the winning run in the hour and forty minute opener. Jimmy "Chicken" Wolf, who had hit an inside-the-park home run in Louisville in '83 when the right fielder had awakened a dog that was sleeping by the fence and the mutt had grabbed a hold of his leg, was in the crowd and he umpired the second game when Tim Hurst took ill. Del drilled four singles and a triple and the Phillies won it 9-7.

the greatest batsman in the land

"Nine hits in one day!" exclaimed Jack Boyle after the game. "Oim lucky to make that many in a week. Wait. Make that two weeks. I ain't exactly bin Jack the Ripper with the bat lately. What's yer secret?"

"Clean livin' and pure thoughts, Jack."

"You've got *murderous* thoughts when it comes ta pitchers."

"*Mush is the* greatest batter there is if you ask me," said George Wheeler. "I've seen Keeler and Hamilton - they're nothing but a couple of bandy hitters - and I've seen Lange and Burkett too. None of them can hold a candle to Del. When you watch him bat his eyes light up and his tongue runs out and pokes out over his lip and he's so happy he can't stand still. There's not a man alive who lives to bat like Mush."

On July 17th the players boarded a train for Chicago at 10:30. It pulled out at midnight. When they awoke the next morning after the 283-mile trip from St. Louis they and the other passengers, mostly businessmen, were able to shave without having to worry they'd cut their throats during a bumpy ride on a cheap railroad and perform their absolutions at their leisure before de-training for the ballpark at ten. In the game that afternoon Del had three hits to knock in five runs, but was stranded all three times on base by Lajoie and Clements in a 7-6 loss.

The *Brooklyn Daily Eagle* opined that,

> *"the great and only E.J. Delahanty is on the warpath and Keeler and Burkett et. al. had better watch out. Delahanty is on such a pace he's bound to shoot his batting average beyond the .400 mark and will not be headed in the batting line."*

Del had two hits in each of the last two games in the Windy City, both Philly wins, and he was a major contributor to their only win in Cleveland with one, two, and three-baggers. The Phillies surprised even themselves when they went into Pittsburgh and swept the Pirates. Del kept up his torrid pace with six hits in the three games. The *Philadelphia Times* proudly reported that "Delahanty's work with the stick has been phenomenal" and noted that he had clustered hitting streaks of nine, twelve, ten, eleven, and twenty-one games. With hits in 67 of his last 72 games he led all batters

The Only Del

with a .424 average. Keeler was second at .397. Del ranked second in the league in outfield work behind Duff Cooley.

On August 11 the Phillies were described as playing in a "semi-somnolent state" as if they were "hired men waiting for the dinner bell." Cooley, Lajoie, and Brewery Jack Taylor showed up drunk. Lajoie and Taylor slept in the clubhouse. Cooley was thrown out twice, having tripped both times. The Phillies lost 6-0 and Stallings fined each of the men fifty dollars. Two days later Del learned that a pair of his teammates had been arrested for public intoxication. Three Phillies spent the next night in a station house after being charged with disorderly conduct. No names were printed but Del knew it had been Nap, Cooley, and Taylor.

It wasn't as if those three were the only big drinkers on the team. The Phillies had been dubbed "the Staggering Stallingites." Del was glad there was no speculation that he'd been one of the offenders. In the *Sporting Life* Horace Fogel made a point of informing his readers that Delahanty was not one of the trouble-makers. "No player has more friends than Delahanty. He is greatly admired for his sterling qualities." He related how when his former teammate Joe Sullivan had died of consumption Del had collected money from every team to pay Sully's funeral expenses.

The Phillies snuffed out any chance they had of making it into the first division - much less winning the pennant - when they lost their next twelve straight. A big part of the collapse was that Del had strained his knee pulling up short on a sinking line drive and his batting had fallen off dramatically. On Friday the 20th Stallings' charges finally snapped their string of futility, winning the first game of a Friday double header with the Reds. A baseball note in the *Times* that day warned that ball players in bar rooms should not talk so loud that they can be heard on the street.

On Thursday, August 26 the Phillies lost to Pittsburgh. Napoleon Lajoie staggered into the clubhouse an hour late the next day. He almost fell down trying to get his legs into his pants. Everyone looked at him, but no one said anything.

"Where's my damn glove?" he growled, screwing his cap on.

It was sitting on the bench right in front of him.

the greatest batsman in the land

In the first inning Pink Hawley hit a grounder to third. Lave Cross fielded it and threw to first. Lajoie didn't see it. He was ogling a pretty girl in the crowd. The ball rolled to the grandstand. Ed McFarland, who had been backing up first, picked it up, glared at Nap, and tossed the ball to the pitcher.

"What's your problem, McFarland?" yelled Lajoie.

"Nice play, Frenchie," called a crank in a linen suit and a straw boater.

Lajoie wheeled around and hollered, "Who said that?"

The crank said nothing.

"Which one of you gutless bastards said that?" snarled Lajoie, storming toward the box seats.

George Stallings hurried from the bench and pointed Napoleon back to his position. "Get your head in the game, Lajaway," he chided.

Seeing the condition Lajoie was in, the next batter, Bones Ely, bunted down the first base line. Napoleon ran in, bent to pick up the ball and fell forward, flat on his face. The stands exploded in laughter.

"*Now* you've got your head in the game," yelled the crank.

Napoleon looked around for his cap and finally located it. He jammed it on his head crookedly and stood up. He glared into the stands. "Who is the low-down, piece of shit that's yelling at me?"

The crank stood up. "It was me, you lousy sot! You wanna do somethin' about it?"

Lajoie threw down his glove and stormed toward the seats. Two park policemen grabbed him before he got there and guided him to the bench.

"You're out of the game, Lajaway," said Stallings. "Go sleep it off."

The Phillies lost the game to the Pirates and the next two as well. When Colonel Rogers, at his summer home in Cape May, read of Lajoie's disreputable behavior, "wolfish thirst for liquor," and foul language he suspended him without pay indefinitely. "The man has had only brief lapses of sobriety this year," snorted Rogers.

The Only Del

When asked by O.P. Caylor if anything was the matter of late Del didn't mention the knee. He said, "When we played that exhibition game in Atlantic City one uv their men stole me favorite bat." Most people felt that *Lajoie's* slump could be attributed to bottles, not bats. Del fell off drastically the final weeks of the season. He ended up batting .377, fourth in the league. His September swoon at the plate was attributed to his being overly anxious and trying to hit the cover off the ball but besides his strained knee Del had been deeply saddened by Sully's death, even though he'd known it was only a matter of time.

Chapter Twenty

"They Do Get in the Way"

The Phillies went back to Cape May for spring training and returned to the Aldine. Only Del, Sam Thompson, and Jack Boyle still remained from the 1893 team. The players had been hoping to stay at the Chalfonte but it was too expensive for Rogers. At least at the Aldine young women were allowed to flirt with the players. At the Chalfonte, protective mothers with an eye to finding their daughter a duke, lawyer, or future captain of industry forbade their debutantes from even laying eyes on a lowly ball player.

Stallings set the tone from the start when he talked to Jules Jurgensen of the *Inquirer*, who'd come to cover the limbering up. The manager was already in a foul mood because the new uniforms weren't ready even though the company'd had five months to sew and deliver them. Mike Scanlon was trying to figure out what the players would wear. Del had made Scanlon aware that he might be getting wires intended for him from a man named Carr and that he would be sending packages to the man in return.

"I have had all the experience I care for on the kind treatment order," Stallings told the reporter. "I tried to make it agreeable for everyone. This year I'll try the opposite tactics."

"Will that start here in Cape May?" asked Jurgensen.

"The men will be ousted from their beds at seven sharp and I expect them to be sound asleep by eleven."

The new uniforms arrived by train the next day, plain white tunics with a dark red collar and a large *P* on the left breast. The players took turns in the Aldine's new vapor bath after dinner and then held a singsong in the lobby. There was a talented newcomer among the Yannigans this spring,

The Only Del

a dark-haired, clean-shaven, 22-year-old named Elmer Harrison Flick. He'd prepared for the professional ranks by making his own bats on his father's lathe, something he would continue to do throughout his career. His biggest difficulty was judging the distance of fly balls. Stallings had hoped to use Flick as the club's fourth outfielder, but when Thompson's back went, Flick was pressed into service in right.

Ed got talking with the owner of the Aldine one morning when it looked as though training would be scrubbed for the day because of the foul weather.

"What's the huntin' like around here?" asked Ed.

"Not great," admitted the owner. "Except for woodcock that is. They travel down the coast and get funneled into the peninsula and pile up at the tip to wait for a favorable wind before they make the cross over Delaware Bay. I've seen three hundred or more in the space of a few hours. You can plug away at the things 'til your barrel's red hot and your bird dog's run ragged. With those butterball bodies of theirs they make mighty fine eating. The cook does them up in garlic with a strip of bacon, fleur de sel, and his favorite rub. They're delicious."

Ed was the most popular man on the team when he brought back eleven of the birds to share that night.

"The man's a regular Buffalo Bill," the cook told Ed's teammates, who were too busy chomping on roasted woodcock breasts to comment.

In November the Phillies had sent Jack Taylor, Tommy Dowd, now 33-year-old Jack Clements, and Lave Cross to St. Louis for William "Klondike" Douglass, Red Donahue, and Philadelphia-born shortstop Montford Montgomery Cross, whose nickname unsurprisingly was Monte. He'd trimmed his errors from eighty-five in '96 to a slightly less egregious seventy-five in '97. He'd approach the century mark in Philly. By contrast, Klondike Douglass was a terrific first baseman, one of the best in baseball. Now the Phillies could move Nap Lajoie to second base where he would be brilliant.

the greatest batsman in the land

But there was no sign of Lajoie at Spring Training. He was home sulking over the sobriety clause in his new contract and a fine he'd been given just before the end of the season. He said he wouldn't report unless the money was returned to him and the clause removed. Rogers wasn't budging on either score. Lajoie finally capitulated, but he was bitter about having no alternative.

In the first exhibition back in Philadelphia Del rapped three hits, stole three bases, and make a spectacular catch that brought the small, half-frozen crowd to its feet. In a Regulars vs. Yannigans game two days later he scored three runs and made two sensational plays.

"He hasn't slowed down one step," Bill Shettsline told Stallings after the second play.

"He's not the most *obedient* player I've ever managed," grumbled Stallings.

"You want a man who runs like a gazelle, hits the ball harder than anyone alive, and can throw out a runner from the farthest reaches of the park Delahanty's your man. You want obedience, get yourself a dog."

Stallings huffed and walked away.

Before the April 16 home opener against Brooklyn the Regimental Band, which had been left behind by the Regiment when it shipped off to Cuba to fight President McKinley' war, played the customary patriotic airs including the Star Spangled Banner. The gamblers stopped placing bets and removed their hats and the vendors took a breather from selling their penny scorecards and cigars. The bugs stopped talking and milling about and stood at attention. After the anthem the teams took turns taking batting practice and the buzz in the stands resumed. It would be hard to stop when umpire Emslie yelled "Play."

"They should play the anthem *after* batting practice. To get everyone to shut up and be still so the game can start," Del told Nap.

"I wonder why no one's thought of that," said Elmer Flck.

Jealous of the ovation Ed McFarland received when he drove a ball over

The Only Del

the right field fence in the fourth Del humped a ball farther over it in the fifth. It was "a beauty bright," crowed the *Courier-Journal*. "Delahanty is mighty with the stick." He stole three bases even though the knee he'd wrenched sliding into third late in September was still bothering him and scored three times in the second game of the season, a gratifying 13-3 win.

The first road trip of the Phillies' 1898 season began on Saturday, April 30 in Brooklyn. Del had decided to bring his bride along on the trip - at his own expense of course. Norine waited at the hotel while he smacked two singles, "business-like affairs of the true Delahanty brand," and threw a strike to Billy Nash to nab Fielder Jones when he was foolish enough to take a chance against Del's arm.

"We simply *must* go shopping," Norine told Del when he came through the door after the game. She was reading the *Brooklyn Eagle*. All the talk in the papers was of how Commodore George Dewey's ships had captured Spain's Pacific fleet at Manilla Bay, but Norine wasn't reading the front page. She was looking at an advertisement in the "Latest Fashions" section. "Listen to this. A beautiful selection of braids, loops, frogs, and ornaments in black and colors. All the newest creations in silk, velvet, and ribbons designed to match the latest dresses."

"Do you not have enuff clothes already, me pet?"

She laughed. "Don't be silly, darling. A woman can never have enough fine things to wear. Besides, the new summer line's about to come out."

"Oh, well then. Why didn't you say so?"

The Phillies lost 11-10 on Monday when Red Donahue tired in the late-going and got shelled for five runs. They lost the first game of a double header the next day, but led the second game 12-0 when, in his clipped British accent, umpire Tom Connolly mysteriously called the game due to darkness at 4:55. With sunset due at 6:54 there were at least two hours of light left even on a cloudy day like this.

"You'd better go back to cricket," Billy Nash yelled at Connolly, whose services were soon no longer required by the National League.

the greatest batsman in the land

The Phillies played a single game in Baltimore on breezy May 4. Del picked up a program from behind the bench that must have blown out of some rooter's hand. He chuckled as he saw portraits of John McGraw and Wilbert Robinson atop an advertisement that read *"The Diamond. 519 N. Howard St., Robinson & McGraw Props. Bowling Alleys, Billiards and Pool Parlors, Wine, Liquors and Cigars."*

Del went hitless but threw out mouthy John McGraw twice, once when he'd overrun second, the other time when he tried to stretch a two-bagger into a triple. McGraw had kicked both times and umpire Curry had been intimidated and let him away with it. Norine had gone back to Philadelphia so after the game Del and Nap went to the Diamond Cafe. The place had a dining room, a reading room that stocked all the papers that covered baseball, a billiard room, an alley for duckpin bowling, and a gymnasium where McGraw worked out and Robinson watched him, beer in hand. Its most popular feature was an electronic scoreboard that showed the progress of out of town games.

McGraw was behind the bar when they went in. Uncle Robby was sitting at it with a beer and a whiskey chaser in front of him along with a half-eaten pork sandwich. It looked as though he'd started drinking while watching from the bench.

"If it isn't Napoleon and the mighty Ed Delahanty," roared Robinson when Nap and Del approached the bar. "To what do we owe this magnificent honor?"

"We're thirsty," said Lajoie, taking off his boater and setting it on an unoccupied stool.

"Come ta wet our whistles is all," added Del.

McGraw didn't seem happy to see them. But then, Del thought, he was rarely happy - unless he was getting away with some act of chicanery on the diamond.

"Your best beer, Mugsy," said Lajoie.

Robinson cringed, shook his head, and put a finger to his lip. Del elbowed Nap in the ribs. "McGraw hates that name."

"Sorry, John, I mean Mister McGraw," said Nap.

The Only Del

McGraw slammed a pair of stubby brown bottles with Maryland Brewing Co. printed on their labels down on the bar. Beer foamed out of their tops from the impact. The four talked for a while about how well the Reds and the Spiders were doing. It wasn't easy making small talk with McGraw but Robinson was as jolly as ever. Lajoie didn't much like the beer so he switched to the hard stuff. After three or four stiff belts and a couple of weaving trips to the john he reminded McGraw of how Del had thrown him out twice.

McGraw turned several shades of red and called Napoleon a fucking frog. Lajoie reached over the bar, grabbed McGraw by the shirt front, and yanked him upwards. McGraw's feet flailed away beneath him. Robinson sobered up and looked on in horror.

"Put him *down*, Sandy," said Del. "Now!"

Lajoie let go. McGraw fell to the floor and scrambled around the bar to get at the much bigger Lajoie. Del, who figured McGraw was a far more ruthless and experienced fighter than Napoleon, managed to get between them.

"I think it's time you boys left," said Robinson. "Before something ugly transpires and we're all on the front page of the Sun. Your drinks are on me."

"Much appreciated," said Del. He handed Nap his boater and hustled him out the door.

Del scorched two doubles and a single and stole a base in the Phillies' 5-4 win over Baltimore on Friday the 13th. He didn't get a chance to throw out John McGraw, Wiley Piatt, a 23-year-old leftie from Blue Creek, Ohio, kept him off the bases. Del did nail another runner with a bullet from deep left center to Billy Nash. Or would have if Nash hadn't dropped the ball. Stallings released Nash after the game. The former captain had never been the same since being beaned in '96 and was batting just .243. Billy Hamilton, the man the Phillies had given up for Nash, would hit .369 in '98.

After going hitless in five at bats in a game in Washington, Sam Thompson complained of stomach and back pains. Days later Dr. Boger, the Phillies' team physician, delivered the stunning news that due to a chronic sprain of the muscles of his back Sam Thompson would never play baseball again.

the greatest batsman in the land

"I'm fed up with Stallings and my back is killing me, Mush," he told Del.

"It's not gointa be the same without you around, Sam."

"Good luck with Stallings and Rogers. Lord knows you'll need it."

Sam hopped on a train to Detroit and never came back.

The Phillies arrived in Cleveland on Friday, June 20 for a weekend series, the start of an abbreviated nine-game road trip. There were a lot of Delahanty boosters - handsomely-dressed "Lace Curtain" Irish and drabbier but louder "Shanty" ones from the Bend as well - in the rain-spattered crowd. They cheered when Del lined two run-scoring singles off droopy-eared Zeke Wilson. The Phillies took a 6-3 lead into the ninth in the first game but the Spiders mounted a rally and had two men aboard when Bobby Wallace drove a ball to deep left. Del raced back through the wet grass, caught the liner for the second out, and fired to Lajoie to nab Wallace at second and snuff out the comeback attempt.

Del met up with Fergus Maloney and Shaymus Finnegan after the game.

"Yer money's no good tonight, lads, whatever we get up to oim payin' fer the whole shebang."

"Well oim famished," said Fergus. "Let's haul our arses over ta Otto Moser's and get a bite and a jar or two."

"Where are you stayin'?" Shaymus asked Del as they hopped into a cab pulled by a skittish bay.

"The Colonial. It's not quite finished yet so we're gettin' a deal."

After quenching their appetites the three went to a burlesque show. They liked the scantily-clad dancers, though Del considered that his young wife was far prettier and shapelier than any of them, but weren't as thrilled with the contortionist, the sword swallower, the mime, or the comic and his lame puns. They took an electric trolley to their next destination. They sat in the back with young smokers who rocked the car back and forth to the disgust of other passengers until Del grabbed one of them and threw him into the street to cheers and applause.

The Only Del

The bedraggled waiter behind the bar rail at the saloon they'd chosen looked as though he'd been at work since dawn. When Shaymus ordered beer he brought three bottles that had "Made to Perfection by the Cleveland & Sandusky Brewing Corporation" on their gold labels.

"You call this *lager*?" asked Del after he tried the local beer. "Shite. There are more hops in a dead frog than there are in this."

The place got louder and louder. More than once Del had to duck as a Cleveland & Sandusky Brewing Corporation bottle flew past his head.

"They're a lot better to throw than ta drink," yelled Fergus.

When the police arrived to break up a fight and hauled away six combatants Shaymus shouted over the din, "There's a reason they call um *paddy* wagons."

The skies threatened on Saturday and Del was glad most of his rooters weren't on hand to see him go hitless in both games of the doubleheader. Fergus and Shaymus were in no condition to go anywhere. Del didn't even reach base in two of three losses in Pittsburgh, though he doubled twice and was robbed off an extra-base hit in the other one.

At the end of May the Phillies went back home to face the Colonels. Del was impressed by a big 24-year-old German named Honus Wagner that the Louisvilles had playing shortstop after trying him in the outfield. He had huge hands and when he fired the ball to first he sent a handful of dirt and pebbles along with it. Wagner's uniform was covered in mud, blood, and tobacco juice stains. He never cared much how he looked and rarely spent the money to have it laundered.

Del made a magnificent catch of a short fly in the second inning of the first game of the series. With two out and two on he thundered in from left, hurled himself forward and managed to get his glove under it just before it hit the spongy grass. In the afternoon game he made an even more remarkable catch of a drive from Wagner's big bat. The *Times* was ebullient in its praise. "Del's catch of Wagner's drive brought every spectator to his feet. It was the kind that only the Only Del can make."

the greatest batsman in the land

Ed was happy to read what the *Times* said. Right beside the account of the double header was a piece on the Eastern League game between Allentown and Lancaster. The Allentown Peanuts featured three of Ed's brothers in the infield, Tom at second, Jimmy at short, and little Joe at third. They played error-free ball in a 3-1 win and Ed was happy for them, but the fact that none of the three had managed a hit spoke volumes about why they hadn't followed their big brother to the big time.

The brothers stopped in at Ed and Norine's apartment in the Divine Lorraine that night. They gave Ed a hard time about being called "the only Del."

"There's five uv us and they call you the only one," said Joe.

"It's not right, Ed," said Jimmy.

"Don't yas go gettin' yer dander up at *me*," replied Ed. "It's not as if oim tellin' the reporters ta call me that."

Norine cooked the brothers liver and onions. She wore a tight-fitting, dark rose shirtwaist blouse and a gray skirt.

"It's one uv the few meals she can't ruin," Ed whispered to his brothers.

Norine looked at the food, knowing it wasn't likely to be very tasty. "I kiss better than I cook," she said.

"With looks like that who the hell cares if the girl can cook," Joe whispered to Tom.

"If she were my wife I wouldn't care if she burned the water fer me tea," said Tom.

"That's quite the pair uv *nursers* your bride's got," Joe told Del after Norine had left the brothers alone. "Oill bet you hate playin' with those beauties."

"They *do* get in the way when we try ta hug," said Del.

They all stared at him and then burst out laughing. Del punched Joe's arm and got out a bottle of whiskey.

"Duffy's Pure Malt Whiskey," Tom read from the label. "For medicinal use. Contains no fusel oil."

The Only Del

"What in the name uv Pete is fusel oil?" asked Jimmy.

"It's the stuff that gives you a hangover," Del told him. "Er so they say."

Tom turned the bottle around to read the back while his brothers tinked their glasses and then drained them in unison. "Made in Rochester, best known remedy for indigestion, dyspepsia, and all similar ailments."

"No wonder our big brother drinks it," chuckled Joe.

"It's purely fer me health," Del swore. "God's own truth."

"It's a hundred and twenty proof," read Tom. "This stuff'd put a shock uv hair on a cue ball."

"Purely medicinal, Thomas," Del reminded him.

"It must be," said Tom. "It says not to let your druggist or grocer persuade you to drink anything but Duffy's."

"Well we'd best drink some more then," said Jimmy.

They finished off two more bottles of the healthy elixir.

Del misjudged a routine fly, had a ball carom off the end of the bicycle track and bound over his head, and got caught napping off second with the bases loaded the next day to cost his club a win. He had a terrible hangover - but no indigestion or dyspepsia.

O.P. Caylor saw Colonel Rogers muttering to himself after the game. "What's eating you today, Colonel?" he asked.

"In a word?"

"Sure."

"Delahanty."

"*Delahanty?*"

"Did you see the condition he was in today?"

"He's not like that very often. Delahanty likes to go out on the town and sometimes he hoists a few, but he's usually ready and raring to go the next day. Of course he's strayed a little more since you got Lajoie. I heard Del's brothers were in town last night."

the greatest batsman in the land

"They must have swallowed half the whiskey in Philadelphia," grumbled Rogers.

"Well, Colonel, you could go out and get a dozen men who would follow all your rules and bat a hundred points less than Delahanty, or you could have a half a dozen more of him and your hair would turn gray but you'd leave Boston and Baltimore so far behind you couldn't see them with a telescope."

The Quakermen lost three out of four to the lowly Browns and then went to Boston and did the same. The only win was a 9-0 shutout by Al Orth on June 14th. Del, who was struggling to keep his average above .300, went hitless. Cooley had three hits, Lajoie a pair. After the win the two were in a mood to celebrate.

"Let's go see what sort of mischief we can get up to, Mush," said Napoleon as he combed pomade into his thick hair after the tally-ho brought the team back to their hotel.

"Sorry, Sandy, oim not in much uv a mood fer hijinks tonight," said Del.

"I'll go paint the town with you," Cooley told Napoleon. "We don't get to celebrate a win very often."

Cooley and Lajoie stayed out the whole night.

As bleary-eyed as they were the next day Cooley had another trio of hits and Napoleon another pair. The Beaneaters banged sixteen of them off three different Philly hurlers though and Stallings was in a foul mood after a 12-6 loss. He fined Cooley and Lajoie $25 each. Del was glad he'd stayed at the hotel last night. Stallings fumed the next day in New York when Cooley and Lajoie both failed to hit a ball out of the infield in an 11-3 loss. Their reveling had caught up with them.

"As we Irish uv learned, it's often not the day after that does a fella in," Del told Napoleon. "It's the day after that."

There was starting to be a lot of grumbling in the clubhouse. The *Times* opined, "there is definitely trouble between Stallings and his men." The

The Only Del

Phillies turned things around and won six in a row and climbed within a game of a .500 record, but it didn't cause Stallings to let up on his players. He still berated them in person and in the press every chance he got. Del and Nap were constantly arguing with him. He wanted them to bunt and sacrifice more. Like most of their teammates, they considered him a minor leaguer.

Duff Cooley finally spoke out. "We're fed up with the way Stallings has been riding us. He handles us like a bunch of cattle. We may not be the best team in the league but we don't intend to go on abiding his tactics."

When the team dropped ten of their next thirteen games Reach and Rogers had had enough. Del saw Stallings cleaning out his office before the game on Saturday, June 18. When he went to say something, Stallings growled, "I hope the lot of you are satisfied."

The players were more than satisfied, they were *overjoyed* when Ed told them Stallings was out. The only problem was there was no one to take his place. There were men the Philly owners would love to have hired, but they were all gainfully employed elsewhere. That left only one choice. The players could hardly believe their ears when they learned who the new skipper would be.

Chapter Twenty One

Billy's Phillies

The only baseball job that new manager Billy Shettsline had ever occupied apart from being the long-time club secretary was as a ticket-seller for the Philadelphia Keystones of the Union Association. He came from a family of coach painters.

Shettsline was moving into Stallings' old office when Ed got to the ballpark the next day. "Congratulations, Shetts," Ed told him. He patted him on the back and then helped him put things on the high shelves he was struggling to reach.

"I'm not sure I'm cut out for this," Shettsline told Ed when they stopped for a break. "I push *pencils*, not men."

"Don't worry. You'll be fine. We know what we're doin'. Just fill out the lineup card and we'll take care uv the rest."

Shettsline relaxed a little. "Thanks, Mush."

"Oh. One uther thing."

"What's that?"

"See if you can get some pitchers that can get the ball over the bluddy plate without havin' it knocked inta the middle uv next week."

Shettsline called the team in for a chat. "You fellows know me pretty well. I've been booking your rooms, hustling you into Pullmans, and making sure no one got berth thirteen for a while now. We all know I'm no genius when it comes to field work. Like Del's reminded me, you men know how the game is played and I'm going to leave it up to you to do what needs to be done. I'll just make sure to stay out of your way."

The Only Del

"What time do we have to be in at night, Shetts?" asked Napoleon.

"It was eleven under Stallings, the latest I can make it is midnight."

Lajoie smiled. "Fair enough, Billy. We can't *afford* to stay out any later than that on what Rogers pays us."

Shettsline sent George Wheeler to the slab against New York. He gave up ten hits and five runs but with the Phillies a run down Del belted a two-run double in the eighth to give his new manager his first win.

"Thanks, Mush," Billy told Del after the game.

"I told you we'd take care uv things."

In the first match of a sixteen-game road trip Del stroked four hits and drove in as many runs in a 14-2 bombardment of the Browns. The next day he drove in Douglass with a knock to right in the third, reached base on an error by ex-Philly Lave Cross in the fifth, and plated Cooley with another knock to right to win the game in the ninth. In the third game at Sportsman's Park he doubled and scored in the fifth and doubled, stole third, and scored on Lajoie's single in the sixth. The Phillies were having fun again. It was as if a dense cloud that had been smothering the team had been lifted. Del had a triple and two hard singles in the last game in St. Louis but Wheeler gave up another ten hits and seven runs and manager Shettsline suffered his first defeat.

Del had no hits in the first game in Louisville but three in each of the other two as Billy's Phillies took all three games. Del had another three hits off Wee Willie Dammann in the second game in Cincinnati, a 17-3 laugher on the last day of June. Manager Ewing left Dammann in even though he was beaten up for twenty-seven hits.

Ed and Napoleon met for breakfast the next morning. Nap was late so Ed read the news from Cuba in the *New York World* over a cup of lousy coffee. Nap winked at a fetching girl behind the counter when he came in. They ordered cereals from a new company called Quaker Oats, grape nuts and shredded wheat.

the greatest batsman in the land

"What's the scoop, Mush?" asked Nap, indicating his newspaper. "Anymore word of the flying machines?"

"No, but there's big news about the campaign to capture Santiago de Cuba. The US Army Fifth Corps engaged Spanish forces at El Caney and San Juan Heights."

"How did they do?" asked Nap, smiling as the girl from behind the counter set a coffee in front of him.

"Not so well at El Caney, but a lot better takin' the heights."

"How so?"

"Seems Theodore Roosevelt gave up his post as Secretary uv the Navy and put together a volunteer cavalry. It's mostly cowboys so the press is callin' them the Rough Riders. They arrived in time to take part in the Battle of San Juan Hill but somebody messed up and their horses didn't arrive in time so they had ta go up on foot."

"I guess rough *plodders* doesn't have quite the same ring," chuckled Nap.

"At any rate they've taken the hill. Hey, where's Cooley? I thought the two uv yas were as thick as thieves these days."

"I've decided to take your advice and settle down a might, Mush. I actually stayed in last night if you can believe that."

"I'm not sure I can, but if it's true I'm proud uv ya."

The Phillies went into Baltimore and came out feeling like the Spanish fleet at Manila Bay. The batting was feeble and the twirlers got shelled. Six straight losses ended the road trip that had started so brilliantly.

The *Inquirer* described the team's return to Philadelphia. "The Phillies returned to their home acre not like gladiators crowned with victorious eagles commanding the homage of the fickle masses. On the contrary, they stole into town in the quiet of night unheralded and unsung."

As much as Ed wanted to "be with" his bride he decided not to wake her when he got in at three a.m. When she woke up and wanted to give him a

The Only Del

proper welcome home he told her that he would be a lot more in the mood if he could help the team get back on track. The Phillies won 6-5 but Ed was stymied at the plate. When he got home he told Norine he'd been a bust. "We'd best not celebrate tonight, me luv. It might jinx me."

The next day Ed slammed two balls to the fence and the Phillies won 5-0. When he got home Norine was wearing a house coat and she had her hair up in a bun. Ed thought that rather strange since her makeup was applied with her usual attention to detail and a pair of her prettiest earrings dangled from her lobes. The high heels she was wearing didn't really go with a house coat.

"Did you win?" asked Norine.

"Aye, we did."

"And did you make a hit?"

"Aye. Two uv um."

"And did you make a pretty catch?"

"I did. Two uv *them* too."

"That's all I needed to hear." She reached behind her head and pulled at a blue silk ribbon. Her luxuriant curls fell to her shoulders. Ed smiled.

"Are you any good with knots, Mister Delahanty the hit maker?" Norine asked coquettishly.

"Fair ta middlin' I suppose. Why do you ask?"

She tugged gently at the knot on the belt of her robe and pouted, "You try."

Del didn't have to work very hard. The belt came undone with a slight tug. He slowly opened up the robe. Norine was naked underneath.

"I love your outfit," said Del.

"I thought you might."

She let the robe drop to the floor and stepped into her husband's arms.

the greatest batsman in the land

Ed took Norine and her sister Nettie to Wanamaker's at Eighth and Broadway the next morning. Norine still loved being an attractive ornament on her dashing husband's arm. Nettie was jealous of her sister's luck in finding such a handsome, athletic, successful man. Wanamaker's had a huge circular counter in the center of the store with 129 smaller counters radiating out from it. A swaying sea of shoppers swelled the aisles, their eyes agog at the plethora of goods on display.

Ed and Norine looked at Irish embroideries and linens. At each counter pretty and smartly-dressed sales girls made eyes at Ed. One went so far as to hold a fountain pen in front of her chest so he could admire her breasts along with the pen - until she saw Norine glaring menacingly from behind him and quickly returned the Waterman to its case.

Norine bought some overgaiters and a pair of Oxford tans for occasions when she wasn't trying to be alluring. Nettie bought a jar of Parker's Hair Balsam, some stationery, and - with some embarrassment - a female regulator for her monthly affliction at the drug counter. Del bought two India gauze shirts and a twilled silk umbrella. He spent a long time on the eighth floor, where a monorail snaked through the toy department. When the three were worn out and their arms could hold no more packages they went to the Crystal Tea Room for lunch. Norine kept hoping some man would take an interest in her plain sister but none did.

Del pounded out 24 hits in 48 at bats as the Phillies won six out of seven under their new skipper at the end of June to climb to within two games of the first division. Then they went to Baltimore and suffered five demoralizing defeats. Del ran into the left field wall trying for a foul fly in a game against the Spiders and split two fingers on his left hand. He missed five games and rather enjoyed the vacation. He spent his afternoons surrounded by admirers in the upper pavilion of what the ink-stained wretches were calling "the Colonel's Cantilever." One sun-drenched afternoon he found himself seated behind five elderly clergymen.

"Run, fer God's sake, Duff!" Ed yelled as a fly went over Cooley's head. "That was a bluddy ball and you know it!" he yelled at the umpire when Lajoie watched an outside pitch sail by for strike three. "Get yer arse back

The Only Del

in there and hit," he yelled at an enemy batter who'd stepped out of the box. He let a Philly runner who'd settled for a double when a three-bagger looked more than possible have it with, "Jaysus, Mary, and Joseph! Are ya runnin' the bases or deliverin' groceries?" The cranks around Ed were loving it. What could be better than watching a game with the Only Del in their midst?

The pastors turned and gave Ed disparaging looks. "Sorry, deacons. Oim just tryin' ta help the lads is all."

The rooter on Ed's left patted him on the back. "Don't mind them, men of the cloth don't understand that the fellas need a little encouragement."

Ed held his glass of root beer high and said, "Maybe I'll split some fingers more often. Oim havin' meself a grand old time up here."

His fingers healed, Del went on a tear with seven hits in a double header sweep of Chicago and another trio the next day to push his batting mark over .350. Then he ripped three "crisp bingos" in a 6-2 win over the Senators. A mini-slump at the end of July brought his average back to earth but he was still a wonder in the field, making brilliant plays and going 35 games without an error.

Del wasn't slowing down on the basepaths either. He led the league in steals. And now that Stallings was gone he didn't mind laying down a bunt to move a runner over. Sometimes he did it for a base-hit. He could have done it a lot more since the infielders usually moved back onto the grass when he swung his bat. But he still loved to pound the ball and he couldn't let Lajoie show him up in that department. Del's bat was stone cold the first two weeks of August but finally came to life on the 17th with three hard knocks in a 13-1 pounding of the Pirates and two more the next day.

"What's that yer readin', me pet?" Del asked Norine when he got home. "It doesn't look like Harper's Weekly."

He went over and looked to see the name of the book. "The Care and Feeding of Children," he read. "Is one uv yer sisters havin' a wee one?" he asked.

"No," Norine answered casually.

"Well who is then?"

"What did you say you were doing when we sneaked into that storage closet at the opera?"

Del stared at Norine, a look of bewilderment on his face. He smiled as he recalled ravaging his wife in the tiny room. Then he remembered. "I told you I was makin' a baby."

"Well it seems you did."

Del's eyes swelled. "I *did*?"

Norine took Del's hand and put it on her stomach.

"There's a wee bump!"

"There's a wee Delahanty."

Del played every game the last two months of the '98 season and finished at .339, sixth best among the league's depressed averages. Thanks to playing weak teams the last two weeks of the season the Quaker men climbed to fifth place but Del was getting more and more frustrated that he didn't have a single championship or even a close second to show for all his great years. Just as depressing was the fact that the top players in the league were making less now than they had ten years ago. Colonel Rogers was telling everyone who'd listen that the team had made $10,000 less in '98 even with the new 154-game schedule.

Del took Norine to New York at the end of October. She loved the city and the splendor of its hotels. She talked, or rather pleasured Del into taking her to Café Martin for dinner their first night. Jean and Louis Martin had taken over a lease on 26th Street when the building's owner had moved to Fifth Avenue and had refurbished it with the latest Art Nouveau design flourishes. The neighborhood around Madison Square Park was losing some of its luster after being the center of New York's social scene for twenty-five years. Some of its leading hotels and restaurants had begun to close.

The Only Del

When the tall, thin as a rake waiter arrived he said, "Bienvenue au Cafe Martin. Il me fait plaisir de vous servir ce soir."

Del gave him a blank look.

Norine asked the waiter, "Avez-vous une table près de la cheminée?"

Now Del gave *her* a blank look.

"Mais, oui," answered the waiter. He picked up the menus he'd set down and led Del and Norine to a table by the crackling fireplace.

Del couldn't make heads nor tails of the menu. He wasn't sure he didn't have it upside down.

Norine ordered for them both. "La soupe de Poison Marseillaise et le Gigot d'Agneau Dauphinoise pour mon mari. Et pour moi, la Petite Marmite et la Poule au Riz."

"You never told me you spoke French," said Del after the waiter had left them alone.

"If one aspires to travel in the best company, mon cher, one simply must learn French," she said as she daintily placed her napkin in her lap.

Del just shook his head and tried to guess what he'd be getting when the waiter brought his Gigot d'Agneau Dauphinoise.

They went walking hand-in-hand after breakfast the next morning. Norine carried a Taffeta silk parasol to block the rays of sunlight that occasionally broke through the tall buildings. She wore a yellow afternoon dress with a high neck, a wasp waist, and puffed sleeves. She hoped her outfit hid the bump in her belly, which was expanding rapidly now. She had thought it might bother Ed but he wanted her as much and as often as ever. He always stroked her stomach before moving up to her breasts, which were larger than ever.

They shopped in the fashion district that had been designed to approximate Le Bon March in Paris. They went to Lord & Taylor, Bloomingdale's, and Macy's. Norine looked at jewelry and Evangeline hats. She bought a pair of imported patent enamel russet "King Calf" shoes, some elaborate hat trimmings, and some things for the baby that was on

the greatest batsman in the land

the way. They concluded their shopping at Rogers Peet. Norine had seen their clever advertisements. The store, which sent salesmen to golf clubs to display their clothes to men who hated shopping, catered to people who enjoyed being treated like a millionaire but couldn't afford to spend like one. They cleverly made their labels tiny so that buyers could pretend their purchase had been made at a more expensive store. Norine picked out a dark blue smooth-twilled cassimere suit for Del that made him look like a muscular young bank president and a mauve four-in-hand tie.

The fifteen to thirty pounds of manure left behind by each of New York's 150,000 horses every twenty-four hours meant that the city needed to dispose of more than three million pounds of it each day! There were also the three dozen dead horses which had to be cleared from Gotham's streets and the 40,000 daily gallons of equestrian urine. The stench of it all was overpowering. A prognosticator who'd observed that every vacant lot featured piles of manure that reached heights as high as fifty feet had just calculated that by 1930 the horse droppings would rise to Manhattan's third-story windows. Ed paid a "crossing sweeper" twenty-five cents to clear a path through the disgusting minefield so he and Norine could get across the street to Rector's.

The ostentatious eatery had been open for less than a year but it was already the talk of the the town. Rector's catered to financiers, gamblers, the theater crowd, the racing set, and anyone else with money to burn. If you wanted to 'be seen', this was the place. Norine had told Ed she wanted to come here instead of Delmonico's, the first restaurant in America in which diners could order from a menu, because of the food. He knew better. He also knew that Rector's, which reminded prospective diners that ladies "without escort" would not be admitted, would cost a lot more than Café Martin and *it* had cost a small fortune.

Norine positively beamed when they walked in. She looking chic and radiant and Del was very dapper in his new cassimere suit. One man after another whispered, "That's Ed Delahanty. And that's not a society princess or a showgirl from the Follies he's with, that's his *wife*." Paunchy stockbrokers yelled at one another about the killer deal they'd pulled off

The Only Del

that day and gamblers called out the odds on the night's boxing matches to diners in all corners of the room. White-shirted teenage boys bussed towering trays of barely touched and outrageously-priced meals to the kitchen at breakneck speed while bejeweled celebrities held court.

"*She* certainly knows how to make an entrance," said Norine as Helen Dauvray swept in on the arm of her new husband. He looked rather out of place in his Admiral's uniform. Dauvray paused for a round of applause, which she accepted with false modesty. Tongues started wagging about how the only stage productions Dauvray was in these days were ones she financed and promoted herself.

A shady-looking man in a striped suit came over. "Well if it isn't the only Del," he said. "You must be here to talk to Eddie Talcott about playin' for the Giants."

"Oim just here ta spend some time with me beautiful bride is all," said Del.

The man ogled Norine. "I heard you'd robbed the cradle. Now I can see why. She's a stunner."

"And smart as a whip too," said Del.

Ed was happy to let Norine order for the two of them again. The snooty waiter looked surprised but Ed didn't care. He knew Norine had read all about dining in fancy restaurants. She glanced up and down the menu and told the waiter, "Sorbet to cleanse the palate to begin of course. My husband will have the saddle of lamb with beans and mushrooms, stuffed artichokes, and roast quail. I would like lamb chops with green peas."

The waiter couldn't help but be impressed. Ed smiled as Norine continued. "For dessert ... timbale Madison for me and banana mousse for my husband. And to finish, coffee and liqueurs served with fruit and petits fours."

"Diamond Jim and Lilian Russell are here!" someone called out.

"Have you heard her sing her hit If the Tables at Rector's Could Talk?" a woman at the next table asked Ed and Norine. "It's part of the new show at Ziegfeld's Follies."

the greatest batsman in the land

A huge jewel in the handle of Diamond Jim's umbrella glistened as he and Miss Russell sat down at a table near Ed and Norine's.

"That set him back fifteen hundred dollars," Norine heard someone say. "And that watch he's wearing cost nine *thousand*. He's got jewels on his garter clasps, his suspenders, even his underwear."

Ed could hardly believe what Diamond Jim ordered.

"I will have three dozen oysters - the Lynnhavens - to start. And then a dozen hard-shelled crabs, the terrapin soup, a sixteen-ounce steak, rare, with fried potatoes, onions, and mushrooms," he told the senior-most of three waiters. "And to drink, my usual, two carafes of orange juice."

The man who had described Jim's jewelry shared with his dinner companions that the gourmand generally feasted on game birds at Delmonico's after the theater, along with a pound or two of bonbons. When Diamond Jim polished off everything he'd ordered the waiter brought the dessert cart. "Leave it," said Diamond Jim. Lilian Russell grabbed an éclair. Jim ate the rest.

Ed and Norine were staying at the Waldorf. The Windsor, the Fifth Avenue, and St. Nicholas were out-of-date now. Norine had read that no one chic stayed there anymore. When they got back to their room the bed had been turned down and there was a chocolate on each pillow. A bottle of champagne sat in a bucket of ice.

"If I have anything else to drink I'll turn into a lustful strumpet," Norine warned Del.

He took off his suit jacket and stroked his chin. "I know exactly what I need to do then," he said. He poured champagne into a crystal glass and handed it to her. "Drink this." Norine took the glass.

The Only Del

In November the *Sporting News* lamented the decline in offense in baseball.

"*The remarkable reductions in batting averages and the increase in the number of shut out games demonstrate that this great sport needs a change that will restore hitting. The leading batsmen show a remarkable falling in their work this year as follows:*"

	1897	1898
Keeler, Baltimore	.432	.381
Clarke, Louisville	.406	.318
Kelley, Baltimore	.389	.239
Delahanty, Philadelphia	.377	.334
Lajoie, Philadelphia	.363	.328

We can see no reason for deferring experimentation with the rules. Changes cannot be effected any too soon."

Chapter Twenty Two

"Yer Liable ta Fall In"

Over the winter Boston made a pitch for Del and so did Chicago, offering Bill Lange once again. Billy Shettsline wanted no part of it, pointing out that Del was as good in the field as Lange and far stronger at bat. Del was glad the Phillies had found another terrific hitter in Roy Thomas but what they still needed was a first-rate twirler or two. Thomas, a skinny, long-nosed, 25-year-old, grew up in Sheetz's Creek, a little mill town on the Schuykill River, near Morristown, Pennsylvania. After earning a degree from the University of Pennsylvania he played for the Orange Athletic Club. He was a terrific bunter and slap hitter but he'd had a tough time making contact off a high schooler that pitched for one of the club's regular opponents, Christy Mathewson of the Honesdale Reds. Roy would foul off pitch after pitch until he got one he could drive. Thomas drew a lot of walks. He would make an excellent leadoff hitter.

Del read in the *Sporting News* that in 1898 the average club had spent $39,000 in player salaries and paid $18,000 to the league for administrative costs and umpires, $17,500 for grounds-keeping, $13,285 for travel, $4,000 for the manager's salary, and $1,000 for insurance.

"Just over half in salaries," Del muttered to himself. "I'm no business tycoon but it seems as though that figure should be a lot higher than that."

He was delighted to read Frank Hough's column in the *Inquirer* the next day. Hough told his readers that the baseball magnates' greed would come back to haunt them, that with no other league to compete with them they were taking advantage of the players who filled their parks and coffers. He called them "a coterie of pocketbook snatchers as devoid of sporting blood as an egg is of hair."

The Only Del

Del spent his mornings at the gym with Napoleon and his afternoons and evenings with Norine and their baby daughter. Del had rented a modestly furnished townhouse for the three of them on North 18th Street three blocks west of the ballpark. They couldn't carry on living in their hotel apartment forever. Norine was looking forward to decorating the townhouse while her husband was on the road. They'd named the baby Florence and she was the apple of her daddy's eye. Del loved to dandle his wee girl on his knee and tell her Irish yarns, even though he knew she didn't understand a word he was saying.

"Enough with the blarney, Edward Delahanty," Norine would say.

Del kept on telling Florence the tall tales anyway and sang her Irish ditties as well. "Tura lura lura, tura lura lie, tura lura lura, hush now don't you cry. Tura lura lura, tura lura lie, tura lura lura, That's an Irish Lullaby." He usually put his exhausted wife to sleep faster than the baby.

When Del received his contract for the league maximum of $2,400 he found a letter attached. Billy Shettsline wanted each player to let him know his measurements so new uniforms could be ordered. Shettts was leaning toward white and bottle green. "*Bottle* green. That'd sure enough suit some uv the boys," Del told Florence. She just giggled and drooled.

On March 15 at 1:10 nineteen Phillies departed for Charlotte, North Carolina. Del wasn't one of them. He knew he needed less practice than most to get ready for a new season. Spring training was for Yannigans, not veterans. Besides, he wanted to spend a little more time with his wife and baby. With the team was a reporter from the *Inquirer* who would be filing stories as "The Man Behind the Plate." Del finally tore himself away and the *Inquirer's* man in Charlotte was able to tell his anxious readers that "The Great Delahanty will arrive today."

The mercury cavorted near seventy so the players had no trouble working up a sweat. There were a lot of sore arms and "a great run on the witch hazel bottles." Del shed several pounds of "adipose tissue and superfluous flesh." As he looked around the practice field he considered that, though Billy Hamilton and Sam Thompson were gone, this might be the best nine the Phillies would field since he'd become a Quaker a decade ago. With

the greatest batsman in the land

McFarlane behind the plate, young Thomas at first, the now sensational fielding Lajoie at second, Monte Cross at short, and Cooley, Flick, and himself in the outfield their only weakness was at third base - and on the mound as usual.

The team had the entire third floor of the Trade side of the Central Hotel as well as four bedrooms on the second floor, one of those, right next to a makeshift Turkish bath, being Del and Nap's. The day after the sauna was set up they made sure to be first in the steamer after practice and first on the cots for a rubdown from trainer Mike. Nap was in a foul mood. He'd made a comment about how Elmer Flick could probably have reached a pop up if he'd been more alert and gotten a better jump on the ball. Flick had called Lajoie names that he generally reserved for umpires and Nap had told Flick he should go and perform a physical impossibility. Del figured it might be a while before they spoke to one another in anything but curses.

The *Inquirer's* diligent correspondent occupied a table in the dining room across from where the team ate so he could even report on what he called their "table clearing."

> "Manager Shettsline has asked for substantial food and plenty of it. The players are good doers when it comes to eating. If the table does not suit the ball tossers they're apt to register a holler that can be heard in the lobby. They have acquired epicurean tastes. Delahanty would no more think of eating a pate de foi gras before his berries than he would of wearing a high hat with a sack suit."

The morning after Del's arrival the players were leaving the hotel to walk to the practice grounds when a horse raced toward them pulling a driverless wagon. The *Inquirer* man, who was just getting into a carriage, witnessed and reported on the scene.

> "The runaway charged at the group and Del jumped out in front to stop it. But the horse swerved and dashed the wagon against a tree, smashing it into atoms. The released runaway roan reared up and jumped toward Del, but he cleverly side-stepped and allowed the horse to continue making good its escape."

The Only Del

The reporter added that the Phillies have accepted an invitation to attend a social session of the Elks and would attend a colored cake walk on Thursday evening. The Phillies' brain trust had bought Chick Fraser from Cleveland during the off season. His record to-date was 36-56. "Another ace," Del had thought when he'd read of the latest acquisition in the *Sporting News*. Fraser's specialty it appeared was hitting batters.

One of the more interesting of the Yanningans this Spring was Pearce "What's the Use?" Chiles, who bore a resemblance to Honus Wagner and at 33 was no spring chicken. He'd been a real helion as a youth. After playing for teams in Lawrence, Topeka, and Little Rock, Chiles returned to his hometown of Deepwater, Missouri for his mother's funeral in 1895 and got into trouble. When he went to Phoenix that fall the authorities there were after him. He was wanted in Missouri for illicit relations with a sixteen-year-old girl. As the age of consent in that State was eighteen years, the charge against him was "constructive rape." Chiles got the jump on the local authorities and lit out of Phoenix just ahead of the arrest papers. He managed to get in some playing time with Shreveport and Galveston and acquired his unusual nickname. He had a habit of taunting opposing batters when they hit pop-ups to him by shouting "What's the use?" before stylishly catching the ball.

After successful stints with the Lancaster Maroons and the Waco Tigers, Chiles was invited to try out for the Phillies. Even though there didn't seem to be a spot for him in the lineup he was playing great for the Yannigans and meshing well with the regulars.

"I heard about what happened to you," Del told Chiles one night after a round of pinochle. "A lot uv us did. Did ya beat the charges or are they still after ya?"

"The thing of it was the girl had been rollicking under the sheets with most of the fellas in town. I was the only one stupid enough to let her think it was serious. That's why she got her daddy to charge me. When he found out just how many men his precious daughter had been with he dropped the charges and sent her to a convent."

Chiles and Duff Cooley were acknowledged as the best billiards players in camp. Cooley started up a singing Quintette consisting of himself,

the greatest batsman in the land

third baseman Billy Lauder, Red Donahue, Monte Cross, and Klondike Douglass. They performed old-time classics like "The Bridge the Heart Burned Down" and "You'll Get All That's Coming to You." Cooley's Quintette began to steal so much attention from the local women that reserve catcher Morgan Murphy conspired to start his own musical group.

Chiles joined him, along with Del and Flick, to form a quartet more interested in clowning than harmonizing. They sang "Honey on My Lips" and "She May Have Seen Better Days" and "You've Been a Good Wagon but You've Broke Down Now." By the time the club returned to Philadelphia for the start of the season, they'd stolen the hearts of their Charlotte hosts.

The only change to the rules for '99 was that pitchers could no longer feint a throw to first base to hold a base runner. The team benches were to be moved father away from the stands to reduce interactions between players and patrons.

Del got off to a flying start and so did Billy's Phillies. They swept three from the Senators and Del went 7-for-12. When he and Norine were tucking baby Florence into her crib Del's first night back in Philadelphia she said, "Mister Delahanty do you realize that you have not attended to your husbandly duties in almost a week?"

"Has it been that long?"

"Could it be that you have taken to thinking of me as an old married woman?"

Del looked at his beautiful nineteen-year old wife. He noticed that she had her hair styled the way she did when they were going out. "I thought it was all about the baby now," he pouted.

"It is. Until she goes to sleep. Then it's all about us." She kissed Del and pushed herself up against him.

The next morning when Del got out of bed he grinned as he navigated through a crooked line of shirts, trousers, stockings, and petticoats on his way to check on Florence and then make breakfast. Norine woke up a few

The Only Del

minutes later. She yawned and stretched. Her hair was tussled but luxuriant and it glistened in the sunlight that poured through the windows Del had thrown open to wake her up. The tops of her breasts, still swollen from nursing, peeked out alluringly from the top of the sheets. "I'd have to say that last night you succeeded rather well and often in proving you're still fond of me, Mister Delahanty," she yawned contentedly.

"I might as well warn you, my sweet. If the wee one's down for her nap when I get home from the Grounds this afternoon I might have an urge ta prove it to you *anuther* time er two."

The Brooklyns came to town for a four game set. Ed Robison, streetcar baron and co-owner of the Cleveland Spiders had bought the St. Louis Browns from Chris von der Ahe over the winter. Robison's partner, who was also his brother, allowed him to move all the best Spiders to St. Louis. Robison changed the the name of the team to the Perfectos and the team color to red. The color proved so popular that fans and sportswriters began referring to the team by their shade of red - Cardinal.

The shady manouever had inspired Harry von der Horst, the owner of the Baltimore Orioles, to pull the same stunt. He'd bought into the Brooklyn club and moved four of the Orioles' stars - Willie Keeler, Joe Kelley, Hugh Jennings, and 28-game winner Joe McGinnity - over to it. With the injection of the four players and Bad Bill Dahlen from the Colts the Bridegrooms now played under the nickname Superbas, which was drawn from a vaudeville troupe of daredevil acrobats.

Del had three hits in the second game against Brooklyn's stacked lineup and four in the fourth. The Phillies were happy to split the series. They took two of three from Boston to move within a game of first place and headed to New York. Ed knew that Norine wanted to go, but she thought it was too soon for Florence to make such a trip and it wasn't as if they could take her to Rector's or Delmonico's. The visitors won two, lost one, and tied one in New York.

In the last game, on Wednesday, May 3, Del called for something that had never been tried before. With one out and Giants on second and third in the eighth inning and hard-hitting Tom O'Brien coming to the plate, Del

the greatest batsman in the land

ran in from his outfield position to talk to Jack Filfield, who was nursing a four-run lead.

"What is it, Mush?" asked Filfield before sending a stream of tobacco juice toward first base.

"O'Brien's a pretty fair slugger, Jack," said Del.

Fifield wiped his mouth with his sleeve and nodded. "Don't I know it, he's sent more than a few of my best shoots to the fences."

"Hartman's due up next," said Del as Shetts ran out from the bench to see what the two were talking about. Ed McFarland took off his mask and followed him. Duff Cooley, the team captain, stayed put at first base. He looked to be more concerned with how much longer it would be until he could get a drink.

"What of it?" asked Fifield.

"Why don't ya serve up four balls to O'Brien and take your chances with Hartman, he doesn't hit worth a lick."

"You mean walk O'Brien *intentionally*?" asked Shetts. "Is that allowed?"

"Uv course it's allowed. Oive never heard tell uv it bein' done, but there's no law against it."

"What do you think, Jack?" asked Shetts.

Fifield took off his cap and scratched his head. ""Well, it puts another man on base, but I'd sure as hell rather pitch to Hartman."

"Give O'Brien four wide ones then," said Del. "With O'Brien on first, you'll set up a double play inta the bargain."

"I hadn't thought of that," said Shetts. "Hartman runs like a plow horse."

"And he's battin' two-thirty," said Del. "O'Brien's closin' in on three hundred."

"Makes sense to me," said Fifield.

Del smiled and ran back to his position. McFarland went back behind the plate and winked at O'Brien. "Don't expect much, O'Brien," he told him. O'Brien looked at him queerly.

Fifield's first pitch was two feet outside. McFarland jumped to his right and caught it.

The Only Del

"Must have gotten away from him," O'Brien told McFarland, digging in again.

The next three pitches were in the same location. As O'Brien flung his bat toward the bench in disgust and trotted to first, John Day, the Giants' rookie manager, flew off the bench. "What the hell was that business?" he demanded of the umpire.

"Looked like Fifield walked your man on purpose," the umpire told him.

"O'Brien didn't have a chance in hell of hitting any of those throws," growled Day.

"Well he got himself a free pass to first out of it, didn't he?"

"But ..."

"No but's about it. Get back to the bench and send your next man up."

Fred Hartman came to the plate looking nervous. He waved at the first pitch, a high shoot, and grounded the next one to Nap Lajoie, who scooped the ball up and lobbed it to Monte Cross who was covering second. Cross stepped on the bag and then wheeled and fired a strike to Duff Cooley and the inning was over.

Del caught up to Nap as he jogged off the field beaming. "Clever move, Mush. Worked like a charm."

The Phillies were tied for first when they took on the decimated Orioles. Del hit a home run over the centerfield fence, a line drive double, and another two-bagger that came within an ace of leaving the grounds. On Friday, May 12 Del, the only outfielder in the league not to have made an error, doubled and singled in the opener, an 11-0 laugher for the home side. He went 1-for-4 in the matinée and his batting average after a month of play fell to .453. The papers said he was playing the best ball of his career - which was saying something.

Del bought a bottle of Imperial Cabinet rye from Thomas Massey & Sons on his way home. It was $1.25 but he thought he would splurge.

"Why don't ya try a wee dram, darlin?" he asked Norine when they finished the delicious dinner Amy had made.

"Ladies do not drink whiskey," Norine told him.

the greatest batsman in the land

"Is that so?"

"It most certainly is."

"How about we play a wee game then?"

"What sort of game?" Norine asked. She had a feeling her husband was up to no good. He had the same twinkle in his eye he'd had in Atlantic City.

"You could be Kitty, a naughty girl who's slipped away to see Dangerous Dan the notorious riverboat gambler."

"And you think Dangerous Dan could talk Kitty into having a drink of whiskey, do you?"

"I think he might."

She undid the top two buttons of her shirt-waist. "Then *you* pour the whiskey and *I'll* turn into naughty Kitty."

"There's one thing you need to know about Dangerous Dan," said Del as he poured the expensive whiskey into two crystal glasses.

"What's that?"

"He never spills a drop."

"Is that so? Then Florence might just have a baby brother this time next year."

The next day Del hit a ball so hard he loosened its seams. Lajoie followed with a long drive of his own and when Kid Gleason picked up the ball he was astonished to see that it was warped and cracked.

"In my eleven years in the league I've never seen a ball knocked to pieces like that," he told reporters. "I guess no ball was ever hit as hard as Delahanty and Lajoie bashed that one."

When the Phillies arrived in Cleveland they were determined to sweep the devastated Spiders, who were 3-18 on the season and had lost eleven straight. Del's leg was hurting from a nasty collision he'd had with Cooley and he pulled himself after one at bat. Norine massaged his sore thigh Saturday night when the team returned home. It soon felt a lot better, but significant swelling developed in a nearby location and that was the end of the massage.

The Only Del

"I'm sorry, darling. You'd better have Mike rub your thigh the next time," said Norine as she put her clothes back on and attempted to restore a semblance of order to her hair before checking on Florence. "He won't get distracted and touch you improperly like I just did."

With Del still on the bench, the Phillies lost three in a row to Chicago. He was back in the lineup on June 1st in the last game against Chicago and clubbed three hits. The cranks were delighted to have him back and he got enough pats on the back to last a lifetime. He and Nap accounted for seven runs in a much-needed 10-7 win. In the Saturday game Del was "the cynosure of all eyes." The *Press* scribe was so taken with his work in the field he was inspired to write that "there were many star performers, but the work of Delahanty stood out in such stark contrast to that of the other leather-chasers that they were beaten to a pulp by comparison."

On Sunday Del and Norine showed off their adorable daughter at church. Her eyes had stayed blue, though not the remarkable shade of her mothers. Then they took her to the park so she could point and giggle at the squirrels and ducks. Lajoie had four hits off Billy Rhimes in the Monday game against Pittsburgh. Del had a single, another stolen base, and a home run in the 13-3 romp to boost his league-leading average to .424.

Del took Norine to Keith's Playhouse in his new Pittsburgh Coupe Rockaway after dinner that night. George E. Bogle, the theater manager, was presenting "a program of merit and novelty" that featured Ching Ling Foo, the Chinese magician, the Gotham Four comedy team, and a juggler from France whose name was Henri. Norine liked Robert Browning in the arena scene from "The Gladiator." Del's favorite act was a pair of boxing kangaroos.

Norine wore a low-cut dress that attracted a lot of admiring looks. When Del came back from getting sodas there was a well-dressed, pimple-faced, seventeen-year-old boy standing in the aisle beside their seats. He pretended he was looking for someone but was actually staring wide-eyed down at Norine's ample cleavage.

"Careful, me sun, yer liable ta fall in," Del told Norine's latest admirer. The embarrassed lad wheeled around. His face turned so red his pimples disappeared.

The Quakers shellacked the Senators 9-1 Friday, June 9 and then the teams got rained out on Saturday before heading to Washington for a Tuesday double header. Del smashed a triple and a homer in the first game, an 11-10 win for Philadelphia. He singled but uncharacteristically grounded into a double play in the second game, which didn't start until 4:46 because the first match had lasted two hours and twenty minutes. Wiley Piatt tossed a three-hit shutout and the Phillies coasted into third place.

"If only we got pitching like that more often," Del told Nap after the game. "We could be right bluddy world beaters."

The next day Shetts saw a wagon stacked with empty barrels and whistled his way to the Grounds knowing his club would win. Del led off the sixth inning with another home run. The twirler drilled him in the shoulder his next time up. Del wasn't upset, that was how the way the game was played. A 6-4 Philly win took away some of the sting. Shettsline's crew took three out of four from the Reds. Del led the charge with three hits in the third game and a pair in the last.

After a rainout and a 6-4 loss in which Del had another three hits the Phillies traveled to Louisville to face the tenth-place Colonels. Chick Fraser won the Wednesday game 3-1 with little help from Del or Nap. Del was even less help on Thursday, going hitless and letting Honus Wagner stretch a double into a triple as 25-year old rookie Jack Fifield got shelled for eleven runs. Piatt was almost as bad on Saturday but Del and Nap knocked in Thomas and Cooley six times as the Phillies won 13-4. Ed was focused on getting back to his wife and daughter as they dropped the last game in Louisville 10-4 before heading home for a Fourth of July double header with Brooklyn.

To give Norine a break Ed took Florence for a long walk and a play in the park when he arrived home. Norine's beautiful eyes had lost some of their sparkle from lack of sleep, Florence had been colicky. When they returned, Norine was fast asleep on the settee and Ed decided not to wake her. He told Florence some more of his far-fetched old Irish tales and

The Only Del

then took her back out and bought her some toys she was still too young to play with and a bottle of Hoff's Malt Extract for nursing mothers that the chemist had recommended for Norine.

The salesgirls thought the father and daughter were adorable.

"I'd give my eye teeth to marry a man like that," one girl said to another. "Do you see the way he dotes on the wee one?"

"Isn't he Ed Delhanty, the famous ball player?" asked the other girl.

"He is," said their boss, who had overheard. "Now get back to work or you'll *have* to find husbands because you'll be out of a job."

When Ed and Florence got back from their shopping expedition she was fast asleep and her mother was her lively self again. Norine put the baby to bed, freshened up, and joined her husband in the sitting room.

"Were the women in Saint Louis as beautiful as you remembered?" she asked Ed.

"Every bit. And *friendlier* than ever as well. Seems they just can't get enough uv ball players. And the girls in Louisville were quite accommodating as well."

"I'm so glad they could attend to my husband's needs. I suppose you've no desire to bed down your boring wife then."

"Well I had thought we could take a wee nap together, but I see you've just taken one without me."

"That's true. I'm quite refreshed now. I won't need to lie down again for ..."

"Come her, you wee vixen. I want ta show you how much luvin' oive got stored up after three weeks away from me boring wife. Then oill show ya the pretty things I bought you while I was avoidin' temptation."

The Phillies took both ends of the double header from the Superbas. The biggest crowd ever for a morning game in Philadelphia turned up to give the home team a warm reception. Del had five hits on the day including a home run off the top of the fence beside the flagpole to boost his average, which had dipped to .415 before the start of the festivities.

the greatest batsman in the land

After the games Ed went to collect his Pittsburgh Coupe Rockaway from the stable.

"What took so long? Was everything all right with the Rockaway?" asked Norine when he got back.

"'Twas all good. But with me bein' away so long they'd moved it all the way to the back."

They dropped Florence off at Nettie's and went to the Walnut Theatre to see James O'Neill play Edmund Dantes in "The Count of Monte Cristo." Then Ed took Norine for a slow ride through Fairmount Park under a cloudless sky and a full moon. They held hands and snuggled like they had on their first dates, each glad to be back in the other's company.

"Will we always be this much in love?" Norine asked Del as he steered the carriage along the lane beside the river. The moon reflected off its inky surface.

"I expect so. I know I'll never want anyone but you."

"How about when I get old and ugly?"

"Do you really think I'd throw ya over just fer gettin' on in years? OiIl always be a fair site older than you."

"Then we'll grow old together. And have a few more babies while we're at it."

"Ach! That means we'll have ta keep on rustlin' under the covers like we do all the time."

"It doesn't always have to be under the covers."

"No?"

"Did you notice the lane we just passed?"

"What uv it?"

"It looked as though no one could see down it."

"So we could park down it and be all alone?"

"That's right. And we could do a scientific experiment."

"A scientific experiment?"

The Only Del

"That's right. A mechanical one. To find out how much *rocking* this Rockaway can stand?"

It turned out it could stand a lot.

Del had two hits the next day as the Phillies swept the series from the front runners and pulled within three games of them. The Superbas came to life though when the two teams traveled to Brooklyn for four more games, winning the first three. Del socked two doubles and a triple and scored three runs in the finale in Brooklyn, a 10-0 rout the Phillies badly needed to stay in the hunt. The Quaker crew was happy to get out of Brooklyn and go home to host the Spiders, who had won only four of their last thirty-two games. With half the season still to go the Clevelanders were already thirty-six games from the lead. Del stood first in batting at .410 and led the league in total bases as well. He was glad to see that Napoleon, who had settled down a lot under Del's wing, stood second, not Keeler. The Phillies took all three games from the sad-sack Spiders.

The seventh-place Reds were next in line and the Phillies swept them too. No one could recall the last time they'd been this close to first place so far into the season. But in the series opener Napoleon went hard into second base and then swerved to avoid spiking the Reds' rookie shortstop Harry Steinfeldt. Nap's knee struck Steinfeldt's head hard. The rookie lay unconscious for five minutes and there was grave concern. He'd complain of headaches for a while but Nap's injury was worse. The knee had suffered such trauma that he couldn't put the slightest bit of weight on it. The diagnosis was synovitis, water on the knee. The tissue above and below it swelled to twice its normal size. He was lost to the team for weeks, a crucial blow.

Duff Cooley was out too. His reflexes shot, he'd been hit in the mouth during batting practice and the wound had needed stitches. The exact same thing had happened to him two weeks before. He wasn't hitting a tinker's dam and the bleacher cranks were badgering the thin-skinned field captain mercilessly. Colonel Rogers stripped Cooley of the captaincy and suspended him without pay for violating his temperance pledge. Duff denied that he was drinking but Rogers knew better, he'd had him followed. Del reluctantly took over as captain. He was the obvious choice, but he didn't want the job.

the greatest batsman in the land

When Del opened his mail on Monday, July 17, the morning of the Phillies' seventh straight win, he was astounded to find a letter from Colonel Rogers addressed to each member of the team informing them that if they succeeded in winning the championship flag they would split $5,000. If they came second they'd divide $2,500. It was so out of character for Rogers Del had to read it four times.

He had two hits in each game against Louisville but the Phillies won only one of the three contests. Things went from bad to worse in Pittsburgh. They lost all five games there. Pearce Chiles had taken over at second and he was making two or three errors a game. The Phillies were glad to get out of the Steel City on the 25th. They had only an hour to grab a bite to eat, hustle to the train station, and jump on a sleeper for the trip to Chicago. They'd fallen to fourth place, eight games back. They needed to turn things around, and fast.

Del scored three times in the opener in the Windy City, a satisfying 7-5 win. But the next day the Phillies got clobbered 9-1. The score was tied through eight in the Friday game and neither pitcher showed signs of cracking. As usual, Thomas fouled pitches off until he drew a walk and Lauder reached on an error. Del drove the ball over the infield and both of the speedy runners scored for a 4-2 triumph. On Saturday he tripled and scored in the first, singled in a run in the fifth, and hit a long fly to center in the eighth that Sam Mertes couldn't handle. Pearce Chiles crossed the plate with the winning run.

The Phillies came home at the end of the month for a nineteen-game home stand beginning with five against the Spiders. They hoped to take at least four of them. After splitting the August 1 doubleheader Del led the way with three hits and scored twice in an 8-5 win in the third tilt. He tripled, singled, and threw out a runner from deep left in the first game of the Thursday doubleheader, which ended 6-1 for the home side, and singled and scored in the Phillies 4-0 shutout in the afternoon game.

The August 9 game with the Pirates was described as "a most wonderful exhibition." The *Inquirer*, which remarked upon "the running of the mighty Delahanty," told its readers that in the future old men would gather their

The Only Del

grandchildren and tell them of "one of the most exciting finishes in the history of baseball."

The Phillies led 7-4 after seven and 8-6 after eight. The Pirates scored seven runs in the ninth and the Phillies came back with a half a dozen of their own for a tumultuous 14-13 win. Del, who had four hits on the day, scored the winning run on a daring slide. The *Inquirer* claimed that "future cranks will aver that the new players are just as good as the old ones were, but old men will shake their heads deprecatingly and say 'Yes these new players of yours are pretty fair but you should have seen the Only Del in the summer of '99.'"

The Phillies took three out of four from Pittsburgh and edged to within three games of the lead. On Saturday, August 12 in the first game against the Chicago Orphans Del strained his neck diving for a low fly but socked three hits in support of Red Donahue's three-hit shutout. Red may have struggled in the past, but he was having a banner season. Del sat out the Monday and Tuesday games but was back for the first game with the Perfectos on Wednesday and he slashed a double to show that his batting eye hadn't suffered. He still led the league, though his average had dipped to .404.

Del had two hits in the next game, the Phillies' fifth straight victory. In the first game of the series-ending double header the Perfectos sent eight runs across the plate. It would have been nine but Del gunned down Cupid Childs at the plate in the fourth. Ed McFarland had to leave the late game after being struck by a foul tip and Elmer Flick dislocated his knee when he tripped over first base. The Phillies were now without the services of Flick, McFarland, Cooley, and Lajoie, who told Ed, "I just want to get back out there and swipe at the ball, Mush. It'd to a lot more for my knee than a month of hazel baths and massages."

The men now surrounding Del in the batting order were Billy Goeckel from the Wilkes-Barre club, Chiles, and light-hitting Bill Lauder. Del was still swinging hard and trying to make long hits but now they just weren't coming. It didn't take him long to figure out the problem. With no other dangerous batters in the lineup he wasn't getting any decent pitches to hit. He'd have to adjust and change his swing.

the greatest batsman in the land

The Phillies managed to win three of four in New York but Del was awful, a bitter disappointment for his legions of Gotham City boosters. He did no better in three straight losses in St. Louis before finally regaining his touch with three hits in the fourth game to move the Phillies back into second place.

"The Only Del was wicked with the willow" in the first game in Louisville, a 12-0 romp, banging two doubles and a three-bagger. He doubled and wafted a ball over the right field fence the next day in an 8-7 squeaker. "The big captain" was making terrific plays in the field as well.

Del led the way again with three hits and two runs in the first game in Cincinnati. He singled and hit one off the top of League Park's centerfield wall in the second game, but Fraser was bludgeoned for ten runs. "Delahanty, as usual, carried off the batting honors" in the Saturday game. He singled twice and put another dent in the centerfield wall with the bases loaded.

The injury-riddled, Delahanty-driven Phillies were winning against all odds. The problem was that the connivingly-constructed Superbas never seemed to lose. They'd fashioned a 20-1 string in June but had allowed several clubs back in the hunt with eight consecutive losses that had led tongues to wag about fixes. Now they were in a stretch of twenty-six wins in twenty-nine games. Now the contenders were vying to *place* rather than win. Splitting $2,500 would be better than nothing at least, thought Del.

With his club a run down in the seventh in the first of six against Washington Del drew a walk - now a common occurrence - and promptly stole second. When the Senators' second baseman took his time fielding McFarland's grounder and throwing to first Del tore around third and scored. The cranks went nuts. In the third game against Washington the play of the day was "Ed Delahanty's wonderful one-hand running scoop and a hard peg to nail the runner at home." At the bat he rapped three singles and two doubles in an 18-5 win. The Phillies captured five out of six from the Senators to put a little distance between themselves and Boston and Baltimore and then swiped all four games from Cleveland.

Lajoie was back at last, though still hobbled, but Thomas was out due to an unexplained off-field accident. The team badly needed Cooley to

The Only Del

return to action, but the imperious Rogers wouldn't even consider it. He refused to trade or sell the former captain as well, even though other teams were certainly interested. It reminded everyone that they were indentured servants, just as they had been before the Players League experiment.

The Phillies struggled to play .500 ball the last two weeks of September, losing key games they badly needed to the Giants and Reds. As they did, the Beaneaters won ten straight to climb to within a half game of them while the stacked Superbas surged into an eight-game lead. On October 7th the Brooklyns clinched the pennant with a win over the Giants. The Beaneaters arrived in Philadelphia for a three-game set to be followed by a season-ending four game one in Boston. Del cracked three hits in a 6-1 win on Saturday and hit a double with two aboard on Monday to give the Phillies a 3-1 victory. The teams were tied for second. He singled and tripled in the last game at home to Boston, but the Beaneaters prevailed. The Phillies would have to win three out of four in Boston.

On Wednesday, Oct 11 the Phillies "failed to make solid contact with the benders of Vic Willis." They beat the Beaneaters the next day, but Kid Nichols shut them out on Friday to clinch second place. Playing on a bad ankle, Del had two of the Phillies' three hits. In the crucial series Chiles batted 1-for-17 and Lajoie went 3-for-15. Del was 8-for-16. He'd batted .434 in the last thirty games of the season. He was crestfallen that the club had finished third. But they had won more games than any other Phillies team and he had clearly established himself as "the top notch hitter of his profession." The *Inquirer* wrote a tribute to the hometown hero. "Del is the personification of strength. He is brawn and muscle from tip to toe and swings on the horsehide like a triphammer, slamming the ball on the nose nearly every time he bats." President Young said that Delahanty's average of .410, twenty-nine points better than Keeler's winning mark the year before, was one of the most brilliant achievements accomplished with the bat in the history of the game and "almost beggars belief."

In spite of not being among the top ten players in plate appearances, Del had led the way in hits, doubles, total bases, and slugging, and would have ranked first in a lot of other statistics like On Base Plus Slugging and Runs Created that no one would be calculating for a long time. To top it all off, he'd thrown out twenty-six runners even though few players dared trying for an extra base when they hit a ball Del's way.

The Spiders finished the season a whopping 84 games back of Brooklyn. Their twirlers had all suffered seasons they'd have trouble forgetting. Coldwater Jim Hughey had gone 4-30, Charlie Knepper 4-22, Crazy Schmit, who had acted as his own attorney after being accused of throwing a brick at a neighbor in '92 and had told the judge, "Your Honor, that the man still lives is sufficient evidence that I, who have such splendid control, did not throw a brick at him", 2-17, Harry Colliflower 1-11, and Frank Bates 1-18. Bid McPhee, the last holdout, retired. He'd finally started wearing a glove in '96 after a scalding grounder had mangled one of his fingers. The next year he'd set a record for fielding and conjectured that maybe he should have tried a glove earlier after all.

Del and Ned Hanlon arranged a six-game exhibition series between their clubs. The winners would get 75% of the proceeds, the losers the rest. The Phillies and Superbas won three games each so the money was divided equally. Each club got $2,500, which made up for what Colonel Rogers had promised the Phillies if they finished second. The day after the series ended the two teams attended an Irish-themed gala at Brooklyn's Academy of Music. William Cahill recited "Casey at the Bat", James Byrne sang "Off to Philadelphia" and John L. Sullivan and James Corbett sparred like tiger cubs to the delight of the players and their wives. Among the honors and awards presented before a sumptuous repast and many drinks was one recognizing Del's remarkable season.

Norine had her hair up in elaborate waved side-locks and wore a Nile-green velvet dress with a line of rhinestone rosette ornaments along its low sweeping neckline. The skirt of the dress was gored and created an elongated trumpet bell shape like the gently opening head of a longiflorum lily. It was trimmed around the bottom with tiny rows of silk drawn in careless folds and held at intervals by large bows. She wore buff-colored gloves and gently waved a fan of ostrich feathers. Men's eyes were nailed to Norine the whole night and they passed her and Del's table every time they went to the bar or restroom even if wasn't even slightly on their way. Del was afraid they were going to wear a path in the carpet.

"You are an absolute vision tonight, Norine," Nap told her admiringly as he breathed in her expensive perfume. "If you were my wife I'd never

The Only Del

want to leave home."

"How would you take me shopping?" asked Norine.

Nap burst out laughing. Hearing him, Del asked what she'd said.

"Your breath-taking but candid wife has pointed out very succinctly why she and I could never have married."

Norine put her hand on Del's arm and smiled up at him. "My *husband* sees that all of my needs are satisfied, especially when it comes to diamonds. You know a girl can never have enough."

"I'll have to remember that when I get serious about courting," said Nap.

Del winked at him and said, "My friend, the twinkle of the jewelry you buy a girl means more than the twinkle in your eye."

Chapter Twenty Three

"Why Not a Baker's Dozen?"

There was still a buzz in the newspapers about Del's wonderful batting a month after the '99 season ended. He left Norine and Florence for a few days and went to Cleveland, where he had a carpenter make him a pair of 48-ounce bats, and then went to his parents for some "Irish turkey." After spending some time at his brother Tom's downtown "wet emporium" he went to see the gang at Fire Hall Number Five.

"Well if isn't Edward Delahanty, the grandest bat wielder in the hemisphere," teased Mike Whalen, who'd retired but came in for a visit when he'd heard Del would be stopping by.

"Begorrah! It's none uther. Come ta see the wretched likes uv us then, can you just imagine," added Sean Murphy.

"Stop yerselves," said Del. "Where's the captain? I brought him a box of cigars."

"Away at some big meeting," said Murphy. "You can leave um with us."

"Not on yer life," said Del. "They'd go up in smoke like most uv the buildings you lot are supposed ta save." He went to the hansom he'd rented and got a crate. "I brought *this* for you fellas."

"Imperial Cabinet Rye," read Mike Whalen. "Well, well, well, oive heard tell uv this stuff. They call it the *devil's* cut."

"'Tis," said Del. "It can make a man do outlandish things. A woman too."

On January 24 the National League's Reduction Committee met to outlaw the kind of transfer of players that Brooklyn and St. Louis had engineered the year before and to secretly discuss the elimination of

The Only Del

Baltimore, Washington, St. Louis and Cleveland from the league. They voted in favor of going with eight teams. The committee had no idea that it was playing right into the hands of the embryonic American League. A week later the new league's owners assembled at the Hanover Hotel in Philadelphia. Lurking in the hallways were several players interested in their deliberations. They included Sam Clements, Bill Hallman, Cub Stricker, Art Irwin and several players from Philadelphia. Del was one of them.

Sixteen Phillies boarded the 1:12 train for Charlotte on March 13, even though Del had warned Shetts that leaving that day would be unlucky. He was very nearly right, the train was delayed when the one in front of it derailed. The players didn't reach Charlotte until early morning the next day and attacked the breakfast table like wild dogs. Del and Nap had each reported lighter than they had in '99, the result of a lot of hours spent in the gym and on handball courts with Mike Grady and Kid Gleason. The players shot pool after dinner most nights. Lajoie and Chiles were the best of the bunch. Del, who shot cunny-thumbed, struggled.

There was a lot of optimism that the Phillies could finally win a championship in 1900. Piatt, Donahue, and Fraser had won twenty games each in '99 and Orth had finished a terrific 14-3. Reach and Rogers had purchased Jim "the Rabbit" Slagle, who'd batted a modest .272 in his rookie season but covered a lot of territory, from the Senators to play left field. Del would move back to first base and he said he was fine with that. Since he was the captain now, it would make it easier for him to help the umpires.

Things started badly for the Phillies. In the first match between the Regulars and Yannigans Donahue and Fraser surrendered twenty-one Yannigan safeties. Three days later Colonel Rogers declared that if the work of Delahanty at the initial station continued to improve the Phillies would have no reason to worry about first base.

Word reached Charlotte that Ned Hanlon had offered Rogers $8,000 for Del's services. The *Inquirer* said Rogers would go out of business before parting with America's greatest batsman. The next day, between ads for Hunter's Baltimore Rye and Dr. Sander's Electric Belt, which was guaranteed to generate a great volume of electricity while you slept and

the greatest batsman in the land

cure any weaknesses in your body, Shetts read that Ewing had offered Rogers $15,000 for Del and Lajoie.

"With all this interest in us do you not think it's about time we were paid what superior players deserve?" Nap asked Del one afternoon while they were getting their rubdowns.

When the Phillies returned home the disgruntled players who had been holding out for more money met with Rogers. They'd learned that their tightwad owner had cleared $65,000 for the '99 season - as much as all the other teams combined. Piatt was threatening to open a bar back home in Lexington. Flick was planning to go back to Cleveland to help manage his father's chair factory. Goeckel was going to open a law practice and McFarland said he was going to be a shoemaker.

But they fell in line one after the other and signed contracts for the 1900 season. All except Billy Lauder, Nap, and Del. It had always bothered Lauder when players' shirttails hung out, so he'd invented an arrangement of belt loops to keep the shirt and trousers connected. Irate that Rogers had reneged on a promised bonus, he quit the team to go off and manufacture the devices he modestly called billauders. They never caught on and he returned to ball playing, but not for Rogers.

Nap and Del wanted an increase from the league maximum to $3,000, which it was widely-held they deserved. They were well aware of the interest in their services among owners of the American League clubs. The *Inquirer* conjectured that with the pair of them in their lineup the Phillies would have a hard row to hoe just to finish third again but that *without* them the team would cut no figure at all. The two sat out exhibition games against Montreal and everyone expected they'd be fined.

"I'm so fed up that if I could get a good-paying position in any other business I'd quit baseball altogether," Del told Norine.

Norine thought for a moment. "I'm no expert in such matters, darling, but it seems to me that if you are far more valuable to the team than the other players you should be making a lot more than they do. I'm quite certain the general manager of a railway makes ten times what a brakeman does and I know Lilian Russell makes *twenty* times what a girl in the chorus does."

The Only Del

Del met with Colonel Rogers and left his office with his still unsigned contract in his suit jacket pocket and a sour look on his face. Rogers wasn't about to budge, even though it was well known that other teams were paying their stars more than the $2,400 he was paying Del. He told reporters that he would not be placed at the mercy of the players - he was paying more than a thousand a year for them to ride trains and buses and as much as $2.50 a night for them to stay in hotels. Rogers finally compromised with his two stars. Del would get $2,400 as his base salary plus an additional $600 for his duties as captain. He lied to Lajoie about what Del was getting and tricked him into signing for $2,600.

More than ten thousand cranks showed up for the 1900 season opener in Boston. It was a wild affair with three Boston pitchers and the Phillies' Orth surrendering forty-four hits. Philadelphia led 14-4 after six and many of the Boston boosters gave up on their pets and headed for the pubs. The Beaneaters scored three in the seventh to the Phillies' two and added another run in the eighth. In the ninth the Beaneaters scored *nine* runs and the Phillies scored one to tie the mad affair at 17-17.

When the Phillies scored a pair in the tenth Del finally took out Orth and put in 205-pound "Strawberry Bill" Bernhard, a dark-eyed twenty-nine-year-old who'd seen limited work in '99. Bernhard shut down the Beaneaters in the tenth and the Phillies won at last - after two hours and ten minutes of play. Del had made twenty-one putouts at first without a single miscue and figured his new glove must already be broken in.

The next morning came news that the Phillies had bought third baseman Harry Wolverton from Chicago. When Billy Shettsline introduced sloped-shouldered Wolverton to his captain, Del, who thought Harry looked more like an accountant than a hard-nosed ballplayer, asked him if he was a college man.

"I was, but I got kicked out. There was an annoying kid in my dormitory and I was given the job of getting rid of him. I decided to make a bomb out of twine, piping, and gunpowder to scare him out. It worked a little better than I planned. The blast tore apart the pest's room and a chunk of the building as well."

the greatest batsman in the land

Del laughed. "So you went out with a bang, then. Why is it they call you Fighting Harry?"

"From when I played in Columbus. A runner spiked me when he slid into third."

"Why did you do about it?"

"I broke his nose," Wolverton explained matter-of-factly. "I could've got gangrene or lockjaw for Christ sakes."

On May Day Del made his third error of the young season. Lajoie was the star of the 11-8 win with four hits. In the Wednesday game Del made another error but handled sixteen chances efficiently and swiped two singles in a 7-5 win. Quakerdom was delighted that their heroes had put themselves a game ahead of the pack. Wolverton had three hits and made two strong throws to Del at first as the Phillies took their first game in Boston. In the second game Del made two errors but cracked a double and a home run and drove a ball to the wall in the ninth that looked like a game-winner until Stahl ran it down.

After breakfast and shaves at the barbershop their first morning in Pittsburgh Del and Nap went back up to their room. Del opened the envelope containing his month's pay and took out the check. He left the envelope and check stub on the table and went to find his tooth powder. While he was attaching a new collar to his shirt Nap looked at the stub. He assumed the amount would be exactly the same as he was getting, $216.66 a month. It read $250.

"What the hell!" he shouted as Del came back into the room.

"What's the matter?" asked Del, spearing Essex Crystal cufflinks into his sleeves.

"Rogers *lied* to me. He swore up and down I'd be getting the same as you. I'm not letting the fucker get away with this. The first chance I get … I'm going somewhere else. *Anywhere* else! Mark my words."

The Only Del

Ray Donahue had a rough day in the first of three in Steeltown. Barney Dreyfuss, the former president of the Colonels, had seen the writing on the wall and bought his way onto the Pittsburgh organization. When the National league eliminated Louisville he moved to Pittsburgh and took Fred Clarke, Honus Wagner, and outstanding young twirlers Rube Waddell and Jack Chesbro with him. In the second game against the Pirates, manager Clarke picked the wrong young ace to start. Chesbro gave up three runs in the first. Waddell came in and allowed the Phillies just one score from then on. Del was pretty sure he'd never seen a twirler throw as hard as the huge southpaw.

When he wasn't pitching, Waddell coached first. Apparently he bothered the hell out of everybody if he was on the Pirates' bench, especially humorless Fred Clarke. Waddell paid no attention whatsoever to his job. He caught bugs, did spot-on impersonations of the pitcher, drew patterns in the dirt with his spikes, and asked boosters if they would get him a soda. When runners were circling the bases Waddell made cow and pig noises or waved his arms and pretended he was stampeding a herd of cattle. Clarke tried to remove him, but the crowd howled in protest and he was forced to leave him there. Wagner and Waddell had two hits each. The rest of the Pirates did nothing. Piatt, who'd had a bitter argument with Del on the bench between innings about how to pitch to Wagner, held on for a 4-3 win.

Clarke started Chesbro again on Friday and he gave all of the Phillies fits expect Del, of whom a scribe had just written, "he is playing a far faster game at first than anyone imagined." He ranged far to his right to knock down a hot grounder in the fourth and made a perfect toss to Bernhard who had hurried over to cover the bag. Umpire Hurst called Cooley safe. Del kicked, but to no avail. The lousy call put Bernhard off his game and the Pirates started teeing off on his shoots. The result was an 11-4 loss that cut the Philly lead over the Superbas to one game.

Del and Shetts were glad when the Saturday game was rained out. The team was headed to Chicago and they were able to take an early train so the players could go out on the town after checking into their hotel. Chi Town had a different look than when Del had first come here in the late

'80's. The population had doubled since then for one thing. The buildings erected or quickly rebuilt after the Great Fire didn't look quite so fresh anymore and the trees that had been planted in its aftermath were a lot taller. Thanks to the bicycle boom, most of the roads were now paved all the way out to the countryside.

The city *smelled* different too. The just-finished Sanitary and Ship Canal had reversed the flow of the Chicago River and it now carried its industrial wastes away from Lake Michigan instead of toward it. It had been the biggest enterprise since George Pullman's army of laborers had placed 6,000 jackscrews under buildings and literally lifted the city out of the mud in the 60's. Other buildings had been dug up, put on rollers, and hauled to new locations.

Frances Willard, the ardent temperance leader, was no longer around to torment the downtown's raucous saloons. Del, Nap, Al Orth, and "Strawberry Bill" Bernhard went to a bar on Western Avenue on Saturday night. On the front was a large bell with a globe inside it with *SCHLITZ* wrapped around the equator. The place was one of the many tied houses, saloons that had gone into partnership with breweries. After being badgered by Willard and her milk-drinking cronies the town fathers had raised the license fees for taverns in an effort to drive them out of business. Instead of shutting their doors, saloon owners had gone into partnership with the highly competitive breweries. The beer makers provided the bar with pool tables, furniture, and whatever other accouterments they desired on the understanding that only their products would be on tap.

There was a sign over the highly-polished mahogany bar between the intricately patterned tin ceiling and the wainscoted wall paneling. Orth read it aloud, "Don't treat your friends at my expense. What do you suppose that means, Mush?" he asked.

"It's a warning to the bartenders not to pour their pals free drinks," Del explained.

After a couple of jars of the sudsy Schlitz and a game of darts, Del and Bill went to see "Captain Jinks of the Horse Marines" which was playing at the Garrick Theatre. Nap and Al went to a place where one of the bar's patrons had said young women stripped down to their underwear for

The Only Del

groups of men for fifteen dollars.

Lajoie got back to the hotel late. He told Del the women had actually gotten naked but were far from alluring and then climbed into bed. Nap was a big man. Del was glad he wasn't a bed hog.

Nap shook Del awake an hour later. "Mush! Wake up!"

"What?" asked Del wearily. He was drenched in sweat.

"You were having another nightmare. Were you falling again?"

"I was. It seemed like forever."

"Maybe you oughta see somebody about it. Seems like they're getting worse."

The next morning after breakfast the two friends sat in the lobby looking for unusual items in the newspapers as they often did. This time it was the classified ads.

"A young gentleman of noble family with every manly accomplishment and brilliant prospects desires to meet a lady between eighteen and twenty-five, not fat but not too lean, sound wind and mind, a good set of teeth, decent, clean, and not too talkative or overfond of dress. Object matrimony," read Del from the *Tribune's* Personal Ads.

"A refined and educated gentleman of pleasing appearance, aged forty-eight, with strict business integrity, would like to correspond with a refined lady aged between thirty and forty-five who has one hundred thousand dollars in savings in addition to a ten thousand dollar income," read Nap. "My, oh my, you can't get much more romantic than that."

Del chuckled. "Here's one, Sandy. Refined young woman of nineteen wishes to meet well-bred man who can appreciate and afford the luxury of a well-groomed companion."

"What's her address?" asked Nap. He flipped to the next page. "Say, here's something *you* could use, Mush. Joseph Fleming and Brothers are advertising their new restorative. It's called Cupidene. This great vegetable vitalizer, the prescription of a famous French physician ... curious that if he's famous they don't give his name ... will quickly cure you of all diseases of the generative organs, such as constipation, lost manhood, and

the greatest batsman in the land

exhausting drains. Prevents quickness of discharge which if not checked leads to spermathorrhoea and the horrors of impotency."

"Very funny, but *you're* the only exhausting drain I know."

Ned Garvin, the Orphans' sallow-cheeked, six-foot-three right-hander, took the mound for the Monday game. His first two pitches to Del were around his neck. The next pitch was an old school underhand rise. Del missed it by two inches. He did little better with the next two, a floater and a low curve. Garvin fanned Del his next time up, the one after, and very nearly the one after that. Del was pretty sure he'd never struck out three times, even as a rookie or after a night on the town. His teammates did a little better and the Phillies won 2-1. The two teams split the other two games and the Phillies headed to St. Louis for the last leg of their month-long road trip. Del couldn't wait to get home to his baby girl and voluptuous bride.

His mind elsewhere, Del was hitless in five at bats in the first game, a disappointing 10-5 loss. He didn't hit the ball out of the infield the next day but the Quakers eked out a 2-1 win thanks to Bernhard. On Monday Del singled off the first baseman's shin, bunted for a base hit, and ripped a pair of three-baggers to lead the Phillies to an 11-4 win and a jolly train trek home. He had begun what would be a nineteen-game streak during which he would bat .476.

Del was glad it was almost dark when he got to the town house. No kids had bugged him on the walk from the station. He'd slept well on the long ride from St. Louis. No nightmares of falling this time.

"Do you remember how we used to carry on like a couple uv love-starved rabbits when I'd get home from a long road trip?" Del asked Norine after he'd played peek-a-boo with Florence, given her a teddy bear he'd bought her, read her a story, and put her to bed.

"I do," said Norine.

Del noticed that she had her rouge and lipstick on and her hair up the way he liked it.

The Only Del

"Can you believe we were that ravenous?"

"We were *awful*. You should have been locked up as a decadent scoundrel and I should have been hauled off to a convent."

"Didn't we do the deed ten times one night?"

"I believe it was only nine but I could be mistaken. In any event, we should be more restrained tonight." Norine took off her robe. She wore nothing but a black velvet choker studded with tiny diamonds that glistened in the flickering gaslight and a seductive smile.

"Just how *restrained* were ya plannin' ta be?" gulped Del, loosening his tie and drinking in his wife's curves.

"Why don't we make it an even dozen this time?" suggested Norine.

"Why not a *baker's* dozen? I don't think thirteen'd be unlucky in the bedroom."

"We're not going to the *bedroom*."

"We aren't?"

"No. I've fixed us a love nest in the attic - so Florence won't hear you moaning."

"Or you calling out, 'Don't stop, don't you *dare* stop!'"

They only made it to eleven that night, but twice more in the morning did the trick. "And me with a double header today," Del groaned as he grabbed Norine and kissed her on his way out the door.

"You shouldn't have been so greedy," Norine scolded him.

"*Me?* I was ready to take a break after the seventh round."

"Well I wasn't. Would you like to file a complaint?"

"That me beautiful wife won't leave me alone? I don't think I'd get a whole lot uv sympathy."

Chapter Twenty Four

Drinking Alone

There was a festive parade before the Memorial Day double header. Originally called Decoration Day, the tribute to those who had died in the Civil War was now being celebrated in all the Northern cities. The first game was attended by more than 10,000 cranks delighted that their pets stood atop the league standings. Del got hit by a pitch and scored in the first game. Red Donahue's control was terrific and he needed little help.

The rooters were ushered out and more than 20,000 cranks, many of them returnees, filed through the turnstiles at Fifteenth and Huntingdon for the 4 o'clock game. To get a better view of the action, the occupants of the cold storage plant under the left field bleachers lifted the moorings off the cover of the bicycle track. Then the flooring was turned over and the boosters beneath poured out like rats being driven from the hold of a ship. Del got thunderous ovations when he slashed four hits and batted in four of the Phillies thirteen runs.

The next day, after reporting that Orth had tossed a four-hit shutout and driven a home run to win his own game and move the Phillies four games ahead of the Perfectos, Pirates, and Superbas who were all tied for second place, the newspapers told their anxious readers that Lajoie and Flick had collided on the field during the morning practice and Lajoie had been hurt. It didn't take long for the *real* story to emerge.

Del had been doing his best to maintain cordial relations among the players, but the submerged tension between Flick and Lajoie erupted when Flick picked up Lajoie's lucky bat in the clubhouse and announced that he would be using it today. Lajoie begged to differ. Flick dared Nap to stop him. In the ensuing exchange, Lajoie punched Flick a few times and Flick gave Nap a black eye and opened a cut on his face. Nap shoved Elmer into a corner and aimed another punch at his jaw. Del and the other spectators

The Only Del

to the fight cringed when Flick ducked and Nap's fist smashed into the locker behind him. Everyone could tell in an instant that Lajoie's thumb was broken.

"Serves the prick right!" yelled Fick. "I'll never play for this team again as long as that fucking Frenchman's around!"

"There are a few of us that ud be glad to see him strut around like a peacock for some other club," muttered Jimmy Slagle.

With Flick out of the lineup for a while, Chiles got the chance to fill in for him in right field. Flick was soon back in the lineup and Chiles back on the bench. Nap was suspended for his actions. Del knew it didn't matter. His friend was going to be out of the lineup for several weeks.

Del took his wife and daughter shopping the next morning at Snellenbergs. Norine bought three little dresses, a mull cap, flannel sacques, a gauze vest, and a cashmere coat for Florence and picked out a natty plaid sack spring suit with narrow cut trousers for Del. He bought a pair of black wax calfskin Oxfords and a shoe stretcher for himself, diamond-studded gloves, two summer corsets, and a golden sunburst necklace for Norine, and a white cap trimmed with bees that had little diamonds in the centers for Florence. The mining of two million carats of diamonds in South Africa had made them relatively inexpensive and Del knew how much Norine loved to wear them. He imagined his daughter would too.

The Phillies lost their last game with Chicago, split a four-game set with the Pirates, and lost two out of three to the Reds. Their lead was down to a game and a half. With Lajoie out, Del wasn't getting many good pitches to hit and he was in a slump. He broke out of it in grand style with a game-winning double off the wall in the first game against St. Louis on June 12. He had two hits in the second game, an 11-7 victory, and three in an 11-5 win in the third.

On Friday, in the first game against New York, Del threw out a runner at the plate, his fourth assist of the day, and then made a remarkable catch of a line drive down the line with the bases loaded to preserve a 3-2 win.

the greatest batsman in the land

On Saturday he went from first to third after his second single of the afternoon and deftly evaded Hickman's tag.

"Out!" declared Emslie from behind the plate.

Del reached into his mouth, pulled out his wad of Sensation Cut Plug, and threw it into left field. He glared in at Emslie. "Are ya stark-ravin' mad, Bob? Hickman missed the touch." Hickman stared off into space.

"Not from where I was," said Emslie.

"That's the problem. You needed ta be out on the bases. Whose bright idea was it ta go back to one umpire anyway?"

"Your boss, Colonel Rogers. He cost half of the men their jobs."

"Penny-clutchin' son uv a bitch," Del muttered to himself as he stomped to the bench.

The Phillies led by two runs in the ninth but the Giants loaded the bases with two outs. The game would have been over if Hickman, who'd been tagged out trying to steal, had been called out instead of safe. The Giants ended up winning.

"I hope the miser's happy," Del said to Al Orth. "Emslie's one uv the best there is and he can't call the game properly from behind the plate. A second man woulduv been right there at second ta make the damn call and we'd have won."

The Monday game was scoreless until the eighth when each team notched a run. Del singled, executed a double steal with Ed McFarland, and then scored the winning run on a high fly ball from Chiles. The Phillies clung to first by a whisker. Del and his teammates heard via telegraph the next afternoon that the Superbas had made it four straight over Boston. It was a two-team race now, the Pirates and Perfectos had fallen by the wayside. On Tuesday the Phillies knew they had to win to stay in first, but by the time Del pulled Piatt in the sixth he'd walked five batters and allowed seven runs. Del had three hits, but none that drove anyone in. He hoped the 7-1 loss wasn't a sign of things to come.

They wouldn't need to check the telegraph wires to see how the champions did in their next series. The Superbas were in town for a head-to-head

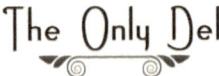

The Only Del

battle. Del singled and scored on Flick's four-base belt as the home town heroes triumphed in the opener and the Quaker crew was back in first. They led 6-3 going into the ninth in the second game but the Brooklyns scored five in the final frame. The Phillies scored four runs in the eighth and another four in the ninth to tie the third game at 13-13 only to see the Superbas win it in the eleventh. Del had tried to get the umpire to call the game on account of darkness to no avail. His club fell a game and a half behind.

As the darkening landscape of northern Pennsylvania swept past his window on the train ride to Boston Friday night Del couldn't help but think that the upcoming eighteen game road trip would be do-or-die for his club. He had little hope that the Superbas would cave anytime soon. Chick Fraser got things off on the right foot in Beantown. He stymied the Boston bats on Saturday afternoon and had three hits of his own in a 10-4 win. Del worshiped at the Church of the Holy Cross on Franklin Street on Sunday morning. He was in a foul mood having just read that Colonel Rogers had lambasted him for attempting to have the game called on Friday.

The Beaneaters lit Bill Bernhard up like a Christmas tree on Monday. It got so bad that Del sent Roy Thomas in to try his luck. Del had three hits but it scarcely mattered, Boston won 20-4. Bernhard tried again on Tuesday. He did better this time, but not much, giving up seventeen hits and losing 10-6.

Before the opener in Pittsburgh Fred Clarke made a deal with Del to play the game as fast as possible. Storm clouds were competing with the usual clouds of chimney smoke above the field. The groundskeeper had stretched large pieces of canvas over home plate and the pitching rubber. Fred Clarke had devised them. He told Del he called them tarpaulins.

Del and Shetts talked about having Lajoie test his bad thumb, but Shetts decided to give it another day or two. Chick Fraser allowed Clarke, who was in a terrible slump but happened to be married to Chick's sister, a pair of hits. The Pirates' workhorse, Sam "the Goshen Schoolmaster" Leever, held the entire Quaker team to just a pair hits in a rainy 3-0 win on Thursday. The Phillies bunched seven singles off Pittsburgh's eccentric

Rube Waddell on Friday for 4-2 win, but Deacon Phillipe held the visitors to six hits, none by Del, in the rubber match and it was be a gloomy ride to Chicago that night.

To get his mind off baseball, Del got a newspaper from the smoking car and read about the Republican National convention that was distracting Philadelphia's attention from their team's recent performance. It had just wrapped up at the Exposition Auditorium near the University of Pennsylvania. Mark Hanna, Del's fellow opera buff from Cleveland, had opened the convention. As expected, President McKinley was unanimously nominated for reelection, though Admiral Dewey had apparently given some thought to opposing him. War hero Theodore Roosevelt of New York had been nominated Vice President.

The Orphans took the Monday opener 6-0 and the Tuesday contest, which wasn't much of one at all, 9-3. West Side Grounds was the hottest place "this side of Mephistopholes' dominions" for the Fourth of July double header on Wednesday. The hosts scored six runs in the sixth and prevailed 10-4. The afternoon game was tied at threes in the ninth when Danny Green dribbled a grounder to Wolverton, who threw to Del in time for the second out. The overflow crowd implored the young umpire to declare Green safe and to the Phillies' disgust he did. Barry McCormick bunted one toward the mound. Orth fielded the ball, dropped it, retrieved it and fired it at Del's feet. The ball rolled into the spectators that stood along the first base line. Flick ran in to try to help Del find the ball. The cranks kicked it further and further out of sight as Green crossed the plate with the winning run.

The four straight losses in the Windy City left the Phillies five games back of the Superbas and just two ahead of the Pirates and Orphans. The only good news was that their next stop was in St. Louis. Even with Lajoie - wearing a plaster cast on his thumb - back in the lineup the Phillies managed just two runs, both unearned, and the Cardinals tied things in the ninth. Sudoff singled and Criger tapped a high bouncer to Piatt, who threw the ball well over Del's head. Del chased it down and fired to Wolverton at third. Unfortunately Wolverton wasn't there. The ball rolled to the bleachers and Sudofff and Criger scored. Luckily Thomas tripled in the eleventh and Del smashed one over the shortstop's head for the win.

The Only Del

Del and Nap were a combined 1-for-10 in the second game but Thomas and Slagle had three hits each as the Phillies won 10-6. The score was the same on Friday but this time it was in favor of the Cardinals.

The Phillies' visit to Cincinnati was an absolute disaster. Homesick and depressed when he arrived, Del organized a trip to the Over-the-Rhine. Nap, Ed McFarland, Pearce Chiles, Ed Orth, Bill Bernhard, and Ray Donahue agreed to go along. At the corner of Vine and McMillan they bought bratwurst and frankfurters from everyone's favorite vendor, Wienerwurst Mike. They followed them up with corn in the husk and a generous slab of melted butter from Simon the Hot Corn Man. Then it was time to wash it all down at Schuler's. The floors were sawdust and tanbark and hanging lights swayed above the drinkers. The waiters sang and the pretty dancing girls wore tights.

"Twenty-vun beers for a dollar," said the Bavarian bartender. He had plastered down hair and a handlebar mustache and he was slightly cross-eyed.

Del tossed a dollar on the bar. "That's three for each uv us, gents."

They drank their Pilsners and enjoyed the music and the dancing girls. The three pitchers decided they should head back to the hotel. McFarland, Chiles, and Nap would have gone with them, but Del persuaded them to move on to the Atlantic Garden, a popular spot for sporting types. Bob Fitzsimmons, Kid McKoy, and John L. Sullivan had all been in over the last few weeks. They staged $50 prize fights at a nearby gym. The four players had a couple of drinks there and that was enough for Chiles and McFarland. They were surprised when Del wanted to keep going.

"Come on then, there's more than a hundred saloons between McMillan and the canal," Del told them. "We've only hit two. The night is still young."

Only Nap went with Del to Gabriel's.

"I've got flips, slings, sangarees, and comperres," said the husky female bartender. "What's your pleasure?"

"They all sound good," said Del. "But oill have a double bourbon and a beer chaser."

the greatest batsman in the land

Nap stared at him. He couldn't remember the last time his friend had behaved like this. "Being captain and the team playing so terrible is really getting to you, isn't it, Mush?"

"I don't want to talk about it," grumbled Del, tossing back his bourbon.

Nap had one more drink, shrugged, and left. Del stayed.

The next day Billy Shettsline had Del sit out. The Phillies lost in the eleventh.

Del went out alone after the game. He had kidney soup, cornmeal dumplings, beef goulash, and hasenpfeffer at Foucar's on Walnut Street before heading to drown his sorrows at more of the establishments on Vine. He went to Wierlert's Garden and heard Rose Sydell sing "She Was Only a Bird in a Gilded Cage" and May Howard perform "After the Ball."

After the show he went to the Stag. "That's called the Sirens," said the owner, Dan Murphy, pointing to the painting of three nymphs frolicking in the sea above the bar. "I bought it in Paris. Set me back five thousand dollars."

Del whistled. "What's that?" he asked, pointing to a small hole on the thigh of one of the nymphs.

"A bullet hole. We had quite a ruckus in here a while back."

Del had a couple of drinks and went to Henry and Ollie's. He'd heard he could get a game of poker there. He'd been warned to be careful though, a government paymaster had been taken for $85,000 one night. Del bet carefully - until he'd had a few more drinks. Then he started to lose. The player who won most of the pots was a sad-looking fellow across the table.

"Who's that man?" Del asked the bug-eyed waiter.

"That's Frank James."

"Jesse's brother?"

"One and the same. I hear tell he's been selling shoes and taking tickets at burlesque shows since he got out of prison. Goes ta show you how far the mighty can fall."

Realizing he'd lost close to forty dollars and shaking his head about the

The Only Del

depth to which the famous Frank James had sunken, Del went to Weber's, where a strapping hellcat who introduced herself as Joanna McNamara said she could lick any man alive, and then to the Coliseum, where Del told a flirty Floradora girl he wasn't interested. He slurred when he said it. He was well into his second bottle of rye.

He went to Shickling's next. The sign out of front said, "Our doors never close." Shickling's turned out to be one stop too many. When a large, drunken teamster with a thick German accent learned that the man at the end of the bar was Big Ed Delahanty he started sounding off loud enough for everyone to hear that Hans Wagner was ten times the batter that Irish prick ever thought of being. Del ignored the galoot for a while, but when he made a few more choice remarks about the Irish being the bottom of the barrel he told the loudmouth he should go suck the kaiser's sausage and the man jumped up and took a swing at him. Del ducked and punched the man in the stomach but he hit Del hard in the jaw and staggered him a little. Before any more blows could be exchanged or the police called the barkeep intervened. Del snarled at the German, threw a bill on the bar, and left.

He sat out the second game of the series the next day, a 5-2 loss. Nap asked him where he'd gone last night and Del said, "Never mind." He played but went hitless in the third game and the Reds scored four times in the ninth to win. Del was the only Phillie to reach second after a walk and a stolen base in the fourth game. Sophomore southpaw Noodles Hahn pitched the season's first no-hitter, striking out Del and Flick twice and retiring the Phillies on five pitches in the ninth. They were eight games off the lead now.

Lajoie, Flick, and McFarland each had four hits and Wolverton had five in a make-up game in Pittsburgh on the way back home from the awful road trip. Honus Wagner took the mound for the Pirates after the visitors had scored a score of runs. The Phillies ended up winning 23-8 to make their road trip record 5-and-13.

"What happened in that saloon in Cincinnati?" Norine asked Del when he got home Friday night. "The papers just said you were sick the next day."

"I don't want to talk about it," Del grunted. He looked around and noticed some colorful new embellishments to the townhouse, Morris chairs, a carnival glass vase, chintzware pottery, a high pile Axminster carpet, feather pillows, and French shawl drapery. "I see you've been busy." He looked around again. "Where's me baby girl?"

"I took her to Nettie's. I thought you might need some time to wind down after all that happened."

Del loosened his collar, pulled off his tie, and slumped into a chair. "'Twas miserable on the road, luv. Absolutely miserable. Here I thought we were finally gointa win a championship and we're just as far back as we always are this time uv year. I'm bluddy sick uv it I am."

"Have you eaten, Del?"

"Aye. They fed us on the train."

"Then we can relax. Just the two of us. We'll go and pick up the baby and go somewhere after the game tomorrow."

Del got up and opened the window.

"You might want to pull the shade, darling," said Norine.

"Why?"

"I thought we could play your favorite game."

"Pinochle? It's not really a game for two."

"Not pinochle, silly. Your *favorite*."

"Oh, the one *you* invented," said Del, his face brightening. "Yer special version uv backgammon."

"That's the one," said Norine, going to an ornate new sideboard and getting out the teak backgammon set she'd bought Del for his birthday. "Lose a game, lose a garment."

"Can I ask ya somethin' before we start?"

"Of course."

"You're such a clever girl. How is it you lose all the time?"

"What makes you think I consider that losing?"

The Only Del

The Phillies won six straight the third week of July to move back into second place, five games back of Brooklyn and three up on Pittsburgh. In August, with Del going 9-for-63, the worst stretch of his big league career, they lost twelve out of fifteen and slid back into third, eleven games out of the lead. The newspapers were documenting the struggles of the mighty Delahanty. One scribe said, "the memory of the oldest local rooter fails to recall a season in which Del was as low on the list." By late August his average had dropped to .326. At least he was still playing a fast game at first, making remarkable stops of line drives, turning double plays, and hauling down wild throws no one expected he could reach.

He finally snapped out of his doldrums with the bat and went on a tear. He notched three hits against Brooklyn on August 28, had four in a September 3rd double header, and nine in three games against Chicago. After the September 4th game Harry Wolverton leaned out of the trolley car he took home from the park and smashed his head against a pole. The papers reported that he'd been killed. Del found out which hospital Harry had been taken to and was relieved to find that he was alive even though he had a fractured skull.

"What possessed you to do it?" Del asked Harry when he finally came to.

"A pretty woman on the street. I whistled at her and she looked to see who'd done it. She couldn't make me out so I stuck my head out the side of the trolley and the damn thing started moving. I was staring at her and didn't see the pole coming."

Wolverton returned to the lineup a few days later. His head was still sore but it was a bit wiser.

Del missed the last few games of the regular season with a split finger. Lajoie was on the sidelines too. His arm had been broken by a pitch. When the season results were announced Del's name was well down the lists of top achievers. He ranked tenth in batting at a disappointing .323 and was eighth in total bases. The only categories in which he had fared as well as he usually did were his second place finish in runs batted in and his third place showing in doubles. He took some solace in the fact that he had been among the league's best fielding first basemen but told reporters that relearning his old position had been a distraction from his work with the bat.

the greatest batsman in the land

Ed and Norine left the baby with Nettie and went to New York for a romantic get-away. When they stepped off the train they took the Third Avenue trolley to the north end of Highbridge Park and checked into the Fort George Hotel at the crest of a hill that overlooked the Harlem River. A harness-racing speedway ran along it. In the 1870's New York City had become a mecca for "wealthy roadites," fabulously rich men who enjoyed racing along the city's streets. Harlem Lane, which later became Seventh Avenue, was widely considered the best of New York's roadways for racing and wealthy men from William K. Vanderbilt on down had torn along it at breakneck speeds. As the city grew, the excessive speeds of these horsemen and their carriages sparked growing alarm. Trolleys and congested traffic compounded the dangers caused by the sportsmen but the police and the judges were reluctant to sentence the influential roadites for their bad behavior.

Eager to find a solution that would allow New York's elite to engage in their favorite sport, several officials recommended the construction of a speedway through Central Park. But the park, which had opened in 1857, was a favorite of both the wealthy and the poor, who saw it as an oasis within the rapidly expanding city. In '93, the mayor offered a compromise, a 2¼ mile track along the Harlem River. The new speedway would be carved out of the bluffs overlooking the river. Varying in width from seventy-five to one hundred feet and running from 155th Street to Dyckman, the road would allow several carriages to run abreast of one another. The sides of the road were landscaped with deep, tree-lined trenches. When completed, the picturesque nature of the roadway charmed the city's residents and visitors. But the best part of this "magnificent roadway" was the fact that Gothamites of all classes could watch the races from a safe distance on the sidelines.

When the speedway opened in July of 1898 the cream of New York society brought their "trotting and pacing stock" to the track. In coming years the question would arise as to whether the speedway should be opened to automobiles. The race course would eventually be given a more sedate name, the Harlem River Driveway, and it would become one of the most important north-south access roads in the city. When it was opened for automobile traffic many drivers who got stopped for speeding on the

parkway would innocently plead that they were only abiding by the intent of the road's original designers.

As the wealthy racers shot by them Ed thought he recognized a couple of the swells from the Opera Club smoker he'd attended three or four years ago. He'd read about a Gentlemen's Dinner held at Sherry's restaurant by the Turtle Bay Beefsteak Club that had become a scandal in '96. The Seeley brothers, well-to-do nephews of the late P.T. Barnum and members of the Larchmont Yacht Club, had hosted it. They'd begun their preparations for the occasion by obtaining the services of an "entertainment caterer" who specialized in booking acts sure to appeal to gentlemen's baser desires. He'd told the caterer he needed something red hot, not Sunday School fare.

The guests ate a thirteen-course dinner and then listened to the throaty and sexy Lottie Gibson the "Little Magnet" sing "You're Not the Only Pebble on the Beach." Just before 11 p.m. William S. Moore of 207 West Fortieth Street arrived at the Nineteenth Precinct Police station in the tenderloin, where he breathlessly informed the precinct captain George S. Chapman that something indecent was transpiring in a private dining room at Sherry's restaurant. He reported that Little Egypt had been booked to dance naked and that Minnie Renwood would appear in a Trilby costume. Shortly thereafter Captain Chapman arrived on the scene with two detectives but no warrant. Hearing clapping and shouting from rooms upstairs they climbed a fire escape to the source of the excitement. They were met at the top by a waiter. When they asked him the way to the banquet room he took them through a dressing room where they discovered eight half-naked women and some gentlemen who were sans certain articles of clothing.

The newspapers got wind of the raid and expected that several of the attendees would be filing charges against the police captain. The subsequent inquiry ordered by New York Police Commissioner Theodore Roosevelt was greatly impeded by everyone's unwillingness to name body parts that may have been exposed and possibly groped. "Upper and lower quarters" were referred to and "stomach" substituted for loins. When a witness ventured to say breast or thigh his testimony was described as "pure filth." It had been revealed, however, that one man had cut the straps of an entertainer's dress and that at least one gentleman had mauled a dancer.

the greatest batsman in the land

The "gentlemen" had been humiliated and some of their wives hadn't spoken to them for months.

Del was glad he hadn't attended any more smokers. He didn't have much need to look for excitement, his young wife provided plenty of that. Their sleeping room at the Fort George, which set Del back three dollars a night, had a private bath tub. After they got back from watching the roadites they went for dinner. Del had read that the hotel featured "open-air dancing" and he was anxious to waltz with his gorgeous bride. They made a big splash on the dance floor, falling into step with one another as though they were professional dance partners. When they finally stopped for punch on the moonlit veranda Del pulled at his collar.

"It seems we've worked up a sweat, my sweet," Norine told Del.

"It's hot as blazes in there," said Del, downing his punch in one gulp.

"I'm afraid I'll need to use that tub when we get back to the room," purred Norine. "Perhaps you could join me."

Del looked at Norine's breasts. "Will ya be takin' *them* in with you?"

"I suppose I shall have to. Will that be a problem for you?"

"I don't know. The tub looked pretty small," said Del.

"I'll do my best to squeeze you in," Norine whispered in Del's ear.

They went to the Fort George Amusement Park the next day. It featured sideshows, shooting galleries, and penny arcades. Norine wanted to go on the Ferris wheel but knew better than to ask Ed after what had happened in Atlantic City. He bought steaming-hot pretzels and then tried his luck at one of the shooting galleries. He didn't fare too well and decided the gallery was fixed, the targets moving just enough that you missed. After losing twenty-five cents Ed moved over to a booth at which you could win stuffed animals by throwing baseballs through small hoops. Not surprisingly, he did much better with his arm than he had with the gun.

By the time he'd won a big stuffed panda for Norine and another stuffed animal for the baby a small crowd had formed.

"That man sure throws hard," a little boy told his father.

The Only Del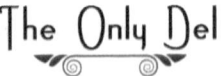

"And he never misses," said a tall man in spectacles who was standing behind the boy.

"Wait a minute," said another man. "That's Ed Delahanty from the Phillies!"

"You're right! It is Delahanty," said the little boy's father.

"No wonder he throws so well," said the boy.

The booth owner was a recent immigrant from Germany. He'd never attended a baseball game but he knew what baseball was and he knew that some of the men who played it were professionals.

"Get out uff here," he yelled at Ed.

"Thanks fer givin' me up, mister," he told the man who'd recognized him.

Deciding that they were thirsty, Ed and Norine went and drank beer from tall, chilled glasses at the German beer garden. Norine didn't feel like sitting for long. She wanted to go to a fortune teller's tent they'd passed. She told her still thirsty husband she'd be only a few minutes and scurried off.

The old woman inside the tent was Hungarian and spoke with a thick accent. Norine gave her a dime and asked her if Nettie would ever find a husband. The fortune teller gazed earnestly into her crystal ball and said that Nettie would, a bookkeeper or bank clerk. Norine asked if Florence would grow up healthy. The woman peered into her ball again and said she could see a teenage girl riding in a horseless carriage.

"Am I with her?"

"Yes."

"How do I look?"

"Older and a little heavier. But still very pretty."

Norine smiled.

"But sad," added the woman.

Norine frowned.

"Is my husband driving the motor car?"

Norine gasped when the woman said, "No. You have no husband."

the greatest batsman in the land

The next afternoon Ed and Norine watched the racers on the Speedway and then had drinks at the hotel's parlor bar. They had steak and lobster for supper in the hotel dining room. Norine hadn't told Ed what the fortune teller had said, or that her words had given her nightmares. After coffee and ice cream they went to the Trocadero music hall, which was packed. They listened to the Perkins Band and danced to the Pantzer Trio. Then they went to the casino. Norine was delighted when Del won a hundred dollars. He didn't tell her that after she'd fallen asleep after their fun in the tub he'd snuck out to the casino and *lost* three hundred.

The Only Del

Chapter Twenty Five

It Still Doesn't Fit

On October 13th Ban Johnson, who had done an enviable job of reducing the incidents of kicking, rowdyism, spiking, and brick-throwing in his new league - primarily by supporting his hand-picked umpires to the hilt - announced that the American League would no longer field teams in Kansas City and Minneapolis. He was on his way to Washington to check out possible sites for a baseball park there. Baltimore and Philadelphia would be his next stops. He also announced that his clubs would pay doctor's bills if a player got hurt during a game. In stark contrast, the St. Louis Cardinals owners refused to pay their players for the last month of the season, citing the late hours they had been keeping. NL President Young stated that his league held exclusive rights to Washington and Baltimore. Arrogant Colonel Rogers told reporters that he'd *welcome* another team in Philadelphia.

In December, the tunnel-visioned National League owners' representatives met with the Players Protective Association leaders, listened to their demands, and rejected every single one of them. Instead, they voted to cut costs by reducing rosters to sixteen in order to pressure players into signing contracts. The *Inquirer* contrasted "the straightforward business practices of the American League to the rubber shoe tactics that the National League magnates had been employing ever since they took control of professional baseball for their own sordid ends."

In March of 1901 the National League owners met at the Fifth Avenue Hotel in New York. In what the *Inquirer* described as "a sickening exhibition of self-stultification" they agreed to limit the hated reserve clause to two years and not transfer a player without his consent. It was too little too late. Once they had finished patting one another's backs they decided upon three rule changes. Catchers would now be required to position themselves

The Only Del

under the bat, a hitter would no longer be awarded first base when struck by a pitched ball, and foul balls would now be counted as strikes, unless the batter had already been assessed two of them. Roy Thomas, who had worked an astonishing number of walks, was the fillip for the new rule. In a game in August enraged Reds' pitcher Bill Phillips had stormed off the mound and punched Thomas in the face after he'd fouled off ten of his best shoots.

In a brilliant ploy, the American League managers agreed not to go after any Pittsburgh players. Their plan was to keep the Pirates so strong they'd make a farce of the National League pennant race. Nap Lajoie's Valentine present to the Philly cranks who'd booed him when he returned from his broken thumb was the news that he had signed to play for Connie Mack, the manager of the new American League team in Philadelphia. It didn't come as news to Del. He'd known ever since his friend found out that Colonel Rogers had double-crossed him and then denied it there was no chance Nap would be a Phillie in '01.

At the end of February, rumors surfaced that Mack was looking to sign more disgruntled Phillies. Ed Delahanty was high on his shopping list. Mack managed to bag three of Rogers' twirlers, Chick Fraser, Bill Bernhard and Wiley Piatt, the core of the staff. He signed Christy Mathewson as well. Mathewson accepted advance money from the Athletics but then reneged.

On March 28 Colonel Rogers filed for an injunction against Lajoie, Bill Bernhard, and Chick Fraser playing for any team but his. Del had no desire to be dragged into court. He sent a telegram to Billy Shettsline that he should send him a contract for the upcoming season and ask Colonel Rogers to send him a $500 advance on his salary.

When Rogers' check arrived, Del packed up Norine and Florence and headed to New Orleans for Mardi Gras and some fun and sun before the start of what promised to be a very chilly spring training. Rogers had decided his team would train in Philadelphia this year. Norine knew there was another reason her husband had chosen New Orleans for their vacation. He'd read her an article by Frank Bryan of the *Evening Journal* that said the Crescent City was "a horse racing point of the first class, offering the most important winter racing in America." Del hadn't mentioned that he'd received some hot tips from Felix Carr.

the greatest batsman in the land

They rode in style on the Washington & Southwestern Limited. The brochure hailed it as "a service second to none in completeness and elegance of detail ... providing all the latest facilities for the comfort and enjoyment of our patrons." The *Vestibule*, so named because it was the South's first all-year train with vestibuled equipment, lived up to its billing. Its drawing rooms, stateroom sleeping cars, dining, smoking, library, and observation cars were the height of luxury. They were gas-lit and equipped with hot and cold running water. The vestibuled platforms proved an interesting novelty; many passengers spent considerable time walking from one car to another just to enjoy the unusual experience of being able to do so without having their hats blown off. Ed and Norine were glad to have a stateroom with a separate bedroom for Florence.

They stayed at the Dauphine Orleans; the more opulent Monteleone was fully booked. Norine was glued to the desk clerk's every word when he warned her and Ed to be on the lookout for the Lost Bride Ghost.

"We think she's the spirit of a young woman named Millie who was a ... courtesan at May Bailey's house of ill repute. She fell in with a young Confederate soldier and he proposed to her. She became obsessed with the wedding preparations, the reception that was to be held in our ballroom, and creating the perfect gown. The morning of the ceremony her groom was shot in a dispute over a poker game. Millie was despondent and took to wearing the gown around May Bailey's. Ever since she died she's walked the halls of the hotel wearing it."

"You've *seen* her?" asked Norine.

"Every time I work the night shift. Gives me the creeps just talking about it, but the manager says I should warn people so they don't have a heart attack."

Ed and the girls had lunch at the Commander's Palace on Washington Avenue the next afternoon. Norine had stayed up late watching for Millie. Then they went for a ride on a riverboat. The next day Florence stared wide-eyed at the strangely-clad participants and the floats - brilliantly-colored replica dragons, Indian tepees, and royal coaches - in the Rex Parade along Canal Street. She was a little frightened by the hooded horses though. Ed caught someone wearing a carnival mask trying to relieve him

The Only Del

of his wallet and turned him over to the police. The pickpocket turned out to be a she not a he, a frail woman in her thirties.

"As I live and breathe. If it isn't Minnie Williams, queen of the pickpockets," said the grizzled policeman when he pulled off the woman's mask. "She's here every year."

"She is?" asked Ed.

"Got yer start at the Diamond Jubilee, didn't you, Minnie," said the cop.

"My, but that was a swell affair," said Minnie. "I made a bloody fortune."

For lunch, the Delahantys went to Antoine's on St. Louis Street for creole fare. Norine read the menu, which was in French, and discovered there wasn't much on it for a baby so they decided to come back another time when Florence wasn't with them. In '93 electric trolleys had replaced the city's mule-drawn streetcars. Norine and Ed, carrying little Florence, boarded one to head back to the Dauphine Orleans and found seats near the back. A lovely girl with light brown skin in a striking dress followed them onto the trolley and sat down beside Norine. They smiled at one another. The middle-age woman on the other side of Norine whispered, "When one of these mulatresses flounces on board in all her finery and then almost sits down on top of a white woman it's enough to make a person's blood boil."

Ed held Florence up to the window so she could see the passing sites and Norine outraged the disgruntled woman by starting up a conversation with the pretty Creole.

"Comment-allez vou?" Norine asked the girl, who appeared to be a couple of years younger than she.

"Je vais bien," said the girl, delighted to have someone to speak with in her childhood tongue.

"Où achetez-vous cette charmante robe?"

"Dans un magasin jusqu'à la rivière à Carrollton, près de la House of the Rising Sun."

"Merci, madamoiselle," Norine thanked the girl. She turned and looked hopefully at Ed.

"I take it a magasin is a store," he said. "Of course you can go there. Did you really think I wasn't expecting you to shop? You're gointa have to take Florence along though, I made a couple uv calls last night and arranged to work out with the Pelicans at Athletic Park."

Ed woke from another nightmare about falling their third night in town and thought a burglar was trying to get into their room. It turned out to be Norine standing in the doorway with a candle. She was watching for Millie.

When he got back from the ballpark the next afternoon Ed asked Mae, their colored maid, if she would watch Florence so he and Norine could step out. Mae was always fussing over Florence and asking Norine if there was anything she could get for the precious child. Ed knew Mae was trustworthy. Twice he'd left money lying around the room and it hadn't disappeared. Mae said she'd been expecting him to ask and that she'd be happy to watch Florence.

Del and Norine, who wore a stunning blue velvet dress, had a light dinner at Tujague's and then went to the Sazarac, a bar in the French Quarter.

"Why aren't there any ladies of the evening here?" Ed asked a jolly-looking man at the next table. "Not that I'm looking for one, it just seems like the kind uv place you might see them."

"They're all in Storyville," the man replied.

"Storyville?"

"Yes, Storyville. Three years ago a city alderman named Sidney Story who'd visited cities in European proposed an ordinance to control prostitution and drugs. The city designated a sixteen-block area in the Fauborg Treme neighborhood as a place where hookers could ply their trade legally and folks started calling it Storyville."

"I'm sure the alderman's thrilled about that," chuckled Del as a comely waitress set a bourbon in front of him and then a glass of cognac in front of Norine, whom she eyed up and down jealously.

The man checked out the waitress and continued. "The establishments in Storyville range from cheap cribs where you can be ... taken care of for twenty-five cents to elegant mansions for well-heeled clientele along Basin

The Only Del

Street where you might pay as much as ten dollars."

"Ten dollars!" said Norine, who couldn't help but be fascinated.

"Saloons and restaurants are opening up between the brothels and they're doing land-office business," the man continued. "I'm told Storyville is getting to be the most popular tourist destination in New Orleans. They've even started selling blue books with descriptions of the services, prices, and stock - from African ebony to Swedish blonde - each house offers. Say, do you folks like music?"

"We *love* music," said Norine.

"Well there are some places on Franklin Street just west of Basin where you can hear the Creole music they're calling jass."

"Can you think of the names of any of the places?" asked Del.

The man thought for a moment. "One's called the pig something. Wait. The Pig Ankle Cabaret. I heard there's a nicer one though. It's got a number. The Twenty Eight Club I think it's called. I haven't frequented any of the whorehouses in Storyville ..."

Del and Norine smiled. "*Obviously not*," said Del.

"But I'm *told* they've hired colored musicians to play this jass for their customers while they wait for their favorite girl. That's why the white folks are calling jass *bawdyhouse* music."

Del and Norine took a hansom cab to Franklin Street, where they were relieved to see a large number of policemen on duty, and went to the Honky Tonk. They listened to the raunchy music and had French onion soup, catfish and fried pig's feet, and then walked to The Hot Cat, which was full of drunken packet captains and roustabouts from the riverboats who ogled Norine lasciviously. They declined the Irish bartender's offer of a new drink made of California claret and something he said could be purchased at any of the drug stores in town called cocaine. They finished off their night at the Twenty Eight Club, enjoying the jass and listening to spasm bands play "Funky Butt" and "My Bucket's Got a Hole in It" but finding the music unsuited to any kind of dancing they knew.

the greatest batsman in the land

The next afternoon Ed and Norine left Florence with Mae and headed to the track. They were amazed to see that there were close to eight thousand people at the Fair Grounds. Women were admitted free and there were a lot of pretty ones with old-fashioned bustles, enormous bonnets, and colorful parasols. Ed bought a program and poured over it while Norine sipped on her sherry cobbler and tried to pick out the richest people in the stands. Then he checked what the *Breeder and Sportsman* had to say about the mounts.

When he was still reading twenty minutes later and Norine was getting bored she asked Ed why he was taking so long. He set down the program and looked at her. "Have I ever told you that you're beautiful," he asked.

"All the time. Now why are you reading so earnestly?"

"There's a lot you need to know before you place your bets. How long the race is, whether it's a dash or a heat race, a heavy or light track, whether a horse is built for speed or endurance, how old it is, how many races it's been in and won, who the jockey is, how good his record is, whether he uses the long stirrups and stands up old style like Fred Taral or Snapper Garrison or Isaac Murphy or crouches like Todhunter Sloan. Sometimes a clever rider can win with a second-rate mount."

Ed bought another sherry cobbler for Norine and a bourbon and branch water for himself and went to one of the nineteen bookmakers' booths to place a bet. His horse did well and Ed won twenty dollars. After he won fifty on a daily double a man with horn-rimmed glasses came up and introduced himself.

"Aren't you Ed Delahanty?" the man asked.

"I am," said Del.

"I thought so. I was just telling Frank Thorp from the Evening World I thought I'd seen Ed Delahanty in the crowd."

"And you are . . ."

"Sorry. I'm Frank Bryan, from the Evening Journal."

"He's the man who wrote that article you read to me last week," said Norine.

The Only Del

Bryan looked at Norine for the first time. "I'm a reporter so it's my job to pry. Does your *wife* know you're down here sashaying around with a gorgeous model, Ed?" Bryan asked.

"This is me wife," said Del.

"It is? I mean you are," he said to Norine. "I *knew* I should have tried harder on those sandlots."

Norine smacked Bryan lightly with her parasol.

"Why don't the two of you come down to the reporters' apartment," suggested Bryan, pointing to a large tent between the finish line and the Western Union stand where the race results were being wired to billiard parlors and gaming houses up north. "We write nice things about the racetrack and they supply us with a smorgasbord of food and potables."

"I *would* like to get out of the sun for a bit, Del," said Norine.

When they got to the 'apartment' they saw that Bryan had not exaggerated. Salmon, oysters, cheese, and roast beef were chilling on ice and there was a lot of beer on ice as well. Del recognized a man standing in the corner. He put out his arm for Norine and led her over to meet him.

"This is Frank James," he told Norine.

"The train robber?" blurted Norine. She blushed. "I am so sorry, Mister ..."

"Never mind. I get that wherever I go. I did my time and there's no point lying about who I am."

"I'm Ed Delahanty, I play for the Phillies. And this is my wife Norine. How did you do at Henry and Ollie's?"

James looked puzzled.

"I saw you there a while ago when we played in Cincinnati."

"I did very well that night. Won enough to come down here and play the ponies."

"Glad to hear it."

"Say, Ed," whispered James. Del leaned closer. "You need to be careful. There are some nefarious characters around here. The Crescent City Jockey Club is investigating some of its members. They've heard veiled

the greatest batsman in the land

suggestions of dirty money and shady practice."

"You know I could uv sworn I saw one uv the jockeys holdin' his mount back when he could uv won. Thanks for the warning, Frank."

Another man was coming over so they broke off their conversation. He was tall and had small bags under his eyes. "Why if it isn't the Only Del. I'm Frank Thorp from the Evening World. Frank Bryan told me you were here. And he said I should check out … I mean *meet* your lovely wife. A pleasure to meet you Missus Delahanty."

Norine shook his hand and excused herself to get a glass of wine and some salmon. "I'm one of the many New Yorkers who would love to see you playing at the Polo Grounds, Del," said Thorp. "And I don't mean for the Phillies."

"I've heard there are a few people that'd like me to go over to the Giants," said Del.

"A *few*? Try a few *thousand*. Pretty well every baseball crank in Gotham is dying for the club to get you."

"We'll see what happens this year with the new league and all. I'm not gointa be in a rush to sign back on with the Phillies next fall."

After tucking Florence in that night Norine disappeared. Ed figured she must be off on the hunt for the ghost bride again. It turned out she'd been in the bathroom all along. She came out dressed in the French Coutel corset she'd worn on their honeymoon.

"It still fits," announced Norine, with a twinkle in her eye.

Del looked at his wife's breasts, which were spilling out of the top of the corset. "You mean it still *doesn't* fit," he chuckled.

When the Phillies played their usual exhibition games against the Montreal club at the beginning of April, Del was at first base and batting in his familiar spot behind Thomas and Slagle, but with Flick batting behind him now instead of Lajoie. The club hadn't been able to practice much. As the players had expected, it was too damn cold. Del was more

The Only Del

concerned about the Phillies' decimated pitching staff than he was about the temperature. Shetts had brought in "Frosty Bill" Duggleby, who didn't make the slightest effort to learn the names of his new teammates. The surly Duggleby wore a black suit everywhere he went. Del thought it matched his mood. In stark contrast was another new addition, carefree "Happy Jack" Townsend. He was also known as "the Whirlwind" because of his blazing shoots. Problem was Jack had little idea where they'd go. He'd once walked seventeen men in nine innings.

At 3 o'clock on Opening Day in Philadelphia, after a concert by the First Regiment band, captains Joe Kelley and Ed Delahanty pulled the halyards and unfurled Old Glory to wintry blasts that blew hundreds of colored balloons aloft. In Box 13 Colonel Rogers handed the ball to Mayor Ashbridge who proceeded to drop it. The umpire picked up the no longer snow white sphere and threw it to the Phillies' twirler Jack Dunn. He'd scarcely pitched last year and this would be his only appearance of '01. He gave up six runs in the first inning and Dunn was done for the season. Years later, as owner of the Baltimore Orioles of the International League, he would discover and sign a teenage pitcher from St. Mary's Industrial School named George Herman Ruth who would quickly be nicknamed Dunn's Babe. Duggleby took over and gave up another half dozen. Del, who struck out twice on slow balls and got hit by another one, was one of six Phillies not to bat one out of the infield the next day as Townsend lost 10-2.

With the score knotted at twos on Monday Del corked a bases-loaded triple to give Al Orth his first win. Del went hitless in a 4-3 loss on Friday after two days of cold April showers. A few blocks away at Columbia Park Napoleon Lajoie had three hits in the Athletics' first game. He had another three in their next game as well. The pitching in the infant league was not of the highest quality and Nap was going to feast on it.

The Phillies took three out of four from the Giants and then lost five of their next six. Their lone win came on Saturday, May 3 when Del had just his second multiple hit game of the season off the Superbas' Doc McJames. They were swept by the Giants in New York. Christy Mathewson shut them out in the first game on five hits.

the greatest batsman in the land

The seventh-place Phillies finally got going in Boston on Saturday, May 11 off thirty-one-year-old Kid Nichols. The four-time thirty game winner had won only thirteen in '01. Then they split four with the Pirates. Del knocked a two-run double in the tenth to win the second game. He was glad to outshine Honus Wagner, who went 2-for-15 in the series. Del, who was 8-for-18, thought about what the drunken German at Shickling's had said to him and chuckled.

The Orphans came to town on Saturday, May 18. Ed was happy the Phillies had re-signed Bill Hallman, who'd been released by the Cleveland Blues of the rival league. Bill, Del, and Monte Cross turned swift double plays to squelch Chicago rallies in the first game, a 4-0 shutout for Duggleby. Del had no idea why Shetts had signed Shad Berry. He'd been released by Boston after batting just .236 last year and getting off to a .175 start in '01. At least he came in handy when Roy Thomas missed a couple of the Chicago games because he'd cut his hand opening clams. Shetts had Barry lead off in the second game and he predictably went 0-for-4 against Rube Waddell, whom the Pirates had let go because he'd driven Fred Clarke to distraction. Ed managed only a single but Doc White outdueled the Orphans' wacky new ace.

Del drove in three runs in the Phillies 5-3 victory in the third game. It would have been more if Thomas had been leading off instead of the again hitless Berry. Waddell pitched the next day too so he could take a few days off to go fishing and allowed just six hits, two by Ed, but the Phillies scored one run in the seventh and another in the eighth when the southpaw started to flag.

After sweeping the Chicagos the Phillies split two with the Cardinals, took two out of three from the Reds, and downed Brooklyn in a make-up game before heading off on a thirteen-game road trip. They were just a game behind league-leading New York but it was an ominous sign that the formerly hard-hitting Quakers had only one man over .300, Harry Wolverton. As expected, Thomas was struggling with the foul strike rule and so was Slagle. Del just wasn't being Del. The 4-and-9 trip ended with a pair of losses in front of tiny crowds in Boston and the Phillies limped home to lick their wounds.

The Only Del

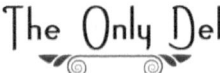

When Ed got home Nettie was there. She told him about an interesting man she had met and he hoped this fellow would be the one. She took Florence from her daddy's arms and said, "I know you two want to be alone tonight to celebrate ..." Norine shot her a disapproving look.

"At any rate, this little dumpling is coming with me. We're going to bake a cake tonight." Florence's eyes lit up. She hugged her father, grabbed her bonnet, and headed out the door with her Auntie Nettie.

Del looked around the townhouse. He didn't notice any new additions this time, not even pillows or knick knacks, only some fresh-cut flowers. "Have you not been to any stores while I was away, me pet?"

"Maybe," she said.

"Which ones? I don't see anything new."

"I'll show you later."

"What was that yer sister was saying about us needin' ta celebrate?"

"Nothing. Just your coming home."

"Are ya *sure*? Do ya not think she might uv be referrin' to our fifth anniversary?"

Norine smiled and hugged Del. "I was afraid you'd forgotten."

"*Forgotten*? *Me*? Not on yer life. I even found out what you're supposed ta give somebody for their fifth anniversary. It's supposed ta be somethin' made uv wood. Isn't that right?"

"Uh ... yes, you're right," said Norine half-heartedly.

Del reached into his left pocket and pulled out a box. He handed it to Norine. When she opened it she found a small wood-carved royal carriage. She looked at the little coach. Del could see the disappointment in her eyes.

"And see?" he said, opening up the back of the carriage. "There's a wee place fer the prince and princess to put their luggage."

"That's very cute," said Norine.

"Do you know what else you could put in there?"

"What?" she asked, puzzled.

the greatest batsman in the land

"This," said Del, taking a velvet case from his other pocket and handing it to Norine.

Her eyes widened. She opened it and found a sparkling silver tiara lined with diamonds and a pair of matching diamond earrings. "Oh, *Del*," she gasped. "They're wonderful. I can't wait to wear them to the opera."

"Did ya get *me* somethin'?"

"Not exactly."

"What's that supposed ta mean?"

"I got *several* things. But for *myself*."

"Fer yerself? I don't understand."

"They're things I'm going to wear. To *entertain* you."

Del was still confused.

"Remember those bachelor dinners you told me you used to be invited to in New York, the ones where the men had women dance for them in slinky outfits."

"Yes."

"Well I went to a costume store and bought myself a few."

Now *Del's* eyes widened. Norine put up her index finger and bent it in toward herself. "Follow me," she said.

She led Del into the bedroom where she pulled a trunk out from underneath the bed. As she held up each of the costumes she'd bought Del recognized them with delight and envisioned his gorgeous wife in them.

Norine beamed and giggled as Del identified them. "A French maid. A genie. Little Red Riding Hood. A belly dancer. An Indian maiden. Cleopatra? *Damn*! Now I'm gointa have the same problem Nap told you he'd have if *he* was married to you."

"You mean you won't ever . . . "

"That's right. I'm never gointa wanna leave the house. Which outfit is it you're wearin' tonight, me little vixen?"

The Only Del

"*That* is a surprise," she teased, starting to unbutton her blouse. "Now get out of here while I slip into one of these."

When she came out five minutes later Del was fully aroused in anticipation. Norine was an exotic belly dancer - with a diamond in her bellybutton.

"Happy Anniversary, Sultan!" she said as she shoved Del back onto the settee and started to writhe in front of him.

Chapter Twenty Six

A Chance at a Championship

Del was worn out but still grinning the next day. Norine had reappeared as an Indian maiden after her belly dance and the passion that had ensued from it. Del slashed three hits and drove in two runs, but the batters behind him were a collective 0-for-8 and the Phillies lost 6-3. After the game Shetts announced that the team had bought Hugh Jennings from Brooklyn. Del was delighted to hear that Shetts planned to use Jennings, who was too old now to play shortstop anymore, at first base so Del could return to left field. It was presumed that Jennings, who'd been a team captain for six years, would take over as the Phillies' captain, but nothing was said of it.

Del was awful at the plate in a double header split with the Cardinals on Thursday. He was 1-for-7 and popped out with the bases loaded in the ninth inning of the late game. Hugh Jennings didn't play on Friday but he did take some groundballs at first base. Del was infuriated when he learned that Rogers had paid $6,000 for the 32-year old and that he would be making more money than Del. As if to show the owner which of his players was the most important to his team Del singled and scored in the first inning, hit the longest home run ever seen at Huntington Grounds in the third, and doubled to the left field wall his last time up.

Jennings went hitless on Saturday. None of his new teammates did much better. Except Del, who had four hits in five at bats. He was one of five Phillies to garner three hits on Monday in a 19-1 decimation of the Reds. Jennings was embarrassed when he was pinned with an 0-for-5 collar. Al Orth shut out the Reds on four hits on Tuesday for a sweep of the Cincinnatis.

A rainout the next day created a double header against Chicago on Thursday. Del led the way in a 16-7 win in the morning game with a walk, two singles, a double, and two three-baggers. The crowd went wild every

The Only Del

time he came to the plate.

Norine and Florence were in the crowd for the afternoon game. Florence had her little hands over her ears when her father batted in the eighth with his club trailing by two runs.

"The people are really excited to see Daddy, aren't they Mommy?" shouted Florence through the din.

"They certainly are," chuckled Norine.

Some of the cranks who were heading for the exits heard a roar and stopped to watch. The *Times* raved about Del's performance.

> The mighty Del appeared at the bat and it sounded as though Bedlam had been turned loose. Cheer after cheer rent the air and the fondest hopes were kindled in the rooters' breasts while the great batsman fouled off five swift ones. The sphere came sizzling across the plate again and Del swung with every once of strength in his muscular frame. Far out across the field he drove the ball and by the time Hartsell relayed it back to the infield both runners had scampered home and Del resided on third.

Flick singled and Del scored the winning run a minute later to a deafening ovation.

"Did Daddy do something good?" Florence shouted at her mommy. "The people sound happy."

Norine hugged Florence and said. "Yes, baby, your daddy likes to make people happy."

"It looks like *he's* having fun too."

Del singled twice and sent a ball to the clubhouse for a triple on Saturday to drive in three of the Phillies' four runs in their third straight win over Chicago. Now they trailed by only two. The *Pittsburgh Press* calculated that Del was leading all National League batters with a .387 average. The Phillies lost two out of three to the first-place Pirates and needed to do better against the Cardinals. Duggleby got roughed up for thirteen hits in the first of two on the Fourth of July. Del hit two balls to the wall. Normally they would have been home runs but with thousands of cranks lining the outfield a special ground rule was in effect and he had to settle for a triple each time. Orth did much better in the matinee, hurling a four-hit shutout. The Phillies headed to the train station for a long ride to St. Louis three games out of first.

A large crowd turned out to see baseball's best hitters face off on Friday. Neither disappointed. Jesse Burkett and Ed Delahanty banged out three hits each. The Phillies led 2-1 in the ninth when with two runners aboard Otto Krueger lined a ball to left. Del fielded it cleanly and fired it to home. It landed in front of rookie catcher Fred Jackslitch but he couldn't handle it. The ball rolled all the way to the backstop and both runners scored. Burkett had another three hits in Saturday's game. Del, who was 20 for 39 with six extra base hits in his last nine games, knocked in four runs with a triple, a single, and a long sacrifice fly. The Phillies lost 2-1 in ten innings in their first game in Chicago but took each of the next three. They won two of three in Pittsburgh to stay in the thick of the six-team battle for first place and took two of three in Cincinnati to wind up an uncharacteristically successful road trip. They looked to do even better at home.

While Del was on the road Norine worked with a group of society women to raise money for the restoration of the Valley Green Inn. She hadn't said anything to Del about it, but when he got back home she delightedly told him that the group's efforts had paid off. The charming little white inn was open for business.

"'Tis a grand thing yuv done," said Del. "Let's go."

"Where?" asked Norine.

"The Valley Green Inn."

"When?" asked Norine.

"Tonight. Bundle up Florence and we'll stay the night and spend tomorrow riding horseback along the Wissahickon."

"Oh, Del! Florence will love that."

Florence had heard her name from the next room. "What will I love, Daddy?"

The Only Del

"Thanks to Mommy and some other ladies there is a beautiful little inn in the forest and we are gointa stay there tonight. Tomorrow we'll let yer muther sleep in and you and I will look for frogs, chipmunks, and deer. In the afternoon the three of us are gointa ride horses along the river."

"Horses! Can I take Molly?" she asked, hugging the teddy Del had bought her in St. Louis.

"Of course, baby. What better place for a bear than in the woods?"

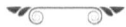

Their room was tiny and even with the window open it was as hot as an oven until long after dark. Del and Florence looked out at the stars and he pointed out the constellations and told her the stories of Diana and Orion, the hunters in the sky. The next morning Florence found and captured a cricket and, with a little help from her father, caught a fish. Norine was none too thrilled when Florence woke her up by holding it up to her face to show it off.

Del had the Valley Green Inn staff make up sandwiches and he and his girls had a picnic lunch in a meadow and then they went to pick out the horses for their ride. Florence was thrilled to get a little Palomino. They rode up one side of the Wissahickon and back along the other, returning just in time for a late dinner on the inn's patio. Florence was asleep before Del had even laid her down on the bed.

"Have we ever gone two nights without making love when I've gotten back from a road trip?" Del whispered to Norine when they went to bed, Florence contentedly snuggled between them.

"Are you serious, Del? We've never gone two *hours*."

"Does this mean we're an old married couple?"

"No, silly. It means you're going to have make it up to me the next two nights." She waited a beat and whispered, "Actually you'll be making it up to Cleopatra and a naughty French maid."

Del hit a run-scoring scorcher the second baseman couldn't handle in the first frame of the Monday game against the Beaneaters. In the fourth

the greatest batsman in the land

he made a deposit into the hanging gardens in left. It was the longest hit ever made on the local grounds. He led off the ninth with a safety to left, worked a hit-and-run with Ed McFarland, and scored the winning run on a wild pitch.

The *Inquirer* stated, "No matter what Delahanty's official position is with Jennings on the scene the fact remains that he is the major part of the works when it comes to the ingredients of which runs are made."

The Phillies took each of the remaining three games from Boston and two of three from Brooklyn before heading back out on the road. Del batted under .200 over the stretch but made a spectacular bare handed catch in the last game with the Superbas. He struck out three times in the first game in Brooklyn and went hitless the next day. After slipping behind Willie Keeler in the list of leading batsmen Del broke out of his slump with a game-winning single in the tenth inning of the August 1st get-away-day game. Batting fourth, with Flick in the three spot, he registered a brace of hits in the first game at the Polo Grounds but neither Jackslitch nor Jennings could bring him home and the Phillies lost 5-3 to fall three games back of Pittsburgh. The Phillies took the next three from New York and two of three from Boston with little help from the silent bat of Ed Delahanty and came home for a pair against the Giants.

Norine could tell her husband was upset. He played with Florence but barely touched his dinner and then went for a walk by himself.

"What is it, Del?" Norine asked when he came home and fired his hat into the front closet.

"I think I've had it."

"What do you mean? The team's got a real chance to win the championship this year, doesn't it?"

"We've had chances *before* and what happens every damn time?"

"Some other team goes on a tear and you get left behind."

"That's right."

The Only Del

"But the cranks still love you. They've turned on every other one of the team's best players, but never on you."

"I'm still not making much more than I did when I was a goddamn rookie, Norine, and I've been among the league leaders or on top for years. Besides, it looks like Jennings is gointa be the captain and I'll lose out on the six hundred dollar bonus."

"Would any of the teams in the new league pay you more?"

"Oive got a feelin' they'd give me *plenty* more."

Del pounded out three hits on Friday in a 13-2 win and another three on Saturday in a 5-3 one. The Phillies were breathing down the Pirates' necks.

"Call Nettie on the telephone," he told Norine when he got home.

"What for?" asked Norine.

"To see if she'll take Florence tonight. I want to take you out for dinner and a show and then play some games when we get back."

Norine frowned. "Are you sure we can afford it? You said we were overdrawn at the bank."

"Not since my end uv the month pay went in we aren't. Besides, next year oill be makin' a helluva lot bigger deposits. I promise."

Norine smiled. "I don't know which I'm looking forward to the most … dinner, the show, or the games after." She went over and gave Del a passionate kiss. "Wait, yes I do."

They went to Dante and Luigi's, a new Italian restaurant that had just opened on Tenth Street. They started with Zuppa di Vongole. Del had red snapper livornese arancini with mozzarella and basil and vitello parmigiano. Norine had the seared tuna with sweet and sour Cipollini onions. Del had tiramisu for dessert, Norine had mascarpone. After dinner they went to see "Ladies Paradise" at the Walnut.

When they got home Norine said she was going to put on a new outfit. Del was disappointed. He liked the ones he'd already seen her in. He wasn't disappointed anymore when she came out of her change room as little Annie Oakley. She was a lot prettier than the real one.

the greatest batsman in the land

The Phillies traveled to Brooklyn for a three-game set and lost all three. Del was a non-contributor. But back home against Boston he went 5-for-10 and his club swept the Beaneaters. The newspapers were full of rumors that Jimmy Manning, the owner of the Washington Senators, was after some of the Phillies. Ban Johnson had amassed a war chest from which owners could draw to entice National Leaguers to come over to his league. Manning planned to dip into it with both hands. He was said to have been talking with Harry Wolverton, Al Orth, and Happy Townsend. There was also a lot of suspicion that he was after Ed Delahanty too. The Washington owner had heard that the Only Del was no longer happy in the City of Brotherly Love.

The Phillies lost three at home to New York and then returned the favor beating the Giants three straight in New York. Del made as many errors and base-running gaffs as he did base hits. Dispirited and disgusted, he relinquished the captaincy to the heir-apparent Hugh Jennings. That morning he'd read what Rogers was paying Jennings in the *Inquirer*.

> *"Notwithstanding that Rogers had a pair of $15,000 beauties of his own, the owner of the Philadelphia club valued each of them at $3,000 per annum or less, while Jennings, who is only a $6,000 beauty, is being paid $6,750. Del has given the best years of his brilliant career to the Philadelphia club and he has never been paid half of what is being given to Jennings."*

The Phillies came home for a double bill against the Cincinnatis and took them both. Del dressed quickly after the late game and headed straight to the Bingham House. Noodles Hahn and four of the other Reds showed up minutes later. In hushed voices in a corner booth of the lobby bar they talked of the greener pastures and piles of greenbacks to be enjoyed in the American League. The Reds noticed that Del seemed nervous and was drinking harder than any of them had seen him drink before.

"Can you boys keep a secret?" he asked after his fourth glass of whiskey.

"Sure, Mush," said Hahn. The other Reds nodded in agreement. "What is it?"

"I met with Manning the uther day and signed a letter uv agreement. It

The Only Del

says the day the season ends oill sign a contract ta play fer his Senators."

"Would ya mind tellin' us for how much?" whispered Hahn as the others leaned in to hear.

"Four thousand," said Del.

The Reds whistled.

"There's no fuckin' salary limit in the new league, boys," Hahn told his excited teammates.

Norine was delighted when she heard that her husband would finally be making the kind of money he deserved. She was excited they'd be moving to Washington too. She'd heard a lot about the swirling social circle there.

"What other teams are there in the American League?" Norine asked Ed.

"Let me think. Washington and Philadelphia of course. And St. Louis, Boston, Chicago, Cleveland, Detroit, and Baltimore."

"They don't have a team in *New York*?"

"Sorry, me pet, they don't. Not yet anyway."

Del started hitting again and the Phillies won some games, but to no avail. Beginning August 31st the Pirates reeled off twenty wins in twenty-three games and the championship was theirs. Harry Wolverton wasn't around anymore. Colonel Rogers had found out he'd signed an American League contract and suspended him without pay. Del missed a couple of games late in the season. He'd taken sick after standing in the rain for hours waiting for the funeral train of President McKinley to pass. He'd been shot by an anarchist at the Buffalo Exposition.

The *Sporting News* announced their unofficial 1901 National League batting records the day after the season ended. Ed Delahanty ranked third in Total bases and On Base Percentage, second in Batting Average, Slugging, and Runs Batted In, and first in doubles and combined Slugging and On Base Percentage. Del bought a gold inscribed watch, chain, and locket for Billy Shettsline. The other Phillies went in on it when they found out what he'd done. Shetts cried when he saw the watch and looked around at the players. He knew he was probably seeing most of them for the last time.

the greatest batsman in the land

That night Del telephoned Jesse Burkett who was in New York.

"Congratulations on winnin' the battin' crown," said Del after the hotel operator had put through his call.

"Thanks, Mush. Good of you to call. What are you up to?"

"Not much. I decided not to go barn-stormin' with the Phillies. Didn't think it'd be right. Besides, I'm hoping not to need the money so much from now on."

"Oh, ya. I hear you're going to Washington for big bucks."

"*Bigger* at least, Jesse."

"I'm hoppin' aboard the gravy train too."

"You are?"

"Damn straight. I signed up with the new league's Saint Louis club."

"Good for you, Crab."

"Speaking of hopping on a train, why don't you climb on one and head here for a couple of days?"

"To do what?"

"To take some dough from the bookies at Aqueduct. Like you always say, Mush, a straight tip's as good as a base hit - with a big killing for a chaser."

"Oive got to go," said Del.

"Where?"

"Ta pack me bag. Oill see ya tomorrow."

Jesse and Del made a killing. Del had to ask for a bag to carry his cash. "How much have you got there?" asked Burkett as Del stuffed the last bundle of bills into the bag."

"A little shy uv two thousand."

"Don't you think it's high time you got yourself a gun, Mush? That's a lot of cash to be lugging around."

"You're right, Jesse. As soon as I get down south I'm buying one."

The Only Del

Del went straight from New York to Washington to meet with Jim Manning at the Oxford Hotel and sign his new contract. Manning told him about his roster. Del knew that the Senators would have a decent lineup with the new additions from the Phillies. They already had Boileryard Clarke to catch, slick-fielding Scoops Carey at first, three-time .300 hitter "Wagon Tongue Bill" Keister at second, "Scranton Bill" Coughlin, a coal miner who had a deadly fear of rodents, at third, and Bones Ely at short. Del's friend Pony Ryan would be in centerfield and Watty Lee, who could hit but wasn't much of a fielder, would be in right.

Manning had lured Happy Jack Townsend, Harry Wolverton, and best of all Del's buddy Al Orth away from the Phillies. In addition to Chick Fraser and Bill Bernhard, Connie Mack had signed Bill Duggleby and Monte Cross to join Nap Lajoie, who'd lent a lot of credibility to the American League. Ed McFarland and Wiley Piatt were off to play for the Chicago Americans and Red Donahue was going over to the St. Louis Browns. Del had no doubt that the new league would draw its fair share of rooters, maybe even more than the badly and deservedly depleted National League.

"Colonel Rogers has gone from having a hell of a team to a *shell* of a team," chuckled Manning.

"Serves the bastard right," said Del.

He stared at the amount on the contract and Manning told him that he would be getting the same amount each pay as he had this year.

"How can that be?" asked Del.

"Because here's a check for one thousand dollars in advance," said Manning.

Del cashed his check and bought two fur coats - a little rabbit one for Florence and a luxurious mink for Norine. She often wore it around the house at night as soon as Florence went to sleep. There was never anything underneath it but jewelry.

Chapter Twenty Seven

"Guinevere Might Relish That."

In January, after a trip to Cleveland to show his parents how cute and clever their granddaughter had grown, Del took his girls to New Orleans - for two months this time. They stayed at the St. Charles. The monthly rates for a suite at the Dauphine Orleans and the Monteleone were exorbitant. Del went to the Dauphine Orleans their second day in town and hired Mae to take care of Florence full-time so he and Norine could paint the town red. Then he found a gun shop and bought a Derringer with a 2½ inch barrel and a holster that attached to the top of a boot.

The Delahantys had made something of a splash on their first trip to New Orleans and the handsome, free-spending couple were fast becoming accepted members of the social scene, Del as a major player among the "horsey set" due to his uncanny success as the track, and Norine for her beautiful dresses, diamonds, and above all her heritage of southern aristocracy, which she tended to embellish a little. Invitations to dinner parties and galas arrived at their hotel almost daily. Their first big event was the lavish Twelfth Night Revelers Ball at the French Opera House. Norine learned that the theme for 1902 was "Cupid on Vacation." Couples were expected to dress as famous lovers. Del went as a dashing Lancelot and Norine looked stunning as his Lady Guinevere.

Del tried not to get too jealous as one man after another inquired as to whether or not Guinevere's dance card was full. He wasn't sure whether it was her youth, her charm, her graceful dancing, her sparkling eyes, or her décolletage that attracted them the most but he had his suspicions. He finally led her out of the middle of a group of male admirers before another one could claim her for the next quadrille and took her out onto the balcony.

The Only Del

She waved her fan in front of her face and tried to catch her breath. "It's great to be popular, but hell to be the rage," she breathed, a bit immodestly.

"I can't say as I blame them," said Del, resignedly. "If I was here with one uv their sour-pussed wives that'd needed three servants to squeeze her inta her gown oid be clamorin' ta dance with ya too, me pet."

Norine kissed him. "Thank you, Del."

"For the compliment? Oive given you grander ones than that."

"No. For our life together. When I was a little girl I always dreamed of wearing diamonds and fancy clothes, and eating at French restaurants, and staying in elegant hotels, and attending galas with a handsome, rich, and charming husband and now I have all of that thanks to you."

"It makes me heart soar ta hear ya say such things and oim glad yer havin' a wonderful time, but I'm afraid oive got to disagree with ya."

Norine looked confused.

"I'm not exactly rich. At least not yet anyway. But oill admit ta bein' handsome and charmin' if you insist."

Norine pulled Del close. "Kiss me you fool."

He pulled back a little.

"What's wrong?"

Del looked around. "If we get ta huggin' and spoonin' out here oim liable ta want ta use me lance a lot."

Norine smiled, pulled him close, and cooed, "Even though she's a lady, Guinevere might relish that."

When they got back to their hotel suite Norine disappeared. Del lit a fire, as he always did, knowing there was a pretty good chance that his bride - she loved that he still called her that - would return with very little on. She reappeared wearing nothing but the pointed hat from her Lady Guinevere costume and a Bolero jacket. She slowly undid the top two buttons, looked down at her breasts and then into Del's eyes and asked, "Do you want to put him between them?"

"You know I hate that."

the greatest batsman in the land

After sleeping in until noon the next day they took Florence and Mae, who at first refused the invitation, to a matinée at the Vitascope Hall. The show was called "Niagara Falls: Shooting the Chutes." It was flickering and grainy but they all stared in wonder at the screen.

"Wouldn't it be fun to ride through the water like that, daddy?" asked Florence.

"A might chilly I'd imagine, but a lot uv fun, sweetie."

"It looks awfully dangerous if you ask me," said Norine. "A person could get killed doing that. Look at those sharp rocks."

Ed and Mae laughed when Florence whispered, "Mommy wouldn't do that. She'd get her beautiful hair wet."

After the show they took Florence to the arcade and then ate at Fabacher's Marble lunch counter next door. Then they went shopping. Ed bought two silk cravats and a cashmere vest at Lacroix's and a "Porous" Hat at J.W. Valentine's. Florence started to get bored so Ed paid for his purchases and told her she would like the next stop a lot better. It turned out to be Miller & Dielmann's Chocolate Factory. Ed left the girls there and went across the street to Hernsheim's for some fifteen-cent cigars. At Mercier's on Dauphine Street Mae loved helping Norine pick out clothes for Florence, but she put up a fuss when Norine insisted on buying her two new dresses.

"My husband ain't gonna recognize me," said Mae.

"He might find it fun to be with a different woman," teased Ed.

Norine hit him over the head with her parasol.

They went back to the hotel, stopping on the way so Ed could buy some bourbon and claret. Mae took Florence to play in her room. Ed and Norine got dressed and went to Denechaud's for dinner before heading to the Twenty-Eight Club. Ed wore one of his new cravats and Norine wore one of the beautiful dresses she'd bought at Merciers.

The next night Ed went to a function at the Crescent City Jockey Club. He wore his best suit, his gold watch and chain, an expensive ring Norine

The Only Del

had picked out for him, and diamond stickpins. He pretended to be drunk so he could surreptitiously listen in on conversations among the owners of thoroughbreds.

The next afternoon while Norine and Florence were at the zoo he went to the Fair Grounds and hung around the paddock area to identify the mounts he'd heard about at the party. He scribbled in his notebook and put his purloined information to good use later. That night he had an awful nightmare. He was shooting the Niagara River rapids and it was anything but fun.

In March the *Washington Evening Star* reported the exciting news that five of Ed Delahanty's "wallopers" had arrived at the ballpark wrapped in cotton and informed its readers that the club's great new batsman was reported to have won close to $6,000 at the race track in New Orleans. It was true. Del was not having to rely entirely on his handicapping skills, overheard confidences, and cables from Felix Carr. Wally Fessenden, whom Del remembered calling him on the Infield Fly rule in his first game in the Players League, was now a trainer at the Fair Grounds and he kept giving Del tips. The *Star* also reported that Jim Manning, frustrated that Ban Johnson had refused to let him to dip into the American League's war chest one more time to sign Willie Keeler, had sold his interest in the Senators to the club president Fred Postal, a hotelier from Detroit.

Two weeks before the season was due to begin Del started going to the Pelicans' park right after breakfast. He had the minor leaguers hit him fungos, ran full-tilt around the bases, and had the Pelicans' ace twirler pitch to him. When he got back to the hotel on March 25 there was a telegram from Felix Carr waiting for him. It listed three horses he should bet and an address where Carr wanted to meet him for a payoff if the horses won.

Each one paid off handsomely and Del went to the meeting place. It turned out to be a sleazy, dimly-lit bar in which Del was the only white patron. He and Carr went out into the garbage-filled alley behind the saloon and Del gave Carr a large wad of bills. The next day Del paid his hefty hotel bill and he and the girls headed to Washington.

the greatest batsman in the land

Norine liked the city that was to be their new home. Not just the social scene, but the city itself. It had the feel of a southern town, not a big industrial city like Philadelphia. For one thing, while it did have electric streetcars, there weren't ugly telephone and telegraph wires strung along every street. The only problem was that Washington had a very small Irish population. People said they always managed to find the money to buy beer or whiskey, but they also found enough coins to pay their way into baseball grounds as well. A good deal of Washington's citizens were Negroes who were far too poor to take in a ball game or even afford the two-cent trolley ride to get there. Unlike Philadelphia, the capital's baseball teams, almost always of the second division variety, had drawn more than 200,000 spectators only once.

No one seemed very upset when Del arrived a few days later than expected at the hastily re-sodded American League Park on the grounds of the Washington Brick Machine Company at Trinidad Street and Florida Avenue. He donned his new home uniform, a white jersey with a navy blue collar and a rectangular patch with a cross between an ink blot and a W on the left side, white pants, and navy blue stockings. The uniform fit fine, Del had lost twenty pounds over the last few weeks and he was back down to his playing weight.

He met easy-going Tom Loftus, the diminutive, slate-eyed, moustachioed manager. Loftus introduced Del to the teammates he didn't already know and proudly told him, "There's not a single lusher on the club. Very few of the boys even drink beer." Not quite sure why Loftus had chosen to tell him that, Del shrugged and rekindled his friendships with Al Orth, Happy Jack Townsend, Harry Wolverton, and Jimmy Ryan.

Loftus had played only a handful of games in the major leagues but he was an expert on the rules of baseball. He'd been in the game for twenty-five years, first as a teammate of Old Hoss Radbourne with the Peoria Reds in the 70's and later as captain of a Nine in Dubuque that featured young Charlie Comiskey at first base.

"Think uv it, Pony, we're finally playin' together after all these years," Del told Jimmy Ryan.

The Only Del

"And makin' a lot more ta do it," chuckled Ryan. "Whad'ya think uv Loftus?"

"I like him. Seems ta know what he's doin'. That'll take a load off me as captain."

"O, my Lord," gasped Del as he read the evening paper that night.

"What is it?" asked Norine.

"Someone I know's been murdered. A colored fella I knew from the track."

"That's terrible," said Norine. "Did I ever meet him?"

"No. Never."

Del didn't want to explain his relationship and dealings with the man who'd been killed. An hour or so after Del had handed him the large bundle of cash, Felix Carr had been mugged, knifed to death, and thrown into a river.

On April 21, two days before the Senators' home opener, came startling news that the Pennsylvania Supreme Court had reversed a lower court's decision and granted a permanent injunction that barred jumpers from playing for any team other than the Phillies. The decision included Del, Lajoie, Flick, Orth, Wolverton, and Townsend. To a man, each of the new Senators assured their new manager that they had no intention of returning to the Phillies. Feeling he had no choice but to comply, Nap Lajoie went to work out at the Huntingdon Grounds. Then he went to see Colonel Rogers.

"As you are well aware, I was paid a great deal more by the American League," Nap told Rogers. "But I would be willing to sign with the Phillies for thirty-five hundred."

"Not a penny more than you made last year, Lajoie," snarled grim-faced Rogers. "And you're lucky to get that. I generally have no truck with contract jumpers."

Nap clenched his fists and struggled to maintain his composure. "I'm prepared to quit baseball if I don't get at least close to what I deserve."

the greatest batsman in the land

"Twenty-eight hundred is all you'll get. I'll have the papers ready in the morning."

Napoleon grabbed his hat and got up to leave. "You can shove your papers straight up your miserable, tightwad ass. Go to hell."

Nap went to see Connie Mack, whose attorney was with him. He was reading over the Pennsylvania Supreme Court's decision.

"Is it binding?" Connie asked the lawyer.

"I'm afraid it is."

"Then I suppose there's nothing we can do," shrugged Mack.

"I really *will* have to quit baseball," moaned Nap.

"You do realize that the injunction is only in effect in the state of Pennsylvania, don't you?" asked the lawyer. Nap and Connie stared at one another.

"Do you mean . . . "

"Mister Lajoie is quite within his rights to play for whomever and against whomever he chooses, so long as he does not do so in the state of Pennsylvania."

"So I can't play for the Athletics then," said Nap.

"As dearly as I would love to keep you, I'm afraid not," said Mack. "But you don't have to go back to the Phillies." He saw that Nap hadn't caught on. "You can play for any other American League club, you'll just have to take a little vacation whenever they come here to play the Athletics."

"I see," said Nap.

"Let me make a couple of calls," said Connie.

Charles Sommers, the owner of the Cleveland Bronchos, was desperate for talent after three years of tiny crowds and woeful performances. He'd made a big pitch to get Del. Sommers had been Ban Johnson's biggest benefactor in providing and raising the funds he'd needed to challenge the National League moguls. After Connie Mack called Johnson, the league

The Only Del

president called Sommers and told him that the American League simply had to keep Napoleon Lajoie. Sommers got out his checkbook and signed Nap, Elmer Flick, and Bill Bernard to lucrative contracts.

Norine and Florence were among the overflow crowd of 9,000 that included congressmen, admirals, and generals at the Senators' home opener. The atmosphere was lively but tense. Twenty-five policemen were on hand to make sure no one tried to serve papers on any of the ex-National Leaguers. Colorful advertisements for several different brands of whiskey populated the outfield fences. Del grinned when he saw one for Duffy's Pure Malt. He waved to his girls when he took his place in left field in front of the rickety grandstand to clamorus applause.

Florence looked around. "Are they cheering for my daddy?" Florence asked her mother.

"Yes they are, sweetie."

Del singled, doubled, and scored three times off Boston's Bill Dinneen in a 7-2 win that delighted the Washington baseball bugs. They hadn't had a winning team in years. "Doughnut Bill" Carrick gave up seventeen hits to lose the second game of the four-game series. Del did no great work at the plate but he made a circus catch of a foul along the left field stand. Carrick's defeat was hardly front page news. He'd lost seventeen in a row in '01. Del had three hits including a triple and stole a base as the Senators thrashed the Boston Americans 15-4 the next day. In the Saturday curtain-closer he delivered two doubles and a single to go 8-for-17 in his first four games. The Senators triumphed 15-7 and got out of the gate with a three-out-of-four start. Del was already the talk of the town.

Norine and Del moved into the just completed Beaux-Arts Highlands Apartments on Connecticut Avenue NW. She hired a nursemaid to help take care of Florence so she could shop and start developing social contacts. She and Del were invited to a dinner party at the home of a cabinet secretary who was a baseball booster their second week in town. The atmosphere was somewhat tense since both Ben Tillman, South

Carolina's senior senator, and John McLaurin, the state's junior senator, were in attendance.

In February McLaurin had raced into the Senate Chamber and pronounced that Tillman was guilty of a willful, malicious, and deliberate lie. Tillman, who had been standing nearby, had spun around and punched McLaurin square in the jaw. The chamber exploded in pandemonium as members struggled to separate the two men. Tillman's actions had caused President Roosevelt to withdraw an invitation to a White House banquet and Tillman was still stewing about it. After several glasses of champagne McLaurin told his former combatant that, as a president, Roosevelt made a good police chief. Tillman put his arm around McLaurin's shoulders, they laughed, and everyone relaxed.

The after-dinner amusement was a table tennis tournament. The hostess had ping pong tables set up under swaying strings of paper lanterns on the back lawn. A spread of rackets, balls, champagne flutes, and appetizers was neatly arrayed around a huge punch bowl. Del was careful not to hit the ball too hard when he played against the host, who was thrilled that Washington's man of the hour was at the party. When Norine played, her opponent, an octogenarian French ambassador in a tuxedo, hit a ball that bounced off her chin, fell straight down, and lodged itself in her cleavage. The ball was so light she wasn't able to tell where it had gone and started to look around for it.

The French ambassador chuckled, "La balle repose - très heureusement je suis certain - dans votre décolleté."

Norine looked down, blushed, and extracted the ball.

"Je m'excuse, Monsieur," she said.

"No apology is necessaire, Madamoiselle. I have never enjoyed following the flight of a ball or its landing as much as I just did that one."

"Now *there's* a story that'll be goin' round the gentlemen's clubs for a while," Del told Norine that night when she related what had happened. He went to the kitchen and came back with a bowl of grapes. He took one out of the bowl and, with a determined look on his face, said, "Now let me see if I can recreate that shot the ambassador made."

Norine looked daggers at Del. Then she giggled and said, "Fire away."

The Only Del

Chapter Twenty Eight

Still on Top

Like his friend Napoleon Lajoie, Ed was barred from playing for any team but the Phillies in the state of Pennsylvania. After the Senators had dropped three out of four to the Athletics in Washington the two teams - minus Delahanty, Orth, Townsend, and Wolverton - shared a train to Philadelphia for a four-game series.

"What are you going to do while the team is in Philadelphia, darling?" Norine had asked when she'd seen the Senators' schedule.

"Al and Harry and Happy Townsend and I are going to the track."

"Do you mean the one in the east end? What's it called, Benning's?"

"That is the name uv the track in the east end uv Washington. But that's not where we're headed."

"Oh. Which one then? Brightwood?" asked Norine as she pulled a brush out of her etui and began brushing her hair.

"No."

"Ivy City then?"

"No."

"Those are the only ones I know of."

"We're goin' ta Morris Park, me pet. I thought you might like ta come along."

"I suppose I could. Where is Morris Park?"

"It's in New York."

"It *is*? What would we do in New York besides go to the track? And make love of course."

The Only Del

"I was thinking we might do some shopping?"

"Oh? I hadn't thought of that."

"Oim sure it hadn't occurred to you," teased Del.

"I suppose it might have crossed my mind *eventually*. I'll be packed in twenty minutes."

Florence stayed behind with the nursemaid. On the train ride, Happy Townsend had some fun. He usually carried two white mice in his pockets. He let them go in the Pullman and shrieks could be heard all up and down the aisle. He turned them loose in the dining car and a couple of dowagers nearly jumped out the window.

Norine spent $350 at the shops in New York. The first night in town, while Norine was trying on the clothes and jewelry she'd bought, Del read the *Racing Form* - from cover to cover as usual.

Before the Metropolitan Handicap Race for thoroughbreds at Morris Park the next day Del tried to talk Orth, Townsend, and Wolverton into betting on Arsenal. "The jockey is Johnny Daly and the trainer is Julius Bauer, they're two uv the best," Del told the others as they stood under the grandstand because of the steady rain that fell. "And Arsenal's a mudder. He loves the slop."

"How old is he?" asked Wolverton, expecting Del would have to look it up.

"Three."

"Didn't a six-year-old win this thing last year?" asked Townsend.

"Aye. But a three-year-old has won three times since the first race in Ninety-One."

"What's so special about this horse?" asked Worth.

"His daddy was Lamplighter."

"What are the odds?" asked Harry.

"He's twenty to one."

"Twenty to one!" I'm not betting on a horse that's going off at twenty to one," said Orth.

the greatest batsman in the land

"If you think he's that good, I'll put a dollar on him," said Wolverton. "But not to finish first. To win, place, or show."

"How much are you gonna bet, Mush?" asked Happy Jack.

"Twenty-five dollars," said Del.

"Twenty-five dollars!" gasped Orth. "Have you lost your mind?"

Harry squinted at the board through the driving rain. "What about Bonnibert or Colonel Madden?" he asked Del. "They're five to one."

"Twenty-five dollars on Arsenal," repeated Del. "To *win*."

Neither Bonnibert nor Colonel Madden ran well. Water Color led at the quarter. Far Rockaway had pulled ahead at the half. With a furlong left Whisky King had passed both of them. Arsenal was fourth.

"Too bad, Mush," said Harry.

"I guess you can't handicap 'em *every* time," said Orth.

"Just wait," said Del.

The others shrugged their shoulders. Harry looked at his one dollar win, place, or show ticket and thought about ripping it up.

"Do ya see that?" asked Del.

Harry looked back at the track. Arsenal had made his move.

"Here comes Arsenal," they heard the track announcer call through his megaphone. "Johnny Daly has given him his head and he's passed Water Color and he's gaining fast on Far Rockaway."

"Damn!" said Townsend.

"And Arsenal continues his late charge from the outside," called out the announcer.

A few minutes later the pretty cashier finished counting out Del's winnings. Arsenal had won by a nose. "Four seventy, four eighty, four ninety, five hundred." She looked up and smiled at Del. "Do you have a special girl to spend all this on?" she asked suggestively.

The Only Del

"Two uv them," Del told her.

Billy Shettsline walked up to the four Senators.

"I forgot the Phillies were in town," said Del, shaking his former manager's hand and smiling when he saw that Shetts was proudly wearing the watch, chain, and locket he'd gotten for him.

"I *heard* you fellas were here," said Shettsline.

"Mush just took the place for five hundred, Billy," Wolverton told Shetts.

"Is that so? Well I've come to take the four of you in," said Billy.

Orth, Wolverton, and Del smiled. "Ya did, did ya," teased Del.

Happy Jack didn't look very happy. He looked scared. "What are you saying, Shetts?"

"The sheriff's on his way up. He'll be here with the handcuffs any time now."

Harry, Al, and Del laughed. "Good one," said Del. "Looks like we're spendin' the night in the crowbar hotel, boys."

"And back to Philly in chains first thing in the morning," said Harry.

"The colonel really wants young Townsend here back," Shetts deadpanned to the others.

Beads of sweat appeared on Jack's forehead. He tugged at his collar and gulped. The others were having a terrible time not bursting into fits of laughter.

Jack elbowed Del in the ribs. "Show him your gun, Mush!" he implored.

Del lifted his pant leg. "Didn't bring it today, Jack. Sorry."

Jack stared in disbelief and then turned and ran full-tilt into a crowd of people, knocking some over as he madly dashed away.

The other men laughed until their sides hurt.

"Well done, Billy," said Del. "You oughta be on the stage."

the greatest batsman in the land

"The poor boy was awake all night," Harry told Del the next morning while they were having breakfast together at the hotel. Norine was still in bed. She and Del had made love in the sitting room of their suite, up against the balcony railing, in the tub, and finally in the bed.

Del believed Harry. Jack had come into the restaurant and spotted Del and Harry and was walking slowly toward the table. He looked awful. "Should we tell him?" Del asked Harry.

"Tell me what?" asked Jack.

Harry shrugged his shoulders. "I suppose it's time. Shetts was just teasing. I'm sure he'd love to have us all back, but he's not about to have us arrested and forced at gunpoint to play for the Phillies."

Jack smiled, but just a little.

Del teased Jack, his roommate on the road, about his paranoia for weeks. But it was no laughing matter for the Athletics who'd jumped ship. Bill Bernard, Elmer Flick, and Napoleon often wore disguises and had to sneak around like they were on the Underground Railway whenever they tried to rejoin the rest of the Athletics at the state line on the team's way out of Pennsylvania. They often hid in the woods or in a rowboat, jumping out into the moonlight like bank robbers only when they saw the smokestack of an approaching train.

Minus their additions from the Phillies, especially Del, the Senators lost three out of four to the Athletics in Philadelphia. Del rejoined his new club in Boston on May 7. He bashed three hits and scored two runs in the first game, but Townsend struggled to get his pitches in the strike zone for a change and got shelled. The Senators lost 12-8. Del had two hits in the second game, a 5-1 victory. He scored twice in a 5-4 win in the third game and got one of the Senators' four hits in a 3-1 loss to Cy Young in the last game in Boston that lasted all of sixty-five minutes.

Del singled, doubled, and tripled on Monday, May 11 in Baltimore, but his new team went down 9-4. On Tuesday he doubled and tripled, but Doughnut Bill Carrick got hammered and the Senators fell 10-3. Del was

The Only Del

the American League's top batter with a .397 average. He was glad the league hadn't adopted the fouls as strikes rule. Ban Johnson wanted to give the bugs more runs to cheer about.

The Senators took two of four from the Cleveland Bronchos, with Del homering in each of the wins. He felt pretty young for a 34-year-old, but he was starting to experience some aches and pains. He'd pushed himself a bit too hard tuning up for the season and his throwing arm hurt like hell. He knew he'd lost a bit of his speed. He was no longer able to circle the bags after a long hit. If he wanted a home run now, he needed to put the ball over the fence.

Del homered again in the first game of a double header with the White Sox on May 30. The crack of his bat making contact with a trick delivery from Clark "the Old Fox" Griffith was said to be so loud it could be heard a half a mile away. The ball sailed out of the ballpark and ran along the sidewalk for an entire block. On June 2 he hit another home run, singled twice, and scored three runs in Al Worth's 12-0 trouncing of the White Sox. Two days later he pounded out three hits as Carrick downed the Tigers 13-6 to boost the Senators within five games of the league lead, heady territory for a team from Washington.

Del wowed the crowd in St. Louis on June 11. He had three hits and made a terrific stop of "Wallace's fast traveler". The *St. Louis Republic* reporter wrote that,

> "McCormick was the author of a stinging liner toward the foul line. Delahanty sprinted for it at full speed, thrust out his lunch hook, and to the amazement of the crowd and himself the ball lodged in his big bare paw to an avalanche of applause."

The next day Boileryard Clarke, Scoops Carey, and Del, who was running the team while Tom Loftus saw to his ailing wife, had three hits each as the Senators outscored the Browns 9-8 on the strength of a three-run ninth. Del had a pair of hits and a sacrifice fly to push his league-leading average to .404 on Friday the 13th in an 11-1 shelling of former Philly Red

the greatest batsman in the land

Donahue. At home on the 25th of June it was only on account of "the ability of Capt. Delahanty to hit the ball all over the lot that the home side had any chance for a white alley." Del doubled in the third, launched a ball far over the left field fence in the sixth, and tripled in the ninth to account for all of the Senators' tallies in a 4-3 win over the Boston Americans.

On Thursday, July 3 Del tripled, singled twice, stole a base, and scored two runs in an 8-3 win over Boston. He and the other former Phillies left Beantown and headed for Baltimore. They wouldn't be traveling by train through Pennsylvania to play the Fourth of July doubleheader in Philadelphia like the rest of the Senators. They traveled in the hold of a steamer inside crates that were labeled "Bananas, consigned to T. Loftus, Boston."

Orth, Jack, and Del felt cramped and suspected there were more than a few bugs in the hay that surrounded them, but Harry was suffering something awful. He was shaking with chills and even though it was cold inside the hold he was sweating like a pig.

"Are you gointa be all right, Harry?" Del shouted.

"I think I'm going to wretch, Mush," answered Wolverton.

"It's no wonder Harry's been playin' so bad," Jack whispered to Al. "He's having terrible headaches too."

"He never made errors like that in Philadelphia," Worth whispered back. "And he was a hell of a lot better hitter too. I sure wish the bugs would lay off booing the man. Mind you they don't know he's got malaria."

Once the ship was well out of harbor the four climbed out of their crates. Del found a blanket to wrap around Harry's shoulders and, after throwing up into a bucket, he felt a bit better.

"I'm done with all this," Harry told the others.

"Done with what?" asked Del. "Tossin' your cookies?"

"No. All this fucking sneaking around. I feel like a damn criminal. It's not just that though, the cranks in Washington have turned on me. I can't blame them. I've been horrible."

The Only Del

"What are you gointa do, Harry?" asked Al.

"I'm going back to the Phillies."

As the other three looked at Harry and then one another they heard someone coming. The steamer's night watchman was more than a little surprised to discover Ed Delahanty and three other 'Bananas' engaged in hushed conversation. Del gave the man five dollars to ignore what he'd seen and the watchman accepted gladly, scared up a couple of bottles of whiskey, and joined them in a game of poker.

Without their former Phillies, the Senators lost both games of the double header in Philadelphia. Colonel Rogers cringed when he read that the Athletics had drawn 23,000 cranks to the games. He sure wasn't getting crowds that size to watch his remnants play. The only saving grace for the Senators was the play of newly-signed 32-year-old "Dirty Jack" Doyle from Killorglin, County Kerry. He'd been released by the Chicago Orphans due to his .232 average and clumsy work at first base. Now the Giants had turned him loose. Ed knew Doyle was well past his prime but he'd always liked him and he was glad to have another horse racing enthusiast on the club.

"What happened in New York, Jack?" Ed asked Doyle after introducing him to the Senators who'd never played against him. Ed knew that changes were on the horizon for the Giants. They'd finished second-last for the past three years but now they had a new man at the helm. John T. Brush, who'd made a fortune on his department store in Indianapolis, was a gaunt man with a crooked nose and sheepdog countenance who suffered from locomotor ataxia, a painful affliction of the nervous system that forced him to walk with two canes. He'd sold his shares in the Cincinnati club and bought a majority stake in the Giants. Freedman would remain president in name only. Brush would run things from now on.

His new field manager was none other than tempestuous John McGraw. Mugsy had been forced out of the American League as part owner/player/manager of the Orioles in July of '02. Ban Johnson had made his life a living hell by instructing his umpires to banish him from the premises after even the slightest amount of kicking. Brush had scooped him up to master-mind his rebuild of the struggling Giants. Brush's next act had been to meet with reporters and inform them that he would make every effort to acquire the best players money could buy. "New York is entitled to the best team that can be gotten together," he told the scribes. "I have equipped Mister McGraw with sufficient resources to land whatever players he requires to build a winning club."

"Fucking McGraw released me as soon as he took over, Doyle told Ed. "Brush asked him which players he didn't want to keep and Mugsy went down the list and crossed nine uv us off. Shite, I was battin' three hundred, I was. The bugger's still holdin' a grudge from that time I accidentally spiked him. I told McGraw oid be happy ta go play fer me old pal Tom Loftus in Washington where I might be able ta hear somebody crack a joke once in a while."

"How's the meat hook?" asked Ed, looking at Jack's right hand.

Doyle flexed the fingers and then grimaced as he tried to make a fist. "When I socked that crank in the kisser at the Polo Grounds it still hadn't healed from when I punched Emslie fer callin' me out in Boston," said Doyle.

"What did the crank call you?"

"A bog-dodgin' lily-livered coward."

"No wonder you hit him."

"Cost me a night in jail, but it was worth it." he chuckled. "What's the matter with Wolverton?" asked Doyle. "He looks awful."

"Man's got malaria he does."

"John McGraw bought his own release," Ed told Norine when he saw the headlines about him abandoning the Orioles. "He's signed on to manage the Giants. For eleven thousand a year if you can believe that."

"They must have deep pockets in New York," replied Norine.

"They must indeed."

The Only Del

After identifying the nine players he had no use for, McGraw had told Brush which players he needed to rebuild his team around.

"I'd like to get Kid Elberfeld from Detroit and George Davis from the White Sox," Mugsy told him. "Most of all, I want Ed Delahanty."

The next day McGraw sent a letter to Del asking if they might get together to chat about him coming over to the Giants. He followed it up with a telegram two days later.

WESTERN UNION   July 11, 1902

To: E. Delahanty, Washington

Important that we meet. Have offer sure to be of interest. Wire back convenient time.

J. McGraw, N.Y.

Chapter Twenty Nine

Put Salt On It

The Senators won five straight after returning home. Happy Townsend had slipped one of his pet mice into the back of Bill Coughlin's collar on the way and to the amusement of his teammates Bill had let out a blood-curdling scream. Del homered in two of the games against Baltimore and made a sensational catch in another. The Senators' boosters were delighted to have a team with talent to root for after so many years of frustration. On Saturday, July 19 Harry Wolverton rejoined the team. As his teammates were welcoming him back a telegram arrived. Tom Loftus assumed it was for him. It wasn't. It was another message for Del, from John McGraw.

"I suppose he wants me to go to the track with him the next time we're in town," fibbed Del. He declined this offer to meet with McGraw as he had the first.

Two days later Del received a long distance telephone call. He went down to the lobby of his hotel, picked up the receiver, and awkwardly put it to his ear.

"Hello."

"Hello. Is that you, Del?"

"Aye, 'tis. Is that you, John?"

"Yes, it's McGraw. We need to talk."

"It's a might strange you tryin' ta woo players away from their teams, John. Didn't you punch a man in the face when he was tryin' ta get players ta jump from the Orioles last year?"

"Never mind about that. Are you going to meet with me or not?"

"I know what you want to talk about and I might as well tell you, oim pretty happy here in Washington."

The Only Del

"We're prepared to offer you fifty-five hundred, Del. We really want you here in New York."

"Believe me, John, oim flattered, *real* flattered. But oim stayin' put right where I am."

The Cleveland Bronchos came to the nation's capital on the 23rd and there was a lot of talk about the rivalry for the batting championship between Ed Delahanty and Napoleon Lajoie. They were both hovering around the .400 mark. A week later, after Napoleon had gone on a tear, he was twenty points above Ed, who was playing first base in the absence of the injured Scoops Carey. Ed outhit Nap when their teams met at the end of the first week of August and enjoyed his first three-hit game in two weeks against the league-leading White Sox in Chicago, a pair the next day, and another two the next.

Ed took Norine to the Opera House to see "A Gambler's Wife" on Saturday night. A debonnaire, perfumed man in his mid-twenties was talking to Norine when he came back with their brandy and sodas after the entr-act.

"Je suis enchanté, Madamoiselle. Vous êtes facilement la plus belle femme ici."

"Merci. C'est très galant de vous dit," replied Norine.

"Tes yeux sont comme les étangs de crystal bleu. Je pourrais me perdre en eux."

Ed reddened. He didn't know what the man was saying but he knew he didn't like it. "Name's Ed, Ed Delahanty. And the lady yer sweet-talking is me wife."

"Je m'excuse, monsieur," said the man. "I should have known such a beauty must be married."

"What was that fellow telling you?" Ed asked Norine as they went back to their seats, her arm in his.

"Just that am the most beautiful woman here."

"So he was just statin' the obvious then."

Norine smiled and squeezed her husband's arm.

"What else did he say?"

"That my eyes are like crystal blue ponds and he could lose himself in them."

"That was a good line. Oill have ta remember that one in case I run into a blue-eyed gal while yer off visitin' yer sister."

"That is going to cost you, Ed Delahanty."

"What this time?"

"I just happen to have seen a lovely necklace the last time Nettie and I went window shopping."

"I see. Can I afford it?"

"*Barely*. Which is just what I'll *be* when I try it on for you."

"Well it couldn't ask for a finer setting."

The Browns and Senators traveled back from St. Louis together on August 13. Their train, which was soon to be put out of service, jolted and swerved the whole way and Del was one of the several players who looked terrible and stumbled across the platform when they reached Washington twenty-eight hours later. Reporters speculated that Del had been drinking the whole way home when he went 0-for-4 the next day.

"How do you account for your club's terrible play today?" Paul Eaton, a cub reporter from *Sporting Life*, asked Del after the game.

"Oill not speak for the uthers," said Del. "I was simply dead. Didn't hit a single ball out uv the infield. But as to the talk that I imbibed on the way home, that story's made uv whole cloth."

"Is it true you're thinking of going over to the Giants, Del?"

"No. Oim well fixed and comfortable here in Washington, me sun. Oill not do business with New York. Oid rather play here for a thousand dollars less than go to any uther club in the country."

The Only Del

"Brush would do well to keep his fingers out of the Washington sugar bowl," wrote Eaton the next day.

In a rare Friday double header on the 15th Del socked a double and a single in the opener and a crowd-thrilling, fence-rattling, game-winning twelfth inning triple in the late game. The hits pushed his average up to .388. Lajoie was in a slump and down to .370. Del outperformed his former roommate when the Bronchos rolled into town for three, going 6-for-11 to Nap's 2-for-10.

The *Washington Times* left no doubt as to who was responsible for the Senators' win over the White Sox on August 21.

> "To big Ed Delahanty is due the credit for today's victory. It was he who came along in the first with a two-bagger that sent Ryan home. It was he who sent Lee home ahead of him in the fifth when he placed a ball over the fence and it was Del that sent the same man home in the seventh with a double to right."

"No wonder the Giants are after him," one booster said to another as they made their way out of the park."

The next day Ed tripled, singled twice, and stole a base. The *St. Louis Dispatch* reported that they had it on the authority of a close friend of John McGraw that Ed Delahanty had signed a contract to play for the Giants. Two days later Ed rapped four hits in a double header against Detroit. The *Indianapolis News* said "Ed Delahanty, who maintains a twenty-point lead on Lajoie in the batting race, will go to New York next season and he will draw the biggest salary ever given a ball player. Put salt on it."

Del went to church on Sunday and prayed that he wouldn't go to hell for playing ball that afternoon. He decided the Lord would forgive him and banged out four hits against the Tigers' Ed Siever, who led the league with the fewest runs allowed. Del's third hit cleared the left field fence and was reported to have met up with a passenger train and be en route to Toledo. He homered again in the first game in St. Louis, but Lajoie was on a tear, just six points back.

the greatest batsman in the land

Del garnered three hits in a 3-2 win over Cy Young in the Senators' first game in Boston. As always, Bill Coughlin left his glove in the grass behind third base when he went to the bench and Happy Townsend slipped a mouse into it. Coughlin nearly feinted when he went to put it back on. Del singled and scored in the seventh and did the same thing again the next inning in the last game in Beantown. He notched a single, double, and triple in the first game in Baltimore on the 12th and missed hitting for the cycle by inches when Stahl corralled his fly to center in the ninth. Del started the Monday, September 15 double header in Baltimore four points behind Lajoie. He tripled in the fifth inning and singled in a three-run tenth in the first game and had two hits in the second game before it was called due to darkness after four innings. The rest of the Senators headed off to Philadelphia. Del, Townsend, and Orth headed home to Washington.

"What are these?" Norine asked Del as some pieces of paper fell out of his pocket when he got home and took off his coat. They were handwritten notes written on Willard Hotel pink stationery. She held them up to her nose. They smelled of perfume. She read the first one aloud. "I must have you, Del." She read another, "I only have eyes for you, Del. You're the best man I could have." She raised her eyebrows when she read the third. "What will it take for me to win you? This woman is obviously desperate to have you. Why haven't you told me about her?"

"Because oim not interested, me pet. Not in the least."

"But who are they from? I have a right to know who she is."

"*She* is Charlie Ebbets. And Charlie isn't short for Charlotte or Charlene. It's short for Charles. Ebbets is president of the Brooklyn Superbas."

"That's a relief. I won't need to use your pistol after all."

Del smiled and picked up the mauve candlestick telephone. "Operator? Could you connect me with Plain Twenty-Eight Twelve Dash Y?" He waited a minute and heard a series of clicks. "Is this Mertz and Mertz Fine Tailors? It is? Could ya tell me if me fall suits are ready? That's right, two imported worsteds, one gray, the uther dark blue. Forty-two large chest. They are? Terrific. Oill be right around ta pick them up."

The Only Del

"You didn't tell me you'd bought two suits, Mister Delahanty," said Norine. "I suppose I shall have to get two fall *dresses*."

The Senators lost all three games to the Athletics sans Del and Company. They played a double bill with the Orioles on Saturday, September 20 to make up for the game that had been called after four innings. The day before the *Detroit Free Press* had speculated that McGraw has given up on the idea of landing Delahanty. Ed slammed four hits, two in each game. He was coaching third base late in the afternoon game when the batboy ran out and handed him a telegram.

"Is that from New York, Del?" a crank called out.

"How much are they offering you now?" yelled another.

The only Senator who could handle Snake Wiltse's benders in the first of another two on Monday was Del, who hammered a single and a double in a losing cause. He had two more hits and scored three times in the late game. The next morning he slipped out of the suite just before dawn and headed to Benning's Race Track. There were a couple of thoroughbreds he wanted to check out. He stood in the cold for three hours and when he showed up at the ballpark his neck was so stiff he could hardly move it. He took some Dr. Miles' Anti-Pain pills but they didn't help one bit. Loftus put a local kid named Joe Stanley he'd just signed in to tend the left garden in Del's place. Stanley played the final two games of the season as well. Del had played more games than any man on the team and it wasn't as if the last two made much of a difference.

A statistician in Chicago had calculated the averages for the '02 season. Ed Delahanty was the leading batsman with a figure of .385. The *San Francisco Chronicle* disagreed. They had "Napoleon La Joie taking the plum." It wouldn't be until December that Ban Johnson would finally release the official records for the season. Del had won the race with a .376 average - ten points better than Lajoie. He'd led the league in doubles and Slugging and was among the leaders in extra base hits with fourteen triples, ten home runs, and 96 runs batted in.

the greatest batsman in the land

Graying, pudgy, but extravagantly clad Fred Postal invited Del to his club, the Washington Club, when the figures were released. When Del arrived, one of the men sitting with Postal was telling the story of a ping pong ball lodging itself in the ample cleavage of a shapely guest at a cabinet secretary's party. He hushed when Del approached.

"Here he is, gents. Big Ed Delahanty, the only Del, in the flesh. The first player to win the batting title in both leagues."

"Pleasure ta make yer acquaintances," said Del, removing his hat and taking a seat."

"What can we get you?"

"The season's over, Mister Postal, so I suppose it'd be all right with you if I indulge in a glass or two uv spirits."

The other men at the table chuckled.

"Brandy, cognac, ten-year-old whiskey? Name your poison, Del," said Postal.

"I imagine a snifter uv brandy'd warm the cockles uv me heart. As an Ulsterman that tends bar in Saint Louis would say, 'It's a might chilly out the night.'"

"Brandy it is then." Postal snapped his fingers and a young, curly-haired server hurried off to get the drinks.

"Could I ask a wee favor of you, Mister Postal?" said Del in a low voice.

"Name it, Del. And for heaven's sake, do call me Fred."

The server arrived and Del waited until he'd set down the snifters and embroidered cloth napkins and left.

"It's cost a tad more ta live here in Washington than oid expected and oid luv ta take me wife and wee girl on a couple uv trips this winter. Is there any chance you could see yer way clear ta givin' me an advance on me salary fer next season?"

Postal smiled and thought for a moment. He reached into the inside pocket of his tweed suit and pulled out his check book. "How about I go ahead and pay you the amount you receive as captain, six hundred dollars."

The Only Del

Relieved that it had been so easy, Del said, "That ud be grand, Mister Postal, I mean Fred."

Postal began to fill in the amount on the check and then paused. "Say, why don't you come out to the Chevy Chase Club for a spot of shooting some Sunday afternoon, Del," said Postal. "It's just north of town, near Bethesda. It's a great escape. The grounds are beautiful and we have a fine bunch of fellows."

"That'd be grand, Fred. Oid luv to."

The girls had already packed when Del got back to the hotel warmed by the expensive brandy. He was taking them to New York for the last few weeks of the racing season. Jack Doyle, still a carefree bachelor, was going with them.

Doyle read the *Sporting Life* on the train. "Del, you've been named as one of the outfielders on their Ideal Team of Players - along with Willie Keeler and Honus Wagner."

"Who did they pick as their top twirlers?"

"Cy Young was their top right-hander."

"And their top leftie?"

"Rube Waddell."

"Makes sense," said Del. "He's got the fastest shoots and the best drop ball oive ever laid eyes on."

"And he pitched the Athletics to the American League championship."

"It's a shame Shetts didn't grab the big kid instead of Connie Mack. We could have finally won some titles."

The train stopped for coal and water at a little station in East Windsor, New Jersey. Del and Jack stood on the platform between the cars smoking cigars when a rotund man in a black derby marched out toward them from the station.

"Shetts? Is that you?" asked Del. He shook Billy Shettsline's hand and so did Doyle. "What the hell are you doing out here?"

Shetts looked at Doyle. "Good to see you, Jack. Could we have a minute?"

"Sure, I was just thinkin' I could use a drink," said Doyle, flinging his cigar into the night and heading inside.

"What's this all about?" Del asked Shetts when Jack had gone.

"I talked him into trying to get you back, Mush."

"The Colonel?"

"That's right. It wasn't easy, but we're hurting for a power hitter something awful."

"I imagine you are are, with Shad Barry the only fella on your club knockin' in north uv forty runs."

Shetts handed Del a package. He looked at it for a moment, looked up at Shetts, and tore it open. It contained a contract wrapped around a wad of hundred dollar bills. Del scanned the contract. It was for two years and there was no amount filled in where the salary should have appeared.

"The Colonel says you can fill in any … and I do mean *any* amount that's reasonable," said Shetts. "There's thirty-five hundred in cash there and you'd be allowed to draw against your salary any time."

"Oim real flattered, Shetts. Flabbergasted as well to be honest. But oive got a hard and firm contract with the Senators."

"Well think it over. As far as going to any *other* National League club if the new league were to fold, the Colonel has first claim on you."

"Oim pretty well set just now," said Del, thinking of all the cash in his valise and how much he figured to take the bookmakers for in New York.

"I've got to get back, Mush. Let me know if you change your mind."

Del handed back the package and Shetts scurried off into the station.

In New York the girls shopped and went for walks in Central Park across from the hotel they were staying in. Del and Jack each lost a pile at Aqueduct. Their third morning in the Big Apple the four headed to

The Only Del

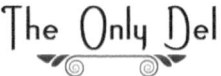

Coney Island and checked into the luxurious four-story Queen Anne-style Manhattan Beach Hotel on the boardwalk.

"Are you sure we can *afford* this?" whispered Norine as Del signed the guest register.

"If I do better on the ponies than I did at Aqueduct we can, and I can hardly help but do better. I found a bookmaker in New York that gave me tips on some mounts at Brighton Beach."

The girls went to the almost-finished Luna Amusement Park. Some of the rides were still being checked for safety and weren't yet up and running. First they rode a miniature railroad to see Hagenbeck's Wild Animals. Then they went on the Razzle Dazzle, Twenty Thousand Leagues Under the Sea, a ride left over from the Sea Lion Park that had closed the year before, and The Teaser, a set of spinning wooden chairs that turned both of them green. The attraction Florence liked the best was Professor Wormwood's Monkey Theater. It featured trained dogs, monkeys, and apes. Norine thought Florence was too young for it, but they went on Shoot the Chutes because it reminded Florence of the show they'd seen at the Vitascope Hall. Pictures of menacing waves and rocky riverbanks racing by were projected on the walls. The ride was save enough, but they both got soaked to the skin.

"Why are all those men staring at you, Mommy?" asked Florence as Norine fussed with her sodden hair.

She looked down and realized that people could see clear through her soaked blouse. She pulled her Irish shawl around herself and shot the men a dirty look.

Del and Jack went to the Brighton Beach Race Track, where Jack won a bit and Del lost big, all of his sure things turning out to be nags, and then to Gravesend. When Del lost another hundred dollars he tore up his ticket in disgust and told Jack, "Gravesend's a good name for this place. It's gointa be the death uv me."

Del wired Postal for more money as soon as he got back to the hotel. Postal wired him another advance on his '03 salary, a thousand dollars this time. Del and the girls headed back to Washington after he'd lost another three hundred dollars on the ponies. He knew he shouldn't be betting so big when he didn't recognize any of the jockeys and the only horses worth taking a chance on were going out at thirty-to-one odds or worse. He stood a better chance at a roulette table.

Del tried his luck at Benning's when they got back to Washington. Ned Hanlon, Joe Kelley, John McGraw, and Wilbert Robinson were there. So was Nap Lajoie.

"It's a regular Who's Who uv baseballists," said Joe Kelley, who had started drinking at breakfast.

"Good to see you, Mush," said Nap. "Even if you did beat me out for the batting title, you lucky stiff."

"Luck had nuthin' ta do with it, Sandy. And it's had nuthin ta do with me bettin' lately either."

"Your picks at Aqueduct didn't pan out?" asked McGraw.

"No. And the ones on Coney Island were worse."

"How much are you down?" asked McGraw.

Wondering why he was being so inquisitive, Del answered, "More than oid care ta say."

"Well I'm putting a hundred down on a three-year old that's due for a win," said Ned Hanlon.

"And I'm wagerin' a hundred on a four-year old that a tout said'll surprise everybody today," said Lajoie.

Del had only planned to bet twenty on his pick, but he couldn't look like a piker in front of the others. Besides, he needed to recoup some of his losses. He bet a hundred on a filly that was running ten-to-one to win, place, or show. It finished fourth.

After the races, at which Del had dropped another three hundred and fifty dollars, the group went to an expensive restaurant for dinner. The food cost enough as it was but the bar tab swelled prodigiously as each

The Only Del

man ordered a more expensive round that the last. Since this was Del's hometown and he wanted to impress the others he picked up the tab. The others fought him for it, but not very hard.

"My pal's the cock of the walk around here," announced Nap.

"Mighty grand uv you, Mush," said Kelley.

"Are you sure you can cover it?" whispered Nap.

"Of course," said Del with a grimace, kicking himself for deciding to pay.

McGraw snuck a peak at Del's wallet as he laid down one twenty-dollar bill after another and, reluctantly, five dollars as a tip. There wasn't much left when he'd finished.

For his birthday Norine gave Del a cloth-lined, steel bound, cowhide suit case with excelsior locks. She asked him how many suits he thought he'd be able to carry in it.

"Only one or two," answered Del.

Norine frowned. "But the man at the store said it should hold six or seven."

"Aye, but when I pack, I'm plannin' ta smuggle *you* inside."

Norine gave him a hug and said, "You always know how to make a girl feel special. Just for that, you don't need to get a birthday present for me next year." She paused and Del grinned. "Unless you see some little outfit you think would look good on me."

"*Every* outfit looks good on you?" said Del, "especially little ones."

In late November Del and Norine left Florence with her nursemaid and went on a second honeymoon to Niagara Falls. They stayed at the four-year-old red brick Lafayette Hotel on River Road just north of the recently burned to the ground Clinton Arms. The advertising in the *Niagara Falls Daily Record* that Del had picked up as they got off the train said the Lafayette was fitted with every modern convenience: electric lights, elevator service, a telephone in the lobby, and private and public baths. There were separate parlors for men, ladies, and couples, a writing room, and even a darkroom where guests could develop their photos of the falls.

the greatest batsman in the land

The hotel's most popular feature was its roof garden observatory. As soon as they'd unpacked Del and Norine took the steam elevator up to it.

"The American side's impressive," said Norine, "but the Canadian falls are absolutely spectacular."

"That surely is a torrent uv water goin' over them," said Del.

"What's that little boat that's going so close to the falls?"

"It's called the Maid uv the Mist, I saw a brochure for it in the lobby."

"Can we go on it, Del? It would be such fun."

"We can, but I might as well warn you ..."

"What? Is it dangerous?"

"I don't expect so. But you're bound ta get your hair wet."

After making love, playing cards, and making love again the next day Del and Norine realized they were famished and went downstairs to eat. The Lafayette boasted an excellent dining room that served the choicest imported wines and liquors. There was a lot of buzz among the diners about Annie Taylor, a 63-year-old music teacher who had announced that as part of the Pan American Exposition she would go over the falls inside a barrel.

The next morning Del took Norine for a ride on the Maid of the Mist. They both got drenched. They got strained necks as well from looking up at the angry swirl of millions of gallons of water poring over the crest a hundred feet above the tiny craft.

"What's that in the water?" asked Norine, pointing over the bow at several loosely attached pieces of wood.

"Used ta be a boat uv some type or uther I suppose," said Del. "There isn't much left of it."

They ate sausages in buns at a stand on the riverwalk that night and mouth-watering hot waffles filled with berries, syrup, and ice cream. Del bought a container of whipped cream. He had a plan for what he would do with it when they got back to their room. Norine had a pretty good idea it would involve her.

The Only Del

Chapter Thirty

Lost Forever

For her birthday Norine, who was making a little money teaching other children in their apartment building how to speak French, bought Florence a box of the twenty-eight color Crayola Young Artists Drawing Crayons that had just come out.

"Craie is the French word for chalk and ola means wax," Norine explained when her daughter looked puzzled.

Florence set down the stuffed horse she'd named Daisy and asked, "What do I do with them, Mommy?"

"You can draw with them or you can color in pictures," said Norine. She handed Florence a book of outlines.

Florence opened to a picture of a duck and took the yellow crayon out of the box. She slowly and carefully turned the duck yellow and then ran to show her father.

"Daddy. I made the duckie yellow!"

"Aren't you the clever girl?"

"You have to put your crayons away for a minute, baby," Norine told Florence.

"Why, Mommy? I love them."

"Your daddy has a gift he wants to give you."

Del went around behind the settee and picked up a huge box. He put it in front of Florence.

"It's really big, Daddy. Is it a baby brother?"

Norine laughed and winked at Del. "No, sweetie, but your daddy and I are doing our best to make you one."

The Only Del

Florence tried to pick up the box but it was far too heavy. Del opened it and pulled out what was inside.

"Is that the thing you put on a horsey?" asked Florence.

"Yes, baby girl. It's a saddle."

Florence looked at her stuffed horse. "You're a silly daddy. That's much too big for Daisy."

"It's not *for* Daisy." He reached out his hand. "Come here."

Florence looked confused but took her father's hand. Del led her out onto the balcony. "Look down there, sweetpea."

Del picked her up so she could see down to the street. An old man in a railroad cap held the reins to a palomino colt that was munching away on a bale of hay.

"The saddle is for *her*. She's your new pony."

Florence turned and yelled, "Mommy! Daddy bought me my own pony! It's just like the one I rode when we stayed at the little hotel."

"Oim sorry, me pet," Del told Norine as she joined him in bed that night.

"Sorry for what?"

"Fer upstagin' yer present with the pony. Oive never seen them before but the … whad'ya call 'em … crayons? They look like great things fer wee ones."

"They were hardly a match for the horse," pouted Norine.

"Aye. And like I said. I'm sorry."

"You can make it up to me by going back to work."

"Goin' back to *work*? The season doesn't start fer anuther four months."

Norine reached under the covers and took Del's member in her hand. "Back to the job of making a baby brother for Florence."

"Not *that* work. It's such awful drudgery."

"That may be, but somebody seems ready to get back to it."

the greatest batsman in the land

Del looked down at his erection. "Aye, the wee lad *does* seem as though he might be talked into it."

"Then I'll start by telling him for the thousandth time him that I'm very fond of him and that he's not wee at all."

"Well he's gettin' less wee every second. Come here, you."

The Delahantys returned to New Orleans in December. Norine renewed her contacts with the leading families and Florence found playmates among their children. Del spent his time at the track. Wally Fessenden was gone and Del could find no other reliable tipsters. He gave up on his system after more heavy losses and started betting on sure things. Even they didn't come in. He wired Fred Postal and told him that some unforeseen expenses had come up and he required more funds. Del received a check two days later but when he went to cash it, Postal had stopped payment.

When Del went to the track the next day he knew he absolutely had to start winning again. He had to pay the hotel bill, Mae, and the stable fees for the pony. He'd just watched another of his picks finish out of the money when a familiar face appeared, that of John McGraw.

"I thought I might find you here, Del. That was a swell dinner we had in Washington."

Del thought back to the number at the bottom of the tab and cringed.

"Has your luck improved any?"

"My luck and my system have both gone fer a shite," groaned Del.

"Listen, Del, I'm still very anxious to get you into a Giants' uniform."

"You know, Norine and I ud luv nuthin more than ta go ta New York, but oive got a contract with Washington."

"Willie Keeler's bolted the Superbas and signed with the New York Americans or whatever it is my old club's going to be called and Wiley Piatt's left the White Sox for the Beaneaters. You need to make hay while the sun shines, Del. Think of how many years you were stuck in Philadelphia batting four hundred and getting paid peanuts. You owe it to yourself and your family to make some money ... serious money ... while you still can."

The Only Del

Del stared at McGraw. "It's no secret oim in some trouble right now, John." He thought of Postal stopping payment on the check. "How much'd Brush be willing to pay me?"

"Six thousand a season. For three years. Eighteen thousand dollars, Del. You'd be set for life."

"I hate ta ask, but did Brush say anything about an advance?"

McGraw reached into his pocket and handed Del a fat envelope. "There's two thousand dollars in here. It's yours if you agree."

Del stared at the cash. "I don't know, John."

"Sleep on it, Del. Talk it over with that beautiful wife of yours. The two of you'd be able to live high off the hog on six thousand a year."

"Telephone me in the morning. Oill have an answer for you."

Del and Norine talked for two hours that night. He badly wanted to live up to his obligations in Washington. The boosters had shown their appreciation of his heavy hitting even though he'd lost a step in the field and on the bases too.

"I know you'd love to live in New York," said Del, pacing the room and fiddling nervously with a cigar lighter.

"I would, but I don't want you to do it for *me*."

Del sat down on the settee and straightened a pillow that didn't need straightening.

"Can I ask you something, darling?"

"What?" asked Del, without looking up. He knew what Norine was about to say.

"How badly off are we? I haven't said anything, but I know you've had some bad luck."

"I suppose there's no point in keepin' it from you, me pet. We're in trouble. Big trouble."

"Then you'll just have to sign with the Giants."

"I have a plan. Oim not thrilled about it, but it's the only way out."

the greatest batsman in the land

"What is it?"

"I'm gointa take the Giants' advance money, win it back on the ponies … me luck's bound ta change soon, and then pay back Brush and stay put in Washington."

Ed and Norine went to New York the next day and he signed to play for the New York Giants. Word was out before the ink had dried. There were a hundred dailies in New York and Brooklyn. Ed disingenuously denied having done anything more than speak with John McGraw on occasion. "I still belong to the Senators," he told reporters.

In a matter of days John T. Brush confirmed to the press that Ed Delahanty had signed a contract to play for the New York Giants. When he heard the news, Colonel Rogers declared that he had no intention of relinquishing his rights to Delahanty. Fred Postal reminded one and all that his batting champion had an iron-clad contract and had accepted a great deal of advance money for the upcoming season. "I assure the baseball enthusiasts of Washington that Mister Delahanty will appear in a senatorial toga again next year. If not, I shall appear in court dressed for battle."

Ban Johnson expressed outrage that the Giants would sign a player bound to one of his teams. John McGraw told reporters that the American League president had a great deal of nerve crying foul when someone stole another league's stars. Brush said that in signing Delahanty he'd simply done what every other National League owner had tried to do. "In war time one must adopt war measures."

A perplexed Paul Eaton chimed in that "Del seems to have gotten himself into a pickle sure enough, but he is a good-natured chap who always intends to do the right thing." Eaton told his readers that a player's value was determined by people like Brush and McGraw who set up temptations a player finds hard to resist. "The men who entice players to jump their contracts are more to blame than the players themselves."

Regardless of anyone's interpretation, it was quite clear that the two leagues were now at one another's throats. If the best players - especially one of Ed Delahanty's caliber - got away with what he'd done no owner could feel safe. Smooth-fielding shortstop George Davis had left the

The Only Del

Giants and signed with the White Sox, had a terrific 1902 season, and then re-signed with the Giants, pocketing $2,700 in advance money. Charlie Comiskey went to court and got an injunction against Davis playing in Illinois.

The National League owners were appalled by what they saw. Stripped of its best players, their league was in shambles. Their attendance was in freefall. And with the Pirates now so strong, there was little chance there'd be a viable competition for the '03 championship. The Athletics promised to dominate the American League and if the Giants kept stealing the American League's stars the Baltimore team that was going into Gotham would be hard-pressed to survive. Many of the AL owners were over-extended. Their cranks needed assurance that the new players that had taken the field in '02 would be back.

Del and Norine headed back to New Orleans. He knew he'd "fallen off the stool" but returned to the Fair Grounds anyway. He paid a hundred dollars for tips and laid down another two hundred. An hour later he looked at his betting card. Every item was a loss.

"Still picking plow horses?" asked Fred Thorp when Del visited the reporters' 'apartment' for a much-needed drink.

"I couldn't call a race between a snail and a steam engine," groaned Del.

He laid one more bet with the now usual result and was about to leave when John McGraw reappeared out of nowhere.

"You know, I feel awful bad about cuttin' loose on Tom Loftus when he's been so good to me," Del told him. "Postal too. Aren't they liable ta take me ta court, John?"

"Listen to me, you've got nothing to fear from Postal or Johnson. Or Rogers for that matter."

"I don't know ..."

"How about I float you another two thousand, Mush?"

Del's slumped shoulders straightened a little. "I could surely use it, John."

the greatest batsman in the land

The National League owners, minus Brush and Rogers, met at the Criterion Hotel in New York in January with an eye to paving the way for peace talks. They elected the Pirates' secretary Henry Clay Pulliam, a thirty-three-year-old newspaperman from Louisville, as the new league president. A moderate and a voice of reason, Pulliam was tired of hearing the pronouncements from on high from Brush and Rogers. He appointed delegates to meet with Ban Johnson and his delegates at the St. Nicholas Hotel in Cincinnati. Johnson, Somers, and Charlie Comiskey sat down there with the NL reps to work out a much-needed truce.

The atmosphere was surprisingly good-natured as the magnates recognized that they had common interests. The first topic was whether they should form a single, 16-team association. Neither side was for that. The American Leaguers decided to adopt the older league's rules and the NL magnates agreed they would raise no opposition to a new American League team in New York. The two sides agreed to work together in the scheduling of games. Then came the thorny matter of what to do about jumpers and the camaraderie was quickly subplanted with tension.

Above all, both sides agreed that the reserve clause must be enforced. From now on it would be strictly hands-off. Any player under contract who signed with another club would be blackballed. The delegates plowed through the list of jumpers. Sam Crawford, who had re-signed with Cincinnati after signing a contract with Detroit, was allowed to stay in the American League. Kid Elberfeld, who'd signed with New York, was returned to Detroit and slant-ball artist Wild Bill Donovan, who had inked a two-year deal with Brooklyn and then jumped to Detroit was allowed to stay with the Tigers. All players who had jumped before 1902 would remain with their clubs. Those who jumped after '02 would be returned. But a heated argument arose when the delegates finally came to the cases of George Davis and Ed Delahanty. After some angry exchanges it was decided that Davis would be allowed to stay with the Giants. But not Del.

"Ed Delahanty will return all of the advance money he has received from the Giants and stay in Washington," announced Pulliam at the end of the meeting. "Delahanty will play in Washington or he will not play at all."

The Only Del

Del could hardly believe it when he read of the decision. "Why does Davis get treated one way and me the opposite?" he asked Norine.

"Because he's not a batting champion and without you the Senators are back to being cellar dwellers," said Norine.

"I was really hoping I could take you to New York, me luv."

Norine hugged him. "I know that Del, it just wasn't meant to be."

To Del's great fortune, Fred Postal was willing to let bygones be bygones and forgave Del for what he'd done. He recognized that his now addictive gambling and downward spiral had led him to do something he knew in his heart was wrong. Postal even worked out a solution for the advance money Del had taken from the Giants. He delivered a check made out to John T. Brush to Pulliam's office. The four thousand dollars would be deducted from Del's salary over the next two years of his contract. He would now be making a thousand dollars a year less than he had playing for Colonel Rogers. It was a bitter pill to swallow. He confessed that he'd had his tail feathers plucked and that he'd had it coming.

Del paid his bills and left New Orleans. He sent Norine and Florence to stay with Norine's parents for a while. On March 24 he finally reported to the Senators' training camp at Georgetown College, where reporters badgered him about his jump to the Giants. Del seemed weary and distracted and looked jowly and middle-aged, with hollowed eyes and suddenly thinning hair. No one had ever seen him this out of shape. Too preoccupied at the track to work out with the Pelicans, he tipped the trainer's scale at a beefy 233 pounds.

His teammates seemed glad to see him and said nothing about his weight or his contract machinations. Tom Loftus said Del was "a royal good fellow at heart." Del was glad to be back on a ball field doing what he did best. Paul Eaton said he looked "like a small boy with a new pair of red-topped boots." He looked good with the willow - he hadn't lost his swing or his batting eye - but he struggled mightily to reach even lazy flyballs. The *Washington Post* opined that, "In spite of all that has transpired over the winter with regards to The Only Del, the Washington patrons will welcome him back with open arms."

the greatest batsman in the land

On April 26 the Senators and Clark Griffith's New York Americans paraded through downtown Washington behind Haley's Band, accompanied by two buses jammed with rooters from the northeast and southwest. More than 11,000 baseball bugs passed through the turnstiles for the windy home opener, the largest attendance for a game in the capital. Del was nervous about how he'd be received but the boosters were apparently as willing to put aside their star's flirtation with the Giants as Loftus and Postal had been. During batting practice, Del smashed one ball after another into the boosters seated on the grass in front of the outfield fences.

"Hit us another one, Del," yelled a man who'd spilled his box of Cracker Jacks when he caught one of Ed's hits after it had bounced off the wall.

"You're the best, Del," yelled the man beside him.

Norine let out a sigh of relief and her eyes moistened.

"What's wrong, Mommy?" asked Florence.

"Nothing, sweetie. I was just worried about your daddy."

"Is something wrong with daddy?" Florence asked nervously.

"No, your daddy is going to be just fine."

When Del came to the plate in the first inning a delegation of men carried a huge horseshoe of American Beauty roses onto the field and presented it to him. "With heartfelt felicitations for the world's greatest slugger" read the ribbon across it.

"The reception given Delahanty was unusually enthusiastic and gratifying," wrote a scribe for the *Evening Star*. "When he doffed his cap in acknowledgement of the shower of applause he was given there was hardly a person in the enclosure who did not join in the hearty shout of 'Welcome Back, Del.' And a tear came to the star's eye."

Del was robbed off an extra base hit on a diving catch by the center fielder a minute later but in the fifth inning he singled home the winning run. Two days later he laced three hits in a 7-1 drubbing of Gotham's new team. In the final game of the series, an 11-0 loss, Del chased balls all over the left garden, made one outstanding catch after another, and was rewarded with ebullient ovations. Three plays bordered on the sensational, especially one all of the newspapers raved about, his "one-handed catch of

The Only Del

Ganzel's long drive in the ninth when after a hard run the big fellow dived after the ball and caught it a few inches above the ground in his ungloved hand."

After the game, a sweat-soaked Del showed a telegram he'd received the night before to the *Washington Times* reporter. It read,

> "Denver Colorado, April 24
> E. Delahanty, Oxford Hotel, Washington, D.C.
> Need you here. Will pay you $4,000 for five months. Wire answer immediately and if favorable come at once as we open the 28th.
> D. Packard, President, Denver Grizzlies Base Ball Club."

The reporter looked up at Del. "Well? What did you tell him?"

"Nuthin'. It'd be a hoot and a half ta play with me bruther Tom … but oim stayin' put here."

The reporter went to hand the wire back. "Keep it," said Del.

May 7 marked the first time Del and the other former Phillies had been able to set foot in Pennsylvania in more than a year. The *Evening Star* reported that "Del no longer needs to wrap his batting average in a faded shawl and slip across the river by dark of night with it pressed closely to his bosom." He swatted two hits and scored twice but it hardly mattered. Al Orth's return to the City of Brotherly Love was a disaster. He allowed the powerful A's 22 hits and lost 19-5.

The next day Del, who'd trimmed down to 205 pounds, had a camera man take his picture to show how much weight he'd lost. He made "a terrific swipe" to the top of the wall just out of the reach of centerfielder Topsy Hartsell and legged out his first three-bagger of the season. The *Washington Times* said that the capital's 'fans' - a reporter's term for boosters that was beginning to take hold - were "in a slough of despond and it was about time that Edward Delahanty pulled himself together and started to swat the cover off the ball. Among the bleacherites there is not a more popular man in the national game and without him the Washington club would draw about as many fans as a vinegar barrel does flies. But Delahanty has not played Delahanty ball this season."

the greatest batsman in the land

Del responded in style the next day, driving in all three runs with a double and two sod-scorching singles in a 3-0 win over the Browns to raise his average to .258. When the Senators arrived in Chicago all of the newspapers ran accounts of Del's four home run game in '97, calling his feat "the most remarkable thing that ever happened on a ball field." Del didn't play, he'd strained ligaments in his right knee doing wind sprints before the first game. He told reporters he'd never had an injury like it. He bought a half dozen Chancellor cigars and four quarts of Keystone Club rye on his way home to wash down some Dr. Miles' Anti-Pain pills.

He went to Mount Clemens for daily sulfur baths in hopes of hastening his recovery and when that didn't help he packed up the family and went to Hot Springs, where they checked into the Waukesha Hotel and Bath House. Ed was delighted when he won enough at the gaming houses to pay for the trip. It was just as well that the Oaklawn Racetrack was still under construction.

Del was back in the lineup a week earlier than anyone expected. In the Patriots Day game against Boston on May 29 he beat out a bunt, moved to second on a sacrifice, and scored on a single to right. His next trip to the plate he singled and then scored on Scoops Carey's two-bagger. In spite of darting pains in his bad leg, he made a terrific running catch and threw a runner out at third as well. But there was sad news for Del that day. The Senators sold his friend Jack Doyle to the Superbas.

He "tore a terrific welt" down the third base line for a double on the third of June and smacked another two-bagger in the ninth in a 9-1 loss to the Browns the next day, but the Senators were mired in last place. Del had two hits the next day in a 3-1 loss to St. Louis. With a hit or more in almost every game Del had lifted his average to .325. He and his mates got some satisfaction in the last game of the series. His single and two doubles, one off the top of the right field wall, were among the Senators' seventeen hits in a 10-0 lambasting of the Browns. Norine was excited when Del told her that night there were rumors making the rounds that Clark Griffith and the New York Americans, who some scribes were calling the Highlanders because they played at Hilltop Park, were after him.

The Only Del

Del had two base hits and threw out another runner at the plate in Cleveland. After the game he went to see his parents and then spent some time at the fire hall. The atmosphere there was somber, the firemen had just returned from Mike Whalen's funeral. When the Senators traveled to Detroit, Del went out drinking, alone. The next night, after checking at the front desk of his hotel to see if there was a letter from Norine and being told there wasn't one, he went out drinking alone again. He didn't play the next day, he'd been 'too sick'.

On Saturday, the Fourth of July, the *Washington Times* reported that

> "Manager Loftus and his senatorial band arrived after a hot forty-eight hours' car ride from Detroit but Ed Delahanty was not with them. His wife was waiting for him at the station. When the club left Detroit on Thursday night Del's baggage and uniform were in his room at the Oriental Hotel, but the big fellow was nowhere to be found."

The writer noted that Del had been drinking and not taking care of himself of late and speculated that he had gone to Hot Springs to bail out. Norine couldn't imagine that Del had gone somewhere without telling her. She was convinced he would turn up soon. He'd apologize for going on a tear and worrying her and he'd hug her with his big arms and everything would be fine.

She knew he had no money to bet with so he wouldn't be at a track. She wired every one she could think of. If he'd gone back to Cleveland to see his parents they would have telephoned her as soon as they'd heard that Del had been reported missing. She had Jimmy Ryan check the saloons she'd heard her husband had begun to frequent in Washington of late but no one had seen him.

She contacted the clubs his brothers played for and came up empty. Then she thought he might have gone to New York and sent telegrams to John McGraw and Clark Griffith. Each of them wired immediate responses that Del had not been to see them. She telephoned the hotels in New York he might have gone to. He hadn't been to any of them. By now there was nowhere else she could think to check and she became frantic. When the

the greatest batsman in the land

telephone rang she nearly jumped out of her skin. She ran to it, hoping desperately to hear her husband's voice on the other end of the line. She was crushed when the voice belonged to Tom Loftus.

"I've received a letter as to Ed's whereabouts, Norine. You need to see it."

"I'll be right there, Mister Loftus." Without giving a thought to how she looked she told the nursemaid to watch Florence, grabbed her bonnet and shawl, and hurried to the ballpark.

The letter was from Car Superintendent Blunett of Buffalo. He told of how a man had been put off a Michigan Central Pullman near Fort Erie, Ontario for disorderly conduct. Blunett related that the same man had tried to cross the International Bridge on foot and had been stopped and questioned by the bridge tender. He related that the man had fallen and the tender had heard a splash in the water below. They'd set up a close watch on both sides of the Niagara River all the way to the Falls but hadn't seen anything yet.

"Why does he think the man was my husband?" asked Norine, tears streaming down her cheeks.

Loftus hated to tell her. "They found a dress suit case ..." he started.

"A cowhide case ... with excelsior locks?" gasped Norine, horrified.

"Yes," said Loftus. "It contained a complementary pass for free admittance to Washington Senators home games."

"Was it number twenty-six?"

"It was, Norine. We both know that was the pass Del was given for you to use. And they found a suit with the initials EJD on the label."

Norine shuddered and began to sob.

Two nights before, after leaving the hotel in Detroit with a grip containing $200 and the dress suit case Norine had given him, Del had bought a Michigan Central train ticket to New York. He was going to see Clark Griffith and John McGraw to find out if either of them could find a way to get him out of his contract with the Senators. He was very anxious about what he'd tell them and about what they would have to say. He went to the

The Only Del

smoking car and had a cigar but it didn't help to calm his nerves. He went to the bar car and had a whiskey. He thought about how George Davis and Kid Elberfeld had ended up playing in New York and he hadn't. His face turned red and he slammed his glass down on the bar. He ordered another whiskey and thought about how much money he owed. He was $1,300 overdrawn on his salary. Then he thought about what had happened to Felix Carr.

He went to the dining car and ordered a steak and another whiskey. He poked at the steak for a while without eating much of it. Then he pushed his plate aside and stared out at the barren, gloomy landscape through the window. He finished his drink and asked for another. The nervous waiter considered telling Ed he thought he'd had enough, but shrugged and went to get it.

"Where does the Michigan Central get its steaks?" he asked the waiter when he set down the glass.

"I'm not sure," said the waiter. "Why?"

Ed pointed at his plate. "That one tasted like horsemeat," he said, loud enough that other diners turned to stare.

"Isn't that Ed Delahanty?" a woman asked her husband.

"What are you starin' at?" Ed demanded of the couple.

The waiter came back with his manager, who told Ed that he had instructed the waiter not to serve Ed any more alcoholic beverages. Ed snorted at him, got up, and shoved his chair against the wall. He strode purposefully but unsteadily to the bar car and when the bartender left to serve a table in the corner, Ed grabbed a glass and a whiskey bottle and poured himself a tall drink. He took a sip and then stared at his glass.

He thought about Joe Sullivan. Then he thought about Norine and about how men stared at her wherever they went. He remembered the men ogling her at the Brooklyn Academy of Music gala and every man at the Twelfth Night Revellers Ball wanting to dance with her. He thought about how often she wanted him inside her - to the point that she'd pretended to be a nurse and sneaked into his hospital room. He wondered if she'd finally resorted to satisfying her yearnings with other men when he was on the road.

the greatest batsman in the land

Then he wondered why she hadn't written to him in a week. He had no way of knowing that she had. The carrier who took the mail from the train to the Detroit post office was usually careful to shake the bag to ensure there were no letters left in the bottom. The day Norine's letter had arrived in Detroit he'd been in a hurry and hadn't done so.

Her letter had began by telling Del how well little Florence was doing in nursery school. After a brief update on her sister, Norine had written that Del had made her the happiest girl in the world and that he would always be the only man for her, healthy or sick, rich or poor. She'd signed it, "Yours forever, darling."

Then Del remembered that he still owed $400 on a necklace he'd bought her and that the final payment on Florence's pony was well past due. Then he thought about what a rotten scoundrel Pulliam was.

"Fuckin' owners are all alike," he growled much too loud. "Oughta be lined up and shot, the whole god damned lot uv um."

The bartender stood over him. "Where did you get that bottle, sir?"

"Where do ya think? From behind the bar."

"You're not permitted back there."

"Oill remember that the next time."

The bartender went to pick up the bottle and Ed grabbed his arm and pushed it away.

"Oill be needin' that ta help me sleep tonight."

"Well I can't let you have it."

"Would you like to see what'll happen to ya if you try again to take it away?"

The bartender went to the door and signaled for the conductor. The conductor, a punctilious little man with tiny spectacles, followed the bartender to where Ed was sitting.

"You fetched *this* pipsqueak ta fight yer battle?" roared Ed.

"Be quiet, sir," demanded the conductor.

"I was bein' quiet ya damn fool. I was just sittin' here havin' a wee bit uv whiskey and this ... this tarbender tried ta steal me bottle."

The Only Del

The conductor looked at the bottle and the Michigan Central stamp on it. "That is the *railroad's* liquor. Not yours."

"It's mine *now*, isn't it?"

"I'm afraid I'm going to have to put you off the train at the next stop, we simply cannot abide such conduct."

"The hell you are!" stormed Ed. "Oim goin' ta take a nap."

He wobbled out of the bar and crashed into an emergency tool cabinet, shattering its glass and headed towards a sleeping car. He went to climb into a berth and found a woman in it. "This is my berth!" he yelled. He grabbed the woman by the legs and she let out a scream. The conductor stared in disbelief and blew his whistle.

Two burly guards arrived. The conductor didn't need to point out which passenger they needed to deal with. Ed was put off the train minutes later when it pulled into the Bridgeburg station on the outskirts of Fort Erie, Ontario.

"Shouldn't we turn him over to a constable, what with it being nighttime and all?" one of the guards asked the conductor.

"He can fend for himself," said the conductor brusquely. The three men got back on the train and it pulled away.

Ed slumped onto a bench on the empty platform and watched as the train disappeared out of sight. He looked up into the clear sky and saw a lacework of stars twinkling above him.

"They ain't me lucky stars anymore," he muttered.

As he said it a large, black cloud that seemed to appear out of nowhere obscured the stars. Del shuddered as it did and a sense of foreboding overcame him.

Del struggled a while to keep his eyes open and then fell asleep. He dreamed of racing toward an outfield fence and hauling down a long drive to a round of hearty huzzahs and applause. Then he dreamt of helping Florence up onto her pony and of Norine and her dazzling smile when he took her in his arms. Then he dreamt of falling through the air into water and woke up with a start.

the greatest batsman in the land

Del wiped his eyes and straightened his collar and necktie. He'd made up his mind. He wasn't going to New York. He was going home to his girls. He spotted a blinking light approaching up the Niagara, an approaching train no doubt, and an enormous bridge spanning the river a short distance from the station. He pulled himself up and began walking toward it. When he neared the structure he saw that it was a railroad bridge.

"Buffalo/Fort Erie International Bridge. No foot traffic," he read aloud from the sign on its base. "If I can get across there, I can catch that train."

He leaped up onto the bridge and started across on the narrow path along the side of the tracks. He'd gone half of the way across when he heard a voice, a gruff one.

"Who's there?"

"Ed Delahanty."

"You are, are you? Then I'm the Queen of Sheba," said the voice.

A flashlight was pointed at Ed's face.

"Another smuggler is it then?" said the man, a bridge tender whose name was Sam Kingston.

"Oim no smuggler, ya damn fool. Do ya see me carryin' anything?"

"Maybe you're fixing to bring something back."

"Get that light out uv me eyes. Yer blindin' me."

"Foot passengers are not permitted on this bridge."

The approaching light Del had seen was not a train. It was mounted on the prow of the steamer Ossie Bidell. It was close enough now that the draw section toward the American side was being opened for it. Kingston instinctively turned around as it did and Del ran past him.

"No! Come back! The draw's opening!"

Still partially blinded by the flashlight, Del ran right though the opening he hadn't seen in the dark and fell sixty feet into the roiling water below. The impact rendered him unconscious.

The Only Del

Del's body emerged from the base of the Horseshoe Falls minutes later, after being whisked at breakneck speed through the water and striking several rocks. It floated into one of the nearby eddies. The next morning it was spotted by horrified passengers on the Maid of the Mist.

When Norine read in the newspapers what had happened to Del she was too overcome with grief to go to identify the corpse. Del's brother Frank went and somberly relayed the news that it was indeed Del.

A gloom fell over the Senators' clubhouse when they heard. Al Orth and Happy Townsend could scarcely believe that their fun-loving friend was gone. Jimmy Ryan took the news the worst.

"He was a better friend to others than he was to himself," said Jimmy.

"I never met a squarer man," said Orth.

"'Twas a terrible end for a wonderful player. A better fellow never lived," said Ryan.

The players wore black armbands the rest of the season, the Phillies wore bows of crepe. The funeral was held at the Church of Immaculate Conception in Cleveland. It was painful for everyone to look at Norine, whose heart they knew occupied the bottom of a deep abyss of grief, and little Florence, who had no idea why her daddy wouldn't be coming home like he always had.

Years later, a grown up Florence recalled the glorious days when she was a little girl - a non-stop, joyful pageant she called them - the first-class Pullman trains, the best hotels, and a life filled with "ease, luxury, and fun" with her famous father. Norine was certainly young enough to remarry, but chose not to. She taught French, modeled from time-to-time, and worked as an inside decorator for the rich. She and Florence adapted to a simpler, more frugal lifestyle. Norine wished that she and Del could have had more children, but she thanked God for Florence. Del was gone, but he had left his girls and his admirers with a lifetime of wonderful memories.

The Only Del

other books by

Rube Waddell
King of the Hall of Flakes

Babe Ruth
& the 1927 Yankees have the Best Summer Ever

available worldwide at

AMAZON
and others

hardcover | *paperback* | *e-book*

About the Author

As a boy, Will Braund's life revolved around baseball. He played every day after school and from 8 until 8 on weekends. He hung up his glove at 39 as the third baseman and manager of a men's league team but later worked as an instructor for the Toronto Blue Jays at their summer camp for teenagers.

After earning an Honors degree in History he taught for several years, during which he was nominated for the Governor General's Award for Excellence in Teaching. After being promoted to principal he was elected Chair of the 1,100 member Toronto School Administrators' Association. Later he was named to the Executive of the Ontario Principals' Council.

Will retired a few years ago but still fills in for principals a few days a month. He lives north of Toronto with his beautiful wife Trudy and their son Tyler and close to Ty's older brother Matthew and his children "Spud" and "Muffin". Will reads voraciously about the history of baseball. His first book, "King of the Hall of Flakes," is based on the crazy life of the remarkable Rube Waddell. His second historical novel, "Babe Ruth & the 1927 Yankee's have the Best Summer Ever ," was released in 2016.

www.ingramcontent.com/pod-product-compliance
Lightning Source LLC
Chambersburg PA
CBHW021930290426
44108CB00012B/782